sexual borderlands

Constructing an American Sexual Past

Edited by
KATHLEEN KENNEDY
AND SHARON ULLMAN

THE OHIO STATE UNIVERSITY PRESS
COLUMBUS

Library of Congress Cataloging-in-Publication Data
Sexual borderlands : constructing an American sexual past / edited by Kathleen Kennedy,
Sharon Rena Ullman.
    p.   cm. — (Women and health : cultural and social perspectives)
Includes bibliographical references and index.
   ISBN 0-8142-0927-0 (cloth : alk. paper)
   ISBN 0-8142-5107-2 (pbk. : alk. paper)
1. Sex customs—United States—History. I. Kennedy, Kathleen, 1963-
II. Ullman, Sharon R. (Sharon Rena), 1955- III. Women and health
(Columbus, Ohio)
   HQ18.U5 S488 2003
   306.7'0973—dc21

                                                        2002014783

Cover and text design by Jennifer Shoffey Carr
Typeset in Adobe Sabon.

The paper used in this publication meets the minimum requirements of the American
National Standard for information Sciences—Permanence of Paper for Printed Library
Materials. ANSI Z39.48-1992.

9 8 7 6 5 4 3 2 1

To Lilian Ullman and Denise Seibert, with love

CONTENTS

ACKNOWLEDGMENTS

The editors would like to thank Janet Goldman, Heather Lee Miller, and The Ohio State University Press for their admirable patience, Bryn Mawr College and Western Washington University for financial support, Brigitte Glaser and Denise Seibert for their emotional support, and Bob Moeller on general principles. The editors would also like to thank Denise Seibert, John Roeder, and Eula Roeder for their assistance in preparing this manuscript.

We gratefully acknowlege the publishers for permission to reprint the following essays:

Ramón A. Gutiérrez, "Honor, Ideology, Marriage Negotiation and Class-Gender Domination in New Mexico," *Latin American Perspectives* 12:1 (Winter 1985): 81–104. Reprinted by permission of Sage Publications.

Jacqueline Peterson, "Women Dreaming: The Religiopsychology of Indian White Marriages and the Rise of Metis Culture," in *Western Women: Their Land, Their Lives,* edited by Lillian Schlissel, Vicki Ruiz and Janice Monk (Albuquerque: University of New Mexico Press, 1988): 47–76. Reprinted by permission of University of New Mexico Press.

Cornelia Dayton, "Taking the Trade: Abortion and Gender Relations in an 18th-Century New England Village," *William and Mary Quarterly,* 3rd Series XLVIII (1991). Reprinted by permission of the William and Mary Quarterly.

Norma Basch, "Marriage, Morals and Politics in the Election of 1828," *Journal of American History* 80:3 (December 1993): 890–918. Reprinted by permission of the Organization of American Historians.

Martha Hodes, "Wartime Dialogues on Illicit Sex: White Women and Black Men," in *Divided Houses: Gender and the Civil War,* edited by Catherine Clinton and Nina Silber (New York: Oxford University Press, 1992): 232–42. Reprinted by permission of Oxford University Press.

Cheng, Lucie, "Free, Indentured, Enslaved: Chinese Prostitutes in Nineteenth Century America," *Signs* 5:1 (1979): 3–29. Reprinted by permission of The University of Chicago Press.

Lisa Duggan, "The Trials of Alice Mitchell: Sensationalism, Sexology, and the Lesbian Subject in the Turn-of-the-Century America," *Signs* 18:4 (Summer 1996). Reprinted by permission of The University of Chicago Press.

George Chauncey Jr., "Christian Brotherhood or Sexual Perversion? Homosexual Identities and the Construction of Sexual Borderlands in the World War I Era," *Journal of Social History* 19 (1985). Reprinted by permission of the Journal of Social History.

Peggy Pascoe, "Miscegenation Law, Court Cases, and Ideologies of 'Race' in Twentieth-Century America," *Journal of American History* 83:1 (June 1996): 44–69. Reprinted by permission of the Organization of American Historians.

Ruth M. Alexander, "'The Only Thing I Wanted Was My Freedom: Wayward Girls in New York, 1900–1930," in *Small Worlds: Children and Adolescents in America, 1850–1950,* edited by Elliot West and Paula Petrik (Lawrence: University of Kansas, 1992): 297–300. Reprinted by permission of The University of Kansas Press.

Joanne Meyerowitz, "Women, Cheesecake, and Borderline Material: Responses to Girlie Pictures in the Mid-Twentieth-Century U.S.," *Journal of Women's History* 8:3 (Fall 1996). Reprinted by permission of Indiana University Press.

INTRODUCTION: Sex on the Borderlands

Kathleen Kennedy and Sharon Ullman

Since the French philosopher Michel Foucault produced his ground-breaking *History of Sexuality* in 1976, historians have swept ceaselessly through the cobwebs of dusty archives seeking out evidence of sexual practices both hidden and ignored.[1] The thousands of books, mono-graphs, and articles that have subsequently emerged testify to the extraordinary success of this endeavor. In the call to research and recover, historians have rewritten not only specific histories of sexuality but also expanded the range of what constitutes appropriate historical subjects and categories as well.

Not surprisingly, this new research has made its way into college class-rooms. As our students, you have clamored to study subjects you view as "relevant" to your lives. At times this relevance can come at the expense of the intellectual rigor insisted upon by those who have fought to have this work received by the academy. It is often difficult to resist substituting the history of your own sexuality for that of the subject under discussion.

To some extent this is the fault of the discipline itself with its far-flung interests and individual fascinations. To the scholar this provides an exciting open field; to the student it can be a confusing mess. What should you know? How can you get a handle on this engaging but often chaotic emerging canon? How can you "relate to" a discipline steeped in difficult theoretical language and ideas? For those of us who teach in the field, these questions have challenged us to develop narratives and theo-retical paradigms that bring coherence to a field that often resists such attempts at order.

This collection attempts to respond to these concerns. Like many faculty who teach courses in the history of sexuality, we have searched for an appropriate reader for an undergraduate course. As the discerning reviewer no doubt immediately noted upon seeing this title, this is hardly the first such collection on the subject. Yet it was our sense that earlier collections had not served our purpose. Some seemed too specialized; some reprinted only the same few venerable chestnuts in the field; a few were insufficiently historical for an undergraduate course; still others required a few sessions at the gym before you could even lift them.[2] None seemed specifically geared toward an actual course taught to actual undergraduates.

We decided to write our own. Our goal is to provide a manageable collection of essays particularly suited for undergraduates. We want to engage you with an exciting specific theme while simultaneously introducing you to the significant empirical and theoretical debates in the field. To that end, we have designed this book with a course in mind. We wanted this reader's coherence to come from our concerns over how to teach the field and your concerns over how to study it.

This reader is for a course that constructs the history of sexuality in America as a story of "sexual borderlands." In this, we are influenced by the recent work on the American frontier which has posited that confrontations on the borderlands helped shape major historical processes such as colonialism, state formation, class formation, and modernization.[3] We think the history of sexuality is equally central to those transformations and find this line of thinking particularly useful in revealing that centrality.

What do we mean by "sexual borderlands"? Here, we are following recent scholarship in feminist and race theory that examines the borderland *not* as some arbitrary line marking a tight boundary between two different cultures. Instead, to paraphrase Kathleen M. Brown's definition of a "gender frontier," we think of the borderland as a "site of creative and destructive processes resulting from confrontations of culturally-specific" (in this instance) constructions of sexuality.[4] This idea is very helpful as we think about the way that sexuality often propels ideology as well as cultural exchange. Sexuality is one important way in which individuals and groups define themselves and their relations to others. Sexuality is clearly one of the most contested arenas in which these groups and individuals negotiate their identities and differences.

Those of you who have studied the American West will find all this quite familiar. Over the past few years, historians have redefined the "frontier" that once was thought so essential to the formation of American identity. But rather than viewing the frontier as the border between "civilization" and "savagery," this new western history examines the frontier as "the drama of life on the edges of where people and places meet."[5] It is on these borderlands that the basic stuff of sexuality—intimacy, marriage, courtship, love—are all in flux.

One of the reasons that this model is especially evocative for our purposes is that it acts as an effective counter to the stubbornly persistent vision of a linear "progress" to the history of sexuality in America. In this tale, once upon a (colonial) time, sexuality had been somewhat "open." Then came the repressive Victorian age followed by the liberating twentieth century. (Miniature versions of this can be found within more narrow time periods as well.) As students you may be initially drawn to this conception since, by the very fact of being able to study all this, your time period seems to look "the best."

We ask you to suspend such preferences and instead consider how the concept of a "sexual borderlands" throws this idea into chaos. At the most basic level, it questions the criteria used to judge what constitutes a "more progressive" (or for that matter, more regressive) view of sexuality. Rather than viewing American history as a march toward (or even against) a more inclusive democracy in which a liberation of sexual views and practices is but one more component of a liberal utopia, we encourage you to view the history of sexuality as a series of encounters fueled by contests over power. The results of the contests were uneven and determined less by the official "powers that be" than by relations across the "borders" of class, gender, and race.

Indeed, we have selected essays that require you to focus on these relations in order to understand the history of sexuality and the pivotal role that sexuality plays in the narrative of American history. Although sexuality helps define the boundaries and hierarchies of gender, class, and race differences by encoding beliefs about normalcy and degeneracy, it does not, cannot, operate in a vacuum. Sexuality is not the only axis upon which these relationships are based, but *is* integral to the process by which Americans produced new identities, social practices, and structural changes. This approach reiterates that the history of sexuality is not simply an interesting, even entertaining, elective course option, but is instead an indispensable guide to understanding the evolution of American society.

That evolution is one that both springs out of and is importantly differentiated from the Western enlightenment. Historians and cultural critics link the modern development of sexuality to how men and women began to define their identities. Foucault, for example, argued that in the late nineteenth century, the enlightenment "crisis of the subject" culminated in the development of modern sexual identities.[6] As some historians have claimed, the key issue in the history of sexuality has been "the way that sexuality has increasingly become a core element of modern social identity, constitutive of being, consciousness, and action." [7]

While our reader presents essays that do explore how sexuality became an essential part of our being, the borderlands model inevitably broadens Foucault's paradigm. Sexuality is placed in relation not only to such important institutions as the state and capitalism, but also to racial and gender identities on the North American continent.

We begin this collection with essays that examine how colonizers in the new world used sexuality to define themselves as "civilizers" and to portray indigenous peoples as "savages." Yet in keeping with our belief that formation of sexual identities took place along a sexual borderland, we also include an essay that shows how Amerindians' reconstruction of themselves drew from both traditional and European sources. The American identities that followed were neither stable nor monolithic but protean and capable of incorporating a variety of sometimes contradictory values.

The borderlands that propelled and defined the emerging American nation rested in the realms of class and race. The profoundly moving and disturbing American nineteenth century has properly been the subject of much anguished research, yet sexuality has rarely occupied its appropriate place in these historical narratives. Class formation—the mainstay to American historiography for this period—focused intensively on moral order and sexual regulation; racial narratives rooted in sexual tales dominated the tragic discourse of American identity. In this volume we return sexuality to its original place in the hearts and minds of those who constructed the evolving American nation—not an invisible diminishing factor buried under the prohibitions of a Victorian Age but an energetic motivator in the public discourses of nation, race, and class making.

If the notion that sexuality is central to the eighteenth and nineteenth centuries somehow seems alien to us, we immediately shift gears and agree to its twentieth-century dominance. Historians have sought out and documented what has come to be known as the "modernization of sexuality"—in other words, its increasing resemblance to a world we recognize. As this volume helps clarify, personal recognition is not the only way to see sexuality's central place in American history. Indeed, by defining it thusly, scholars have often been as trapped as our students— we "see" the importance of sexuality only when it reminds us of ourselves.

While remaining aware of the intellectual limitations this approach has engendered, it still helps to note those moments when "we" seem to appear in the story. Indeed, by focusing on sites of conflict—the frontiers of emerging sexual definition—we see more clearly the links to the past that have often been denied in this tale of transformation.

The sexologists—the medical and psychological professionals—who cemented their social authority and dominated public definition and dissection of sexual practice in the early twentieth century—are not so different from the preachers of moral order who constructed the middle class itself in the nineteenth century. This replacement of church by "science," as represented by such figures as Freud and Havelock Ellis, is in line with the general secularization of social authority that characterized the first part of the century (and the increasing reversal of this trend which so flummoxed the latter part).

In America, the forces of "science" and class joined hands in the growing power of the state to define and regulate sexual practice. Although sexual regulation has a longstanding history, the energetic clashes over its twentieth-century application provide an exceptional view to a history marked more by conflict than by success and whose regulatory "failures" were ultimately as likely to end up in a department store window display as in jail. The social reformers who dotted the early century's landscape could hardly have imagined that their attempts to solidify a social and sexual order would lead instead to sexual chaos demanding new, and ever more contentious, notions of order.

"Modern" sexuality's anarchy stretches the concept of borderlands past the physical, or even metaphysical, and into the virtual—as identity itself becomes fluid and, perhaps, neither attainable nor desirable. This volume does not take on this developing trend but offers a history to help situate you—the current student of sexuality. As twenty-first-century forces gather and attempt to smash the borders of nation, race, and self through the powers of corporate globalization and an information economy, we are reminded that these borders are not so easily dissipated and that for many the borderlands have been sites of transformation and the home of voices that needed to be heard.

NOTES

1. Michel Foucault, *The History of Sexuality: An Introduction* (New York: Vintage Books, 1990).

2. For example, see Henry Abelove, Michele Aina Barale, and David Halperin, eds. *The Lesbian and Gay Studies Reader* (New York: Routledge, 1993); Martin Bauml Duberman, Martha Vicinus, and George Chancey Jr., eds., *Hidden From History: Reclaiming a Gay and Lesbian Past,* (New York: Meridian Books, 1989); Kathy Peiss and Christina Simmons with Robert A. Padgug, eds., *Passion and Power: Sexuality in History* (Philadelphia: Temple University Press, 1989); and Domma C. Stanton, *Discourses of Sexuality: From Aristotle to AIDS* (Ann Arbor: University of Michigan Press, 1992).

3. See for example, Andrew R. L. Clayton and Fredrika J. Teute, *Contact Points: American Frontiers From the Mohawk Valley to the Mississippi, 1750–1830*

(Chapel Hill: University of North Carolina Press, 1998); Leonard Thompson and Howard Lamar, *The Frontier in History: North America and South America Compared* (New Haven: Yale University Press, 1981); and David J. Weber, *The Spanish Frontier in North America* (New Haven: Yale University Press, 1992).

4. Kathleen Brown, "The Anglo-Indian Gender Frontier," in *Negotiators of Change: Historical Perspectives on Native American Women,* ed. Nancy Shoemaker (New York: Routledge, 1995), 27.

5. David Weber, *"The Legacy of Conquest,* by Patricia Limerick: A Panel Appraisal," *Western History Quarterly* 20 (1989): 317.

6. Foucault, *The History of Sexuality.*

7. Kathy Peiss and Christina Simmons, "Passion and Power: An Introduction," in *Passion & Power: Sexuality in History,* ed. Kathy Peiss and Christina Simmons with Robert A. Padgug, eds. (Philadelphia: Temple University Press, 1998), 4.

part one

Constructing a "New World"

CONSTRUCTING A "NEW WORLD"

Constructions of sexuality and sexual relationships between Europeans and Amerindians were essential to how these different groups conceived of the "new world" they were making. Europeans used sexual metaphors—the English named Virginia after Elizabeth I, their "virgin queen"—to naturalize their colonial relationships with Amerindians and the land. The sexual practices of Amerindians, especially the ease of divorce, an acceptance of homosexuality, and transgendered practices and premarital sexuality in Amerindian cultures, appalled European colonizers. Europeans used these differences to distinguish themselves from Amerindians by defining themselves as civilized and Amerindians as savage. In spite of their efforts to transplant "old world" sexual practices and values to the "new world," "new world" conditions led to important changes in the sexual practices and values of European colonizers.

Ramón A. Gutiérrez examines how the building of a "new world" changed traditional sexual and family bonds among Spanish colonizers. His essay describes the central role of marriage and family relationships to a class hierarchy that maintained the hegemony of those of pure Spanish blood in Spanish New Mexico. As in Spain, parents controlled the marriage choices of children and those choices reflected social and political concerns. But, Gutiérrez argues, contradictions within the Spanish marriage traditions and changes in Spanish imperial policy eventually undercut those values. By the nineteenth century, love rather than family honor, played a more significant role in children's marriage choice and in doing so, may have disrupted the traditional relationships in Spanish societies.

In spite of Europeans' efforts to distinguish themselves from Amerindians through their sexual practices, sexual intimacies played a central role in constructing the borderlands in which Europeans and Amerindians met. Many Amerindian tribes integrated newcomers into their societies through marriage and captivity. Such relationships were integral to Amerindian diplomacy and to French and English fur traders. The French in particular relied on people in this middle ground to create and preserve economic relationships with Amerindian people. Of special importance were male traders who had married Amerindian women. Such marriages led to the construction of a border culture—the Metis. The majority of the Metis defined themselves as French but held significant kinship relationships with Amerindians. This position in the borderlands enabled the Metis to serve as key negotiators between Amerindians and Europeans.

In her contribution Jacqueline Peterson takes a new look at the development of Metis culture. While most historians have examined interracial relationships from the perspective of European men, Peterson examines why Amerindian women might choose a European husband. She argues that their choices are best explained when examined through the lens of their Amerindian cultures. Her work illustrates the importance of Amerindian culture and decision making in the raising of Metis children and hence the development of this sexual borderland.

1

Honor, Ideology, Marriage Negotiation, and Class-Gender Domination in New Mexico, 1690–1846

Ramón A. Gutiérrez

The ways in which societies organize marriage provide us an important window into how economic and political arrangments are construed. When people marry, they forge affinal alliances, change residence, establish rights to sexual service, and exchange property. Besides being about the reproduction of class and power, however, marriage is about gender. The marital exchange of women gives men rights over women that women never gain over men. This feature of marriage provides a key to the political economy of sex, by which cultures organize "maleness" and "femaleness," sexual desire, fantasy, and concepts of childhood and adulthood.[1]

With these theoretical moorings in mind, I present here an essay on the history of marriage in a colonial setting, New Mexico between 1690 and 1846, an environment in which class domination was culturally articulated and justified through hierarchies of status based on race, ethnicity, religion, and gender. My major concern will be to examine the key role that control over marriage choice played in the maintenance of social inequality, focusing on changes in the mode of marriage formation during the period under study—a decline in the incidence of parentally arranged nuptials and an increase in those freely contracted by adolescents on the basis of love and personal attraction. Rather than discussing the roots of these changes abstractly, I will explore how parents and children negotiated their behavior; the disparities of power that constrained their actions; and the ambiguities, tensions, and contradictions within the ideological superstructure that gave historical agency meaning.[2]

HISTORICAL SETTING

Once the ancient temples of Mexico City had been leveled and cities of gold had failed to materialize, the business of colonizing Mexico's central plateau began. The 1548 discovery of silver at Zacatecas quickly moved the frontier north and set the pace for the establishment of a rapid succession of towns: Guanajuato, Queretaro, San Luis Potosí, Durango. The far north, the areas we know today as New Mexico, California, and Texas, was explored in the first half of the sixteenth century by such men as Álvar Núñez Cabeza de Vaca, Fray Marcos de Niza, and Francisco Vásquez de Coronado. Nonetheless, it remained a fantasy of future enrichment in the Spanish imagination until the end of the century. Then, in 1598, Don Juan de Oñate, the son of one of Zacatecas's wealthiest silver miners, mustered 129 soldiers and together with their dependents ventured into the land of the Chichimecas—the fierce, nomadic Indian tribes that had effectively curtailed Spanish expansion north—to establish the Kingdom of New Mexico.

Arriving in August of 1598 armed with the cross of Christ and the sword to impose it, the soldier-settlers and friars quickly set about the task of "civilizing" the Indians through baptism, the introduction of European seeds and livestock, and the imposition of Spanish mores of comportment and dress. To ensure the presumed physical and spiritual wellbeing of New Mexico's Pueblo Indians, they were divided into forty-one *encomiendas* awarded to notables of the conquest. For this "entrustment" to the protection and spiritual care of the Spanish, the natives paid dearly in tribute, labor, and, often, lives.[3]

Though "savages" were all the Spaniards saw when they arrived in the Rio Grande Valley, the word is hardly adequate to describe the Indians living there. Since the thirteenth century, the river basin had been occupied by the compact agricultural villages of the Pueblo Indians. The ninety pueblos—so named by the Spanish because their multistoried dwellings resembled Aztec cities—were economically independent, politically autonomous, and best described as city-states. In 1598 the Pueblo population totaled approximately sixty thousand. Though several nomadic Indian tribes, notably the Apache and Navajo, hunted in the surrounding plains and mountains, their low level of material culture and social organization spared them the yoke of subjugation until the early 1700s.[4]

The years 1598 to 1680 were brutal ones for the Pueblo peoples. Their food reserves were depleted by the colonists; their lives were disrupted by Spanish labor demands; their religious images were desecrated by the friars and their rituals suppressed. Many saw their kin driven to the point of death; women were raped and children enslaved. In 1680 the Pueblo peoples formed a confederation and routed the Spanish from the area, a feat that reverberated throughout New Spain and spurred other Indians to similar action. When the fury of the Pueblo Revolt was over, twenty-one out of thirty-three Franciscan friars were dead and 380 settlers had lost their lives. The twenty-three hundred white survivors fled south to Paso (Texas), where they regrouped and remained until 1693.[5]

Don Diego de Vargas was charged with the reconquest of the territory and in 1693 led one hundred soldiers, seventy families, and eighteen friars to reestablish Spanish presence in Santa Fe. A second Spanish town, Santa Cruz de la Cañada, was founded in 1695,[6] followed by Albuquerque in 1706.[7] Colonists who did not live in one of these three towns resided in small dispersed ranches or hamlets situated along the banks of the Rio Grande. The white population in 1700 was perhaps no more than three thousand. The Pueblo population by that year had declined to fifteen thousand.[8]

The period following the reconquest saw a major readjustment in Indian-white relations. Realizing that there was a limit to the exploitation the Pueblo would tolerate and that they would not be cowed into abandoning their native religious beliefs easily, the crown abolished the *encomienda* and replaced it with the *repartimiento*, a less onerous rotational labor levy. New Mexico's governors were ordered to observe Indian rights strictly, and the martyrdom of their brothers impressed on the friars that their evangelical zeal would have to be tempered.[9]

But the problem of extracting labor and wealth from the native population in its various forms remained. The revolt had not altered the practice of using political office as a vehicle for personal enrichment. Someone still had to construct the imposing mission compounds that were to dot the landscape, and the aristocracy's sense of preeminence was still dependent on the labor of others. For these ends, then, a new enemy was necessary. The "Apaches"—as the Spanish called all the nomadic Indians whose hunting grounds bordered on the agricultural settlements of the river basin (Jicarilla, Mescalero, Navajo, Ute, and Comanche)—were quickly defined as Satan's minions; this status made them eligible for "just war." Scores of men, women, and particularly children were brought into Spanish villages enslaved as prisoners of war. Some *genízaros*, as these detribalized Indians became known, were retained in local households for the performance of domestic tasks, while others were traded for luxury goods in the mining centers of northern New Spain. The growth of this commerce in captives during the eighteenth century was directly responsible for the constant warfare the kingdom's colonists were to experience.[10]

In this environment, the Spanish colonists of the post-reconquest period fashioned a society that they perceived as ordered hierarchically by honor, a prestige system based on principles of inherent personal worth.

Honor was a complex gradient of status that encompassed several other measures of social standing, such as descent, ethnicity, religion, profession, and authority over land.[11] The summation and ordering of these statuses and the pragmatic outcome of evaluations of honor resulted in the organization of society into three broadly defined groups: the nobility, the landed peasantry, and the *genízaros*.

The status hierarchy did not completely encompass class standing as structured by relations of production. The Pueblo Indians on whose labor and tribute the colonists so heavily relied fell outside the groups to whom honor mattered and refused to accept, cherish, and validate the ideals by which Spanish society organized its interactions. From the colonists' point of view, the physical tasks the Pueblo Indians performed were intrinsically dishonorable and conquest by a superior power itself dishonoring. Obviously, the Pueblo did not consciously share this view. In colonial New Mexico, honor and class were nevertheless interdependent. Social power ultimately gained its effectiveness from the combination of the two.[12]

The nobility consisted of fifteen to twenty families that intermarried to ensure their continued dominance. Their sense of aristocracy was rooted in the legally defined honor granted to the kingdom's colonizers by King Phillip II in their 1595 charter of incorporation.[13] As the colony developed, nobility gained a broader social meaning and was claimed by individuals who acquired large amounts of land, by military officials, and by bureaucrats—wealth and power acting as the determinants of intragroup mobility. By comparison with the titled peerage of central Mexico, New Mexico's nobility at best enjoyed the life of a comfortable gentry.[14] Yet, perhaps because of its isolation—and the attendant belief that it was a cultural oasis in a sea of barbarism—New Mexico's aristocracy considered itself second to none. Bearing Old Christian ancestry, harboring pretensions of purity of blood, and eschewing physical labor, it reveled in its rituals of precedence, in ostentatious display of lavish clothing and consumption of luxury goods, and in respectful forms of address and titles. Needless to say, such habits were buttressed by force of arms, wealth, and a legal superstructure premised on the belief that the social order was divinely ordained.

Landed peasants who were primarily of mestizo origin but considered themselves "Spaniards" were next in the hierarchy of honor. They had been recruited for the colonization of New Mexico with promises of land, and in 1700 all enjoyed rights to *merced*, a communal land grant consisting of private irrigated farmlands, house plots, and commons for livestock grazing. By 1800 the progressive subdivision of private plots had resulted in parcels too small for subsistence. Under these circumstances, owners of morseled holdings increasingly turned to wage labor.

Their ranks were swelled by persons who had not gained access to land as part of their patrimony. Though the land area of New Mexico may seem boundless, it was constrained by limited water sources, by the previous and competing water and land claims of the Pueblo Indians, and by the resistance to geographic expansion offered by hostile tribes.[15]

Lowest in prestige, dishonored and infamous because of their slave status, were the *genízaros*, a diverse group of Indians who resided in Spanish towns and performed the community's most menial and degrading tasks. Between 1694 and 1849, 3,294 *genízaros* entered Hispanic households.[16] Early in the seventeenth century, New Mexicans had been granted the privilege of warring against infidel Indians and retaining them in bondage for ten years as compensation for the costs of battle.[17] Though many *genízaros* remained slaves much longer, they were customarily freed at marriage. Lack of access to land and the development of emotional dependencies on their masters, by whom in most cases they had been raised, meant that even after manumission *genízaros* had few options for social mobility. Remaining in the household and employment of their former owners was common.

Genízaros (from the Turkish *yeni*,"new," and *cheri*, "troops") were truly New Mexico's shock troops against the infidel. Stigmatized by their former slavery, lacking kinship ties to the European community, and deemed devious because of their lack of mastery of Spanish, the increasing numbers of free *genízaros* were segregated in special neighborhoods such as Santa Fe's Barrio de Analco or congregated in new settlements such as Belén (1740), Abiquiu (1754), Ojo Caliente (1754), and San Miguel del Vado (1794). All of these genízaro communities—communities now of landed peasants of *genízaro* origin—were strategically established along the Indian raiding routes and were to serve Spanish settlements as buffers against attack.[18]

THE IDEOLOGY OF HONOR

"Honor" was a polysemic word embodying meanings at two different but fundamentally interrelated levels, one of status and one of virtue. Honor was first and foremost society's measure of social standing, ordering on a single vertical continuum those persons with much honor and differentiating them from those with little. Excellence manifested as territorial expansion of the realm was the monarchy's justification for the initial distribution of honor. Yet, "the claim to honor," as Julian Pitt-Rivers notes, "depends always, in the last resort, upon the ability of the claimant to impose himself. Might is the basis of right to precedence, which goes to the man who is bold enough to enforce his claim."[19] The children of the conquistadores gained their parents' honor through ascription and maintained and enhanced it through behavior deemed appropriate to a highly esteemed person.[20]

The second dimension of honor was a constellation of virtue ideals. Dividing the community horizontally along prestige group boundaries, honor-virtue established the status ordering among equals. Definitions of virtue were gender specific. Males embodied honor (the sentiment of honor) when they acted *con hombría* (in a manly fashion), exercised authority over family and subordinates, and esteemed honesty and loyalty. Females possessed the moral and ethical equivalent of honor, *vergüenza* (shame), if they were timid, feminine, virginal before marriage and afterward faithful to their husbands, discreet in the presence of men, and concerned for their reputations. Infractions of the rules of conduct dishonored men and were a sign of shamelessness. Shamelessness accumulated around the male head of household and dishonored both the family as a corporate group and all its members.

The maintenance of social inequality was central to the way in which status and virtue were defined to interact, the aim being the perpetuation of the nobility's preeminence. An aristocrat of however low repute was always legally more honorable than the most virtuous peasant. Because precedence at the upper reaches of the social structure guaranteed more material and symbolic benefits, it was usually among the nobility and elites that the most intense conflicts over honor-virtue occurred. Family feuds and vendettas were frequently the way sullied reputations were avenged and claims to virtue upheld.[21]

Consensus seems to have existed among New Mexicans of Hispanic origin regarding the behavior deemed virtuous and worthy of honor. Among the nobility and the peasantry alike, men concerned for their personal and familial repute, judged by how well they resolved the contradictory imperatives of domination (protection of one's women-folk from assault) and conquest (prowess gained through sullying the purity of other men's women), hoped to minimize affronts to their virtue, thereby maintaining their status. Female seclusion and a high symbolic value placed on virginity and marital fidelity helped accomplish this aim.

Yet only in aristocratic households, where servants and retainers abounded, could resources be expended to ensure that females were being properly restrained and shameful. The maintenance of their virtue was made easier because *genízaro* women could be forced into sexual service. As slaves they were dishonored by their bondage and could therefore be abused without fear of retaliation, for as one friar lamented in his 1734 report to the viceroy, Spanish New Mexicans justified their rapes, saying: "an Indian does not care if you fornicate with his wife because she has no shame [and] . . . only with lascivious treatment are Indian women conquered."[22]

Inequalities in power and status kept peasant men from honorably challenging aristocrats. Both because of this disparity in status and because of the excesses of the nobility in asserting their virility, ideals of female virtue were as intensely cherished by peasants. Manuel Alvarez, the United States consul in Santa Fe, alluded to this when he wrote in 1834: "the honorable man (if it is possible for a poor man to be honorable) has a jewel in having an honorable wife."[23] Among the peasantry, gender prescriptions undoubtedly had to be reconciled with the exigencies of production and reproduction of material life. The required participation of all able household members in planting and the harvest meant that there were periods when constraints on females of this class were less rigorously enforced. Juana Carillo of Santa Fe admitted as much in 1712 when she confessed to enjoying the affections of two men her father had hired for their spring planting.[24] Again, in households where men were frequently absent, such as those of soldiers, muleteers, shepherds, and hunters, cultural ideals were less rigid. The fact that females supervised family and home for large parts of the year, staved off Indian attack, and cared for the group's public rights meant that it was difficult for them to lead sheltered and secluded lives. It was not uncommon for these women to lament that they had been assaulted, raped, or seduced while their husbands or fathers were away from home.[25]

HONOR AND MARRIAGE

Marriage was the most important ritual event in the life-course, and in it the honor of the family took precedence over all other considerations. The union of two properties, the joining of two households, the creation of a web of affinal relations, the perpetuation of a family's symbolic patrimony—its name and reputation—were transactions so important to the honor-status of the group that marriage was hardly a decision to be made by minors. The norm in New Mexico was for parents to arrange nuptials for their children with little or no consideration of their wishes. Filial piety required the acceptance of any union one's parents deemed appropriate or advantageous.

The 1786 marriage of Francisco Narpa and Juana Lorem in Sandia provides a glimpse of the familial motivations involved in an arranged union. Appearing before the provincial ecclesiastical judge to explain how he had married, Francisco reported: "Having agreed with Juana Lorem that we wished to marry, I asked her grandmother Tomasa Cibaa, and with her permission and that of her relatives, I married." Juana Lorem had a slightly different understanding of the events that led up to her marriage to Francisco. She told the judge, "It is totally false that I agreed to marry the said Francisco. I never wanted to marry the said Francisco. But for fear of my grandmother Tomasa Cibaa I contracted the marriage." Finally, Tomasa Cibaa explained: "I ordered my granddaughter Juana to marry the said Francisco Narpa because he is moderately wealthy, and it is true that I pressured Juana to appear before the priest [for the matrimonial investigation] and say nothing that might provoke questioning." The details of this marriage surface as part of an ecclesiastical investigation into the allegation that the union was incestuous. Francisco had fathered a child by Maria Quieypas, Juana's mother, and therefore his marriage to Juana was invalid. The marriage was annulled, dotal and patrimonial property were confiscated, the three were publicly flogged, and Narpa was exiled from New Mexico.[26]

Of course, I do not wish to suggest that arranged marriage was an inflexible rule. The extent to which parental preference for arranged marriage could be enforced was mediated both by the person's status and by each family's particular fertility history. The number of children in a family, their birth order, and their sex dictated the options available to parents to secure their son or daughter an acceptable or advantageous spouse. These and other variables also conditioned the range of filial responses possible—whether a son or daughter acted as if bound by duty or sentiment, or resisted, or attempted to manipulate the situation so as to appease everyone's concerns.

From a father's point of view, a round of poker is an excellent metaphor for the way in which limited resources (the patrimony) were manipulated to maximize the gains associated with marital alliance. Pierre Bourdieu has applied this metaphor to the marriage of a family's children.[27] Success at enhancing and perpetuating the family's status is based not only on the hand one is dealt (whether the nuptial candidate is an only child, the eldest of several sons, or the youngest of many daughters) but also the skill with which one plays it (bids, bluffs, and displays). The patrimony was the material resource a father had to apportion among its claimants at strategic moments to maximize reproductive success. Although legally every legitimate child in New Mexico was entitled to an equal share of this wealth, practice varied by class. Aristocratic holders of large landed estates preferred male primogeniture as a way of keeping their property intact. The eldest son, as the heir to the household head's political rights over the group and the person responsible for the name and reputation of the family, was the individual to whom a disproportionate amount of parents' premortem resources was committed. As first in importance, even if preceded by older sisters, he could not suffer a misalliance without lowering the entire family's public rating and diminishing the possibilities of securing honorable partners for his unmarried brothers and sisters. Therefore, he was the child of whom parents expected the most and the child disciplined most severely to ensure obedience but allowed the greatest excesses in other matters. He was also perhaps the most predisposed to bow to duty.

If the eldest son had married well and the family's position had thus been attended to, filial participation in the marriage process was tolerated in subsequent cases. Because younger sons were unlikely to fare as well in the acquisition of marital property and could expect only enough money and movable goods to avoid misalliance, fathers might be more open to their suggestions regarding eligible brides.

Daughters of the nobility were a potential liability on the marriage market, dissipating the material and symbolic patrimony by having their dowries absorbed into their husbands' assets. Every attempt would be made to dispose of nubile females as quickly as possible and at minimal expense. If a daughter experienced a prenuptial dishonor, such as the loss of her virginity, additional resources would have to be committed to secure her an appropriate mate. Thus large amounts of time and energy were spent ensuring that a maiden's sexual shame was being maintained. Undoubtedly, the result was that a woman's freedom to object to a marriage, to express her desires in spouse selection, was more limited than that of her brothers.[28]

Peasants enjoying rights to communal land grants practiced partible inheritance. Sons were given their share of the family's land when they took a bride and were assigned a certain number of *vigas* ("beams"—a way of dividing the space in a house) in the parental home. If space limitations prohibited such a move, assistance was given in the addition of rooms to the house or the construction of a separate edifice in the immediate vicinity. For females, premortem dowries usually consisted of household items and livestock. Daughters seldom received land rights at marriage because parents fully expected the husband's family to meet this need. The authority relations springing from this mode of property division meant that parental supervision over spouse selection and its timing was as rigidly exercised as among the nobility.

For landless freed *genízaros*, the institution of marriage itself was of no consequence. Many preferred concubinage, as they held no property to transmit and the alienation from their Indian kin that accompanied enslavement made the issue of perpetuation of family name irrelevant. Wage earners and landless peasants were in a similar situation with regard to marriage. Once children were old enough to leave the familial hearth in search of a livelihood, parental control over their behavior all but ceased. Their only concern in the timing of marriage, if in fact they chose matrimony for cultural reasons, was the necessity to accumulate a nest egg with which to establish a conjugal residence.

MARRIAGE AND THE CHURCH

The settlement of the Kingdom of New Mexico was a joint venture of church and state. In all the remote areas of the Spanish empire, in which civilization was to be brought to the Indians, it was by the religious orders, through the institution of missions, that the task was accomplished. Acting as defenders of the Indians, as guardians of community piety and morality, and as a counterpoint to the power of the state, the church at one and the same time legitimated and buttressed the colonial system and challenged certain tenets of its rule. Nowhere was this tension among the authorities of God, of the family, and of the state clearer than on the issue of marriage.

Until 1776 the Catholic Church enjoyed exclusive jurisdiction over the ritual, sacramental, and contractual aspects of matrimony. Ecclesiastical law, articulated as a theory of impediments to marriage, was dominated by two concerns: the prohibition of incest and the determination of the exercise of free will. The latter principle drew on the Roman legal tradition that a nuptial contract was valid only if the parties had given free and absolute consent. The use of persuasion and coercion to arrange marriages of children could place patriarchs in direct confrontation with the church and its clerics.

Arranged marriage was a complex issue for the church. Scripture and canon law were fraught with ambiguities and contradictions on the matter. Christian ideology reinforced the honor code regarding the obedience and personal subordination children owed their parents. "Honor your father and mother," orders the fourth commandment. "Children, obey your parents in the Lord," enjoins St. Paul in his Epistle to the Ephesians (5:22). The church maintained that the law of nature bound parents and children in a relationship that entailed reciprocal rights and obligations. The authority of man over his wife, children, and servants emanated from God's power over creation, and therefore his was the right to guide and discipline his children as necessary. Filial submission, St. Paul promises, will be reciprocated with paternal love, protection, and guidance.[29]

But the vexing question clerics were obliged to ask, in the case of marriage, was at what point paternal guidance and filial obedience simply became coercion. The issue was of some importance because forced marriages, or those contracted under duress, were invalid. Matrimony was the sacramental union of free will based on mutual consent. Ideally it was the work of God, and "what God has joined together, let no man separate." The autonomy of individual will, responsibility, and conscience in undertaking marriage was central to Catholic thought. In arranged marriages, in which conflict between obedience to parents and obedience to one's conscience existed, the will of the individual was to take precedence.[30] The scriptural justification for limits on the authority of the father and the freedom of Christ's message rested in the following: "Call no man your father upon the earth: for One is your Father, which is in heaven" (Matthew 23:9). And again (Matthew 10:34–37):

> Think not that I am come to send peace on earth: I came not to send peace, but a sword. For I am come to set a man at variance against his father, and the daughter against her mother, and the daughter-in-law against her mother-in-law. And a man's foes shall be they of his own household. He that loveth father or mother more than me is not worthy of me: and he that loveth son or daughter more than me is not worthy of me.

A mechanism for the determination that a person was marrying freely existed in canon law. If the slightest hint of coercion surfaced, the local priest had the power to remove the candidate from his/her home for isolation from parental pressures. Once the person's wishes became known, the priest was legally bound either to marry the person, even against parental wishes, or to prohibit a forced union. Don Salvador Martínez of Albuquerque, for example, availed himself of ecclesiastical intervention when he sought Vicar Fray Manuel Roxo's help in his 1761 matrimonial bid for Doña Simona Baldes. Though Martínez had twice asked for Doña Simona's hand in marriage, his proposals had been ignored. Moved by the evidence, the vicar sequestered Doña Simona, who admitted she wanted to be Martínez's bride. The marriage occurred despite parental objections, which may have been due to a gross age difference. Don Salvador was a sixty-two-year-old widower; Doña Simona was only nineteen.[31]

The freedom that the Catholic Church might grant the sexes in the selection of conjugal mates formed the legal foundation for the subversion of parental authority, but, as the experience of all areas of the Spanish colonial empire testifies, the law and its execution were two very different matters. It was not uncommon for clerics charged with the interpretation and execution of canon law to enforce it selectively or to bend its dictates to avoid misalliances or subversion of the social order. If a friar believed an arranged marriage was a good match, he might uphold parental prerogatives and rationalize that the natural authority of a father over his children was in full accord with the will of God.

A variant of such an alliance between priest and parents occurred in Santa Fe in 1710. María Belasquez and Joseph Armijo appeared before Fray Lucas Arebalo that year claiming that her parents would not allow her to marry Joseph. They asked the friar to take María into his custody so that she could express her true wishes. María was sequestered but was returned to her father shortly after Joseph left the rectory. Joseph immediately appealed to the provincial ecclesiastical judge, who agreed that Fray Lucas had not upheld the marriage canons of the Council of Trent. The two were sequestered anew and were finally joined in wedlock after affirming their desire to be husband and wife.[32]

From the evidence in the ecclesiastical archives, "absolute" legal liberty to choose a spouse meant, in fact, freedom to select a mate from *within* one's class and ethnic group. No examples exist in the Archives of the Archdiocese of Santa Fe of clerics' sanctioning a cross-class marriage over parental objections. The church might subvert the particular authority of parents, but it would not subvert the social order at large.

CULTURAL CONTRADICTIONS AND THE DIALECTICS OF SOCIAL ACTION

Marriage was a ritual event with meanings derived from several interrelated and interpenetrating ideologies. For the state, it was a way of perpetuating status and property inequalities in their hierarchical order. In Christian thought, it prefigured the love between Christ and the church and was of necessity the union of free wills. The sacrament preserved community morality by providing a sanctioned arena for the expression of sexual desires. The emotions of parents and children regarding affinity and connubiality figured in behavior, as did fertility histories and demographic realities.

The cultural system in which marriage was enmeshed was diverse and divisive, resting on symbols that were ambiguous and polysemic. The head and the heart were two such equivocal symbols that synthesized beliefs about hierarchy, honor, and desires and allowed their translation into behavior. According to the native cognitive model of New Mexicans, behavior was the outcome of interplay between several realms. Individual actions were the result of mediation between external forces—such as social rules, values, chance—and internal physical drives, such as sentiments and emotions.

External factors were comprehended through the head. Reason, probity, and the conscience were perceived to be located there. The head was the symbol of personal and collective honor. The king's honor was exhibited through a crowned head, the honor of the bishop through his miter. Honor and precedence were paid by bowing one's head, taking off one's hat, or (for women) covering one's head. Decapitation was a dishonorable punishment. Honor challenges were frequently initiated by a slap to the face. Manuel Martín of San Juan in 1766 punished his daughter for bearing an illegitimate child by cutting off all of her hair; a bald head was to serve the community as a sign of her shamelessness.[33] Catholic priests cut a tonsure in their hair as a sign of their vow of chastity and pledge to sexual purity.[34]

Just as the reason's source was the head, its antithesis, emotion, was rooted in the heart. The heart was the organ through which "natural" urges were experienced and heartfelt. "I wish to marry for no other reason than to serve God and because it comes forth from my heart, without it being the result of any other motivation," said Sebastiana de la Serna of her 1715 marriage bid.[35] For Fray José de la Prada, concupiscence sprang from the heart. Writing the governor of New Mexico concerning the sexual laity of his congregation, Prada complained that "their customs and heathen friskiness have sunk very deep roots into their hearts."[36] Another friar in a sermon on lust warned his congregation of the metabolic repercussions of an unregulated heart. "It is from the heart that we must displace this monster of sensuality . . . it is the cause of so many sudden deaths, infectious disease, and numerous maladies of the liver."[37]

The heart as a natural symbol for love had been enmeshed in the popular consciousness of Western Europeans since at least the thirteenth century.[38] The songs and poetry of courtly love diffused to the New World cast the heart as the well of sentiment. As roving troubadours performed their medieval romances in New Mexico's villages, the motifs of their repertoire—the all-consuming love that torments the courtier, the impossible desires of an inferior man for a married lady, the discovery of an adulterous liaison that ends in death for the two lovesick individuals—certainly resonated in the imaginations of young and old alike.[39]

The tensions between external forces and personal desires symbolized as conflicts between the head and the heart, between reason and sentiment, between collective responsibility and individual will, provided Hispanics in New Mexico with a variety of options and explanations for their behavior. One sees in the 1715 statements of Sebastiana de Jesús of Santa Fe the equivocation over such ideals. Appearing before the local priest to complete the matrimonial investigation necessary so that she could be joined in wedlock with Gerónimo Ortega, she was asked if she truly wanted to marry. She said:

> When the mother who raised me, whose name is Lucia Ortis, asked me about the marriage the first time, I said no, I did not want to marry; but later, so that my mother would not be angry I said yes. But now, the desire to marry him does not spring from my heart . . . and having heard that the father of Gerónimo de Ortega has become a public ward in Santa Fe, I refuse to marry him. And if I marry him it will be only because my mother forces me to. I must do as she wishes,

and will do it only to please her. . . . I do not wish to marry, it is not of my heart. . . . Before it was not of my heart and it is even less so now.

Fray Antonio Miranda was uncertain whether Sebastiana was being forced into matrimony, so he ordered a new declaration taken. When asked again, she said blankly that she wanted to marry Gerónimo "of my absolute liberty."[40]

The individuals—be they clerics, family heads, or bureaucrats—who articulated the ideals of marriage formation that opposed arranged marriage to marriage choice, hierarchy to egalitarianism, had a vested interest in presenting the cultural system as rigidly circumscribed by these dichotomies. In reality, much behavior fell along a continuum of which these oppositions were the extremes. After all, our information on these prescriptions comes largely from litigation before the civil and ecclesiastical courts, which established the outer limits of proper conduct. In their daily lives, individuals negotiated their behavior pragmatically in dynamic relationships with one another using the ideals of the cultural system as anchors. Thus, for example, on the continuum between arranged marriage and marriage choice, children of the aristocracy may all have their marriages arranged; children of the peasantry may vary between the two forms depending on their sex and birth order; and *genízaros*, wage laborers, and landless peasants would be relatively free to choose their own partners.[41]

The dialogue that undoubtedly occurred between the generations while negotiating a marriage match was seldom voiced and rarely recorded. Folk songs alone give us a hint of the interaction that must have been central to the selection process. "The Recent Bride," an early nineteenth-century song from Taos,[42] explores the tensions between parents and children over marriage choice. Parents, having themselves at one time perhaps experienced the same feelings, can articulate the child's view but do so negatively, casting duty and sentiment, reason and passion, paternal love and romantic love as irreconcilable. The parental objective is clearly the subversion of individualistic filial behavior. By describing the consequences of ignoring parental counsels, the singers hope to have their expectations fulfilled:

A recent bride and woe is me
I weep the livelong day
To think I'm wed so unhappily
Nothing can my fate allay.

Before I wed my mother dear
Did try to turn me from my course,

Her counsels wet with many a tear
I now regret with great remorse.
But willful was I, I paid no heed
And God has fully punished me,
But willful was I, I paid no heed
And God has fully punished me.
For my husband I have found to be
A man who drinks and drinks and drinks,
He has already forgotten me
Of his young bride he never thinks. . . .

In "La Señora Chepita,"[43] the nature of the generational conflict is more explicit:

Oh what times these are, Señora Chepita;
Oh what things are happening these days!
Laboriousness is no longer prized, Misery engulfs us all,
Progress itself is lost.
Oh what times these are, Señora Chepita!

In my time commerce bleated
And the crafts with much to do.
Lovers were always constant,
No woman was ever false.
Women in times past
Spent their time only caring
For their children, husbands and servants
And of none did they gossip.

Today it is common to see
That honor is snatched from one another
In others defects are found
While ignoring one's own, Senora Chepita.
If a young man made a conquest
He would hide it with just reason
So that none would know
The secrets of his heart.

From the parents' point of view presented above, their society is orderly and rule-bound, whereas that of the new generation is chaotic and ruleless. The song is not a statement of fact. If we took them literally, the folk songs in which the older generation laments the shortcomings of the new—a lament so common in every historical period—would lead us to believe that society was constantly in a state of breakdown. These songs are instead comments about what parents would like their children to do. Parents refuse to legitimate the norms that guide filial behavior by denying that such norms exist. The songs express parental displeasure. They attempt to persuade sons and daughters to conform to parental ideals and do things the way they used to in "the good old days."[44]

The bishop of Durango in 1823 attested to the fact that children, though constrained in their marital options, did not sit by passively and always accept parental will. They manipulated the symbols of marriage, of honor and love, to obtain a desired spouse. Given the bishop's concern that maidens were being deflowered as part of youthful schemes "undertaken to facilitate" marriages that might otherwise have been unacceptable to parents,[45] we can speculate on what actions may have been taken by adolescents. A young man and woman might be aroused by a genuine love for one another and desire matrimony. Fearing that parents would object to a union, they might devise a ploy to maneuver an acceptable solution within the limits of familial honor. The woman might allow her virginity to be taken, claim that her honor had been sullied, and demand marriage simply as a way of forcing parents to consider a mate who might otherwise never have been ideally acceptable. The discourse in such a case would take place entirely in the idiom of honor, but only because this strategy allowed the parties to maneuver within the parental value system. Such ploys were popular resolutions to conflicts of honor in Golden Age Spanish theater.[46]

Parents and children negotiated with different amounts of power. The dynamics of the process were clearly skewed in favor of the elders in both conscious and unconscious ways. Sons and daughters were familiar with the options available to them in marriage formation and knew exactly what was expected to ensure property transmission, to satisfy the requirements of the family's symbolic patrimony, and to avoid scandal and ostracism. Norms and the authority of custom buttressed parental prerogatives, as did the socialization process. Personal "tastes" were learned in infancy and reinforced through avoidance of contact with certain persons. Thus a child's desire for a certain mate was just as much the result of interaction with persons of similar status, race, education, and subcultural traits as it was of "individualistic" urges.[47]

SOCIAL CHANGE

From the years following the reconquest to the early 1770s, the Kingdom of New Mexico was peripheral to the empire. Isolated on the northern margins of New Spain, the colony's only link to "civilization" was a yearly mule train to Mexico City, which traveled over several thousand miles of territory inhabited by hostile Indians. New Mexico contained no significant mineral deposits, its population's material culture was rudimentary, and its cash crop production (wheat, cotton, corn, pine nuts) was insignificant. In fact, had the Franciscan order not pleaded passionately before the crown for the privilege of converting New Mexico's Indians, colonists might never have been sent there in the first place.[48]

The isolation of the province slowly began to crumble in the 1760s. Frightened by the increasing levels of Russian, Anglo-American, and French encroachment into Texas, New Mexico, and California, King Charles III ordered a series of economic, military, and administrative reforms, commonly known as the Bourbon reforms, to safeguard the territory. The reform project began in 1765 when the Spanish Royal Corps of Engineers was sent to the northern frontier of New Spain to map the area thoroughly, to identify its mineral and hydraulic resources, to assess the feasibility of textile production, to propose methods for increasing agricultural production, and to outline the military changes necessary to fortify the frontier.[49] On the basis of the expedition's recommendations, northern New Spain was reorganized in 1776 into one military and administrative unit called the Internal Provinces. New *presidios* were constructed to ward off foreign attack, and vigorous campaigns were staged to subdue the "Apaches," who made trade and communication difficult. It was precisely in this period that permanent settlements were finally established in California, the first mission being built in 1769 at San Diego.[50]

The crown believed that New Mexico could be retained as part of the empire only through fuller integration into the market economy centered in Chihuahua. To achieve this aim, trade and travel restrictions were abolished, New Mexican products were given sales tax exemptions, and agricultural specialists, veterinarians, and master weavers were sent to the area to upgrade local production and improve the competitive position of the kingdom's products. Within a few years the frequency of mule trains to and from Chihuahua increased, money began to circulate more widely, and new colonists from north-central Mexico migrated into the area.[51]

Imperial economic reforms coincided with a period of demographic growth in New Mexico, which resulted in intense land pressure. Between 1760 and 1820, the Spanish and mixed-blood population of New Mexico grew from 7,666 to 28,436. By the 1780s, many of the land grants to the initial colonists were insufficient for subsistence. A few new *mercedes* were conceded in the late 1780s, but not enough to meet the population's needs. Governor Fernando de la Concha noted this in his 1796 report to the commandant of the Internal Provinces and estimated that there were 1,500 individuals without land to till.[52] The inevitable upshot of this situation was the expansion of wage labor. A comparison of the occupational structures of the kingdom in 1790 and 1827 reflects this expansion of wage laborers. In 1790, Albuquerque had an adult working population of 601. Farmers constituted 65 percent (391), 25 percent (151) were craftsman, and 10 percent (58) were day laborers. By 1827, 610 persons were listed as full-time-workers: 66 percent (397) were farmers, 14 percent (85) craftsmen, and 19 percent (113) day laborers. The 1790 census of Santa Fe listed 413 individuals with occupations. Farmers represented 85 percent (350), craftsmen 7 percent (28), and day laborers 8 percent (34). By 1827, of 846 workers, 55 percent (467) were farmers, 12 percent (101) craftsmen, and 31 percent (264) day laborers. An expansion of the day laborer category in both size and proportion also occurred in Santa Cruz during this period.[53] The end result of the Bourbon reforms and the land pressure that accompanied them was the expansion of socially autonomous forms of labor and increased mobility for a significant portion of the population.

To complete the picture of changes that occurred in the last quarter of the eighteenth century, we must also examine church-state relations as they affected New Mexico. During the reign of Charles III many of the formal aspects of the Patronato Real, the partnership between church and state that had been so effective in the colonization of the Americas, were abolished. The religious orders, perceived as independent and powerful because of their relationship to the indigenous population, were first to lose their privileged status. In New Mexico, where the Franciscan friars and the area's governors had battled incessantly since the 1600s over the extent to which each could exploit Indian land and labor, the Bourbon attack on clerical rights put an end to the feud. The missions were gradually secularized; where thirty friars had administered the sacraments in 1760, by 1834 none remained.[54]

The loosening of the Franciscans' grip on the population of New Mexico, part and parcel of the growth of secularism and the diffusion of rationalism throughout Europe and its colonies, bred an indifference toward moral theology, the scriptures, and the authority of priests. One of the first changes one notes in this increasingly secular society is a linguistic change in the ecclesiastical marriage records. Whereas between 1690 and 1790 most individuals married ostensibly "to save my soul,"[55] "to serve God and no other reason,"[56] or motivated by similar religious convictions, after 1790 nuptial candidates are moved by "the growing desire we mutually have"[57] and by "the urges of the flesh, human wretchedness and the great love we have for each other."[58] Increasingly, individuals mention personal desires such as love as the reason for marriage.

The Bourbon reforms and the growth of a landless population dependent on wage labor for its reproduction had increased social differentiation. This in turn brought into open question the ideological consensus that had formerly existed between the nobility and the landed peasants regarding ascribed honor as a sign of social status premised on family origin and control over means and instruments of production. For free *genízaros*, mestizos who could not boast of "Spanish" origin, and landless peasants, honor was of little material consequence. Their social status was obtained primarily through individual achievement; under such circumstances patriarchal control over marriage formation was of no functional significance. After all, parental sanction for arranged marriage had been effective because familial honor had carried with it property and social privileges. Once children were able with their own wages to accumulate the necessary resources to establish a household, and could not in any way count on significant inheritance of property, generational relations were placed on a new footing.

Examining the period from 1690 to 1848, the major change that occurred in marriage formation was an increased preference for unions based explicitly on romantic love over those arranged by parents pursuing economic considerations. This change was not sudden; it was an ongoing process. Love matches were possible from the earliest days of Spanish settlement but occurred infrequently among the landed classes concerned for the perpetuation of their patrimonies. Children had plenty of parental counsels, ballads, folktales, laws, and sermons to make them realize the disastrous consequences of placing desires over reason.

The history of marriage in a colonial social formation such as New Mexico reveals the centrality of patriarchal control for generational, gender, and class forms of domination. Arranged marriages that enhanced honor provided the nobility and the landed peasantry with a tool by which to protect their status in an unequal society. The various ideologies by which gender and class hierarchies were comprehended and legitimated, however, were not monolithic and static. The partnership between the church and state so instrumental in the conquest of Latin America created distinct views on the meaning of marriage. Though the positions of church and state frequently converged, differences between them enabled children to challenge parental authority without danger to the social order. Similarly, the meanings attached to the system of status and prestige varied by class and changed in response to larger economic forces that themselves transformed relations of production and the power relations between church and state. By the 1800s, the material underpinnings of the honor code had been eroded, creating the conditions that allowed individual urges such as romantic love to exert greater influence on marriage formation.

NOTES

1. Gayle Rubin, "The Traffic in Women: Notes toward a Political Economy of Sex," in *Toward an Anthropology of Women*, ed. Rayna Reiter (New York: Monthly Review Press, 1975), 166–210.

2. The generalizations presented in this article are derived from extensive reading of documents in the Archives of the Archdiocese of Santa Fe, the Spanish Archives of New Mexico, the Mexican Archives of New Mexico (deposited at the New Mexico State Records Center and Archives, Santa Fe), sections of the Archivo General de la Nacíon in Mexico City that pertain to New Mexico (History, Provincias Internas, Inquisicíon, Californias, Hacienda), and the folklore collections housed at the Museum of New Mexico in Santa Fe and the University of New Mexico's Zimmerman Library in Albuquerque. The major portion of my source material dates from 1690 to 1846 and consists primarily of court cases heard by the civil and ecclesiastical authorities on seduction (or the loss of female virtue), affronts to a person's honor, parental opposition to marriage, impediments to matrimony, dowry negotiations, concubinage, rape, adultery, spouse mistreatment, and divorce. By examining points at which behavior deviated from prescriptions, I have attempted to reconstruct the society's ideals. Where my evidence is thin, I have been forced to turn to Mexican proscriptive literature that, though not produced by New Mexico's residents, was undoubtedly available to its literate members and reflected the broader cultural milieu of New Spain. Readers desiring more extensive documentation of my sources should consult Ramón A. Gutiérrez, "Marriage, Sex, and the Family: Social Change in Colonial New Mexico, 1690–1846" (Ph.D. dissertation, University of Wisconsin, Madison, 1980).

3. See Lansing B. Bloom, "The Vagas Encomienda," *New Mexico Historical Review* 14 (1939): 367–71; also David H. Snow, "A Note on Encomienda Economics in Seventeenth-Century New Mexico," in *Hispanic Arts and Ethnohistory*, ed. Marta Weigle (Albuquerque: University of New Mexico Press, 1983), 347–57.

4. Edward Dozier, *The Pueblo Indians of North America* (New York: Holt, Rinehart and Winston, 1950), 43–52.

5. Jesse B. Bailey, *Diego de Vargas and the Reconquest of New Mexico* (Albuquerque: University of New Mexico Press, 1940).

6. Archivo General de la Nacíon, Historia (hereafter cited as AGN-HIST), 39-5.

7. Lansing B. Bloom, "Albuquerque and Galisteo: Certificate of Their Founding," *New Mexico Historical Review* 10 (1935): 48–50.

8. Dozier, *Pueblo Indians*, 122.

9. D. W. Meinig, *Southwest* (New York, 1974), 27–32; John F. Bannon, *The Spanish Borderlands Frontier, 1513–1821* (Albuquerque: University of New Mexico Press, 1974), 28–48.

10. Lynn Robinson Bailey, *Indian Slave Trade in the Southwest* (Los Angeles: Westerlere Press, 1966), 1–89.

11. Ferdinad Tönnies, "Estates and Classes," in *Class, Status and Power: A Reader in Social Stratification*, ed. R. Bendix and S. Lipset (New York: Basic Books, 1953), 12–21.

12. Anthony Giddens, *Capitalism and Modern Social Theory* (Cambridge: Cambridge University Press, 1971), 166–67.

13. George Hammond and Agapito Rey, *Don Juan de Onate: Colonizer of New Mexico, 1595–1628* (Albuquerque: University of New Mexico Press, 1953), 50.

14. Doris M. Ladd, *The Mexican Nobility at Independence, 1780–1824* (Austin: University of Texas Press, 1976).

15. Olen E. Leonard, *The Role of the Land Grant in the Social Organization and Social Processes of a Spanish-American Village in New Mexico* (Albuquerque: Calvin Horne, 1970).

16. David M. Brugge, *Navajos in the Catholic Church Records of New Mexico 1694–1875* (Window Rock, AZ.: The Navajo Tribe, 1968), 30.

17. Mario Góngora, *Studies in the Colonial History of Spanish America* (Cambridge: Cambridge University Press, 1975), 128.

18. Frances Leon Swadesh, *Los primeros pobladores: Hispanic Americans of the Ute Frontier* (South Bend: University of Notre Dame Press, 1974), 31–35.

19. Julian Pitt-Rivers, "Honor," in *Encyclopedia of the Social Sciences*, 2nd ed. (New York: Macmillan, 1968), 505.

20. A general understanding of honor can be obtained from J. G. Peristiany, *Honor and Shame: The Values of the Mediterranean* (Chicago: University of Chicago Press, 1966); J. K. Campbell, *Honor, Family, and Patronage: A Study of Institutions and Moral Values in a Greek Mountain Community* (New York: Oxford University Press, 1976); Pierre Bourdieu, "Marriage Strategies as Strategies of Social Reproduction," in *Family and Society*, ed. R. Forster and C. Ranum (Baltimore: Johns Hopkins University Press, 1976), 117–44; Verena Martinez-Alier, *Marriage, Class, and Colour in Nineteenth-Century Cuba* (Cambridge: Cambridge University Press, 1974); Jane Schneider, "Of Vigilance and Virgins: Honor and Shame and Access to Resources in Mediterranean Societies," *Ethnology* 10 (1971): 1–23; Julius Kirshner, *Pursuing Honor While Avoiding Sin* (Milan: Quaderni di "Studi Senesi," 1978); Alfonso Garcia Valdecasas, *El Hidalgo y el Honor* (Madrid: Revista de Occidente, 1948); Gutiérrez, "Marriage, Sex, and the Family"; also Gutierrez, "From Honor to Love: Transformation of the Meaning of Sexuality in Colonial New Mexico," in *Interpreting Kinship Ideology and Practice in Latin America*, ed. Raymond T. Smith (Chapel Hill: University of North Carolina Press, 1984); and Julian Pitt-Rivers, *The Fate of Shechem, or The Politics of Sex* (Cambridge: Cambridge University Press, 1977).

21. No one has yet adequately explained the origins of honor-virtue. Its history is ancient in the Mediterranean as a cultural template for the maintenance of hierarchy through endogamy and precepts concerning the sacred. Honor antedates Christianity, yet their moral and ethical ideals coincide on many points. The most intelligent discussion of the origins of honor is found in Schneider, "Of Vigilance and Virgins," 1–23.

22. Archivo General de la Nacíon, Inquisicion (hereafter cited as AGN-INQ), 854:253–56.

23. Manuel Alvarez, personal papers, notebook, New Mexico State Records Center and Archives, Santa Fe.

24. Archives of the Archdiocese of Santa Fe (hereafter cited as AASF), 51:735–58.

25. AASF 60:270; Spanish Archives of New Mexico (hereafter cited as SANM), 18:579; AASF 60:376.

26. AASF 64:706–7; 52:773–74.

27. Bourdieu, "Marriage Strategies," 122.

28. SANM 10:4–25, 868–72.

29. Jean-Louis Flandrin, *Families in Former Times: Kinship, Household, and Sexuality* (Cambridge: Cambridge University Press, 1979), 118–19.

30. Ibid. 122.

31. AASF 62:311–14.

32. AASF 60:680–92.

33. SANM 9:943.

34. Pitt-Rivers, *Fate of Shechem*, 23.

35. AASF 61:209.

36. SANM 15:617.

37. Archivo General de la Nación, Hacienda (hereafter cited as AGN-HACIEN-DA) 29-8:2.

38. Johan Huizinga, *The Waning of the Middle Ages* (Garden City, NY: Double-day, 1949), 77–84.

39. Arthur L. Campa, *Spanish Folk-Poetry in New Mexico* (Albuquerque: University of New Mexico Press, 1946), 29–90; Aurelio M. Espinosa, "Romancero Nuevomejicano" *Revue Hispanique* 33 (1915): 446–560.

40. AASF 61:209–12.

41. Lee Drummond, "The Cultural Continuum: A Theory of Intersystems," *Man* 15 (1980): 352–74.

42. Works Progress Administration, New Mexico Folklore Collection, 5-5-19 #26.

43. Campa, *Spanish Folk-Poetry*, 203.

44. Sylvia Yanagisako, "Time, Ambiguity, and the Norms of Filial Relations" (paper presented at the Conference on Theoretical Perspectives on Kinship in Latin America, 1980, sponsored by the Social Science Research Council and the American Council of Learned Societies), 56.

45. AASF 53:790.

46. Donald R. Larson, *The Honor Plays of Lope de Vega* (Cambridge, MA: Harvard University Press, 1977), 17–37.

47. Bourdieu, "Marriage Strategies," 140–41.

48. Eleanor B. Adams, *Bishop Tamaron's Visitation of New Mexico, 1760* (Albuquerque: Historical Society of New Mexico, 1954), 3–4.

49. Janet R. Fireman, *The Spanish Royal Corps of Engineers in the Western Borderlands: Instrument of Bourbon Reform, 1764 to 1815* (Glendale,CA: Arthur K. Clark, 1977).

50. Bannon, *The Spanish Borderlands Frontier*, 143–90.

51. AGN-HIST 25-31:252–53; 25–36:297; Archivo General de la Nación, Californias (hereafter cited as AGN-CALIF), 17-7:228; 17-10:325–27; SANM 10:931–33, 1020–37; Juan Aguatin Escudero, *Noticias estadíticas del estado de Cihuahua* (Mexico City: Juan Ojeda, 1832), 37–38.

52. AGN-CALIF 17-7:226.

53. SANM 12:319–502; H. Bailey Carroll and J. Villasana Haggard, eds., *Three New Mexico Chronicles* (Albuquerque: The Quivera Society, 1942), 88.

54. David J. Weber, *The Mexican Frontier 1821–1846* (Albuquerque: University of New Mexico Press, 1982), 43–82.

55. AASF 61:404.

56. AASF 61:68.

57. AASF 66:18.

58. AASF 79:122.

2

Women Dreaming: The Religiopsychology of Indian-White Marriages and the Rise of Metis Culture

Jacqueline Peterson

So recent is the inclusion of the term *Metis* in the collective vocabulary and consciousness of historians of the American West that scholarly discourse still centers on the fundamental and seemingly perplexing question of Metis origins. Whence did this numerous, biracial people spring? The question, however naive, both stings and amuses. It has called forth the rejoinder from Antoine Lussier, a Canadian historian of Metis ancestry, that Metis origins can be dated with precision: nine months after the first European male landed in North America![1]

Arguing with this bit of folk biology might be difficult if the term *Metis* were merely a French language designator for the offspring of Indian and white parents. However, the pattern of intermarriage accompanying the westward spread of the fur trade after 1700 contributed to far more than a genetically mixed population. By the early decades of the nineteenth century, a distinctive Metis ethnic identity, culture, and nationality had taken root along the banks of the Red River of the north, branching westward along the river corridors of the Northern Plains. Here, in the heartland of the North American continent, homeland of the Cree, Ojibwa, and Assiniboine, Metis people under their messianic leader Louis Riel waged two unsuccessful rebellions for national independence. The dreams of the "New Nation" died on the gallows with Riel in 1885, and the Metis were plunged into poverty and obscurity.

The history of the Metis is well known to Canadians. As we are belatedly discovering, however, Metis history is not specifically and uniquely

Canadian. The eighteenth-century antecedents of a hybrid Metis cultural complex stretched south and east, to the American Great Lakes. By the mid–nineteenth century, collateral communities of peoples neither Indian nor Euro-American had gathered throughout the northern Plains and Pacific Northwest on both sides of the international border. Some of these survive today.[2]

Over the past century, considerable attention has been paid to the political history of the aspiring Metis nation, but the processes by which Metis identity was formed, the content of Metis culture, and the mechanisms by which it was transmitted intergenerationally still remain obscure. Perhaps this is because, despite Louis Riel's impassioned declaration of Metis consciousness "that we honor our mothers as well as our fathers,"[3] the native women who mothered and nourished the growth of a Metis society have been overshadowed by their white male partners and fathers.

This essay does not hope to answer the larger questions of Metis identity and culture formation but instead explores the motivations prompting native females to marry whites in the early stages of fur trade expansion south and west of the Great Lakes, and seeks to resolve an apparent anomaly with regard to the role of women in subsequent Metis cultural development. On the one hand, as Jennifer S. H. Brown has noted in a path-breaking article, native women were both center and symbol in the emergence of Metis communities.[4] Since Metis daughters of Indian-white marriages were more likely than Metis sons to remain in the West and to maintain close ties with native mothers and kin, they were the primary contributors via their own marriages to incoming whites and Metis males to the rapid growth of a Metis population in the fur trading zone. It is not surprising, therefore, that Metis life appears to have been characterized by matriorganization, with the female and native side exercising the predominant influences over residence and community, behavioral roles, and ethnic filiation. Ultimately, to be Metis was to claim descent from, and the rights of, a native mother, rather than of a white father.

On the other hand, a core denominator of persistent Metis identity has been a strong attachment to Christianity. Especially among French-speaking Metis, Catholic belief and practice did, and often still does, act as the demarcator between themselves and their Indian relatives. Simply put, Metis attend Mass, not the Sun Dance. But if Metis life was matri-centered and native women and their female descendants were the transmitters and translators of Metis culture and identity, what are we to make of the prominence of an intrusive European belief system? How are we to reconcile the apparently mutual influences of strong-minded, perhaps exceptional native women and the religious ideology of the colonizer?

What role, if any, did Christianity play in propelling native women toward white males and why did certain women choose, or so it would seem, to abandon the traditions and lifeways of their own people?

The term *certain women* is deliberate. It may be fairly assumed that the majority or even the preponderance of tribal women did not take white husbands or succumb to the appeals of Christian missionaries at any time during the early contact phase in North America. Carol Devens has argued that among the "domiciled" Indian groups of New France, women led the resistance against missionary efforts at conversion.[5] It may also be assumed, thanks to the remarkable portrait of "women in between" painted by Sylvia Van Kirk and to Jennifer S. H. Brown's seminal ethnohistorical analysis of fur trade families, that the native wives of fur traders and their Metis daughters were neither degraded drudges, commodities to be bought or sold, nor the casual purveyors of sexual favors, stereotypes best buried with the likes of Walter O'Meara's *Daughters of the Country.*[6]

Van Kirk, in particular, has ably illustrated the intelligence and forceful personalities of a number of wives of fur traders, women capable of exerting considerable influence within both native and fur trade circles. Although her sources tend to favor the native wives and daughters of men of rank, or women who aroused comment, the women she describes had their counterparts throughout fur trade country, on both sides of the international boundary.[7] In the western Great Lakes region alone, women such as Madame Cadotte, Susan Johnston, Sally Ainse, Madame LaFramboise, Therese Schindler, Marinette Chevalier, Domitille Langlade, and Sophia Mitchell achieved prominence as traders, church founders and patrons, and leaders of fur trade communities, while their Metis daughters and granddaughters perpetuated many of these traditions, adding the roles of teacher, translator, and interpreter.[8]

Van Kirk and Brown have pointed to a number of factors that may have persuaded native women to marry white traders, among them heightened material comfort and physical security, access to trade goods, and personal role expansion. Other factors—the demographic pressure caused by a possible female surplus among hunting tribes, the benefits to kin of an alliance with whites, the appeal of a more permissive sexual code, a preference for monogamous marriage, and the influence of Christianization—may have been important.[9] Given the slender evidence that has been assembled and analyzed by Van Kirk, Brown, Devens, Peterson and Mary Wright, however, all these variables deserve further elaboration, particularly as they may have selectively applied to women of diverse tribal cultures.

From a Western European perspective, materialist explanations appear especially plausible; yet, it is precisely because such explanations derive from the normative context of the post–Reformation West, rather than North American tribal society, that they must be approached with caution. While ringing true to the historian, they do not link native women's choices and behavior to the belief systems, traditions, and normative role expectations of their native cultures. For the Great Lakes, at least, the tribal world was one in which reality was both seen and unseen, tangible as well as thought or dreamed. Nature was not a sphere separate from the supernatural, and spiritual forces and meanings pervaded all of life. Personifications of sacred power—appearing in visions and dreams as animals, medicinal plants, or other natural phenomena—instructed men and women along the road of life, and most especially in those role choices that were atypical when viewed from a traditional perspective.[10]

The marriages of native women to white fur trade personnel are best viewed in this light. Such behavior was extraordinary, and it may be that the decision, made by only a few, to cross a cultural chasm was fueled by far more than mundane ambition or desire. For some, it may have been a leap of faith.

From the earliest decades of fur trade expansion into the Great Lakes region, native women's impressions of Euro-American males diverged. On the one hand, white men's physical appearance disgusted the sensibilities of some Indian observers. Among the Ojibwa and Ottawa of the upper lakes, natives "disliked the white skins and curly hair [of the French males] and thought beards were loathsome." In contrast to the "soft and delicate" skins of Indian males who plucked their body hair, whites were regarded as "ugly and rude." Similarly, the Eastern Dakota, first visited by Louis Hennepin and Michel Accault at Mille Lacs, Minnesota, in 1680, could scarcely believe that the Frenchmen had managed to garner the affection of any woman. "'How,' they said, 'would you have these two men with thee have wives? Ours would not live with them, for they have hair all over their faces and we have none there or elsewhere.'"[11]

Disgust was not universal, however. Late-seventeenth- and early-eighteenth-century reporters among the Huron and Ottawa at Detroit and Michilimackinac, and among the Illinois tribes to the west, announced that the native women liked "the French better than their own Countrymen," that they liked all men "very much," and "especially the French," and that "they always prefer a Frenchman for a husband to a savage whatever."[12]

Such contradictory female attitudes may be attributed perhaps to cultural differences among Great Lakes peoples and to the length and quality of these groups' contact with Europeans. But women from the same kin group, tribe, or region also diverged in their opinions, ambitions, and behavior. Within the tribal setting, forgetting for a moment the complicating factor of white intervention, were women who hewed closely to role models established by tradition as properly womanly and normal, and those—such as celibates, medicine women, female hunters, warriors, and concubines—who adopted atypical roles.

Acculturation to European ways, moreover, was not a generalized process that affected all tribes or bands evenly. Some groups were more resistant to change than others, just as some individuals were more likely than others to respond positively to external appeals or to new opportunities. Thus, while certain European influences may have worked to persuade Indian women to adopt alien customs and beliefs, there were also tribally based sanctions and precedents for extraordinary female behavior. Possibly the small number of Great Lakes women who were inspired to deviate from traditional female roles at home were interchangeable with those who, when placed in a contact situation, proved most susceptible to innovation and change, however destructive such change might prove to be for tribal society as a whole.

The native wives and consorts of fur traders did not, any more than their partners, comprise a single interest group, or share a common background. They nonetheless possessed qualities, akin to those of medicine and warrior women, that transcended tribal differences and set them apart from the traditional female majority. Marriage to a white stranger—a being initially viewed as an other-than-human person with unknown, hence unpredictable, powers—was a frightening life adventure for which tribally reared women received no preparation. It confounded the imagination of all but the strong-hearted.

If Indian women who married Europeans were unusual, what were the prescribed roles for late-seventeenth- and eighteenth-century Great Lakes women? The paucity of data pertaining to American Indian women of this period and the difficulties in comparing members of dissimilar cultural and linguistic groups (Siouan, Iroquoian, and Algonkian speakers) make generalizations tentative indeed. For the most part, I will focus upon Algonkian-speaking Illinois-Miami, Ottawa, and Ojibwa women, for whom fairly detailed observer accounts exist. These data have been enhanced by the collected oral traditions and insights of anthropologists such as Ruth Landes, Frances Densmore, Inez Hilger, A. Irving Hallowell, Paul Radin, Mary Black Rogers, Beatrice Medicine, and Raymond DeMallie Jr., whose writings based on work among western Great Lakes tribal peoples and the Dakota have been consulted.[13]

Despite variations in the degree of freedom allowed female adolescents in the Great Lakes region, ranging from open sex play among courting Huron youth to an emphasis on premarital chastity and modesty among Dakota and Illinois girls, all females were reared with one end in view: to behave in such a way as to enjoy a long, healthy life free of misfortune. That meant, among Algonkian and Dakota speakers, to behave as became a good woman, that is, as faithful wife and devoted mother. Women's sphere encompassed the cornfield and lodge, the immediate kin group, and, where applicable, the clan or ritual sodality. While along with her brothers she was taught in childhood to fast in order to communicate with "dream visitors" who were the "source of assistance . . . in the daily round of life, and besides this, of 'blessings,'" powerful female visions or dreams bestowing extraordinary gifts were not regarded as vital. Women's usual dream visitors, Antoine Denis Raudot reports, were "lesser spirits," those who taught women how to make themselves irresistible, or to succeed in marriage, childbearing, and the domestic arts. In contrast, men dreamed as if their lives and the life of the community depended upon it. The group could not survive, it was believed, without the help of important other-than-human persons or spiritual allies in the male occupations of hunting, warfare, governance, and religious prediction and intervention.[14]

The female vision quest was nonetheless the most significant event of a young girl's life, coinciding as it often did with the passage into womanhood and eligibility for marriage. It occurred at or prior to menarche, or when girls were about thirteen to fifteen years of age. With the onset of a girl's first menses, she was secluded in a special hut or corner of the longhouse away from the eyes of all but her closest kinswomen and other menstruating girls. During this time, when a woman was regarded as spiritually potent (and threatening to male power), she fasted or cooked only for herself. When her menses ceased and she was purified, the newborn woman returned to her family and a new fire was kindled in the lodge. She was thereafter regarded as marriageable by men who stood in the proper kinship relationship to her and could call her "sweetheart."[15]

Wedlock might occur in several ways, although among late-seventeenth- and early-eighteenth-century Great Lakes people a marriage "with ceremony" was one contracted between kin groups and, at least among the Illinois, one without prior conversation between the prospective spouses. A well-conducted girl avoided gatherings where men were present and did not initiate relationships. Rather, she deferred to the wishes of her parents and male kin. Young women could and did voice their preferences, particularly after a young man's name had been advanced, but ideally they followed the suggestions of brothers, uncles, and parents. More was at stake than a romantic union. Well-arranged marriages secured the cooperation and support of others. Moreover, payment for a bride, whether in the form of goods, services, horses, or food, brought honor to a family and praise to the parents of a worthy woman.[16]

Although women's choices seem to have been circumscribed by their families, in reality women could exercise their desires either through recalcitrance, persuasion, or, if all else failed, elopement. No estimates for the rate of elopement are available for the seventeenth through the nineteenth centuries; however, clandestine marriage was perceived by all Great Lakes people as a valid, if disreputable, marriage form. Parental approval, even if temporarily withheld, usually followed the birth of a first child. Still, the lack of strong family support, the absence of gift exchange, and honorable payment of bride price or bride service probably made such marriages more fragile and susceptible to divorce than those which had been publicly sanctioned.[17]

Once married, a Great Lakes Indian woman was to devote her talents to the woman's domain. If she happened to enter a polygynous household, she was to share her husband's attentions cheerfully and to obey his first wife's domestic dictates dutifully, thankful for the female companionship and the division of labor. She shied from the company of men other than her husband and her male relatives and won her family's and village's esteem by industry and modest and faithful deportment. Although her husband might abandon her for cause—infidelity, sterility, or incompatibility—she rarely left her husband. If her husband preceded her to the grave and if she had loved him, she grieved for the requisite year. At the end of her mourning she was free to remarry; however, a well-reared woman would allow her husband's kinsmen to arrange the match.[18]

During her adult life, a Great Lakes woman might demonstrate special talents as a craftswoman, designer, herbal doctor, or midwife. As a result she might be invited to join, usually through payment, a women's artistic sodality or a medicine society. After menopause, when she was no longer regarded as polluting, she might gain a reputation for healing or, in rare instances, prophecy. In old age, should she live that long, she would be cared for by a son or daughter and admired for her goodness and wisdom—manifest in her longevity.

The above description, based primarily on the seventeenth- and early-eighteenth-century observations by Louis Deliette, Antoine Denis Raudot, Pierre Charlevoix, and Nicolas Perrot, of the Illinois, Ottawa, and Ojibwa is an idealized one. In reality, all Illinois or Dakota women were not chaste before marriage or modest thereafter. Moreover, Great Lakes women could adopt roles other than wife, horticulturalist, and mother and still receive the sanction and tribute of their kinsmen and peers. Female hunters, warriors, seers, prostitutes, and celibates were numerically uncommon, but we can infer from other sources that Great Lakes peoples did not regard such women as necessarily deviant or deserving of punitive sanctions. On the contrary, women who displayed excellence in skills and arts normally monopolized by males seem to have been treated with deference, in the belief that such extraordinary behavior derived from blessings acquired from spiritual allies.[19]

Just as the puberty vision quest verified traditional values and set most women on the right road to marriage and motherhood, dreams and visions could also inspire and sanction unconventional behavior. The importance of dreams and visions as the triggering mechanism for individualistic action cannot be overemphasized. Comparative analysis across time and space is almost impossible because of the self-imposed secrecy surrounding most sacred visions and dreams and because the meaning and power of such dreams unfolded only gradually over the lifetime of the recipient. It is likely, however, that exceptional women dreamers were not randomly distributed, but rather were drawn from among those women who manifested unusual ambitions or talents, or had been singled out and encouraged by members of their families by privileges of birth.[20]

Women who communicated with "stronger" dream visitors were apparently those who approached the adolescent vision quest with the great seriousness and courage expected of young men. Deliette implies that most Illinois girls did not fast the length of their first seclusion, although one sixteen-year-old girl "was foolish enough to remain six days without eating or drinking and whom it was necessary to carry back to her cabin, after thoroughly washing her of course, because she was not able to stand up." When she recovered,

> She made her father and all her relatives believe that she had seen a buffalo, that he had assured her that her brothers who were on an excursion against the Iroquois would make an attack without losing anyone. The thing happened partly as she had said.[21]

The partial success of the young girl's prophecy was lauded by the village shaman; its partial failure was attributed to an unduly short fast! No wonder that few adolescent women risked the physical ordeal of a major power quest or eagerly sought to play the shaman's odds of successful repetitive predictions. In the case of the Illinois woman dreamer, we know nothing more. It is possible, however, that her nearly brilliant forecast propelled her in the direction of medicine and prophecy, roles ordinarily assumed by Illinois men or menopausal women.

It is also possible that we are inferentially witnessing the emergence of a seventeenth-century female Illinois warrior. The guardian spirit that communicated its power and knowledge to the young woman appeared in the form of a buffalo, a sacred ally associated with war among the Illinois. Lacking information about the woman's immediate kin connections, birth rank, or clan membership, we can only speculate about how such unusual spiritual gifts were accorded to an adolescent female. Oral traditions surrounding warrior or "manly hearted" women seem to suggest that exceptionally powerful allies derived from training and preparation begun in early childhood. Predisposition and talent, in other words, went hand in hand with support and tutelage from important male kin.[22]

A century later, on the southern shore of Lake Superior, Oshahgushkodanaqua, daughter of Ojibwa headman Waubojeeg, secluded herself at the onset of menstruation to fast for a vision. The intensity of her quest equaled that of the Illinois woman, and she was similarly gifted with a guardian spirit. Remarkably, however, in this instance, her spiritual ally was not drawn from the range of traditional sources of Ojibwa sacred power, but appeared in the form of a white man.

As Anna Jameson recorded from the lips of her "adopted" mother in 1837:

> [Oshahgushkodanaqul] fasted, according to the universal Indian custom, for a guardian spirit: to perform this ceremony, she went away to the summit of an eminence, and built herself a little lodge of cedar boughs, painted herself black, and began her fast in solitude. She dreamed continually of a white man, who approached her with a cup in his hand, saying "Poor thing! why are you punishing yourself? why do you fast? here is food for you!" He was always accompanied by a dog, which looked up in her face as though he knew her. Also she dreamed of being on a high hill, which was surrounded by water, and from which she beheld many canoes full of Indians, coming to her and paying her homage; after this, she felt as if she were carried up into the heavens, and as she looked down upon the earth, she perceived it was on fire, and said to herself, "All my relations will be burned!" but a voice answered and said, "No, they will not be destroyed, they will be saved"; and she *knew* it was a spirit, because the voice was not human. She fasted for ten days, during which time her grandmother brought her at intervals some water. When satisfied that she had obtained a guardian spirit in the white stranger who haunted her dreams, she returned to her father's lodge.[23]

The import of Oshahgushkodanaqua's vision likely was not immediately clear to her. However, shortly thereafter, her father arranged her marriage to a wealthy and influential Irish trader, John Johnston. Not without trepidation did she enter this species's lodge with its European stove. For more than a week she slept huddled in a corner rolled in her blanket, finally running away. Her father, dreaming that she had abandoned her husband, found her out and sent her back to John Johnston, launching a happy and much-noted marital relationship in which Oshahgushko-danaqua's talents and leadership qualities flowered.[24]

Oshahgushkodanaqua's vision, narrated many years after the event and after she had been baptized a Christian and taken the name of Susan, comes to us in translation as a secondary and possibly altered source. It is nonetheless extremely suggestive, containing not only the sanction for a special relationship with whites and an unusual influence over her own relations, but a recognition of the possible dire consequences (world on fire) that might result from overreaching ambition or the protection of a nontraditional source of power. Significantly, however, the other-than-human white guardian assured her that her relations would "not be destroyed," but rather "saved."[25]

The favored eldest daughter of a headman, and a woman of great personal strength and intelligence, Oshahgushkodanaqua probably would have been regarded as exceptional by her own people even if she had not married John Johnston. Yet in her dreams she had found a white spiritual ally, just as the medium through which her unusual abilities were exercised was marriage to such a person in his human form and the management of a bicultural household at the center of the Sault Sainte Marie, Michigan, fur trade community. What had disposed Oshah-gushkodanaqua to envision an alien god? Was his protection the sanction for her marriage to Johnston?

Let us look first at influences generated by the contact experience and at missionization in particular. It may be that some Indian women in the Great Lakes region had been sufficiently acculturated or "Frenchified" by the final decades of the eighteenth century to regard marriage to a Canadian male as a natural and desirable state. The numbers of such acculturated females would have been small, however. West of Lake Huron, missionaries did not staff permanent stations until the final decades of the seventeenth century, and, even then, conversion and civilization efforts reached only a portion of the native population, making inroads in the lower Illinois country among the Ottawa at Michilimackinac and the refugee Huron farmers gathered near Detroit after 1701. French observers like Raudot quickly sensed the futility of short-term expectations of success; Indians were reluctant neophytes.[26]

Still, what gains occurred, beyond superficial mass baptism of infants, the sick, and the dying, were sex specific. Throughout the eighteenth century, most Algonkian-speaking Christians west of Montreal were female. Apparently, this was so because the Algonkian- and Siouan-speaking tribes of the region engaged in a diverse annual round of planting, gathering, hunting, and fishing. Native males' preoccupation with the winter hunt was intensified by fur traders reliant on Indians to gather peltry. Thus, while native males devoted themselves to the peripatetic occupations of hunting and warfare, the burden of nearly all subsistence-centered work fell on women. Their tasks argued for a fairly sedentary life and left them exposed to manipulation by outsiders. The Jesuits perceived that "occupied and humbled by work," Indian women were "more disposed to accept the truths of the Gospel."[27]

Christian missionaries enjoyed their greatest success in the Illinois country, where, by 1714, most of the Illinois tribes were at least nominally Christian converts. One Jesuit father alone baptized over two thousand individuals within a six-year period, and by 1711 all of the inhabitants of Kaskaskia professed themselves Christians.[28]

In 1699, Father Julien Binneteau claimed that the young men and their religious leaders were opposed to the progress of Christianization. But "'the women and girls, on the contrary,' Father Marest noted, 'are very well disposed to receive baptism, they are very constant and firm, when once they have received it; they are fervent in prayer, and ask only to be instructed.'" Deliette affirmed the Illinois women's ready conversion. Instruction caused them "to mock at the superstitions of their nation," which "greatly incense[d] the old men."[29]

The causes for a sex-specific response to Christian instruction are difficult to pinpoint, aside from the greater availability of women at any given mission village. Possibly, the elevation of a female deity, the Virgin, appealed to and was easily understood by women accustomed to ritual taboos surrounding childbirth. On the other hand, Christianity, as the French missionaries practiced it, was more than a set of religious beliefs. The Christian fathers attempted to teach an ethical and cultural system as well, whose prescriptions often conflicted with native concepts of right behavior. Surprisingly, however, Illinois women exhibited a disposition to affect European politenesses. According to the Jesuits, that disposition made them all the more desirable as wives for French Canadians.[30]

The acculturation of native women to French ways and beliefs is difficult to measure beyond superficial changes in demeanor. The social arrangements and customary beliefs of Great Lakes tribes varied, as did missionary techniques and their effectiveness. Nonetheless, missionary documents suggest an intriguing clue to the pedagogical force of at least one conversion tool in the Illinois country: liturgical art.

Natives were subjected repeatedly, often from an early age, not only to a litany and catechism, but to pictorial and emblematic aids that the Jesuits found useful in refurbishing the religious imagination of American Indians. When Marquette first visited the large Kaskaskia village on the Illinois River in 1675, he called a general assembly of the more than five thousand inhabitants. Then, "having directed them to stretch out upon Lines several pieces of Chinese taffeta, [he] attached to these four large Pictures, of the blessed Virgin, which were visible from all Sides."[31]

The missionaries who followed Marquette to the Illinois missions brought similar paintings and engravings. Twenty years later, Father Gravier explained the whole of the New Testament by way of "copper engravings representing perfectly what is related on each page." The artwork had a profound effect. Gravier easily admitted that it was "curiosity to see the picture, rather than to hear the explanations that [he] gave [that] attracted a great many." In 1669, Father Marest, at the same mission, wrote that evening instruction "is generally the time that I explain the pictures of the old and of the new testament. Pictures of this kind produce an impression upon the savage's mind and greatly assist him in remembering what we tell him."[32]

Religious art was exhibited without discriminating by sex. Similarly, the six gross of finger rings, many of them containing Christian symbols and the likeness of saints and the holy family, which Father Gravier ordered in 1702, were offered to anyone who would wear them. The opposition of tribal leadership, however, and the frequent absence of males made women the usual recipients of religious gifts and visual suggestion.[33]

Marie Rouensa, for example, daughter of a Kaskaskia headman and later wife of Michel Accault, one of LaSalle's concessionaires at Fort Sainte Louis at Peoria, had so mastered Gravier's teachings that she could explain each picture "singly, without trouble and confusion, as well as [he] would do and even more intelligibly, in their manner." Her persuasive zeal converted both her parents and her profligate French husband, prompting Gravier to lend her engravings so that she could explain them at home "to all the girls who went there," as well as to the men her father assembled in his dwelling.[34]

Marie modeled herself after her namesake, taken in baptism. Her devotion to the Virgin's image, which she and her converted sisters dwelt upon, thrilled Gravier. However, that image had been struck in a European mold. Illinois women were startled, around 1702, by the appearance of the first French woman in the region. Tall, slender, and blonde, Madame LeSueur was not a handsome woman by French standards, but she attracted curious crowds and the envy of Christianized native women. Deliette reported that the wife of a prominent Kaskaskia (possibly Marie's mother) rued the European woman's coming. "I believed," she lamented,

> that our women and our girls could hold their own for beauty with other natives, and we even see that those who are known to us are much inferior to us; but now we know that we are only monsters

compared with your women and still we are told that this is not a
beautiful woman![35]

It was not only the Virgin which Church art idealized. The fair hair and
fine features of Madame LeSueur's small children seemed to the
Kaskaskia matron "like the little Jesus that Father Gravier shows us
every day." Gravier does not explicitly say that Illinois women noticed
the similarity in appearance between the engravings of Christ and the
French men in their midst, or that sacred art worked to soften initial
Indian objections to the strange appearance of Europeans, but there is
little question that the pictures were regarded as magical talismans,
capable of answering dreams and provoking visions. Of Marie Rouensa
Accault, Father Gravier marvelled, "She has such tenderness for Jesus
Christ suffering that she has admitted to me that she often weeps while
gazing at Jesus crowned with thorns,—a picture of whom she keeps in a
sort of apartment that she has made for herself."[36]

It is also likely that sacred pictures tended to reinforce native beliefs
about the other-than-human quality of Europeans, heightening the
attractiveness of a white ally. Marie had acquired her powerful white
Christian guardian through a conversion experience, but that experience
is best understood in terms of the traditional Illinois vision quest. I have
already pointed out that strong spirit helpers were generally sought by
men or by exceptional woman dreamers. Thus, to the extent that missionaries encouraged native women to fast, seclude themselves, and to
pray for Christian grace, they unwittingly provided alternative opportunities to strong-minded and spiritually gifted women who, in the context
of their own cultures, may have been bound to traditional influences. By
acquiring a white spiritual ally, Marie Accault not only received the
sanction for a special relationship with Europeans, but the courage to
marry a white man. Only after intense prayer or vision seeking and conversations with Gravier was Marie reconciled to Accault. Initially, like
other early converts, she had, in her devotion to Christ and her namesake, wished to remain celibate.[37]

It is also noteworthy that Marie gained the power to assume roles
usually ascribed to males in both Illinois and French Catholic societies.
That a young woman in her late teens could zealously instruct her father,
a Kaskaskia headman, and his mature associates in religious matters was
no mean achievement. Whereas Christian, and particularly Pauline, theology has been identified as one of the historical underpinnings of sexist oppression, it may well have served, during the early fur trade era, to
enlarge the scope of women's activities.

To enlarge was not to abandon tradition, however. Far from denying
the cultures of their birth, strong-hearted women dreamers like Marie

Accault and Oshahgushkodanaqua—more often than not sisters, daughters, and granddaughters of tribal *okema* or headmen—interpreted and used the presence of white men and their sources of spiritual power within a tribally sanctioned context. Such women appear not only to have brought to their marriages to white men both influential kin and unusual abilities, but to have been motivated by the potential for the development of their talents that outmarriage and conversion offered. While their marriages were often arranged by male kinsmen eager to cement diplomatic alliances with equally interested traders, the prestige and acclaim accorded many traders' wives by both Indians and whites suggested that these women had sought and received the blessings of a strong supernatural guardian.

It is not surprising, therefore, that in the Metis nursery that was the fur trader's household in the Northwest after 1700, intelligent and forceful native females were to exert as much influence in the education and acculturation of their bicultural children as their "civilized" white husbands. French language, material culture, song and dance, artistic design, and Christianity introduced by traders and missionaries gave way, in the intimacy of the household, to nativized hybrids: Michif language (French-Cree and Ojibwa); Metis fiddling and jigging; brilliantly colored floral beadwork gracing all manner of clothing and accoutrements for man and horse; and, finally, a devotion to Mary, Mother of God, mother of all.

NOTES

1. D. Bruce Sealey and Antoine S. Lussier, *The Metis: Canada's Forgotten People* (Winnipeg, Canada: Pemmican Publications, 1975), 1.

2. See, for example, the diverse regional portraits in Jacqueline Peterson and Jennifer S. H. Brown, eds., *The New Peoples: Being and Becoming Metis in North America* (Lincoln: University of Nebraska Press, 1985).

3. Louis Riel, quoted in Joseph Kinsey Howard, *Strange Empire: Louis Riel and the Metis People* (1952; reprint, Toronto: James Lewis and Samuel, 1974), 44.

4. Jennifer S. H. Brown, "Women as Centre and Symbol in the Emergence of Metis Communities," *The Canadian Journal of Native Studies* 3 (1983).

5. Carol Devens, "Separate Confrontations: Gender as a Factor in Indian Adaptation to European Colonization in New France," *American Quarterly* 38 ("Bibliography," 1986): 46–80.

6. Sylvia Van Kirk, *"Many Tender Ties": Women in Western Canadian Fur Trade Society* (Winnipeg, Canada: Watson and Dwyer, 1980); Jennifer S. H. Brown, *Strangers in Blood: Fur Trade Company Families in Indian Country* (Vancouver: British Columbia Press, 1980); Walter O'Meara, *Daughters of the Country: The Women of the Fur Traders and Mountain Men* (New York: Harcourt, Brace and World, 1968). For the Pacific Northwest, see Mary C. Wright, "Economic Development and

Native Women in the Early Nineteenth Century," *American Quarterly* 33 (winter 1981): 525–36.

7. Van Kirk, "*Many Tender Ties.*"

8. Jacqueline Peterson, "The People in Between: Indian-White Marriage and the Genesis of a Metis Society and Culture in the Great Lakes Region, 1680–1830" (Ph.D. diss., University of Illinois at Chicago, 1981).

9. Peterson, "People in Between," chap. 2.

10. Jacqueline Peterson and Mary Druke, "American Indian Women and Religion," in *Women and Religion in America*, vol. 2 of *The Colonial and Revolutionary Periods*, ed. Rosemary Radford Ruether and Rosemary Skinner Keller (San Francisco: Harper and Row, 1983), 1–41. For an overview of North American Indian cosmologies and religious practice, see Ake Hultkrantz, *The Religions of the American Indians*, trans. Monica Settlerwell (Berkeley: University of California Press, 1979); and Sam D. Gill, *Native American Religions: An Introduction* (Belmont, CA: Wadsworth Publishers, 1982). See also Elisabeth Tooker, ed., *Native North American Spirituality of the Eastern Woodlands: Sacred Myths, Dreams, Visions, Speeches, Healing Formulas, Rituals and Ceremonies* (New York: Paulist Press, 1979).

11. George Irving Quimby, *Indian Culture and European Trade Goods* (Madison: Wisconsin Historical Society, 1966), 5; Louis Hennepinin Doane Robinson, "A History of the Dakota or Sioux Indians," in *South Dakota Historical Collections*, vol. 2 (Pierre, SD: State Publishing Company, 1902–12), 38. See also Father Gabriel Sagard, *The Long Journey to the Country of the Hurons*, ed. George M. Wrong (Toronto: The Champlain Society, 1939), 137; Father Joseph François Lafitau, *Customs of the American Indians Compared with the Customs of Primitive Tribes*, vol. 1, ed. William N. Fenton and Elizabeth L Moore (Toronto: The Champlain Society, 1974), 89; Cornelius J. Jaenen, "Amerindian Views of French Culture in the Seventeenth Century," *The Canadian Historical Review* 55 (September 1974): 261–91; and *Friend and Foe: Aspects of French-Amerindian Cultural Contact in the Sixteenth and Seventeenth Centuries* (Toronto: McClell and Steart Ltd., 1976), 23–24; and *Alexander Henry's Travels and Adventures in the Years 1760–1776*, ed. Milo M. Quaife (Chicago: University of Chicago Press, 1921), 113–14.

12. Baron Louis-Armand de Loin d'Arce Labontan, *New Voyages to North America*, vol. 2 (1703; reprint, New York: Burr Franklin, 1970), 455; Antoine Denis Raudot, "Memoir Concerning the Different Indian Nations of North America," in *The Indians of the Western Great Lakes, 1615–1760*, ed. W. Vernon Kinietz (1940; reprint, Ann Arbor: University of Michigan Press, 1965), 342; Nehemiah Matson, *French and Indians of the Illinois River* (Princeton, Ill., 1874), 125. LaMothe Cadillac, October 18, 1700, in Cadillac Papers, *Michigan Historical Collections*, vol. 33 (Lansing, Mich.:1874/1876–1929), 99.

13. For early beliefs about the other-than-human qualities of white men see, for example, John C. Ewers, "Indian Views of the White Man Prior to 1850: An Interpretation," in *Red Man and Hat-Wearers: Viewpoints in Indian History*, ed. Daniel Tyler (Fort Collins, CO: Pruett, 1976), 7–23. I am indebted to Raymond DeMallie Jr., Department of Anthropology, Indiana University, for suggesting the relationship between dreaming and unconventional female behavior and for allowing me to read his typescript, "Male and Female in Nineteenth-Century Lakota Culture," now in print in *The Hidden Half Studies of Plains and Indian Women*, ed. Patricia Albers and Beatrice Medicine (Washington, D.C.: University Press of America, 1982). See also A. Irving Hallowell, "Some Psychological Characteristics of the Northeastern Indians," in *Man in Northeastern North America*, ed. F. Johnson (Papers of H. S.

Peabody Foundation for Archaeology, vol. 3, 1946), 195–225; "Aggression in Saul-
teaux Society," *Psychiatry: Journal of the Biology and Pathology of Interpersonal
Relations* 3 (August 1940): 395–407; "Psychosexual Adjustment, Personality, and the
Good Life in a Nonliterate Culture," in *Psychosexual Development in Health and
Disease*, ed. Paul W. Koch and Joseph Zubin (New York: Grune and Stratton, 1949);
all reprinted in A. Irving Hallowell, *Culture and Experience* (Philadelphia: University of Pennsylvania Press, 1955), 133–37, 277–90, 291–305. See also A. Irving Hallowell, "The Role of Dreams in Ojibwa Culture," and "Ojibwa Ontology, Behavior,
and World View," in *Contributions to Anthropology, Selected Papers of A. Irving
Hallowell* (Chicago: University of Chicago Press, 1976), 449–74, 357–90; Sister M.
lnez Hilger, *Chippewa Child Life and Its Cultural Background*, Smithsonian Institution, Bureau of American Ethnology, Bulletin 146 (Washington, D.C.: Government
Printing Office, 1951); Frances Densmore, *Chippewa Customs*, Smithsonian Institution, Bureau of American Ethnology, Bulletin 86 (Washington, D.C.: Government
Printing Office, 1929); Paul Radin, "Ojibwa and Ottawa Puberty Dreams," in *Essays
in Anthropology Presented to A. L. Kroeber*, ed. Robert H. Lowie (Berkeley: University of California Press, 1936), 233–64; Ruth Landes, *The Ojibwa Woman* (New
York: The Norton Library, 1971), *The Mystic Lake Sioux: Sociology of the Mde-
wakantanwan Santee* (Madison: University of Wisconsin Press, 1968), and *Ojibwa
Sociology*, reprinted from *Columbia University Contributions to Anthropology*, vol.
29 (New York: Columbia University Press, 1937); Eleanor Leacock, "Women's Status in Egalitarian Society: Implications for Social Evolution," *Current Anthropology*
19 (June 1978): 247–75. Mary Black Rogers, "Ojibwa Power Belief Systems," in *The
Anthropology of Power: Ethnographic Studies from Asia, Oceania, and the New
World*, ed. Raymond D. Fogelson and Richard N. Adams (New York: Academic
Press, 1977), is especially insightful.

14. On the guardian spirit complex and the vision quest, see Ruth F. Benedict,
The Concept of the Guardian Spirit in North America, American Anthropological
Association Memoir 29 (Menasha, WI: American Anthopology Society, 1923); and
Patricia Albers and Seymour Parker, "The Plains Vision Experience: A Study of
Power and Privilege," *Southwestern Journal of Anthropology* 27 (autumn 1971):
203–33. Raudot, Letter 30, in Kinietz, *Indians of the Western Great Lakes*; Dens-
more, *Chippewa Customs*, 72 and 79; Hallowell, "Role of Dreams," 461–71; Hilger,
Chippewa Child Life, 39–55; Nicolas Perrot, in *The Indian Tribes of the Upper Mis-
sissippi Valley and Region of the Great Lakes as described by Nicolas Perrot, French
commandant in the Northwest; Bacqueville de la Potherie, French royal commissioner to Canada; Morrel Marston, American army officer, and Thomas Forsyth,
United States agent at Fort Armstrong*, vol. 1, trans. and ed. Emma Helen Blair
(Cleveland: Arthur H. Clark, 1911–12), 75; Gabriel Marest to Father Germain,
Caskaskias, November 9, 1712, in *The Jesuit Relations and Allied Documents: Trav-
els and Exploration of the Jesuit Missionaries in New France, 1610–1791*, vol. 66,
ed. Reuben Gold Thwaites (New York: Pagent Books, 1959), 231 (hereafter cited as
JR); William H. Keating, *Narrative of an Expedition to the Source of St. Peter's River,
Lake Winnepeek, Lake of the Woods, etc. etc. Performed in the Year 1823, by order
of the Hon. J. C. Calhoun, Secretary of War, under the command of Stephen H.
Long, Major, U.S. T.E. Comp. from the Notes of Major Long*, vol. 1 (Philadelphia:
H. C. Carey & I. Lee, 1824), 229–30; Landes, *Ojibwa Woman*, 3.

15. Raudot, Letters 60 and 61, in Kinietz, *Indians of the Western Great Lakes*,
391–92; Louis Deliette, "Memoir Concerning the Illinois Country," in *Collections of
the Illinois State Historical Library*, vol. 23, French Series 1, ed. Theodore C. Pease
and Raymond C. Werner (Springfield, IL 1903, 48), 355. A copy of this memoir,

attributed to Deliette and thought to have been written about 1712, signed DeGannes and dated 1724, is deposited in the Edward Everett Ayer Collection, Newberry Library, Chicago. See also Hilger, *Chippewa Child Life*, 50–55, 155–56, 166; and Landes, *Ojibwa Woman*, 5–6.

16. *Journal of a Voyage to North America Translated from the French, of Pierre François Xavier de Charlevoix*, vol. 2, ed., Louise Phelps Kellogg (Chicago, 1923), 248–51 (hereafter cited as Charlevoix); Perrot in Blair, *Indian Tribes* 1:67–68; Deliette, "Illinois Country," 330–31; Raudot, Letter 25, in Kinietz, *Indians of the Western Great Lakes*, 345; Lafitau, *Customs of the American Indians*, 341–46; Kinietz, *Indians of the Western Great Lakes*, 205; Densmore, *Chippewa Customs*, 72; Hilger, *Chippewa Child Life*, 157–59, 162.

17. Landes, *Ojibwa Woman*, 56, 123; Landes, *Mystic Lake Sioux*, 128.

18. Perrot in Blair, *Indian Tribes* 1:65, 70–73; Raudot, Letter 25, in Kinietz, *Indians of the Western Great Lakes*, 345; Lafitau, *Customs of the American Indians*, 341; Deliette, "Illinois Country," 330–35; Thomas Forsyth, in Blair, *Indian Tribes* 2:215; Hilger, *Chippewa Child Life*, 161–62.

19. Deliette, "Illinois Country," 331; Kinietz, *Indians of the Western Great Lakes*, 215; Anna Jameson, *Sketches in Canada, and Rambles among the Red Men* (London: Longman, Brown, Green and Longmans, 1852), 191; Landes, *Ojibwa Woman*, 20, 135–77. See also John Tanner, *A Narrative of the Captivity and Adventures of John Tanner (US Interpreter at the Sault de Ste. Marie,) During Thirty Years Residence Among the Indians in the Interior of North America*, prepared for the press by Edwin James (1830; reprint, Minneapolis: Ross & Haines, 1956), 15, 48, and 101, for a courtship initiated by an Ojibwa woman and for his adopted mother's reputation as a powerful dreamer and medicine woman.

20. Hallowell, "Role of Dreams," 462, 465, 471; Hilger, *Chippewa Child Life*, 47, 55; Landes, *Ojibwa Woman*, 8–9. See Radin's "Ojibwa and Ottawa Puberty Dreams," a small dream collection and remarks on this problem. See also Marshall Fisher, "World View as Social Organization: An Examination of the Transmission of Authority Patterns and Leadership Roles in Ojibwa Society," *Alberta Anthropologist* 2 (1968): 23–34, for the importance of dreams in producing leaders. On the manner in which sacred visions link generations and a people to their cosmic past, see Robin Ridington's sensitive "Telling Secrets: Stories of the Vision Quest," *The Canadian Journal of Native Studies* 2 (1982): 213–20.

21. Deliette, "Illinois Country," 353–54; Hilger, *Chippewa Child Life*, 55.

22. The best treatment of this neglected topic is Beatrice Medicine, "'Warrior Women'—Sex-role Alternatives for Plains Indian Women," in *Hidden Half Studies*, 267–280. See also Landes, *Ojibwa Woman*, 135–77; Oscar Lewis, "Manly-Hearted Women: Among the South Piegan," *American Anthropologist* 43 (April–June 1941): 173–87; Valerie Scherer Mathes, "Native American Women in Medicine," *Military Journal of the West* 21 (April 1982): 41–48; and a recent videotape, "All Travel, All the Time," an interview with Ida Nasson, produced by University of Washington Instructional Media Services for the Ellensburg Public Library. Nasson, a ninety-year-old Yakima woman, provides a unique and fascinating account of her mother's spirit quest and subsequent power as a "big doctor." Nasson's mother, Tehanap, was singled out in early childhood as a "favored offspring" by her father, who encouraged and guided her extraordinary development.

23. Jameson, *Sketches in Canada*, 247. Oshahgushkodanaqua (Mrs. Susan Johnston) related her vision to Mrs. Jameson in 1837, some thirty years after it had occurred.

24. Jameson, *Sketches in Canada*, 181, 247–48. For information on the illustrious

union of Oshahgushkodanaqua and John Johnston and their offspring, see Chase S. Osborn and Stellanova Osborn, *Schoolcraft-Longfellow-Hiawatha* (Lancaster, PA: Jacques Cattel Press, 1942), 515–40; a well-researched historical novel, Janet Lewis, *The Invasion: A Narrative of Events Concerning the Johnston Family of St. Mary's* (1932: reprint, Chicago: The Swallow Press, 1960); and a family history prepared by Oshahgushkodanaqua's grandchild, Charlotte E. J. Killaly, "History of John Johnston of Sault Ste Marie, Michigan," Sault Ste. Marie, Mich., Bayliss Public Library.

25. Jameson, *Sketches in Canada*, 247.

26. Raudot, Letters 23, 46, and 72, in Kinietz, *Indians of the Western Great Lakes*, 341–42, 371–72, 408–10.

27. Gabriel Marest to Father Germain, Caskaskias, November 9, 1712, *JR* 66:231; *JR* 65:77; Louise Phelps Kellogg, *The French Regime in Wisconsin and the Northwest* (Madison: State Historical Society of Wisconsin, 1925), 172–75.

28. Jacques Gravier to Father Michelangelo Tamburini, Paris, March 6, 1707, *JR* 66:121–23; Emily J. Blasingham, "The Depopulation of the Illinois Indians, Part 2, Concluded," *Ethnohistory* 3 (fall 1956), 387–88, for missionary success in the Illinois country.

29. *JR* 65:67, 77, 79; Deliette, "Illinois Country," 361.

30. *JR* 66:231, 241; Raudot in Kinietz, *Indians of the Western Great Lakes*, 342–43, 380.

31. *JR* 59:189.

32. *JR* 64:227; *JR* 65:83; Natalia Maree Belting, *Kaskaskia under the French Regime*, vol. 24, no. 3 of *Illinois Studies in the Social Sciences* (Urbana: University of Illinois Press, 1948), 27, for examples of surviving church art in the Illinois country.

33. Jacques Gravier to Rev. Father Jean de Lamberville, March 5, 1702, *JR* 66:25–33; Quimby, *Indian Culture*, 76; Alice S. Wood, "A Catalogue of 'Jesuit' and Ornamental Rings from Western New York: Collections of Charles Wray and the Rochester Museum and Science Center," *Historical Archeology* 8 (1974): 83–104; François-Marc Gagnon, *La Conversion Par L'Image: Un Aspect de la Mission des Jesuites Aupres des Indians du Canada au XVIIe Siècle* (Montreal: Editions Bell Armin, 1975), for missionary art as an acculturation factor. In 1878, an early-eighteenth-century Jesuit medal, struck in Italy, was unearthed near the old Jesuit mission at DePere, near Green Bay, Wisconsin. On one side it bore "the figure of the Blessed Virgin, standing on the moon, her head encircled by stars, with two cherubs . . . on the reverse an orb with the monogram as described, and two kneeling angels." See Rev. Chrysostom Verwyst, *Missionary Labors of Fathers Marquette, Menard and Allouez in the Lake Superior Region* (Chicago: Hoffman Brothers, 1886), 191. Also, for illustrations of Jesuit rings found at the old Fort Michilimackinac site, see Lyle M. Stone, *Fort Michilimackinac, 1715–1781: An Archaeological Perspective on the Revolutionary Frontier* (East Lansing: Michigan State University Press, 1974), 122–30.

34. *JR* 64:299; *JR* 66:25–33.

35. Deliette, "Illinois Country," 338; Claude Charles Le Roy, Bacqueville de la Potherie, "History of the Savage People who are Allies of New France," in Blair, *Indian Tribes* 1:309–311.

36. *JR* 64:215; Deliette, " Illinois Country," 338.

37. *JR* 66:25–33.

part two

American Society Takes Shape

AMERICAN SOCIETY TAKES SHAPE

Class

We begin this section with an examination of how middle-class under-standings of sexuality took shape. While the middle class did not estab-lish its national hegemony until after the Civil War, we can see in an early conflict over abortion and in an electoral scandal, the emergence of those sexual and gender values that would define the middle class. Essential to the formation and propagation of middle-class values was the family. First emerging in the Northeast, the middle-class family was smaller and more nuclear than its predecessor. Unlike the patriarchal family of early modern Europe and America, the middle-class family served as the locus for the socializing of children and was the primary domain of women. Ideally, the family and the women who watched over it, remained apart from the public; thereby, protecting the home from the unpleasant business of economics and politics. This ideal relegated sexuality to the private and hence the margins of public life.

The secularization of colonial society and the adoption of English rule of law were key ingredients to middle-class formation. These changes had important consequences for how men's and women's sexuality entered into the public. Cornelia Dayton examines this issue through her investigation of one of the only fully documented abortions in colonial New England. In 1739 Sarah Grosvenor, her sisters, and her lover tried to conceal Grosvenor's pregnancy through a secret abortion. The abor-tion eventually led to Grosvenor's death and to legal proceedings against the doctor who performed it. Dayton argues that the result of those pro-ceedings indicates the emergence of a new sexual double standard that would underlies middle-class conceptions of the family in the nineteenth century. The efforts by Grosvenor's father to keep this abortion secret in spite of his daughter's death, Dayton contends, illustrates the growth of a secularized public culture of men in which the boundaries between illicit and legitimate sex differed for men and women.

Lest we relegate these conflicts to the private and hence the historical margins, Norma Basch reminds us of how often these private conflicts entered into the most important of public debates, in this case the elec-tion of a president. Her contribution examines the presidential election of 1828 and the meanings that Andrew Jackson's marriage to Rachel Jackson acquired during that election campaign. Supporters of Jackson's opponent, John Quincy Adams, argued that Jackson's "inadvertent" mistake—he married Rachel before her divorce from her first husband was final—threatened the public virtue that he believed preserved liber-ty in the new Republic. Quincy Adams subscribed to a traditional view of the relationship between the family and the political order in which political order was preserved through close ties between organized moral households and public virtue. In contrast, Jackson and his supporters subscribed to a newer view of marriage as a romantic union between individuals and was consequently outside of politics. Basch concludes that the scandal signaled more than political muckraking; rather it signified conflicting values over marriage, love and women's place and their place in the polity. Together Dayton and Basch's contributions demonstrate that the boundary between the public and private that was so essential to the middle class's conception of itself was a contested borderland in which the "private" business of love, intimacy, and sex shaped America's institutions and sense of themselves.

Race

Conflicts over sexuality were at the heart of how Americans came to understand and invent race and racial differences throughout the nineteenth century. Sexuality was central to the slave system, Reconstruction, and the politics of redemption that ultimately disenfranchised African American men. By law, an African American's status as a free person or as a slave was determined by his or her mother, thereby implicating the sexuality of enslaved and free women in the slave system. As the slave trade came to an end, enslaved women's reproductive labor became even more valuable as they produced the slave labor force. Slave holders could determine enslaved men's and women's family choices as he or she could compel marriages and/or sell family members (most often husbands). He, or as Martha Hodges notes, she could also compel enslaved people into sexual relationships. But such power did not go unchallenged. Enslaved men and women resisted the slave holders' hold on women's reproductive labor by running away, withholding labor, performing their own marriage ceremonies, and socializing children into a unique slave culture with its own values of appropriate sexual behavior and family relationships. Despite this resistance, it is difficult to underestimate what Nell Painter has called "the soul murder" of African American peoples that has followed a long history of sexual harassment, rape, and sexual torture.

As we noted in our first section, sexual ideologies were key to European colonization as Europeans defined themselves as different from and superior to native peoples in part due to sexual practices. At the time of initial contact and through much of the colonial period, these differences were understood as cultural—as native people came to accept European understandings of sex, gender, and labor they would be civilized. But by the nineteenth century, scientific racism was gaining hegemony. European

Americans, especially those of Anglo-Saxon descent, were defining race as a biological characteristic and ranking races based on so-called scientific evidence. For example, biological theories defined African American women as having larger sexual organs and consequently a virtually unquenchable sexual desire. White (middle-class) women, on the other hand, were passionless and incapable of sexual seduction. Such ideologies legitimated white men's unlimited sexual access to African American women and defined any sexual contact between white women and African American men as rape.

Martha Hodes's essay mines testimony given by African Americans to the Freedman's Bureau as it investigated sexual relationships between white women and African American men. This testimony was taken at a historical moment in which miscegenation between white women and black men symbolized the worse fears of whites about racial integration. Hodes's essay illustrates the importance of listening to white women's and African American men's voices in our interpretations of how racialist sexual ideologies were constructed and implemented. The racial/sexual ideologies that supported lynchings both became a powerful tool for disenfranchising African American men and symbolically denying to them the patriarchal privileges of manhood. Hodes also suggests that this racial ideology also empowered white women as they could use their racial privilege to force African American men into sexual relationships.

As Hodes's essay demonstrates, the personal sexual choices made by men and women were invested in and could not escape from the various regimes of power of American society. Policy makers used sexuality to control the racial composition of the nation. Immigration laws, in particular, played a central role in this process. Such laws were especially central to the experiences of Asians and Asian Americans. For example, laws regulating Chinese men's ability to form families were central to defining them as outside American society and as a temporary cheap labor force. The most famous of these laws—the Chinese Exclusion laws—forbid most Chinese male immigrants from bringing their families to the United States. Consequently, Chinese Tongs imported women from China to serve the sexual needs of temporary laborers. Yet as Lucy Cheng argues in her contribution to this anthology, laws in the United States were not the only factors affecting Chinese women's conditions. Economic depression and loyalty to family influenced Chinese women's prostitution and the latter provided some protection for those women who worked as prostitutes. Cheng's essay urges us to look across international borders to understand the relationship between constructions of sexuality and race in American history.

3

Taking the Trade: Abortion and Gender Relations in an Eighteenth-Century New England Village

Cornelia Hughes Dayton

In 1742 in the village of Pomfret, perched in the hills of northeastern Connecticut, nineteen-year-old Sarah Grosvenor and twenty-seven-year-old Amasa Sessions became involved in a liaison that led to pregnancy, abortion, and death. Both were from prominent yeoman families, and neither a marriage between them nor an arrangement for the support of their illegitimate child would have been an unusual event for mid-eighteenth-century New England. Amasa Sessions chose a different course; in consultation with John Hallowell, a self-proclaimed "practitioner of physick," he coerced his lover into taking an abortifacient. Within two months, Sarah fell ill. Unbeknownst to all but Amasa, Sarah, Sarah's sister Zerviah, and her cousin Hannah, Hallowell made an attempt to "Remove her Conseption" by a "manual opperation." Two days later Sarah miscarried, and her two young relatives secretly buried the fetus in the woods. Over the next month, Sarah struggled against a "Malignant fever" and was attended by several physicians, but on September 14, 1742, she died.[1]

Most accounts of induced abortions among seventeenth- and eighteenth-century whites in the Old and New Worlds consist of only a few lines in a private letter or court record book; these typically refer to the taking of savin or pennyroyal—two common herbal abortifacients. While men and women in diverse cultures have known how to perform abortions by inserting an instrument into the uterus, actual descriptions of such operations are extremely rare for any time period. Few accounts of abortions by instrument have yet been uncovered for early modern

England, and I know of no other for colonial North America.[2] Thus the historical fragments recording events in a small New England town in 1742 take on an unusual power to illustrate how an abortion was conducted, how it was talked about, and how it was punished.

We know about the Grosvenor-Sessions case because in 1745 two prominent Windham County magistrates opened an investigation into Sarah's death. Why there was a three-year gap between that event and legal proceedings, and why justices from outside Pomfret initiated the legal process, remain a mystery. In November 1745 the investigating magistrates offered their preliminary opinion that Hallowell, Amasa Sessions, Zerviah Grosvenor, and Hannah Grosvenor were guilty of Sarah's murder, the last three as accessories. From the outset, Connecticut legal officials concentrated not on the act of abortion per se, but on the fact that an abortion attempt had led to a young woman's death.[3]

The case went next to Joseph Fowler, king's attorney for Windham County. He dropped charges against the two Grosvenor women, probably because he needed them as key witnesses and because they had played cover-up roles rather than originating the scheme. A year and a half passed as Fowler's first attempts to get convictions against Hallowell and Sessions failed either before grand juries or before the Superior Court on technical grounds. Finally, in March 1747, Fowler presented Hallowell and Sessions separately for the "highhanded Misdemeanour" of attempting to destroy both Sarah Grosvenor's health and "the fruit of her womb."[4] A grand jury endorsed the bill against Hallowell but rejected a similarly worded presentment against Sessions. At Hallowell's trial before the Superior Court in Windham, the jury brought in a guilty verdict and the chief judge sentenced the physician to twenty-nine lashes and two hours of public humiliation standing at the town gallows. Before the sentence could be executed, Hallowell managed to break jail. He fled to Rhode Island; as far as records indicate, he never returned to Connecticut. Thus, in the end, both Amasa Sessions and John Hallowell escaped legal punishment for their actions, whereas Sarah Grosvenor paid for her sexual transgression with her life.

Nearly two years of hearings and trials before the Superior Court produced a file of ten depositions and twenty-four other legal documents. This cache of papers is extraordinarily rich, not only for its unusual chronicle of an abortion attempt, but for its illumination of the fault lines in Pomfret dividing parents from grown children, men from women, and mid-eighteenth-century colonial culture from its seventeenth-century counterpart.

The depositions reveal that in 1742 the elders of Pomfret, men and women alike, failed to act as vigilant monitors of Sarah Grosvenor's courtship and illness. Instead, young, married householders—kin of

Sarah and Amasa—pledged themselves in a conspiracy of silence to allow the abortion plot to unfold undetected. The one person who had the opportunity to play middleman between the generations was Hallowell. A man in his forties, dogged by a shady past and yet adept at acquiring respectable connections, Hallowell provides an intriguing and rare portrait of a socially ambitious, rural medical practitioner. By siding with the young people of Pomfret and keeping their secret, Hallowell betrayed his peers and elders and thereby opened himself to severe censure and expulsion from the community.

Beyond depicting generational conflict, the Grosvenor-Sessions case dramatically highlights key changes in gender relations that reverberated through New England society in the eighteenth century. One of these changes involved the emergence of a marked sexual double standard. In the mid-seventeenth century, a young man like Amasa Sessions would have been pressured by parents, friends, or the courts to marry his lover. Had he resisted, he would most likely have been whipped or fined for the crime of fornication. By the late seventeenth century, New England judges gave up on enjoining sexually active couples to marry. In the 1740s, amid shifting standards of sexual behavior and growing concern over the evidentiary impossibility of establishing paternity, prosecutions of young men for premarital sex ceased. Thus fornication was decriminalized for men, but not for women. Many of Sarah Grosvenor's female peers continued to be prosecuted and fined for bearing illegitimate children. Through private arrangements, and occasionally through civil lawsuits, their male partners were sometimes cajoled or coerced into contributing to the child's upkeep.[5]

What is most striking about the Grosvenor-Sessions case is that an entire community apparently forgave Sessions for the extreme measures he took to avoid accountability for his bastard child. Although he initiated the actions that led to his lover's death, all charges against him were dropped. Moreover, the tragedy did not spur Sessions to leave town; instead, he spent the rest of his life in Pomfret as a respected citizen. Even more dramatically than excusing young men from the crime of fornication, the treatment of Amasa Sessions confirmed that the sexually irresponsible activities of men in their youth would not be held against them as they reached for repute and prosperity in their prime.[6]

The documents allow us to listen in on the quite different responses of young men and women to the drama unfolding in Pomfret. Sarah Grosvenor's female kin and friends, as we shall see, became preoccupied with their guilt and with the inevitability of God's vengeance. Her male kin, on the other hand, reacted cautiously and legalistically, ferreting out information in order to assess how best to protect the Grosvenor family name. The contrast reminds us yet again of the complex and gendered ways in which we must rethink conventional interpretations of secular-ization in colonial New England.

Finally, the Grosvenor case raises more questions than it answers about New Englanders' access to and attitudes toward abortion. If Sarah had not died after miscarriage, it is doubtful that any word of Sessions's providing her with an abortifacient or Hallowell's operation would have survived into the twentieth century. Because it nearly went unrecorded and because it reveals that many Pomfret residents were familiar with the idea of abortion, the case supports historians' assumptions that abortion attempts were far from rare in colonial America.[7] We can also infer from the case that the most dangerous abortions before 1800 may have been those instigated by men and performed by surgeons with instruments.[8] But both abortion's frequency and the lineaments of its social context remain obscure. Did cases in which older women helped younger women to abort unwanted pregnancies far outnumber cases such as this one, in which men initiated the process? Under what cir-cumstances did family members and neighbors help married and unmar-ried women to hide abortion attempts?

Perhaps the most intriguing question centers on why women and men in early America acted *covertly* to effect abortions when abortion before quickening was legal. The Grosvenor case highlights the answer that applies to most known incidents from the period: abortion was under-stood as blameworthy because it was an extreme action designed to hide a prior sin, sex outside of marriage.[9] Reading the depositions, it is near-ly impossible to disentangle the players' attitudes toward abortion itself from their expressions of censure or anxiety over failed courtship, ille-gitimacy, and the dangers posed for a young woman by a secret abor-tion. Strikingly absent from these eighteenth-century documents, however, is either outrage over the destruction of a fetus or denuncia-tions of those who would arrest "nature's proper course." Those absences are a telling measure of how the discourse about abortion would change dramatically in later centuries.

THE NARRATIVE

Before delving into the response of the Pomfret community to Sarah Grosvenor's abortion and death, we need to know just who participat-ed in the conspiracy to cover up her pregnancy and how they managed it. The following paragraphs, based on the depositions, offer a recon-struction of the events of 1742. A few caveats are in order. First, precise dating of crucial incidents is impossible, since deponents did not remem-ber events in terms of days of the week (except for the Sabbath) but rather used phrases like "something in August." Second, the testimony concentrated almost exclusively on events in the two months preceding Sarah's death on September 14. Thus, we know very little about Sarah and Amasa's courtship before July 1742.[10] Third, while the depositions often indicate the motivations and feelings of the principals, these will be discussed in subsequent sections of this article, where the characters' attitudes can be set in the context of their social backgrounds, families, and community. This section essentially lays out a medical file for Sarah Grosvenor, a file that unfolds in four parts: the taking of the abortifacient, Hallowell's operation, the miscarriage, and Sarah's final illness.

The case reveals more about the use of an abortifacient than most colonial court records in which abortion attempts are mentioned. Here we learn not only the form in which Sarah received the dose but also the special word that Pomfret residents applied to it. What the documents do not disclose are either its ingredients[11] or the number of times Sarah ingested it.

The chronicle opens in late July 1742 when Zerviah Grosvenor, aged twenty-one, finally prevailed upon her younger sister to admit that she was pregnant. In tears, Sarah explained that she had not told Zerviah sooner because "she had been taking [the] trade to remove it."[12] "Trade" was used in this period to signify stuff or goods, often in the deprecatory sense of rubbish and trash. *The Oxford English Dictionary* confirms that in some parts of England and New England the word was used to refer to medicine. In Pomfret trade meant a particular type of medicine, an abortifacient, thus a substance that might be regarded as "bad" medicine, as rubbish, unsafe and associated with destruction. What is notable is that Sarah and Zerviah, and neighboring young people who also used the word, had no need to explain to one another the meaning of "taking the trade." Perhaps only a few New Englanders knew how to prepare an abortifacient or knew of books that would give them recipes, but many more, especially young women who lived with the fear of becoming pregnant before marriage, were familiar with at least the idea of taking an abortifacient.

Sarah probably began taking the trade in mid-May when she was already three and a half months pregnant.[13] It was brought to her in the form of a powder by Amasa.[14] Sarah understood clearly that her lover had obtained the concoction "from docter hollowel," who conveyed "directions" for her doses through Amasa. Zerviah deposed later that Sarah had been "loath to Take" the drug and "Thot it an Evil," probably because at three and a half months she anticipated quickening, the time from which she knew the law counted abortion an "unlawful measure."[15] At the outset, Sarah argued in vain with Amasa against his proposed "Method." Later, during June and July, she sometimes "neglected" to take the doses he left for her, but, with mounting urgency,

Amasa and the doctor pressed her to comply. "It was necessary," Amasa explained in late July, that she take "more, or [else] they were afraid. She would be greatly hurt by what was already done." To calm her worries, he assured her that "there was no life [left] in the Child" and that the potion "would not hurt her."[16] Apparently, the men hoped that a few more doses would provoke a miscarriage, thereby expelling the dead fetus and restoring Sarah's body to its natural balance of humors.

Presumably, Hallowell decided to operate in early August because Sarah's pregnancy was increasingly visible, and he guessed that she was not going to miscarry. An operation in which the fetus would be removed or punctured was now the only certain way to terminate the pregnancy secretly.[17] To avoid the scrutiny of Sarah's parents, Hallowell resorted to a plan he had used once before in arranging a private examination of Sarah. Early one afternoon he arrived at the house of John Grosvenor and begged for a room as "he was weary and wanted Rest."[18] John, Sarah's thirty-one-year-old first cousin, lived with his wife, Hannah, and their young children in a homestead only a short walk down the hill but out of sight of Sarah's father's house. While John and Hannah were busy, the physician sent one of the little children to fetch Sarah.[19]

The narrative of Sarah's fateful meeting with Hallowell that August afternoon is best told in the words of one of the deponents. Abigail Nightingale had married and moved to Pomfret two years earlier, and by 1742 she had become Sarah's close friend.[20] Several weeks after the operation, Sarah attempted to relieve her own "Distress of mind" by confiding the details of her shocking experience to Abigail. Unconnected to the Grosvenor or Sessions families by kinship, and without any other apparent stake in the legal uses of her testimony, Abigail can probably be trusted as a fairly accurate paraphraser of Sarah's words.[21] If so, we have here an unparalleled eyewitness account of an eighteenth-century abortion attempt.

This is how Abigail recollected Sarah's deathbed story:

On [Sarah's] going down [to her cousin John's], [Hallowell] said he wanted to Speake with her alone; and then they two went into a Room together; and then sd. Hallowell told her it was necessary that something more should be done or else she would Certainly die; to which she replied that she was afraid they had done too much already, and then he told her that there was one thing more that could easily be done, and she asking him what it was; he said he could easily deliver her. but she said she was afraid there was life in the Child, then he asked her how long she had felt it; and she replyed about a fortnight; then he said that was impossible or could not be or ever would; for that the trade she had taken had or would prevent it: and that the alteration she felt Was owing to what she had taken. And he farther told her that he verily thought that the Child grew to her body to the Bigness of his hand, or else it would have Come away before that time, and that it would never Come away, but Certainly Kill her, unless other Means were used.[22] On which she yielded to his making an Attempt to take it away; charging him that if he could perceive that there was life in it he would not proceed on any Account. And then the Doctor openning his portmantua took an Instrument[23] out of it and Laid it on the Bed, and she asking him what it was for, he replyed that it was to make way; and that then he tryed to remove the Child for Some time in vain putting her to the Utmost Distress, and that at Last she observed he trembled and immediately perceived a Strange alteration in her body and thought a bone of the Child was broken; on which she desired him (as she said) to Call in some body, for that she feared she was dying, and instantly swooned away.[24]

With Sarah's faint, Abigail's account broke off, but within minutes others, who would testify later, stepped into the room. Hallowell reacted to Sarah's swoon by unfastening the door and calling in Hannah, the young mistress of the house, and Zerviah, who had followed her sister there. Cold water and "a bottle of drops" were brought to keep Sarah from fainting again, while Hallowell explained to the "much Surprized" women that "he had been making an Attempt" to deliver Sarah. Despite their protests, he then "used a further force upon her" but did not succeed in "Tak[ing] the Child . . . away."[25] Some days later Hallowell told a Pomfret man that in this effort "to distroy hir conception" he had "either knipt or Squeisd the head of the Conception."[26] At the time of the attempt, Hallowell explained to the women that he "had done so much to her, as would Cause the Birth of the Child in a Little time." Just before sunset, he packed up his portmanteau and went to a nearby tavern, where Amasa was waiting "to hear [the outcome of] the event."[27] Meanwhile, Sarah, weak-kneed and in pain, leaned on the arm of her sister as the young women managed to make their way home in the twilight.

After his attempted "force," Hallowell fades from the scene, while Zerviah and Hannah Grosvenor become the key figures. About two days after enduring the operation, Sarah began to experience contractions. Zerviah ran to get Hannah, telling her "she Tho't . . . Sarah would be quickly delivered." They returned to find Sarah, who was alone "in her Father's Chamber," just delivered and rising from the chamber pot. In the pot was "an Untimely birth"—a "Child [that] did not Appear to have any Life In it." To Hannah, it "Seemed by The Scent . . . That it had been hurt and was decaying," while Zerviah later remembered it as "a perfect Child," even "a pritty child."[28] Determined to keep the event "as private as they Could," the two women helped Sarah back to bed, and then "wr[ap]ed . . . up" the fetus, carried it to the woods on the edge of the farmstead, and there "Buried it in the Bushes."[29]

On learning that Sarah had finally miscarried and that the event had evidently been kept hidden from Sarah's parents, Amasa and Hallowell may have congratulated themselves on the success of their operation. However, about ten days after the miscarriage, Sarah grew feverish and weak. Her parents consulted two college-educated physicians who hailed from outside the Pomfret area. Their visits did little good, nor were Sarah's symptoms—fever, delirium, convulsions—relieved by a visit from Hallowell, whom Amasa "fetcht" to Sarah's bedside.[30] In the end, Hallowell, who had decided to move from nearby Killingly to more distant Providence, washed his hands of the case. A few days before Sarah died, her cousin John "went after" Hallowell, whether to bring him back or to express his rage, we do not know. Hallowell predicted "that She woul[d] not live."[31]

Silence seems to have settled on the Grosvenor house and its neighborhood after Sarah's death on September 14. It was two and a half years later that rumors about a murderous abortion spread through and beyond Pomfret village, prompting legal investigation. The silence, the gap between event and prosecution, the passivity of Sarah's parents—all lend mystery to the narrative. But despite its ellipses, the Grosvenor case provides us with an unusual set of details about one young couple's extreme response to the common problem of failed courtship and illegitimacy. To gain insight into both the mysteries and the extremities of the Grosvenor-Sessions case, we need to look more closely at Pomfret, at the two families centrally involved, and at clues to the motivations of the principal participants. Our abortion tale, it turns out, holds beneath its surface a complex trail of evidence about generational conflict and troubled relations between men and women.

THE POMFRET PLAYERS

In 1742 the town of Pomfret had been settled for just over forty years. Within its central neighborhood and in homesteads scattered over rugged, wooded hillsides lived probably no more than 270 men, women, and children.[32] During the founding decades, the fathers of Sarah and Amasa ranked among the ten leading householders; Leicester Grosvenor and Nathaniel Sessions were chosen often to fill important local offices.

Grosvenor, the older of the two by seven years, had inherited standing and a choice farmstead from his father, one of the original six purchasers of the Pomfret territory.[33] When the town was incorporated in 1714, he was elected a militia officer and one of the first selectmen. He was returned to the latter post nineteen times and eventually rose to the highest elective position—that of captain—in the local trainband. Concurrently, he was appointed many times throughout the 1710s and 1720s to ad hoc town committees, often alongside Nathaniel Sessions. But unlike Sessions, Grosvenor went on to serve at the colony level. Pomfret freemen chose him to represent them at ten General Assembly sessions between 1726 and 1744. Finally, in the 1730s, when he was in his late fifties, the legislature appointed him a justice of the peace for Windham County. Thus, until his retirement in 1748 at age seventy-four, his house would have served as the venue for petty trials, hearings, and recordings of documents. After retiring from public office, Grosvenor lived another eleven years, leaving behind in 1759 an estate worth over six hundred pounds.[34]

Nathaniel Sessions managed a sizable farm and ran one of Pomfret's taverns at the family homestead. Town meetings were sometimes held there. Sessions was chosen to be constable in 1714 and rose from ensign to lieutenant in the militia—always a step behind Leicester Grosvenor. He could take pride in one exceptional distinction redounding to the family honor: in 1737 his son Darius became only the second Pomfret resident to graduate from Yale College, and before Sessions died at ninety-one he saw Darius elected assistant and then deputy governor of Rhode Island.[35]

The records are silent as to whether Sessions and his family resented the Grosvenors, who must have been perceived in town as more prominent, or whether the two families—who sat in adjoining private pews in the meetinghouse—enjoyed a close relationship that went sour for some reason *before* the affair between Sarah and Amasa. Instead, the signs (such as the cooperative public work of the two fathers, the visits back and forth between the Grosvenor and Sessions girls) point to a long-standing friendship and dense web of interchanges between the families. Indeed, courtship and marriage between a Sessions son and a Grosvenor daughter would hardly have been surprising.

What went wrong in the affair between Sarah and Amasa is not clear. Sarah's sisters and cousins knew that "Amasy" "made Sute to" Sarah, and they gave no indication of disapproving. The few who guessed at Sarah's condition in the summer of 1742 were not so much surprised that she was pregnant as that the couple "did not marry."[36] It was evidently routine in this New England village, as in others, for courting couples to post banns for their nuptials after the woman discovered that she was pregnant.

Amasa offered different answers among his Pomfret peers to explain his failure to marry his lover. When Zerviah Grosvenor told Amasa that he and Sarah "had better Marry," he responded, "That would not do," for "he was afraid of his Parents . . . [who would] always make their lives [at home] uncomfortable."[37] Later, Abigail Nightingale heard rumors that Amasa was resorting to the standard excuse of men wishing to avoid a shotgun marriage—denying that the child was his.[38] Hallowell, with whom Amasa may have been honest, claimed "the Reason that they did not marry" was "that Sessions Did not Love her well a nough for [he] saith he did not believe it was his son and if he Could Cause her to gitt Red of it he would not Go near her again."[39] Showing yet another face to a Grosvenor kinsman after Sarah's death, Amasa repented his actions and extravagantly claimed he would "give All he had" to "bring Sarah . . . To life again . . . and have her as his wife."[40]

The unusual feature of Amasa's behavior was not his unwillingness to marry Sarah, but his determination to terminate her pregnancy before it showed. Increasing numbers of young men in eighteenth-century New England weathered the temporary obloquy of abandoning a pregnant lover in order to prolong their bachelorhood or marry someone else.[41] What drove Amasa, and an ostensibly reluctant Sarah, to resort to abortion? Was it fear of their fathers? Nathaniel Sessions had chosen Amasa as the son who would remain on the family farm and care for his parents in their old age. An ill-timed marriage could have disrupted these plans and threatened Amasa's inheritance.[42] For his part, Leicester Grosvenor may have made it clear to his daughter that he would be greatly displeased at her marrying before she reached a certain age or until her older sister wed. Rigid piety, an authoritarian nature, an intense concern with being seen as a good household governor—any of these traits in Leicester Grosvenor or Nathaniel Sessions could have colored Amasa's decisions.

Perhaps it was not family relations that proved the catalyst but Amasa's acquaintance with a medical man who boasted about a powder more effective than the herbal remedies that were part of women's lore. Hallowell himself had fathered an illegitimate child fifteen years earlier, and he may have encouraged a rakish attitude in Amasa, beguiling the younger man with the promise of dissociating sex from its possible consequences. Or the explanation may have been that classic one: another woman. Two years after Sarah's death, Amasa married Hannah Miller of Rehoboth, Massachusetts. Perhaps in early 1742 he was already making trips to the town just east of Providence to see his future wife.[43]

What should we make of Sarah's role in the scheme? It is possible that she no longer loved Amasa and was as eager as he to forestall external pressures toward a quick marriage. However, Zerviah swore that on one occasion before the operation Amasa reluctantly agreed to post banns for their nuptials and that Sarah did not object.[44] *If* Sarah was a willing and active participant in the abortion plot all along, then by 1745 her female kin and friends had fabricated and rehearsed a careful and seamless story to preserve the memory of the dead girl untarnished.

In the portrait drawn by her friends, Sarah reacted to her pregnancy and to Amasa's plan first by arguing and finally by doing her utmost to protect her lover. She may have wished to marry Amasa, yet she did not insist on it or bring in older family members to negotiate with him and his parents. Abigail Nightingale insisted that Sarah accepted Amasa's recalcitrance and only pleaded with him that they not "go on to add sin to sin." Privately, she urged Amasa that there was an alternative to taking the trade—a way that would enable him to keep his role hidden and prevent the couple from committing a "Last transgression [that] would be worse then the first." Sarah told him that "she was willing to take the sin and shame to her self, and to be obliged never to tell whose Child it was, and that she did not doubt but that if she humbled her self on her Knees to her Father he would take her and her Child home." Her lover, afraid that his identity would become known, vetoed her proposal.[45]

According to the Pomfret women's reconstruction, abortion was not a freely chosen and defiant act for Sarah. Against her own desires, she reluctantly consented in taking the trade only because Amasa "So very earnestly perswaided her." In fact, she had claimed to her friends that she was coerced; he "would take no denyal."[46] Sarah's confidantes presented her as being aware of her options, shrinking from abortion as an unnatural and immoral deed, and yet finally choosing the strategy consistent with her lover's vision of what would best protect their futures. Thus, if Amasa's hubris was extreme, so too was Sarah's internalization of those strains of thought in her culture that taught women to make themselves pleasing and obedient to men.

While we cannot be sure that the deponents' picture of Sarah's initial recoil and reluctant submission to the abortion plot was entirely accurate, it is clear that once she was caught up in the plan she extracted a pledge of silence from all her confidantes. Near her death, before telling Abigail about the operation, she "insist[ed] on . . . [her friend's] never discovering the Matter" to anyone.[47] Clearly, she had earlier bound Zerviah and Hannah on their honor not to tell their elders. Reluctant when faced with the abortionist's powder, Sarah became a leading co-conspirator when alone with her female friends.

One of the most remarkable aspects of the Grosvenor-Sessions case is Sarah and Amasa's success in keeping their parents in the dark, at least until her final illness. If by July Sarah's sisters grew suspicious that Sarah was "with child," what explains the failure of her parents to observe her pregnancy and to intervene and uncover the abortion scheme? Were they negligent, preoccupied with other matters, or willfully blind?[48] Most mysterious is the role of forty-eight-year-old Rebecca Grosvenor, Grosvenor's second wife and Sarah's stepmother since 1729. Rebecca is mentioned only once in the depositions,[49] and she was not summoned as a witness in the 1745–1747 investigations into Sarah's death. Even if some extraordinary circumstance—an invalid condition or an implacable hatred between Sarah and her stepmother—explains Rebecca's abdication of her role as guardian, Sarah had two widowed aunts living in or near her household. These matrons, experienced in childbirth matters and concerned for the family reputation, were just the sort of older women who traditionally watched and advised young women entering courtship.[50]

In terms of who knew what, the events of summer 1742 in Pomfret apparently unfolded in two stages. The first stretched from Sarah's discovery of her pregnancy by early May to some point in late August after her miscarriage. In this period a determined, collective effort by Sarah and Amasa and their friends kept their elders in the dark.[51] When Sarah fell seriously ill from the aftereffects of the abortion attempt and miscarriage, rumors of the young people's secret activities reached Leicester Grosvenor's neighbors and even one of the doctors he had called in.[52] It is difficult to escape the conclusion that by Sarah's death in mid-September her father and stepmother had learned of the steps that had precipitated her mortal condition and kept silent for reasons of their own.

Except for Hallowell, the circle of intimates entrusted by Amasa and Sarah with their scheme consisted of young adults ranging in age from nineteen to thirty-three.[53] Born between 1710 and 1725, these young people had grown up just as the town attracted enough settlers to support a church, militia, and local market. They were second-generation Pomfret residents who shared the generational identity that came with sitting side by side through long worship services, as well as attending school, playing, and working together at children's tasks. By 1740, these sisters, brothers, cousins, courting couples, and neighbors, in their visits from house to house—sometimes in their own households, sometimes at their parents'—had managed to create a world of talk and socializing that was largely exempt from parental supervision.[54] In Pomfret in 1742 it was this group of young people in their twenties and early thirties, *not* the cluster of Grosvenor matrons over forty-five, who monitored Sarah's courtship, attempted to get Amasa to marry his lover, privately investigated the activities and motives of Amasa and Hallowell, and, belatedly, spoke out publicly to help Connecticut juries decide who should be blamed for Sarah's death.

That Leicester Grosvenor made no public move to punish those around him and that he avoided giving testimony when legal proceedings commenced are intriguing clues to social changes underway in New England villages in the mid-eighteenth century. Local leaders like Grosvenor, along with the respectable yeomen whom he represented in public office, were increasingly withdrawing delicate family problems from the purview of their communities. Slander, illegitimacy, and feuds among neighbors came infrequently to local courts by mid-century, indicating male householders' growing preference for handling such matters privately.[55] Wealthy and ambitious families adopted this ethic of privacy at the same time that they became caught up in elaborating their material worlds by adding rooms and acquiring luxury goods. The "good feather bed" with all of its furniture that Grosvenor bequeathed to his one unmarried daughter was but one of many marks of status by which the Grosvenors differentiated themselves from their Pomfret neighbors.[56] But all the fine accouterments in the world would not excuse Justice Grosvenor from his obligation to govern his household effectively. Mortified no doubt at his inability to monitor the young people in his extended family, he responded, ironically, by extending their conspiracy of silence. The best way for him to shield the family name from scandal and protect his political reputation in the county and colony was to keep the story of Sarah's abortion out of the courts.

THE DOCTOR

John Hallowell's status as an outsider in Pomfret and his dangerous, secret alliance with the town's young adults may have shaped his destiny as the one conspirator sentenced to suffer at the whipping post. Although the physician had been involved in shady dealings before 1742, he had managed to win the trust of many patients and a respectable social standing. Tracking down his history in northeastern Connecticut tells us something of the uncertainty surrounding personal and professional identity before the advent of police records and medical licensing boards. It also gives us an all-too-rare glimpse into the fashion in which an eighteenth-century country doctor tried to make his way in the world.

Hallowell's earliest brushes with the law came in the 1720s. In 1725 he purchased land in Killingly, a Connecticut town just north of Pomfret and bordering both Massachusetts and Rhode Island. Newly married, he was probably in his twenties at the time. Seven months before his wife gave birth to their first child, a sixteen-year-old Killingly woman charged Hallowell with fathering her illegitimate child. Using the alias Nicholas Hallaway, he fled to southeastern Connecticut, where he lived as a "transient" for three months. He was arrested and settled the case by admitting to paternity and agreeing to contribute to the child's maintenance for four years.[57]

Hallowell resumed his life in Killingly. Two years later, now referred to as "Dr.," he was arrested again; this time the charge was counterfeiting. Hallowell and several confederates were hauled before the governor and council for questioning and then put on trial before the Superior Court. Although many Killingly witnesses testified to the team's suspect activities in a woodland shelter, the charges against Hallowell were dropped when a key informer failed to appear in court.[58]

Hallowell thus escaped conviction on a serious felony charge, but he had been tainted by stories linking him to the criminal subculture of transient, disorderly, greedy, and manually skilled men who typically made up gangs of counterfeiters in eighteenth-century New England.[59] After 1727 Hallowell may have given up dabbling in money-making schemes and turned to earning his livelihood chiefly from his medical practice. Like two-thirds of the male medical practitioners in colonial New England, he probably did not have college or apprentice training. But his skill, or charm, was not necessarily less than that of any one of his peers who might have inherited a library of books and a fund of knowledge from a physician father. All colonial practitioners, as Richard D. Brown reminds us, mixed learned practices with home or folk remedies, and no doctor had access to safe, reliable pharmacological preparations or antiseptic surgical procedures.[60]

In the years immediately following the counterfeiting charge, Hallowell appears to have made several deliberate moves to portray himself as a sober neighbor and reliable physician. At about the time of his second marriage, in 1729, he became a more frequent attendant at the Killingly meetinghouse, where he renewed his covenant and presented his first two children for baptism.[61] He also threw himself into the land and credit markets of northeastern Connecticut, establishing himself as a physician who was also an enterprising yeoman and a frequent litigant.[62]

These activities had dual implications. On the one hand, they suggest that Hallowell epitomized the eighteenth-century Yankee citizen—a man as comfortable in the courtroom and countinghouse as at a patient's bedside; a man of restless energy, not content to limit his scope to his fields and village; a practical, ambitious man with a shrewd eye for a good deal.[63] On the other hand, Hallowell's losses to Boston creditors, his constant efforts to collect debts, and his far-flung practice raise questions about the nature of his activities and medical practice. He evidently had clients not just in towns across northeastern Connecticut but also in neighboring Massachusetts and Rhode Island. Perhaps rural practitioners normally traveled extensively, spending many nights away from their wives and children.[64] It is also possible, however, either that Hallowell was forced to travel because established doctors from leading families had monopolized the local practice or that he chose to recruit patients in Providence and other towns as a cover for illicit activities.[65] Despite his land speculations and his frequent resort to litigation, Hallowell was losing money. In the sixteen years before 1742, his creditors secured judgments against him for a total of 1,060 pounds, while he was able to collect only 700 pounds in debts.[66] The disjunction between his ambition and actual material gains may have led Hallowell in middle age to renew his illicit money-making schemes. By supplying young men with potent abortifacients and dabbling in schemes to counterfeit New England's paper money, he betrayed the very gentlemen whose respect, credit, and society he sought.

What is most intriguing about Hallowell was his ability to ingratiate himself throughout his life with elite men whose reputations were unblemished by scandal. Despite the rumors that must have circulated about his early sexual dalliance, counterfeiting activities, suspect medical remedies, heavy debts, and shady business transactions,[67] leading ministers, merchants, and magistrates welcomed him into their houses. In Pomfret such acceptance took its most dramatic form in September 1739 when Hallowell was admitted along with thirty-five other original covenanters to the first private library association in eastern Connecticut. Gathering in the house of Pomfret's respected, conservative minister, Ebenezer Williams, the members pledged sums for the purchase of "useful and profitable English books." In the company of the region's scholars, clergy, and "gentlemen," along with a few yeomen—all "warm friends of learning and literature"—Hallowell marked himself off from the more modest subscribers by joining with thirteen prominent and wealthy signers to pledge a sum exceeding fifteen pounds.[68]

Lacking a college degree and family pedigree, Hallowell traded on his profession and his charm to gain acceptability with the elite. In August 1742 he shrewdly removed himself from the Pomfret scene, just before Sarah Grosvenor's death. In that month he moved, without his wife and children, to Providence, where he had many connections. Within five years, Hallowell had so insinuated himself with Providence town leaders such as Stephen Hopkins that fourteen of them petitioned for mitigation of what they saw as the misguided sentence imposed on him in the Grosvenor case.[69]

Hallowell's capacity for landing on his feet, despite persistent brushes with scandal, debt, and the law, suggests that we should look at the fluidity of New England's eighteenth-century elite in new ways.[70] What bound sons of old New England families, learned men, and upwardly mobile merchants and professionals in an expanded elite may partly have been a reshaped, largely unspoken set of values shared by men. We know that the archetype for white New England women as sexual beings was changing from carnal Eve to resisting Pamela and that the calculus of accountability for seduction was shifting blame solely to women.[71] But the simultaneous metamorphosis in cultural images and values defining manhood in the early and mid-eighteenth century has not been studied. The scattered evidence we do have suggests that, increasingly, for men in the more secular and anglicized culture of New England, the lines between legitimate and illegitimate sexuality, between sanctioned and shady business dealings, and between speaking the truth and protecting family honor blurred. Hallowell's accountability to men like minister Ebenezer Williams and merchant Stephen Hopkins hints at how changing sexual and moral standards shaped the economic and social alliances made by New England's male leadership in the 1700s.[72]

WOMEN'S TALK AND MEN'S TALK

If age played a major role in determining who knew the truth about Sarah Grosvenor's illness, gender affected how the conspiring young adults responded to Sarah's impending death and how they weighed the issue of blame. Our last glimpse into the social world of eighteenth-century Pomfret looks at the different ways in which women and men reconstructed their roles in the events of 1742.

An inward gaze, a strong consciousness of sin and guilt, a desire to avoid conflict and achieve reconciliation, a need to confess—these are the impulses expressed in women's intimate talk in the weeks before Sarah died. The central female characters in the plot, Sarah and Zerviah Grosvenor, lived for six weeks with the daily fear that their parents or aunts might detect Sarah's condition or their covert comings and goings. Deposing three years later, Zerviah represented the sisters as suffering under an intensifying sense of complicity as they had passed through two stages of involvement in the concealment plan. At first, they were passive players, submitting to the hands of men. But once Hallowell declared that he had done all he could, they were left to salvage the conspiracy by enduring the terrors of a first delivery alone, knowing that their failure to call in the older women of the family resembled the decision made by women who committed infanticide.[73] While the pain and shock of miscarrying a five-and-one-half-month fetus through a possibly lacerated vagina may have been the experience that later most grieved Sarah, Zerviah would be haunted particularly by her stealthy venture into the woods with Hannah to bury the shrouded evidence of miscarriage.[74]

The Grosvenor sisters later recalled that they had regarded the first stage of the scheme—taking the trade—as "a Sin" and "an Evil" not so much because it was intended to end the life of a fetus as because it entailed a protracted set of actions, worse than a single lie, to cover up an initial transgression: fornication.[75] According to their religion and the traditions of their New England culture, Sarah and Zerviah knew that the proper response to the sin of "uncleanness" (especially when it led to its visible manifestation, pregnancy) was to confess, seeking to allay

God's wrath and cleanse oneself and one's community. Dire were the consequences of hiding a grave sin, so the logic and folklore of religion warned.[76] Having piled one covert act upon another, all in defiance of her parents, each sister wondered if she had not ventured beyond the pale, forsaking God and in turn being forsaken.

Within hours after the burial, Zerviah ran in a frenzy to Alexander Sessions's house and blurted out an account of her sister's "Untimely birth" and the burying of the fetus. While Alexander and Silence Sessions wondered if Zerviah was "in her right mind" and supposed she was having "a very bad fit," we might judge that she was in shock—horrified and confused by what she had done, fearful of retribution, and torn between the pragmatic strategy of silence and an intense spiritual longing to confess. Silence took her aside and demanded, "how could you do it?—I could not!" Zerviah, in despair, replied, "I don't Know; the Devil was in us." Hers was the characteristic refuge of the defiant sinner: Satan made her do it.[77]

Sarah's descent into despondency, according to the portrait drawn in the women's depositions, was not so immediate. In the week following the miscarriage she recovered enough to be up and about the house. Then the fever came on. Bedridden for weeks, yet still lucid, she exhibited such "great Concern of mind" that Abigail, alone with her, felt compelled to ask her "what was the Matter." "Full of Sorrow" and "in a very affectionate Manner," Sarah replied by asking her friend "whether [she] thought her Sins would ever be pardoned?" Abigail's answer blended a reassuringly familiar exhortation to repent with an awareness that Sarah might have stepped beyond the possibility of salvation. "I answered that I hoped she had not Sinned the unpardonable Sin [that of renouncing Christ], but with true and hearty repentance hoped she would find forgiveness." On this occasion, and at least once more, Sarah responded to the call for repentance by pouring out her troubled heart to Abigail—as we have seen—confessing her version of the story in a torrent of words.[78]

Thus, visions of judgment and of their personal accountability to God haunted Sarah and Zerviah during the waning days of summer—or so their female friends later contended. Caught between the traditional religious ethic of confession, recently renewed in revivals across New England, and the newer, status-driven cultural pressure to keep moral missteps private, the Grosvenor women declined to take up roles as accusers. By focusing on their own actions, they rejected a portrait of themselves as helpless victims, yet they also ceded to their male kin responsibility for assessing blame and mediating between the public interest in seeing justice done and the private interests of the Grosvenor family. Finally, by trying to keep the conspiracy of silence intact and by allowing Amasa frequent visits to her bedside to lament his role and his delusion by Hallowell, Sarah at once endorsed a policy of private repentance and forgiveness *and* indicated that she wished her lover to be spared eventual public retribution for her death.

Talk among the men of Pomfret in the weeks preceding and following Sarah's death centered on more secular concerns than the preoccupation with sin and God's anger that ran through the women's conversations. Neither Hallowell nor Sessions expressed any guilt or sense of sin, as far as the record shows, *until* Sarah was diagnosed as mortally ill.[79] Indeed, their initial accounts of the plot took the form of braggadocio, with Amasa (according to Hallowell) casting himself as the rake who could "gitt Red" of his child and look elsewhere for female companionship, and Hallowell boasting of his abortionist's surgical technique to Sarah's cousin Ebenezer. Later, anticipating popular censure and possible prosecution, each man "Tried to Cast it" on the other. The physician insisted that "[h]e did not do any thing but What Sessions Importuned him to Do," while Amasa exclaimed "That he could freely be strip[p]ed naked provided he could bring Sarah . . . To life again . . . , but Doct. Hollowell had Deluded him, and Destroyed her."[80] While this sort of denial and buck passing seems very human, it was the antithesis of the New England way—a religious way of life that made confession its central motif. The Grosvenor-Sessions case is one illustration among many of how New England women continued to measure themselves by "the moral allegory of repentance and confession" while men, at least when presenting themselves before legal authorities, adopted secular voices and learned self-interested strategies.[81]

For the Grosvenor men—at least the cluster of Sarah's cousins living near her—the key issue was not exposing sin but protecting the family's reputation. In the weeks before Sarah died, her cousins John and Ebenezer each attempted to investigate and sort out the roles and motives of Amasa Sessions and John Hallowell in the scheme to conceal Sarah's pregnancy. Grilled in August by Ebenezer about Sarah's condition, Hallowell revealed that "Sessions had bin Interseeding with him to Remove her Conseption." On another occasion, when John Grosvenor demanded that he justify his actions, Hallowell was more specific. He "[did] with her [Sarah] as he did . . . because Sessions Came to him and was So very earnest . . . and offered him fivepounds if he would do it." "But," Hallowell boasted, "he would have twenty of[f] of him before he had done." John persisted: did Amasa know that Hallowell was attempting a manual abortion at John's house on that day in early August? Hallowell replied that Amasa "knew before he did anything and was at Mr. Waldo's [a Pomfret tavern keeper] to hear the event."[82]

John and Ebenezer, deposing three or four years after these events, did not mention having thrown questions at Amasa Sessions at the time, nor did they explain why they did not act immediately to have charges brought against the two conspirators. Perhaps these young householders were loath to move against a male peer and childhood friend. More likely, they kept their information to themselves to protect John's wife, Hannah, and their cousin Zerviah from prosecution as accessories. They may also have acted, in league with their uncle Leicester, out of a larger concern for keeping the family name out of the courts. Finally, it is probable that the male cousins, partly because of their own complicity and partly because they may have believed that Sarah had consented to the abortion, simply did not think that Amasa's and Hallowell's actions added up to the murder of their relative.

Three years later, yet another Grosvenor cousin intervened, expressing himself much more vehemently than John or Ebenezer ever had. In 1742, John Shaw at age thirty-eight may have been perceived by the younger Grosvenors as too old—too close to the age when men took public office and served as grand jurors—to be trusted with their secret. Shaw seems to have known nothing of Sarah's taking the trade or having a miscarriage until 1745, when "the Storys" suddenly surfaced. Then Hannah and Zerviah gave him a truncated account. Shaw reacted with rage, realizing that Sarah had died not of natural causes but from "what Hallowell had done," and he set out to wring the truth from the doctor. Several times he sought out Hallowell in Rhode Island to tell him that "I could not look upon him otherwise Than [as] a Bad man Since he had Destroyed my Kinswoman." When Hallowell countered that "Amasa Sessions . . . was the Occasion of it," Shaw's fury grew. "I Told him he was like old Mother Eve When She said The Serpent beguild her; . . . [and] I Told him in my Mind he Deserved to dye for it."[83]

Questioning Amasa, Shaw was quick to accept his protestations of sincere regret and his insistence that Hallowell had "Deluded" him.[84] Shaw concluded that Amasa had never "Importuned [Hallowell] . . . to lay hands on her" (that is, to perform the manual abortion). Forged in the men's talk about the Grosvenor-Sessions case in 1745 and 1746 appears to have been a consensus that, while Amasa Sessions was somewhat blameworthy "as concerned in it," it was only Hallowell—the outsider, the man easily labeled a quack—who deserved to be branded "a Man of Death." Nevertheless, it was the stories of *both* men and women that ensured the fulfillment of a doctor's warning to Hallowell in the Leicester Grosvenor house just before Sarah died: "The Hand of Justice [will] Take hold of [you] sooner or Later."[85]

THE LAW

The hand of justice reached out to catch John Hallowell in November

1745. The warrants issued for the apprehension and examination of suspects that autumn gave no indication of a single informer or highly placed magistrate who had triggered the prosecution so long after the events. Witnesses referred to "those Stories Concerning Amasa Sessions and Sarah Grosvenor" that had begun to circulate beyond the inner circle of Pomfret initiates in the summer of 1745. *Something* had caused Zerviah and Hannah Grosvenor to break their silence.[86] Zerviah provided the key to the puzzle, as she alone had been present at the crucial series of incidents leading to Sarah's death. The only surviving account of Zerviah's belated conversion from silence to public confession comes from the stories told by Pomfret residents into the nineteenth century. In Ellen Larned's melodramatic prose, the "whispered" tale recounted Zerviah's increasing discomfort thus: "Night after night, in her solitary chamber, the surviving sister was awakened by the rattling of the rings on which her bed-curtains were suspended, a ghostly knell continuing and intensifying till she was convinced of its preternatural origin; and at length, in response to her agonized entreaties, the spirit of her dead sister made known to her, 'That she could not rest in her grave till her crime was made public.'"[87]

Embellished as this tale undoubtedly is, we should not dismiss it out of hand as a Victorian ghost story. In early modern English culture, belief persisted in both apparitions and the supernatural power of the guiltless victim to return and expose her murderer.[88] Zerviah in 1742 already fretted over her sin as an accomplice, yet she kept her pledge of silence to her sister. It is certainly conceivable that, after a lapse of three years, she could no longer bear the pressure of hiding the acts that she increasingly believed amounted to the murder of her sister and an unborn child. Whether Zerviah's sudden outburst of talk in 1745 came about at the urging of some Pomfret confidante, or perhaps under the influence of the revivals then sweeping Windham County churches, or indeed because of her belief in nightly visitations by her dead sister's spirit, we simply cannot know.[89]

The Pomfret meetinghouse was the site of the first public legal hearing into the facts behind Sarah Grosvenor's death. We can imagine that townsfolk crowded the pews over the course of two November days to watch two prominent county magistrates examine a string of witnesses before pronouncing their preliminary judgment.[90] The evidence, they concluded, was sufficient to bind four people over for trial at the Superior Court: Hallowell, who in their opinion was "Guilty of murdering Sarah," along with Amasa Sessions, Zerviah Grosvenor, and Hannah Grosvenor as accessories to that murder.[91] The inclusion of Zerviah and Hannah may have been a ploy to pressure these crucial, possibly still reluctant, witnesses to testify for the crown. When Joseph Fowler, the king's attorney, prepared a formal indictment in the case eleven months later, he dropped all charges against Zerviah and Hannah. Rather than stand trial, the two women traveled frequently during 1746 and 1747 to the county seat to give evidence against Sessions and Hallowell.

The criminal process recommenced in September 1746. A grand jury impaneled by the Superior Court as its Windham session first rejected a presentment against Hallowell for murdering Sarah "by his Wicked and Diabolical practice." Fowler, recognizing that the capital charges of murder and accessory to murder against Hallowell and Sessions were going to fail before jurors, changed his tack. He presented the grand jury with a joint indictment against the two men not for outright murder but for endangering Sarah's health by trying to "procure an Abortion" with medicines and "a violent manual operation"; this time the jurors endorsed the bill. When the Superior Court trial opened in November, two attorneys for the defendants managed to persuade the judges that the indictment was faulty on technical grounds. However, upon the advice of the king's attorney that there "appear reasons vehemently to suspect" the two men "Guilty of Sundry Heinous Offenses" at Pomfret four years earlier, the justices agreed to bind them over to answer charges in March 1747.[92]

Fowler next moved to bring separate indictments against Hallowell and Sessions for the "highhanded misdemeanor" of endeavoring to destroy Sarah's health "and the fruit of her womb." This wording echoed the English common law designation of abortion as a misdemeanor, not a felony or capital crime. A newly impaneled grand jury of eighteen county yeomen made what turned out to be the pivotal decision in getting a conviction: they returned a true bill against Hallowell and rejected a similarly worded bill against Sessions.[93] Only Hallowell, "the notorious physician," would go to trial.[94]

On March 20, 1747, John Hallowell stepped before the bar for the final time to answer for the death of Sarah Grosvenor. He maintained his innocence, the case went to a trial jury of twelve men, and they returned with a guilty verdict. The Superior Court judges, who had discretion to choose any penalty less than death, pronounced a severe sentence of public shaming and corporal punishment. Hallowell was to be paraded to the town gallows, made to stand there before the public for two hours "with a rope visibly hanging about his neck," and then endure a public whipping of twenty-nine lashes "on the naked back."[95]

Before the authorities could carry out this sentence, Hallowell escaped and fled to Rhode Island. From Providence seven months after his trial, he audaciously petitioned the Connecticut General Assembly for a mitigated sentence, presenting himself as a destitute "Exile." As previously noted, fourteen respected male citizens of Providence took up his cause, arguing that this valued doctor had been convicted by prejudiced witnesses and hearsay evidence and asserting that corporal punishment was unwarranted in a misdemeanor case. While the Connecticut legislators rejected these petitions, the language used by Hallowell and his Rhode Island patrons is yet another marker of the distance separating many educated New England men at mid-century from their more God-fearing predecessors. Never mentioning the words "sin" or "repentance," the Providence men wrote that Hallowell was justified in escaping the lash since "every Person is prompted [by the natural Law of Self-Preservation] to avoid Pain and Misery."[96]

In the series of indictments against Hallowell and Sessions, the central legal question became who had directly caused Sarah's death. To the farmers in their forties and fifties who sat as jurors, Hallowell clearly deserved punishment. By recklessly endangering Sarah's life he had abused the trust that heads of household placed in him as a physician.[97] Moreover, he had conspired with members of the younger generation to keep their dangerous activities secret from their parents and elders.

Several rationales could have been behind the Windham jurors' conclusion that Amasa Sessions ought to be spared the lash. Legally, they could distinguish him from Hallowell as not being immediately responsible for Sarah's death. Along with Sarah's male kin, they dismissed the evidence that Amasa had instigated the scheme, employed Hallowell, and monitored all of his activities. Perhaps they saw him as a native son who deserved the chance to prove himself mature and responsible. They may have excused his actions as nothing more than a misguided effort to cast off an unwanted lover. Rather than acknowledge that a culture that excused male sexual irresponsibility was responsible for Sarah's death, the Grosvenor family, the Pomfret community, and the jury men of the county persuaded themselves that Sessions had been ignorant of the potentially deadly consequences of his actions.

No family feud, no endless round of recriminations followed the many months of deposing and attending trials that engaged the Grosvenor and Sessions clans in 1746 and 1747. Indeed, as Sarah and Amasa's generation matured, the ties between the two families thickened. In 1748 Zerviah married a man whose family homestead adjoined the farm of Amasa's father. Twenty years later, when the aging Sessions patriarch wrote his will, Zerviah and her husband were at his elbow to witness the solemn document. Amasa, who would inherit "the Whole of the Farm," was doubtless present also.[98] Within another decade, the third generation came of age, and despite the painful memories of Sarah's death that must have lingered in the minds of her now middle-aged siblings, a marriage directly joining the two families finally took place. In 1775 Amasa's third son, and namesake, married sixteen-year-old Esther Grosvenor, daughter of Sarah's brother, Leicester Jr.[99]

It is clear that the Grosvenor clan was not willing to break ranks with their respectable yeoman neighbors and heap blame on the Sessions family for Sarah's death. It would, however, be fascinating to know what women in Pomfret and other Windham County towns had to say about the outcome of the legal proceedings in 1747. Did they concur with the jurors that Hallowell was the prime culprit, or did they, unlike Sarah Grosvenor, direct their ire more concertedly at Amasa, insisting that he too was "a Bad man"? Several decades later, middle-class New England women would organize against the sexual double standard. However, Amasa's future career tells us that female piety in the 1740s did not instruct Windham County women to expel the newly married, thirty-two-year-old man from their homes.[100]

Amasa, as he grew into middle age in Pomfret, easily replicated his father's status. He served as a militia captain in the Seven Years' War, prospered in farming, fathered ten children, and lived fifty-seven years beyond Sarah Grosvenor. His handsome gravestone, inscribed with a long verse, stands but twenty-five feet from the simpler stone erected in 1742 for Sarah.

After his death, male kin remembered Amasa fondly; nephews and grandsons recalled him as a "favorite" relative, "remarkably capable" in his prime and "very corpulent" in old age. Moreover, local storytelling tradition and the published history of the region, which made such a spectacular ghost story out of Sarah's abortion and death, preserved Amasa Sessions's reputation unsullied: the name of Sarah's lover was left out of the tale.[101]

If Sarah Grosvenor's life is a cautionary tale in any sense for us in the early twenty-first century, it is as a reminder of the historically distinctive ways in which socialized gender roles, community and class solidarity, and legal culture combine in each set of generations to excuse or make invisible certain abuses and crimes against women. The form in which Sarah Grosvenor's death became local history reminds us of how the excuses and erasures of one generation not unwittingly become embedded in the narratives and memories of the next cultural era.

NOTES

1. The documentation is found in the record books and file papers of the Superior Court of Connecticut: *Rex v. John Hallowell et al.*, Superior Court Records, bk. 9, 113, 173, 175; and Windham County Superior Court Files, box 172, Connecticut State Library, Hartford. (Hereafter all loose court papers cited are from *Rex v. Hallowell*, Windham County Superior Court Files, box 172, unless otherwise indicated.) For the quotations see Security bond for John Hallowell, undated; Deposition of

Ebenezer Grosvenor, probably Apr. 1746; Indictment against John Hallowell and Amasa Sessions, Sept. 20, 1746; Deposition of Parker Morse.

2. One such abortion was reported in *Gentleman's Magazine* (London) II, no. 10 (August 1732): 933–34; see Audrey Eccles, *Obstetrics and Gynecology in Tudor and Stuart England* (London: Croom Helm, 1982), 70. On the history of abortion practices see George Devereux, "A Typological Study of Abortion in 350 Primitive, Ancient, and Pre-Industrial Societies," in *Abortion in America: Medical, Psychiatric, Legal, Anthropological, and Religious Considerations*, ed. Harold Rosen (Boston: Beacon Press, 1967), 97–152; Angus McLaren, *Reproductive Rituals: The Perception of Fertility in England from the Sixteenth Century to the Nineteenth Century* (London: Methuen, 1984), chap. 4; Linda Gordon, *Woman's Body, Woman's Right: A Social History of Birth Control in America* (New York: Grossman, 1976), 26–41, 49–60; and Edward Shorter, *A History of Women's Bodies* (New York: Basic Books, 1982), chap. 8.

For specific cases indicating use of herbal abortifacients in the North American colonies see Julia Cherry Spruill, *Women's Life and Work in the Southern Colonies* (1938; reprint, New York: Norton, 1972), 325–26; Roger Thompson, *Sex in Middlesex: Popular Mores in a Massachusetts County, 1649–1699* (Amherst: University of Massachusetts Press 1986), 11, 24–26, 107–8, 182–83; and Lyle Koehler, *A Search for Power: The "Weaker Sex" in Seventeenth-Century New England* (Urbana: University of Illinois Press, 1980), 204–5. I have found two references to the use of an abortifacient in colonial Connecticut court files. Doubtless, other accounts of abortion attempts for the colonial period will be discovered.

3. Abortion before quickening (defined in the early modern period as the moment when the mother first felt the fetus move) was not viewed by the English or colonial courts as criminal. No statute law on abortion existed in either Britain or the colonies. To my knowledge, no New England court before 1745 had attempted to prosecute a physician for carrying out an abortion.

On the history of the legal treatment of abortion in Europe and the United States see McLaren, *Reproductive Rituals*, chap. 5; Gordon, *Woman's Body, Woman's Right*, chap. 3; James C. Mohr, *Abortion in America: The Origins and Evolution of National Policy, 1800–1900* (New York: Oxford University Press, 1978); Michael Grossberg, *Governing the Hearth: Law and the Family in Nineteenth-Century America* (Chapel Hill: University of North Carolina Press, 1985), chap. 5; and Carroll Smith-Rosenberg, "The Abortion Movement and the AMA, 1850–1880," in *Disorderly Conduct: Visions of Gender in Victorian America* (New York: Knopf, 1985), 217–44.

4. In 1683, a Newport, Rhode Island, woman was whipped for fornication and "Indeavouringe the distruction of the Child in her womb" (Supreme Court Records, bk. A, 66, Supreme Court Judicial Records Center, Pawtucket; I thank Catherine Osborne DeCesare for alerting me to this case).

5. The story of the decriminalization of fornication for men in colonial New England is told most succinctly by Carol F. Karlsen, *The Devil in the Shape of a Woman: Witchcraft in Colonial New England* (New York: Norton, 1987), 194–96, 198–202, 255. Laurel Thatcher Ulrich describes a late-eighteenth-century Massachusetts jurisdiction in *A Midwife's Tale: The Life of Martha Ballard, Based on Her Diary, 1785–1812* (New York: Knopf, 1990), 147–60. For New Haven County see Cornelia Hughes Dayton, "Women Before the Bar: Gender, Law, and Society in Connecticut, 1710–1790" (Ph.D. diss., Princeton University, 1986), 151–86. See also Zephaniah Swift, *A System of Laws of the State of Connecticut*, 2 vols. (Windham, Conn., 1795–1796), 1:209. A partial survey of fornication prosecutions in the Windham County Court indicates that here, too, the local justices of the peace and annually

appointed grand jury men stopped prosecuting men after the 1730s. The records for 1726 to 1731 show that fifteen men were prosecuted to enjoin child support, and twenty-one single women were charged with fornication and bastardy, while only two women brought civil suits for child maintenance. Nearly a decade ahead, in the three-year period from 1740 to 1742, *no* men were prosecuted, while twenty-three single women were charged with fornication and ten women initiated civil paternity suits.

6. Such also was the message of many rape trials in the mid- and late eighteenth century. See Dayton, "Women Before the Bar," 112–43; trial of Frederick Calvert, Baron Baltimore, as reported in the *Connecticut Journal* (New Haven, June 10, 1768) and in other colonial newspapers and separate pamphlets; and the Bedlow-Sawyer trial, discussed by Christine Stansell in *City of Women: Sex and Class in New York, 1789–1860* (New York: Knopf, 1986), 23–30.

7. For a recent summary of the literature see Brief for American Historians as *Amicus Curiae* Supporting the Appellees 5–7, *William L. Webster et al. v. Reproductive Health Services et al.*, 109 S.Ct. 3040 (1989).

8. In none of the cases cited in n. 2 above did the woman ingesting an abortifacient die from it. If abortions directed by male physicians in the colonial period were more hazardous than those managed by midwives and laywomen, then, in an inversion of the mid-twentieth-century situation, women from wealthy families with access to, and preferences for, male doctors were those most in jeopardy. For a general comparison of male and female medical practitioners see Ulrich, *Midwife's Tale,* 48–66, esp. 54.

9. Married women may have hidden their abortion attempts because the activity was associated with lewd or dissident women.

10. Conception must have occurred sometime in the months of January through March, most probably in late January. Sarah had been pregnant nearly seven months at her delivery in early August, according to one version offered later by her sister.

11. Hallowell's trade may have been an imported medicine or a powder he mixed himself, consisting chiefly of oil of savin, which could be extracted from juniper bushes found throughout New England. For a thorough discussion of savin and other commonly used abortifacients see Shorter, *History of Women's Bodies,* 184–88.

12. Deposition of Zerviah Grosvenor. In a second deposition Zerviah used the word "Medicines" instead of "trade"; Testimony of Zerviah Grosvenor in Multiple Deposition of Hannah Grosvenor et al. (hereafter cited as Testimony of Zerviah Grosvenor). Five times out of eight, deponents referred to "the trade," instead of simply "trade" or "some trade."

13. So her sister Zerviah later estimated. Testimony of Rebecca Sharp in Multiple Deposition of Hannah Grosvenor et al.

14. After she was let into the plot, Zerviah more than once watched Amasa take "a paper or powder out of his pocket" and insist that Sarah "take Some of it." Deposition of Zerviah Grosvenor.

15. Deposition of John Grosvenor; Deposition of Zerviah Grosvenor; Testimony of Zerviah Grosvenor. "Unlawful measure" was Zerviah's phrase for Amasa's "Method." Concerned for Sarah's wellbeing, she pleaded with Hallowell not to give her sister "any thing that should harm her"; Deposition of Zerviah Grosvenor. At the same time, Sarah was thinking about the quickening issue. She confided to a friend that when Amasa first insisted she take the trade, "she [had] feared it was too late"; Deposition of Abigail Nightingale.

16. Deposition of Zerviah Grosvenor; Testimony of Zerviah Grosvenor.

17. Hallowell claimed that he proceeded with the abortion in order to save Sarah's life. If the powder had had little effect and he knew it, then this claim was a deliber-

ate deception. On the other hand, he may have sincerely believed that the potion had poisoned the fetus and that infection of the uterine cavity had followed fetal death. Since healthy babies were thought at that time to help with their own deliveries, Hallowell may also have anticipated a complicated delivery if Sarah were allowed to go to full term—a delivery that might kill her. On the operation and variable potency of herbal abortifacients see Gordon, *Woman's Body, Woman's Right,* 37, 40; Shorter, *History of Women's Bodies,* 177–88; and Mohr, *Abortion in America,* 8–9.

18. Testimony of Hannah Grosvenor in Multiple Deposition of Hannah Grosvenor et al. Hannah may have fabricated the account of Hallowell's deception to cover her own knowledge of and collusion in Hallowell and Sessions's scheme to conceal Sarah's pregnancy.

19. Deposition of Zerviah Grosvenor. Hallowell attended Sarah overnight at John Grosvenor's house once in July; Multiple Deposition of Sarah and Silence Sessions.

20. On Abigail's husband, Samuel, and his family see Clifford K. Shipton, *Biographical Sketches of Those Who Attended Harvard College in the Classes 1731–1735* (Boston: Massachusetts Historical Society, 1956), 9:425–28; Pomfret Vital Records, Barbour Collection, Connecticut State Library. (All vital and land records cited hereafter are found in the Barbour Collection.)

21. Hearsay evidence was still accepted in many eighteenth-century Anglo-American courts; see J. M. Beattie, *Crime and the Courts in England, 1660–1800* (Princeton, N.J.: Princeton University Press, 1986), 362–76. Sarah's reported words may have carried special weight because in early New England persons on their deathbeds were thought to speak the truth.

22. Twentieth-century obstetrical studies show an average of six weeks between fetal death and spontaneous abortion; J. Robert Willson and Elsie Reid Carrington, eds., *Obstetrics and Gynecology,* 8th ed. (St. Louis, MO: Mosby-Year Book, 1987), 212. Hallowell evidently grasped the link between the two events but felt he could not wait six weeks, either out of concern for Sarah's health or for fear their plot would be discovered.

23. A 1746 indictment offered the only other mention of point at which the "instrument" was mentioned in the documents. It claimed that Hallowell "with his own hands as [well as] with a certain Instrument of Iron [did] violently Lacerate and . . . wound the body of Sarah"; Indictment against John Hallowell, endorsed "Ignoramus," Sept. 4, 1746.

24. Deposition of Abigail Nightingale.

25. Joint Testimony of Hannah and Zerviah Grosvenor in Multiple Deposition of Hannah Grosvenor et al.; Deposition of Hannah Grosvenor; Deposition of Zerviah Grosvenor.

26. Deposition of Ebenezer Grosvenor.

27. Deposition of John Grosvenor; Deposition of Hannah Grosvenor; Deposition of Ebenezer Grosvenor.

28. Testimony of Hannah Grosvenor, Alexander Sessions, and Rebecca Sharp in Multiple Deposition of Hannah Grosvenor et al. In a second statement Hannah said that "the head Seemed to be brused"; Deposition of Hannah Grosvenor.

29. Testimony of Rebecca Sharp, Hannah Grosvenor, and Alexander Sessions in Multiple Deposition of Hannah Grosvenor et al.; Testimony of Silence Sessions in Multiple Deposition of Sarah and Silence Sessions.

30. Joint Testimony of Hannah and Zerviah Grosvenor in Multiple Deposition of Hannah Grosvenor et al.; Deposition of Parker Morse of Woodstock, Apr. 1746. Although Pomfret had had its own resident physician (Dr. Thomas Mather) since 1738, Sarah's family called in young Dr. Morse of Woodstock, who visited twice (he

later admitted he was not much help), and a Dr. Coker of Providence (who I assume
was Theodore Coker). On Mather see Ellen D. Larned, *History of Windham Coun-*
ty, Connecticut (Worcester, Mass.: self-published, 1874), 1:354. On Morse: Shipton,
Biographical Sketches, 9:424. On Coker: ibid., 8:19, and Eric H. Christianson, "The
Medical Practitioners of Massachusetts, 1630–1800: Patterns of Change and Continuity," in *Medicine in Colonial Massachusetts, 1620–1820,* Publications of the
Colonial Society of Massachusetts 57 (Boston, 1980), 123.

    31. Deposition of John Grosvenor.

    32. I am using a list of forty heads of household in the Mashamoquet neighbor-
hood of Pomfret in 1731, presuming five persons to a household, and assuming a 2.5
percent annual population growth. See Larned, *History of Windham County,* 1:342;
and Bruce C. Daniels, *The Connecticut Town: Growth and Development,*
1635–1790 (Middletown, Conn.: Wesleyan University Press, 1979), 44–51. Pomfret
village had no central green or cluster of shops and small house lots around its meetinghouse. No maps survive for early Pomfret apart from a 1719 survey of proprietors' tracts. See Larned, *History of Windham County* (1976 ed.), 1:185.

    33. Leicester's father, John Grosvenor, a tanner, had emigrated from England
about 1670 and settled in Roxbury, Massachusetts, whence the first proprietors of
Pomfret hailed. John died in 1691 before he could resettle on his Connecticut tract,
but his widow, Esther, moved her family to their initial allotment of 502 acres in Pomfret in 1701. There she lived until her death at eighty-seven in 1738. She was known
in the community as a woman of energy and "vigorous habits," "skillful in tending the
sick," and habitual in "walking every Sunday to the distant meeting-house." See
Daniel Kent, *The English Home and Ancestry of John Grosvenor of Roxbury, Mass.*
(Boston; reprinted from The New England History and Genealogy Record for April
1918), 10–13, and Larned, *History of Windham County,* 1:353–55.

    34. Kent, *English Home,* 10–13; Larned, *History of Windham County,*
1:200–202, 204, 208–9, 269, 354, 343–44; Charles J. Hoadly and J. Hammond
Trumbull, eds., *The Public Records of the Colony of Connecticut, 1636–1776,* vols.
5–9 (Hartford, Conn: Lockwood & Brainard Co., 1850–1890); Inventory of Leicester Grosvenor, Oct. 29, 1759, Pomfret District Probate Court Records, 2:260.

    35. Larned, *History of Windham County,* 1:201, 204, 206, 208–9, 344; Ellen D.
Larned, *Historic Gleanings in Windham County, Connecticut* (Providence, R.I.: self-
published, 1899), 141, 148–49; Francis G. Sessions, comp., *Materials for a History*
of the Sessions Family in America; The Descendants of Alexander Sessions of
Andover, Mass., 1669 (Albany, N.Y.: Munsell & Sons, 1890), 34–35 (hereafter cited
as Sessions, *Sessions Family*). Nathaniel's inheritance from his father, Alexander, of
Andover (d. 1687) was a mere 2.14.5 pounds.

    36. Deposition of Hannah Grosvenor et al; Deposition of Ebenezer Grosvenor;
Deposition of Anna Wheeler, Nov. 5, 1745; Deposition of Zerviah Grosvenor; Testimony of Zerviah Grosvenor.

    37. Deposition of Zerviah Grosvenor; Testimony of Zerviah Grosvenor.

    38. Deposition of Abigail Nightingale. Contradicting Amasa's attempt to dis-
avow paternity were both his investment in Hallowell's efforts to get rid of the fetus
and his own ready admission of paternity privately to Zerviah and Sarah.

    39. Deposition of Ebenezer Grosvenor. Hallowell revealed this opinion in an
August 1742 conversation with Sarah's twenty-eight-year-old cousin Ebenezer at
Ebenezer's house in Pomfret. In a study of seventeenth-century Massachusetts court
records Roger Thompson finds evidence that when pregnancy failed to pressure a
couple into marriage, it was often because love "had cooled"; Thompson, *Sex in*
Middlesex, 69.

40. Testimony of John Shaw in Multiple Deposition of Hannah Grosvenor et al.

41. For one such case involving two propertied families see Kathryn Kish Sklar, "Culture Versus Economics: A Case of Fornication in Northampton in the 1740s," *The University of Michigan Papers in Women's Studies* (1978): 35–56. For the incidence of illegitimacy and premarital sex in families of respectable yeomen and town leaders see Dayton, "Women Before the Bar," 151–186, and Ulrich, *Midwife's Tale*, 156.

42. Two years later, in Feb. 1744 (nine months before Amasa married), the senior Sessions deeded to his son the north part of his own farm for a payment of 310 pounds. Amasa, in exchange for caring for his parents in their old age, came into the whole farm when his father died in 1771. Pomfret Land Records, 3:120; Estate Papers of Nathaniel Sessions, 1771, Pomfret Probate District Court. On the delay between marriage and "going to housekeeping" see Ulrich, *Midwife's Tale*, 138–44.

43. Sessions, *Sessions Family*, 60; Pomfret Vit. Records, 1:29.

44. The banns never appeared on the meetinghouse door. Sarah may have believed in this overdue betrothal. She assured her anxious sister Anna that "thay designed to mary as soone as thay Could and that Sessions was as much Concarned as she." Deposition of Zerviah Grosvenor; Testimony of Zerviah Grosvenor; Deposition of Anna Wheeler.

45. Deposition of Abigail Nightingale. I have argued elsewhere that this is what most young New England women in the eighteenth century did when faced with illegitimacy. Their parents did not throw them out of the house but instead paid the cost of the mother and child's upkeep until she managed to marry. Dayton, "Women Before the Bar," 163–80.

46. Deposition of John Grosvenor; Deposition of Abigail Nightingale. Amasa Sessions, "in his prime," was described as "a very strong man," so it is possible that his physical presence played a role in intimidating Sarah. See Sessions, *Sessions Family*, 31.

47. Deposition of Abigail Nightingale.

48. Like his wife, Leicester was not summoned to testify in any of the proceedings against Hallowell and Sessions.

49. Zerviah testified that, a day or two after Sarah fell sick for the first time in July, the family heard "that Doctor Hallowell was at one of our Neighbors [and] my Mother desired me to go and Call him." Deposition of Zerviah Grosvenor.
Sarah's mother had died in May 1724, when Sarah was eleven months old. Perhaps Sarah and Zerviah had a closer relationship with their grandmother Esther (see n. 33 above) than with their stepmother. Esther lived in their household until her death in 1738, when Zerviah was seventeen and Sarah fifteen.

50. Laurel Thatcher Ulrich, *Good Wives: Image and Reality in the Lives of Women in Northern New England, 1650–1750* (New York: Knopf, 1982), chap. 5, esp. 98.

51. In Larned's account, the oral legend insisted that Hallowell's "transaction" (meaning the abortion attempt) and the miscarriage were "utterly unsuspected by any . . . member of the household" other than Zerviah, *History of Windham County*, 1:363.

52. Deposition of Parker Morse.

53. Within days of Sarah's miscarriage, the initial conspirators disclosed their actions to others: Hallowell talked to two of Sarah's older male cousins, John (age thirty-one) and Ebenezer (age twenty-eight), while Zerviah confessed to Amasa's brother Alexander (age twenty-eight) and his wife, Silence. Deposition of Anna Wheeler.

54. The famous "bad books" incident that disrupted Jonathan Edwards's career in 1744 involved a similar group of unsupervised young adults, ages twenty-one to twenty-nine. See Patricia J. Tracy, *Jonathan Edwards, Pastor: Religion and Society in*

Eighteenth-Century Northampton (New York: Hill and Wang, 1980), 160–64. The best general investigation of youth culture in early New England is Thompson's *Sex in Middlesex,* 71–96. Thompson discusses the general ineffectiveness of parental supervision of courtship (52–53, 58–59, 69–70). Ellen Rothman concludes that in New England in the mid- to late eighteenth century "parents made little or no effort to oversee their children's courting behavior"; Ellen K. Rothman, *Hands and Hearts: A History of Courtship in America* (New York: Basic Books, Inc., 1984), 25.

55. Helena M. Wall, *Fierce Communion: Family and Community in Early America* (Cambridge, Mass.: Harvard University Press, 1990); Bruce H. Mann, *Neighbors and Strangers: Law and Community in Early Connecticut* (Chapel Hill: University of North Carolina Press., 1987).

56. Leicester Grosvenor's Will, Jan. 23, 1754, Pomfret Probate District Court Records, 1:146. For recent studies linking consumption patterns and class stratification see Richard L. Bushman, "American High-Style and Vernacular Cultures," in Jack P. Greene and J. R. Pole, eds., *Colonial British America: Essays in the New History of the Early Modern Era* (Baltimore: Johns Hopkins University Press, 1984), 345–83; T. H. Breen, "'Baubles of Britain': The American and Consumer Revolutions of the Eighteenth Century," *Past and Present* 119 (May 1988): 73–104; and Kevin M. Sweeney, "Furniture and the Domestic Environment in Wethersfield, Connecticut, 1639–1800," in Robert Blair St. George, ed., *Material Life in America, 1600–1860* (Boston: Northeastern University Press, 1988), 261–90.

57. Killingly Land Records, 2:139; *Rex v. John Hallowell and Mehitable Morris,* Dec. 1726, Windham County Court Records, bk. 1, 43, and Windham County Court Files, box 363. Hallowell paid the twenty-eight pounds he owed Mehitable, but there is no evidence that he took any other role in bringing up his illegitimate namesake. Just before his death, Samuel Morris, the maternal grandfather of John Hallowell Jr., out of "parentiall Love and Effections," deeded the young man a three-hundred-acre farm "for his advancement and Settlement in the World"; Killingly Land Records, 4:261.

58. Hallowell was clearly the mastermind of the scheme, and there is little doubt that he lied to the authorities when questioned. According to one witness, Hallowell had exclaimed that "[i]f he knew who" had informed anonymously against him, "he would be the death of him tho he ware hanged for it the next minit"; Letter of Joseph Leavens, Sept. 1727, Windham Supreme Court Files, box 170. The case is found in Windham Supreme Court Records, bk. 5, 297–98; and *Public Records of Connecticut Colony,* 7:118. One associate Hallowell recruited was Ephraim Shevie, who had been banished from Connecticut for counterfeiting four years earlier. See Kenneth Scott, *Counterfeiting in Colonial America* (New York: Oxford University Press, 1957), 41–45.

59. The authority on counterfeiting in the colonies is Kenneth Scott. His 1957 book on the subject emphasizes several themes: the gangs at the heart of all counterfeiting schemes, the ease with which counterfeiters moved from colony to colony (especially between Connecticut and Rhode Island), "the widespread co-operation between" gangs, "the readiness of [men of all ranks] . . . to enter such schemes," the frequent use of aliases, the irresistible nature of the activity once entered into, and "the extreme difficulty of securing the conviction of a counterfeiter"; Scott, *Counterfeiting in Colonial America,* esp. 10, 35, 36, 123. See also Scott's more focused studies, *Counterfeiting in Colonial Connecticut* (New York: American Numismatic Society, 1957), and *Counterfeiting in Colonial Rhode Island* (Providence: Rhode Island Historical Association, 1960).

For an illuminating social profile of thieves and burglars who often operated in small gangs see Daniel A. Cohen, "A Fellowship of Thieves: Property Criminals in Eighteenth-Century Massachusetts," *Journal of Social History* 22 (1988): 65–92.

60. Richard D. Brown, "The Healing Arts in Colonial and Revolutionary Massachusetts: The Context for Scientific Medicine," in *Medicine in Colonial Massachusetts*, esp. 40–42. For detailed analysis of the backgrounds and training of one large sample of New England practitioners see Christianson, "Medical Practitioners of Massachusetts," 49–67, and Eric H. Christianson, "Medicine in New England," in *Medicine in the New World: New Spain, New France, and New England, ed.* Ronald L. Numbers (Knoxville: University of Tennessee Press, 1987), 101–53. That the majority of colonial physicians made "free use of the title 'doctor'" (ibid., 118) and simply "taught themselves medicine and set up as doctors" is reiterated in Whitfield J. Bell Jr., "A Portrait of the Colonial Physician," *Bulletin of the History of Medicine* 44 (1970), 503–4.

61. Hallowell's sons, baptized between 1730 and 1740, were named Theophilus, Bazaleel, Calvin, and Luther. Killingly Vital Records, 1:3, 24; Putnam First Congregational Church Records, 1:5–7, 14–15. Hallowell may have been one of the "'horseshed' Christians" whom David D. Hall describes as concerned to have their children baptized but more interested in the men's talk outside the meetinghouse than in the minister's exposition of the Word. Daniel D. Hall, *Worlds of Wonder, Days of Judgment: Popular Religious Belief in Early New England* (New York: Knopf, 1989), 15–16.

62. Between 1725 and 1742, Hallowell was a party to twenty land sales and purchases in Killingly; he also assumed two mortgages. During the same period he was involved in county court litigation an average of three times a year, more often as plaintiff than defendant, for a total of forty-six suits.

63. For example, in early 1735 Hallowell made a 170-pound profit from the sale of a sixty-acre tract with mill and mansion house that he had purchased two months earlier. Killingly Land Records, 4:26, 36.

64. Evidence of Hallowell's widespread clientele comes from his 1727–1746 suits for debt, from his traveling patterns as revealed in the depositions of the abortion case, and from a petition written in 1747 on his behalf by fourteen male citizens of Providence. They claimed that "[n]umbers" in Rhode Island "as well as in the Neighbouring Colonies" had "happily experienc'd" Hallowell's medical care. Petition of Resolved Waterman et al., Oct. 1747, Connecticut Archives, Crimes and Misdemeanors, series 1, 4:109.

65. For a related hypothesis about the mobility of self-taught doctors in contrast to physicians from established medical families, see Christianson, "Medical Practitioners of Massachusetts," in Col. Soc. Mass., *Medicine in Colonial Massachusetts*, 61.

66. These figures apply to suits in the Windham County Court record books, 1727–1742. Hallowell may, of course, have prosecuted debtors in other jurisdictions.

67. In December 1749, Samuel Hunt, "Gentleman" of Worcester County, revoked the power of attorney he had extended to Hallowell for a Killingly land sale. Hunt claimed that the physician had "behaved greatly to my hindrance [and] Contrary to the trust and Confidence I Reposed in him." Killingly Land Records, 5:151.

68. Larned, *History of Windham County*, 1:356–59.

69. The petition's signers included Hopkins, merchant, assembly speaker, and Superior Court Justice, soon to become governor; Daniel Jencks, judge, assembly delegate, and prominent Baptist; Obadiah Brown, merchant and shopkeeper; and George Taylor, justice of the peace, town schoolmaster, and Anglican warden. Some of the signers stated that they had made a special trip to Windham to be "Earwitnesses" at Hallowell's trial. The petition is cited in n. 64 above.

70. For discussions of the elite see Jackson Turner Main, *Society and Economy in Colonial Connecticut* (Princeton, N.J.: Princeton University Press, 1985), esp. 317–66; and Joy B. and Robert R. Gilsdorf, "Elites and Electorates: Some Plain Truths for Historians of Colonial America," in *Saints and Revolutionaries: Essays on Early American History,* ed. David D. Hall, John M. Murrin, and Thad W. Tate (New York: Norton, 1984), 207–44.

71. Ulrich, *Good Wives,* 103–5, 113–17.

72. Compare the seventeenth-century case of Stephen Batchelor (Charles E. Clark, *The Eastern Frontier: The Settlement of Northern New England, 1610–1763* [New York: Knopf, 1970], 43–44) with eighteenth-century Cape Cod, where ministers retained their posts despite charges of sexual misconduct (O. M. Bumsted, "A Caution to Erring Christians: Ecclesiastical Disorder on Cape Cod, 1717 to 1738," *William and Mary Quarterly* 3rd series, 28 [1971]: 413–38). I am grateful to John Murrin for bringing these references to my attention. For a prominent Northampton, Massachusetts, man (Joseph Hawley) who admitted to lying in civil and church hearings in the 1740s, and yet who suffered no visible damage to his career, see Sklar, "Case of Fornication," 46–48, 51.

73. See Ulrich, *Good Wives,* 195–201; and Cornelia Hughes Dayton, "Infanticide in Early New England" (paper presented to the Organization of American Historians, Reno, Nev., March 1988).

74. Burying the child was one of the key dramatic acts in infanticide episodes and tales, and popular beliefs in the inevitability that "murder will out" centered on the buried corpse. For two eighteenth-century Connecticut cases illustrating these themes see Dayton, "Infanticide in Early New England," n. 31. For more on "murder will out" in New England culture see Hall, *Worlds of Wonder,* 176–78; and George Lyman Kittredge, *The Old Farmer and His Almanack . . .* (New York: B. Blum, 1920), 71–77.

75. Testimony of Zerviah Grosvenor.

76. Hall, *Worlds of Wonder,* 172–78.

77. Testimony of Silence Sessions in Multiple Deposition of Sarah and Silence Sessions; Testimony of Alexander Sessions in Multiple Deposition of Hannah Grosvenor et al.; Hall, *Worlds of Wonder,* 174. Alexander and Silence may have had in mind their brother Amasa's interests as a criminal defendant when they cast doubt on Zerviah's reliability as the star prosecution witness.

78. Deposition of Abigail Nightingale.

79. Testimony of Zerviah Grosvenor; Deposition of John Grosvenor. Abigail Nightingale recalled a scene when Sarah "was just going out of the world." She and Amasa were sitting on Sarah's bed, and Amasa "endeavour[ed] to raise her up &c. He asked my thought of her state &c. and then leaning over her used these words: 'poor Creature, I have undone you[!]'"; Deposition of Abigail Nightingale.

80. Deposition of Ebenezer Grosvenor; Testimony of John Shaw in Multiple Deposition of Hannah Grosvenor et al. See also Deposition of John Grosvenor. For discussions of male and female speech patterns and the distinctive narcissistic bravado of men's talk in early New England see Robert Saint George, "'Heated' Speech and Literacy in Seventeenth-Century New England," in *Seventeenth Century New England,* ed. David Grayson Allen and David D. Hall, Publications of the Colonial Society of Massachusetts 63 (Boston, 1984), 305–15; Dayton, "Women Before the Bar," 248–51, 263–83, 338–41; and John Demos, "Shame and Guilt in Early New England," in *Emotion and Social Change: Toward a New Psychohistory,* ed. Carol Z. Stearns and Peter N. Stearns (New York: Holmes & Meier, 1988), 74–75.

81. On the centrality of confession see Hall, *Worlds of Wonder,* 173, 241. The

near-universality of accused men and women confessing in court in the seventeenth century is documented by Gail Sussman Marcus in "'Due Execution of the Generall Rules
of Righteousnesse': Criminal Procedure in New Haven Town and Colony, 1638–1658,"
in *Saints and Revolutionaries,* esp. 132–33. For discussions of the increasing refusal of
men to plead guilty to fornication (the most frequently prosecuted crime) from the
1670s on, see Thompson, *Sex in Middlesex,* 29–33; Karlsen, *Devil in the Shape of a
Woman,* 194–96, 198–202; and Dayton, "Women Before the Bar," 168–69. On the
growing gap between male and female piety in the eighteenth century see Mary Maples
Dunn, "Saints and Sisters: Congregational and Quaker Women in the Early Colonial
Period," *American Quarterly* 30 (1978): 582–601. For the story of how the New England court system became more legalistic after 1690 and how lawyerly procedures sub-
sequently began to affect religious practices and broader cultural styles, see Mann,
Neighbors and Strangers, and John M. Murrin, "Anglicizing an American Colony: The
Transformation of Provincial Massachusetts" (Ph.D. diss., Yale University, 1966).

    82. Deposition of Ebenezer Grosvenor; Deposition of John Grosvenor. Although
a host of witnesses testified to the contrary, Hallowell on one occasion told Amasa's
brother "[t]hat Sessions never applied to him for anything, to cause an abortion and
that if She was with Child he did not Think Amasa knew it"; Testimony of Alexander Sessions in Multiple Deposition of Hannah Grosvenor et al.

    83. Testimony of John Shaw in Multiple Deposition of Hannah Grosvenor et al.
One of these confrontations took place in the Providence jail, probably in late 1745
or early 1746.

    84. It is interesting to note that Sessions claimed to have other sources for strong
medicines: he told Shaw that, had he known Sarah was in danger of dying, "he tho't
he could have got Things that would have preserved her Life"; ibid.

    85. Ibid. Shaw here was reporting Dr. [Theodore?] Coker's account of his con-
frontation with Hallowell during Sarah's final illness. For biographical data on Coker,
see n. 30 above.

    86. Testimony of Rebecca Sharp, Zebulon Dodge, and John Shaw in Multiple
Deposition of Hannah Grosvenor et al; Deposition of Ebenezer Grosvenor.

    87. Larned reports that, according to "the legend," the ghostly visitations ceased
when "Hallowell fled his country." *History of Windham County,* 1:363.

    88. For mid-eighteenth-century Bristol residents who reported seeing apparitions
and holding conversations with them, see Jonathan Barry, "Piety and the Patient:
Medicine and Religion in Eighteenth Century Bristol," in *Patients and Practitioners:
Lay Perceptions of Medicine in Pre-industrial Society,* ed. Roy Porter (Cambridge:
Cambridge University Press, 1985), 157.

    89. None of the depositions produced by Hallowell's trial offers any explanation
of the three-year gap between Sarah's death and legal proceedings. Between 1741 and
1747, revivals and schisms touched every Windham County parish except Pomfret's
First Church, to which the Grosvenors belonged; see Lamed, *History of Windham
County,* 1:393–485, esp. 464.

    90. One of the magistrates, Ebenezer West, had been a justice of the county court
since 1726. The other, Jonathan Trumbull, the future governor, was serving both as
a county court justice and as an assistant. The fact that the two men made the twen-
ty-four-mile trip from their hometown of Lebanon to preside over this Inferior Court,
rather than allow local magistrates to handle the hearing, may indicate that one or
both of them had insisted the alleged crime be prosecuted.

    91. Record of the Inferior Court held at Pomfret, Nov. 5–6, 1745. Hallowell was
the only one of the four persons charged who was not examined at this time. He was
in jail in Providence for debt. Apprehended in Connecticut the following March, he

was jailed until the Pomfret witnesses could travel to Windham for a hearing before Trumbull and West. At the second hearing, the magistrates charged Hallowell with "murdering Sarah . . . *and* A Bastard Female Child with which she was pregnant" (emphasis added). See Record of an Inferior Court held at Windham, Apr. 17, 1746.

92. Indictment against Hallowell, Sept. 4, 1746; Indictment against Hallowell and Sessions, Sept. 20, 1746; Pleas of Hallowell and Sessions before the adjourned Windham Superior Court, Nov. [18], 1746; Superior Court Records, bk. 12, 112–17, 131–33.

93. Superior Court Records, bk. 12, 173, 175; Indictment against John Hallowell, Mar. 1746/47; *Rex v. Amasa Sessions*, Indictment, Mar. 1746/47, Windham Superior Court Files, box 172. See William Blackstone, *Commentaries on the Laws of England* (1765–69; facsimile, Chicago: University of Chicago Press, 1979), 1:125–26, 4:198.

94. Larned, *History of Windham County,* 1:363.

95. Even in the context of the inflation of the 1740s, Hallowell's bill of costs was unusually high: 110 pounds and 2s.6d. Sessions was hit hard in the pocketbook too; he was assessed 83 pounds and 14s.2d. in costs.

96. Petition of John Hallowell, Oct. 1747, Connecticut Archives, Crimes and Misdemeanors, series 1, 4:108; Petition of Resolved Waterman et al., ibid., 109. Specifically, Hallowell and his supporters asked that his sentence be reduced to a fine in an amount "adequate to his reduced Circumstances." Such requests for reduced sentences were increasingly submitted by convicted felons in eighteenth-century Connecticut, and some were granted. See ibid., series 1 and 2. Rumors of bankruptcy had haunted Hallowell since he moved to Providence in 1742. As a physician and shopkeeper, between 1742 and 1750 he won a net of 325 pounds in frequent county court litigation (including two substantial executions against Dr. Theodore Coker). However, two 1743–1744 Superior Court judgments against him totaling over four thousand pounds spelled financial ruin. His name last appears in Connecticut records in 1749, and in Rhode Island, as far as I can tell, in 1750. Three of his sons settled in Providence as mariners. These conclusions are based on an analysis of Rhode Island census records, and the record books and indices of the Providence County Court of Common Pleas and of the Supreme Court at the Judicial Records Center, Pawtucket.

97. Note Blackstone's discussion of the liability of "a physician or surgeon who gives his patient a potion . . . to cure him, which contrary to expectation kills him." *Commentaries,* 4:197.

98. Killingly Land Records, 3:99; Estate papers of Nathaniel Sessions, 1771, Pomfret Probate District Court. Although Zerviah bore five daughters, she chose not to name any of them after the sister to whom she had been so close. In 1747, the final year of the trials, Sarah's much older sister, Anna, gave birth to a daughter whom she named Sarah.

99. Pomfret Vit. Records, 2:67.

100. Carroll Smith-Rosenberg, "Beauty, the Beast and the Militant Woman: A Case Study in Sex Roles and Social Stress in Jacksonian America," *American Quarterly* 23 (1971): 562–84. There were branches of the Female Moral Reform Society in several Connecticut towns.

101. Sessions, *Sessions Family,* 31, 35; Larned, *History of Windham County,* 1:363–64. Indeed Lamed refers to the Grosvenor and Sessions families only obliquely, characterizing them as among Pomfret's "proudest," "first and wealthiest families." The only principal in the case whom she identified directly was the culprit Hallowell.

4

Marriage, Morals, and Politics in the Election of 1828

Norma Basch

And then about that Mrs. Robards affair—
That, too, they've told Adams and Clay—
Had it never *leaked* out, I'll make bold to declare
'Twould not be *known* to this day.
Though every objection I've answered enough,
Still the Adams men jabber and squall,
'Bout militiamen—marriages—*moral & stuff*,
And war—and the deuce knows what all.

The foregoing verses, part of a longer piece of anti-Jackson doggerel entitled "Groanings," were created to deride Andrew Jackson's pique at losing the presidential election of 1828.[1] "Groanings," of course, turned out to be a form of wishful thinking; Jackson won the election, garnering almost 56 percent of the popular vote. Yet this ribald projection of his defeat reveals a good deal about the campaign. Signed appropriately enough with the pseudonym Trash, it exemplifies a narrow but virulent strain of anti-Jackson rhetoric that drew on Rachel Jackson's marital problems with her first husband, Lewis Robards, and her allegedly illicit union with the general. Some supporters of John Quincy Adams were clearly convinced that the voters would shrink from electing a candidate so tainted by marital scandal, and although the voters did not respond as anticipated, the Jacksons were deeply distressed by the public scrutiny of their private life. Rachel Jackson was already in declining health, but there is little reason to discount James Parton's assessment that the political exploitation of the Robards affair contributed to her death in

December 1828. The new president neither forgave nor forgot the great personal price of the exposure. He entered the White House in mourning over the loss of his beloved wife and embittered at "the Adams men" who had raked up the scandal.[2]

The broad outlines of the so-called Robards affair, at least as they were sketched by Jackson supporters, portrayed the Jacksons as the innocent victims of a petty legal misunderstanding. Andrew Jackson married Rachel Donelson Robards in Natchez on the lower Mississippi River some time in 1791, on the presumption that she had been divorced from Lewis Robards by the Virginia legislature, only to discover that what they both had believed was a formal divorce decree was merely an authorization for Robards to sue for divorce in a civil court. Robards, however, did not pursue this option until 1793 in the newly admitted state of Kentucky, which had previously fallen under the jurisdiction of Virginia. In 1794, after a final decree had been issued and the Jacksons came to understand that they were not legally married, they participated in a second marriage ceremony. Now in 1828, some thirty-seven years after their initial union, their innocent mistake was being distorted in the vituperative heat of partisan politics.[3]

Supporters of John Quincy Adams proffered a far more sinister script, which they documented with citations from Robards's divorce decree. Their version of the story, as they were quick to point out, faithfully followed the court's conclusion that "the defendant, Rachel Robards, hath deserted the plantiff, Lewis Robards, and hath and doth still live in adultery with another man."[4] The other man, of course, was Andrew Jackson, a candidate now for the nation's highest office. Substituting the treachery of seduction for the innocence of a courtship undertaken in good faith, they accused the general not only of the legal lapse of living with his lady in a state of long-term adultery but also of the moral lapse of being the paramour in the original divorce action. Rachel Jackson in her youth was depicted as not having been a lady at all, but as a loose, impetuous, and immoral woman who willingly cast off her lawful husband for an arrogant and impassioned young suitor. The political implications of her illicit union were readily apparent: a vote for Jackson was a vote for sin. By raising the prospect of a convicted adulteress and her paramour husband living together in the White House, the Adamsites transformed the circumstances of the Jacksons' marriage into an intense and gendered political controversy.

That controversy intersected national politics at an especially critical juncture. The expansion in voter participation, the proliferation of state political organizations, the growing consolidation of party loyalties, and the emergence of local campaign newspapers all contributed to the elements of mass politics that were taking root in the second party system.

The coverage of the scandal was sweeping, transcending both state and sectional lines. The discursive terms on which the scandal was exploited were strikingly uniform, and the audiences that the coverage addressed were more accessible than in prior campaigns. Given the sheer influx of print and the broad spread of literacy among both men and women, people were now able to feed their hunger for sensationalism on an altogether unprecedented scale. Political spins on the Jacksons' early marital problems, then, reached a wide and engaged audience. This point is an important one; if the election of 1828 was both a journalistic and a political watershed, it was no less innovative in its organized manipulation of a sexual scandal.[5]

Adams supporters would insist that their reading of the scandal was neither innovative nor manipulative; it rested on eighteenth-century assumptions about the political import of marital virtue. Inasmuch as marital fidelity stood as a trope for national unity, adultery represented political chaos. In a culture that had thrived on seduction tales and imbued them with a republican ethos, here, after all, was a flesh-and-blood seduction in which the man who would be president had played the serpentlike role of seducer to a woman who was already married. Such a man menaced the entire civic order: his callous disregard for the laws of marriage symbolized the raw power of evil over institutional efforts to uphold virtue. Furthermore, because the woman who was slated to share his bed at the White House was deemed unchaste and the legitimacy of her most intimate relations with him was contested, she too stood as a threat, albeit a lesser one, to the larger civic order.[6]

Such derogatory images of the Jacksons' sexual relations, together with pro-Jackson counterimages, exemplify Joan Wallach Scott's observation that political history has "been enacted on the field of gender."[7] Political historians have drawn on the Robards affair to suggest a more sensational style of politics in this prelude to the second party system, but they have not been attentive to its substance. It is precisely because both parties attempted to appeal to their constituents' most deeply rooted beliefs and understandings about manhood and womanhood, passion and restraint, and divorce and marriage that their competing narratives of the Robards affair reveal important distinctions in their respective views.

Those distinctions make up the focus of this essay, which explores their meaning in the immediate context of the election of 1828 and then speculates on their broader implications. My thesis here is that in the campaign of 1828, political partisans delineated two discrete clusters of ideas about proper relations between the sexes, or, to put it another way, they developed two competing marital codes. One, the pro-Adams or proto-Whig code, was didactic and contractual with a persistent emphasis on the ties between household and polity; the other, the pro-Jackson or proto-Democratic code, was romantic and private with a distinct preference for heartfelt sentiments over precise legal forms.

Such schematic constructions can hardly do justice to the sensibilities of the voters whom they addressed, much less to the intent of the politicians who framed them. Most Americans undoubtedly espoused elements from both codes in an ambiguous and overlapping fashion. Although we should not dichotomize these codes too neatly in linking them to the values of male voters or their disfranchised wives, the contrast between them provides us with a slender shaft of dazzling paradigmatic clarity. Crisply juxtaposed as they were in a campaign that was waged on the threshold of the Victorian era, they shed considerable light on latent nineteenth-century tensions over the boundaries of marriage and the definitions of love. Furthermore, because the two codes embodied the growing instability of key political terms, they afford a fresh angle of vision on changes in the political culture. To the extent that both parties constructed their debate over the Jacksons' marriage and morals as a contest between freedom and virtue, on the one hand, and power and corruption, on the other, they framed it in familiar republican language that they suffused with new and contested meanings.

A sharp calculus was as important in the political constructions of the Robards affair as any transcendent moral vision. At one level, the codes embraced by the two parties were reflexive responses to their immediate electoral needs. Given the apparent youthful indiscretion of the Jacksons, Adams supporters had a compelling incentive to champion strict governmental control over domestic relations, and Jackson supporters had a vested interest in defending the principle of marital privacy. The Adamsites, after all, aimed to take votes away from the ever-popular Jackson by exposing his sexual transgression, while the Jacksonians rushed to defend him against a potentially fatal political assault. At a second and still intensely partisan level, party leaders shaped their appeals to comport with the ethnic and religious stripes of their constituents.[8] Religious outsiders such as the Catholics and freethinkers among the Jackson supporters would have little enthusiasm for encoding rigid moral prescriptions into a reformist Protestant legal system, while evangelicals were bound to find Jackson's lack of sexual self-discipline morally repellent. More was at stake here, however, than transient campaign strategies. At a third and less conscious level, the layers of meaning compressed into the conflicting narratives of the Robards affair embodied the components of competing value systems. As it turned out, the vagaries of the Jacksons' union in the early 1790s served as a highly evocative emblem for profound political and moral tensions in the late 1820s.

Thanks to Daniel Walker Howe's reconceptualization of the reforming role of evangelical Christianity in antebellum political culture, we can link the intense interest that these incipient Whigs demonstrated in the Robards affair to a broader commitment to moral didacticism, self-discipline, and institutional reforms. In the Whig view of the world, which was informed by the fervent moralism of the Second Great Awakening, the state had an important and legitimate interest in delineating and controlling the boundaries around marriage; it consisted in employing law to enhance marriage as a social institution. We can also locate the defense fashioned by incipient Democrats in a larger framework of political secularism, cultural pluralism, laissez-faire government, and broad-based egalitarianism, at least as it pertained to white men.[9] Marriage, by implication, was a matter of individual and local concern.

Adams supporters relied on a characteristically evangelical ideal of masculinity to sing the praises of their Unitarian leader.[10] They celebrated Adams as a responsible, self-restrained Christian gentleman, a man of sincere piety, impeccable purity, and prodigious intelligence, who had devoted himself unstintingly to a spacious and progressive national vision. Jackson supporters, by contrast, embraced a vividly romantic ideal of manhood. They underscored the general's bravery at the Battle of New Orleans, his chivalry as the protector of endangered women, and his closeness to nature as a man of the frontier. By identifying their candidate with the physical prowess and self-sufficiency that Americans associated with westward expansion, they placed him beyond the artificial constraints of formal authority. With regard to womanhood, they were notably muted, relegating its ramifications to a realm outside the political arena. Still, they persistently deployed the concept of feminine weakness in binary opposition to that of masculine strength, thereby using it as a foil for their heroic definitions of masculinity.[11] For Adams supporters, however, who highlighted the role played by male chastity in adhering to the vows of marriage, gender distinctions were more oblique. Both parties extolled the principle of female chastity, but Adamsites imbued it with a more activist cast.

Though rumors about the Jacksons' marriage had long been bandied about, they assumed tangible political shape in the spring of 1827, a full year and a half in advance of the election. In an effort to combat a Jacksonian offensive that began almost as soon as the previous presidential campaign had ended, charges against the Jacksons were launched early and often. Charles Hammond, a friend and supporter of Henry Clay, unleashed what might be considered the first salvo by printing the story in the March 23, 1827, issue of his paper, the *Cincinnati Gazette,* where he named Jackson as the paramour in the affair. He reprinted this version in his special campaign journal, *Truth's Advocate and Monthly Anti-Jackson Expositor,* in January 1828, and he reprinted it yet again in an anonymous pamphlet entitled *View of General*

Jackson's Domestic Relations, in Reference to his Fitness for the Presidency. As Hammond himself avowed, he was committed to disseminating the story as widely as possible. Citing the "large edition" he had published in pamphlet form he proudly proclaimed that his article had been "extensively read amongst the people."[12]

Hammond and editors like him took the lead in exploring the political implications of the scandal and in promoting its exposure as a conscientious public service. According to Hammond, not only was adultery in general an issue of public concern, but the consequences of electing an adulterer to high office were a decidedly public matter. Charges that he was violating the Jacksons' privacy could not obviate the profound influence sexual mores exerted on all other social and political relations. "It will not much longer avail the Jacksonians to denounce the discussion of this affair as an unmanly and dishonorable act," he insisted, linking the authority of government to a respect for the rules of marriage, for "the moral sense of the community begins to assert its proper influence, and assign to seduction and adultery their appropriate estimation."[13]

Hammond's obsession with the Jacksons' sexual transgressions was by no means typical of all pro-Adams editors. The exposure of the Jacksons' marital history unfolded in two forms: one blunt and astonishingly unrestrained, the other rather more refined and covert; only select newspapers carried the story in full.[14] Respectable pro-Adams papers were often reluctant to address the Robards affair directly, but they subtly intensified the damage Hammond had inflicted with inference and innuendo. Sometimes a single issue would to do the job. Around the same time Hammond first published his version of the story, the *Daily National Journal,* an influential Washington paper that had been the beneficiary of Adams's patronage when he was secretary of state, introduced readers to a similar version of the story by reprinting excerpts from a pamphlet written by Thomas Arnold. Arnold, whose animus against Jackson was as intense as Hammond's, denounced the general as a reckless and unstable adventurer who "spent the prime of his life in gambling, in cock fighting, in horse racing," and who, "to cap off all his frailties . . . tore from a husband the wife of his bosom."[15]

This last phrase, which was reiterated throughout the campaign, depicted Jackson's offense more as an abduction than as a seduction. It implied not only that wife stealing was an affair between men, in which one man violated the sexual rights of another, but also that it was one of Jackson's most heinous crimes. It signified his inability to honor the most elemental of contracts, along with his readiness to employ force. Implicit here was the all-important notion that the obligation of sexual fidelity as set out in the marriage contract was more than a metaphor for obligations in the social contract: as the source of all contractualism among men and thus the foundation for social stability, it was one of its most vital components.[16] The *Daily National Journal* asked its readers to imagine the uproar if Adams or Henry Clay "were to take a man's wife from him pistol in hand," and it urged them to give special credence to Arnold's assertions because he was a congressman from Tennessee and would therefore know the facts. The readiness of this paper, one of the two most conspicuous political organs of the day, to reprint such provocative excerpts attests to the thoroughness with which the story was broadcast.[17]

The story was, by any standard of political scandal, a stick of dynamite. As Robert V. Remini has put it, it held "enough ammunition to kill a regiment of presidential candidates."[18] It also, however, carried the potential for backlash. Even in the heyday of freewheeling partisan politics, not all anti-Jacksonians were sanguine about raking up the Robards affair, because to do so was to violate an emerging ideal of domestic privacy. To exploit the story for partisan political purposes was to subvert the conceptual boundaries middle-class men and women were constructing between the vaunted harmony of the home and the competitive turmoil of the outside world; even worse, it was to part the drapes they were drawing around their most intimate relations. As some editors realized, because the exposure ignored the deepening distinction between private and public life, it was at the very least insensitive, if not in fact counterproductive. After carrying the story, the *Daily National Journal* waffled and turned to champion the right of privacy inherent in the doctrine of separate spheres, the differentiation between home and the world. It castigated those writers who were using the "weapons of political hostility to lay waste the happy valleys in which domestic felicity ought to live remote from the feuds and discords of public life."[19] Like competition in the marketplace, political campaigns unfolded a world apart from the quiet recesses of domestic life.

What gave the Robards affair its real clout, what distinguished it from the formulaic and politicized seduction tales of the revolutionary era, and what made it at once so scandalous and so modern was the very same concept of domestic privacy, which was being breached now in an unprecedented torrent of print. As Michel Foucault observes, "What is peculiar to modern societies . . . is not that they consigned sex to a shadow existence, but that they dedicated themselves to speaking of it *ad infinitum,* while exploiting it as *the* secret."[20] It is precisely because sex, according to the new standards of gentility, was to be confined to the private recesses of the bedroom that it could be deployed so effectively in the partisan presses. And it is precisely because this discourse about sex was construed as the revelation of a secret that it could assume titillating qualities. One consequence of this salacious underside of the campaign of

1828 was the transformation of domestic privacy, in the sense of denoting a realm distinct from and unconnected to that of the political order into a very public issue.

By aggressively championing an antipolitical notion of privacy, the politically astute Jacksonians compensated for a shaky factual defense with a compelling ideological offense. Their outrage against the obscene collapse of private-public boundaries blunted traditional republican appeals to the principle of marital virtue. In the end, they definitively depoliticized the republican conception of virtue not so much by feminizing it as by privatizing it. Since their own charges of a corrupt bargain between Adams and Clay during the election of 1824 focused on the public arena, they were able to claim the high road here and denounce every manifestation of the administration's willingness to penetrate the sacred recesses of the Jacksons' domestic life. An early campaign issue of the *Albany Signs of the Times* claimed, "The editor disavows every attempt to destroy private character, or to enter the sacred retreats of domestic life, for the purpose of dragging forth the unsuspecting victims of foul mouthed slander." As the election drew near and the thoroughness of the exposure became apparent, the same editor ventured that few candidates "have suffered more from the tongue of the slanderer, or the pen of a licentious and unprincipled faction, than ANDREW JACKSON."[21]

But the Jacksonians went even further; they construed privacy as constituting an area properly closed off from the scrutiny of any person, political or otherwise, who stood outside the domestic circle. Their protests against the Adamsite presses went beyond conventional notions of slander to anticipate the legal concept of an injury to a person's feelings as a result of the information technologies of mass culture.[22] And Jackson was invariably the martyr in all of this. Verbal assaults on his wife, in this tack that assumed the complete corporatism of marriage, were deemed assaults on him from which he suffered doubly, because they impugned her honor as well as his and because he subsumed her suffering. Since the "inmost recesses of his family, the honor of his wife," and "his domestic peace" had all been invaded "to serve the purposes and prop up the hopes of a falling party," it was evident "no man has been more foully slandered." Substituting the crime of wife slandering for that of wife stealing, a pro-Jackson broadside averred that "the most unfounded calumnies have been invested and reiterated by the *amalgamation* hirelings against the wife of his bosom."[23]

Although Jackson supporters worked to deflect republican analogies between government and marriage, they embraced other elements of republicanism with gusto. By highlighting the motives of the administration in dredging up the Robards story, they counterpoised the hollow partisanship embodied in such a ploy against the cooperative goals of a truly republican ideology. To be sure, both parties denounced the evils of party at the very moment they were creating the second party system, but Jacksonians were convinced that the calculated exploitation of the Robards affair afforded vivid proof that the Adamsites were engaged in a vicious conspiracy. Their insistence on a plot by the administration to corrupt the morals of the nation with the spread of its lurid stories evoked Patriot charges against the British during the revolutionary era. Antebellum voters, like their revolutionary fathers, were exhorted to exhibit the utmost wariness toward so devious an enemy. A voter who finally switched to Jackson wrote that he was deceived for a time by "the base falsehoods" but was later convinced that Jackson "has been traduced and libelled for mere party purposes."[24]

Nevertheless, Jacksonian attacks on the selfishness of party displayed a distinctly modern resonance. The corruption of the political process and thus of the entire nation was viewed as a direct corollary of the administration's willingness to ride roughshod over the sacred domain of a person's private life. The Jacksonian insistence on locating the source of the administration's corruption in its conflation of public and private spheres diverged from the complementarity between spheres that had been assumed in the revolutionary era. And yet the degree to which the Jacksonians departed from an older construction of virtue that had pivoted on a far less dichotomous conception of separate spheres was obscured by the familiar terms in which they denounced the corruption. They avowed that the administration's spreading of licentious stories, driven as it was by insatiable electoral greed, was an intricate conspiracy to deceive the people. As a Maine editor put it, "We view the scurrilous abuse and calumny heaped upon the best citizens of our country, by the coalition party through the administration presses, to be a vile attempt to corrupt the moral good sense of the people, and to defame the general character of the nation." Jackson, who like Adams held himself officially above the political fray, contributed to the notion that the administration was bent on corrupting the public when he signed off at the end of a letter for public consumption with the following: "Trusting to the justice of an intelligent people, I have been content to rely for security on their decision, against the countless assaults and slanders, which are sought so repeatedly to be palmed upon them."[25]

Administration journalists, however, had both republican political theory and evangelical moral fervor on their side. They invoked a man's regard for the fundamental ground rules of marriage as an acid test of his character, and character was the issue that legitimated their carrying the Robards story in the first place. By running for office, the *Daily National Journal* reasoned, Jackson "provoked if not invited an investigation of his character," along with every facet of his life. The Robards scandal, another Adamsite insisted, represented "an affair in which the National character, the National interest, and the National morals, were all deeply involved" and it was therefore "a proper subject of public investigation and exposure." Indeed. *We the People* argued that a candidate should regard the relentless scrutiny of his private life as a test of his republican principles, and if he were unwilling or unable to take that test, he should not run for public office. "If Gen. Jackson cannot withstand investigations of his character, or if his friends shrink from them and threaten violence to the hand that chalks out their imperfection, neither he, nor his party, is calculated for office, or to administer the laws to a republican people." A speech delivered against Jackson in Natchez, the scene of the alleged adultery, relied on the familiar equation of private virtue with the public good: if Jackson's "private life has been a continued scene of rashness and consequent errors, his public life is more deeply stamped."[26]

Adams's private life, on the other hand, presented a pristine contrast. Jacksonians, of course, attacked Adams's character relentlessly, alleging that he had been corrupted by living too long abroad, that he was mesmerized by the trappings of royalty, and that he had used public funds to purchase a billiard table for his own amusement at the White House. But his private life yielded up no scandal that was even remotely comparable to that of the Robards affair. A few random accusations that he prostituted a young American woman to the desires of Czar Alexander I when he served as a diplomat to the czar's court held little credibility and were not pursued with any degree of persistence. The kind of hard legal evidence that accusers used to document the Robards scandal was simply unavailable for Adams; even the most intemperate verbal assaults against him focused largely on his public record. "While his enemies have assailed his political course with a rabid fury," the *Weekly Marylander* observed, "few have ventured to impeach the morals or devotion, in which he is so justly pre-eminent." Those who scrutinized his private life "stood ashamed and rebuked at the brightness and holiness of that which they had intended to injure."[27]

But Andrew Jackson's private life was quite another matter, and its public import pivoted on a set of evangelical convictions about the affinities between self-government and national government. If a modicum of law and order was dependent on the sanctity of the marriage bed, it was no less dependent on the self-restraint of men against the depredations of their own passion. As Charles Hammond put it, until the present political contest, America had been a land "where no man can succeed to a place of high trust who does not respect female virtue: or who stands condemned as the seducer of other men's wives, and the destroyer of female character." Would readers, he queried, "give sanction to conduct, which is calculated to unhinge the fundamental principles of society?" For Hammond self-control and social control were entirely inseparable aspects of the constraints men needed to impose, both on themselves and on others, in order to achieve a higher order of freedom. Moral reform, in other words, depended both on individual conscience and on any external authority that helped to reshape individual conscience. In the absence of a serious reverence for the boundaries around marriage, whether it took the form of lapses by individual men and women or emanated from a failing on the part of institutions, only political chaos could ensue. "Let all inducements to the maintenance of conjugal fidelity be broken down: let all veneration for the marriage state and covenant be destroyed; and let me then ask, what there is in social life worthy of regard?" The answer was clear: "Show to the world your abhorrence of a man, who disregards the laws which even savages revere."[28]

If the ties between conjugal fidelity and law and order were too much of a moral abstraction, there was the more tangible problem of the example an adulterous president would set. Voters were urged to consider both the seriousness of Jackson's offense and the significance of the office. All forms of fornication were deemed despicable, but Adamsites distinguished the severity of the crime with the sex and marital status of the partners. The problem here, they argued, went well beyond a petty indiscretion with an unmarried female that rested "upon a peculiar freedom of manners too little regardful of the restraints of society"; Jackson's offense ranked as "gross adultery," and as such carried dire consequences. Fear of public censure, one powerful incentive to remaining virtuous, would evaporate with the election of Andrew Jackson, and seduction might become the order of the day. It would become impossible to censure a man "who may seduce his neighbours wife, and take her to live with him in adultery," because the dishonor would be obliterated by "his being no worse than the President of the United States."[29]

The obligation to set a good example for the nation extended to the president's wife. Just as her husband stood as a representative American man, she stood as a representative American wife, wifehood being the only proper status for a respectable adult woman. If she were "weak and vulgar," a combination that implicitly linked sexual promiscuity in a woman to a rank in the lower classes, she might become the object of ridicule that would be directed ultimately toward her husband. But even more important was her effect on the members of her own sex, who would look to her as a model. Adamsites urged voters to consider the problematic relationship between all the virtuous women in the nation and the degraded woman who would now be sitting in the White House.

Would the women of the republic abandon their self-respect to humble themselves "before this modern Jezebel?" Framed in the most rhetorically provocative way, the problem Rachel Jackson brought to her husband's quest for the presidency was summed up in this simple question: "Ought a *convicted adulteress* and her *paramour* husband to be placed in the highest offices of this free and Christian Land?"[30]

"American Jezebel," "profligate woman," "convicted adulteress"— the denunciations pulled Rachel Jackson from outside the margins of political discourse toward its very center. Chief matron among matrons, so to speak, she was invested with a specific political function that provided the basis for a public assessment of her morals. Had there been no scandal, she would have taken her place with the wives of other candidates in the peaceful recesses of the domestic sphere. The problem was not only that she had defiled the domestic sphere and, in so doing, forfeited the respect for privacy accorded virtuous women but also that she was an emblem for all women. Because she was cast as a negative model for the members of her own sex, she became, to borrow a phrase from Mary Poovey, a border case, a challenge to the binary logic in the gendered opposition of separate spheres. It was widely understood that, by living in the White House at her husband's side, she would preside "at the head of the female society of the United States."[31]

Furthermore, in a spectrum of representations that ranged from abduction to seduction to unalloyed passion, most Adamsites invested Rachel Jackson with some responsibility for her own sexuality. The acerbity of the attacks against her inferred that she had been an active, willing, and even eager participant in the decision to leave Robards and take up with the general. She too had been passionate. She too had been ruled by her appetites and was therefore beyond the constraints of her own government, not just of those imposed by a government of men. She, like her paramour, was individually responsible for committing the crime of adultery. The problem with her divorce, moreover, was not the emergence of the institution of divorce per se, but that she was the defendant in a divorce action that was the direct and inevitable consequence of her own unbridled passions. A New York pamphleteer warned, "When the rein is so given to indulgence, that it runs the whole race, and ends in divorce and marriage, the most favorable estimate we can make of the parties, is that they are mere creatures of passion, and the victims of its ungoverned predominance."[32]

Almost four decades of domestic tranquility, which even Jackson's most adamant foes conceded were marked by his wife's exemplary behavior, could not erase the fact that she was irredeemably fallen. There was to be no quarter given here. The same pamphleteer, referring to a scandalous murder conspiracy of the day, asked, "Can forty years of exemplary virtue restore the wretched Elsie Whipple to the station she has lost in society? Would we not be startled at the bare suggestion, that forty years hence she might be placed as the wife of our President at the head of the females of our country?" Elsie Whipple was a married woman who had plotted with her lover, Jesse Strang, to put an end to her marriage by putting an end to her husband. After failing in an attempt to poison him and almost killing her son in the process, she goaded Strang into doing the killing. Convicted of the murder in August 1827, Strang, who had abandoned his own wife, poured out his confession in a pamphlet designed to make Elsie Whipple's guilt as manifest as his own.[33]

The most extravagant of the anti-Jackson propagandists, then, compared the act of adultery on the part of a woman to the murder of her husband. That comparison served as a warning that vigilance was required to keep the White House pure. If Jackson bullied his fellow Tennesseans into admitting his spouse "AMONGST MODEST WOMEN," warned the *Massachusetts Journal* in an uncanny presentiment of the tack he would take with Peggy Eaton, the controversial wife of his secretary of war, "HE SHALL MEET A FIRMER RESISTANCE BEFORE HE FIGHTS HER AND HIS OWN WAY INTO THE PRESIDENTIAL MANSION." Tagging Jackson with the sobriquet "the Great Western Bluebeard," the paper projected yet another allusion linking sexual relations to murder. Indeed, so unrestrained were the attacks of the *Massachusetts Journal,* and so confident were some Jacksonians that they would backfire, that they reprinted the paper's harshest denunciations in a pamphlet for their own political distribution, with an appendix citing the dates of their sources. A section entitled "Abuse of Mrs. Jackson" included the following:

> Who is there in all this land that has a wife, a sister or daughter that could be pleased to see Mrs. Jackson (Mrs. Roberts [Robards] that was) presiding in the drawing-room at Washington. THERE IS POLLUTION IN THE TOUCH, THERE IS PERDITION IN THE EXAMPLE OF A PROFLIGATE WOMAN—"HER WAYS LEAD DOWN TO THE CHAMBERS OF DEATH AND HER STEPS TAKE HOLD ON HELL." And shall we standing in a watch-tower to warn our countrymen of approaching danger seal our lips in silence, in respect to this personage and HER PARAMOUR, great and powerful as he and captivating as he renders himself with his "bandanna handkerchief," "his frock coat," his amiable condescentions, and the fascinations of his BAR-ROOM and PUBLIC TABLE TALK.[34]

The fanaticism of this assault suggests the intensity Adamsites could bring to their critiques of the Jacksons' union. At a time of rapid expansion and growing urbanization, when both familial and social relations were readjusting to the demands of the marketplace, the formal ground rules for marriage became ever more important. The profligacy of Rachel Jackson could loom as a deadly pollutant to the political wellbeing of the nation precisely because marriage played so prominent a role in the Adamsites' quest for moral discipline. One consequence of their preoccupation with a strict adherence to the rules for marriage as they applied to *both* sexes, however, was a divergence from the gendered insularity that was the hallmark of domesticity. Despite editors' protests to the contrary, Adamsites viewed marriage less as a cooperative sanctuary affording protection from the turmoil of political life and mitigating the effects of market relations than as a model for the contractualism on which both the future of the polity and the life of the market depended. Since the trust implicit in the promise keeping of a contractual relationship is not without cooperative elements, the distinction here is one of emphasis.[35] Nonetheless, it is an emphasis that clarifies the larger implications of the Adamsites' marital code. From this fundamental premise regarding the sanctity of the marriage contract, or more precisely the sanctity of contract in marriage (given their grudging recognition of divorce), flowed their subtle but persistent subversion of the doctrine of separate spheres.

The Adamsites' impulse to make one sphere more like the other could run in both directions. Their preoccupation with the letter of the law in their moral assaults on Rachel Jackson reflected the new cognitive style that Thomas Haskell has attributed to the experience and ideology of market capitalism. Legal formalism was central to the case Adamsites were making in exposing the Robards affair, which was, among other things, a breach-of-contract story. The clear cause-and-effect rationale employed by the law in adjudicating breaches of contract made it the perfect arbiter of the rules for conjugal morality. To those who attested Rachel Jackson's innocence, her accusers noted that it was the law, the social institution properly designated to handle challenges to marital fidelity, that had pronounced her guilty of the crime of adultery. In making her offense a matter of judicial record, the law made her guilt a matter of incontestable proof. Emphasis on the details in the legal record represented Adamsite fact versus Jacksonian fiction; it set hard Adamsite rationality against hyperbolic Jacksonian rhetoric. Once the verdict was rendered, no "intelligent mind" could "doubt that Mrs. Jackson was unfaithful to her marriage vow with Robards" or "believe that she would have been guilty of the great indiscretion of flying beyond the reach of her husband, with a man charged to be her paramour, were she innocent of the charge."[36]

But the law was no less instrumental in affixing the guilt of her great and powerful paramour, whose responsibility for the affair far outweighed her own. Sensing the backlash they were creating in debasing Rachel Jackson, Adams supporters placed the blame for her humiliation directly at the feet of the general. If she suffered from the crass intrusion of politics into her private life, her husband had only himself to blame for subjecting her to an investigation that was bound to reveal her shame. Were he truly the gallant protector of women he claimed to be, he would not have run for the office in the first place. A caring husband "would never consent that the wife of his bosom should be exposed to the ribald taunts, and dark surmises of the profligate, or to the cold civility or just remark of the wise and good." Instead, he would have devoted his life to sustaining and comforting his "bruised and broken flower." It was Jackson's own supporters, complained the editor of the *Daily National Journal,* who were trying to divert public attention from the general by "making her the shield" with which to deflect the blows against him.[37]

The defensiveness of these responses reveals considerable uneasiness on the part of Adamsites regarding their exposure of the scandal. And yet they pursued it with great persistence because it encapsulated everything they feared about Jackson, and their fears about Jackson went to the heart of their campaign. Those fears were the fulcrum about which they defined and asserted their moral identity as an emerging political coalition. Indeed, Adamsites specifically aimed to be everything that Andrew Jackson was not. Allusions to the scandal were irresistible not only because they meshed so neatly with the lawless facets of Jackson's public career but also because they enabled Adams supporters to contrast Jackson's casual western ways with what Richard L. McCormick has labeled their "styles of Sunday behavior." Thus Adamsites could measure the "warm yet unobtrusive piety" of their man against the vices of an opponent "unfitted by his habits, his temper and his want of civil acquirements for the exalted station of President of the United States."[38]

For these proto-Whigs, who assessed the nation's increasingly sophisticated legal culture as the hallmark of its remarkable progress, the election of a military leader as undisciplined as Andrew Jackson presented a terrifying prospect. His utter lack of self-control, they predicted, would imperil the rights of individual citizens and serve as an influential model for the collective regression of the nation. It was perilous, one pamphleteer reasoned, "to put at the head of our government, a man who was never known to govern himself." His "disregard of the laws," alleged another, demonstrated his complete inability to conform to the government of others. Here was a man, the *Weekly Marylander* noted, who "openly violated the decalogue, and has not even shewn hypocrisy, that tribute which vice pays to virtue." A political orator observed that this man, in his private life, "exhibited the deformity and the danger of the human disposition when uninfluenced by either moral or legal restraints." Cruel, lawless, passionate, impetuous, violent, these were the qualities associated with the Great Western Bluebeard; he carried a sword cane and, according to one broadside, was "willing to run it through the body of any one who may presume to stand in his way." Another broadside pointed out that this was "not the man to take the lead under our refined system of Government, and our WELL REGULAT-ED CODE OF LAW."[39]

Persistently employing an idiom that equated the political "refine-ment" of the nation with its citizens' acceptance of evangelical discipline, Adamsites set out to puncture what the *Daily Nations Journal* deemed "the fictitious splendor" thrown around Jackson's name by exposing his anti-Christian primitivism. There can be no mistaking their moral urgency. "Worshippers of Jackson and *hickory poles*," the Washington paper alleged, "wish to lead this happy people back to barbarism, where no laws were acknowledged but that of the club, or more recently the bayonet pistol." "Between the two candidates," proclaimed *We the People*, explicitly framing the election as a contest between infidel and evan-gelical, "the difference is as wide as between paganism and christianity." With Jackson setting the standard for national morality, predicted the *Daily National Journal*, "Two centuries would then be found to have been sufficient to carry us from puritanism to its antipodes." The Robards affair, as one broadside inferred, served to exemplify "the ungoverned temper, the inflexible resolution, the vindictive spirit, and the long established habits of Jackson." What better signpost of his utter lack of moral refinement than his unchecked erotic impulses? What bet-ter proof of his great capacity for public deception than the story he invented to mask his crime? To place such a man in the presidency along with his fallen woman was tantamount to inviting a confidence man with his painted woman to occupy the White House.[40]

The Jacksonian narrative of the Robards story was a defensive effort rendered necessary by the unremitting activity of the administration presses. Although the Jacksonians did not set out to give conjugal rela-tions a political focus, they appreciated the need to address the moral ramifications of the Jacksons' irregular union. Public documents dam-aging to the Jacksons included both the private bill issued by the Vir-ginia legislature permitting Lewis Robards to proceed with his divorce suit and the complaint and final decree filed in the Court of Quarter Ses-sions in Mercer County, Kentucky. Since this evidence was widely avail-able, creating a defense that went beyond invoking the inviolability of domestic privacy presented a daunting challenge.

The Jacksonians responded with a series of redeeming counterimages celebrating their hero's reliance on the frontier codes of Tennessee, where honor, friendship, and loyalty counted for more than legal fine print. Although it is tempting to define this line of their defense as tradition oriented—an appeal to the values of an older and simpler society—it was liberally laced with the nature-affirming values of nineteenth-century romanticism. Even the language the Jacksonians employed to contest Adamsite definitions of marital legitimacy drew on the cult of sincerity and sensibility that was itself an outgrowth of religious revivals. Indeed, their devotion to the authenticity of emotion and the validity of individual experience embodied sentiments unleashed by the soft, nonrational side of the Second Great Awakening.[41]

It was in this context of authenticity and sincerity that the frontier emerged as Jackson's definitive personal experience. "His strong manly sense, his integrity and warmth of heart, soon gathered a circle of friends around him, of the blunt yeomanry of that district," noted a supporter intent on valorizing the lessons learned in the wilderness over the niceties of the parlor; "he imbibed their frank and generous spirit," he conceded, "and perhaps partook of their faults." Although no political spin could cast the act of wife stealing in a favorable light, emphasis on the wilderness enabled the Jacksonians to recontour the ground rules for divorce to accommodate persons living on the frontier. This slippage, from a strict adherence to the letter of the law to a reliance on its fundamental spirit, not only was the key to their defense but also embodied their more generalized opposition to the excesses of formalism. Their populist appeal to a simpler and more transparent form of justice undoubtedly resonated with hardworking farmers and laborers, who distrusted the burgeoning refinements of the American legal system. The general emerged as a man who intuitively grasped the inner truth of the law buried within its arcane technicalities. An open-hearted, western man like Andrew Jackson, who was the "punisher of *Booty* and the protector of *Beauty*," might very well transcend some specific legal forms because he was in touch with the reality that gave the forms meaning.[42]

A detailed narrative affirming the Jacksons' adherence to the spirit of the law constituted the core of their defense. This project began with the creation in 1826 of the Nashville Committee, which went to work combing Tennessee for depositions validating the Jacksons' story. Tagged by the administration presses as the "Whitewashing Committee," it consisted of nineteen prominent Tennesseans, most of whom were practicing lawyers or appellate court judges. The result of this august gathering of the general's old friends was the publication of a pamphlet designed to refute "the newspaper charges against General Jackson and his lady."[43] Opening with an overview of the Jacksons' marital history and concluding with a series of letters and depositions from longtime friends and neighbors, the pamphlet addressed the most damaging of the Adamsite charges.

The primary goal of the committee was to establish the unqualified guilt of Lewis Robards in bringing his marriage to an end and to obliterate any notion that Andew Jackson won his wife by challenging Robards to a duel and then seizing her at gunpoint. Relying largely on the testimony of Jackson's old lawyering companion, John Overton, who offered his version as the real story underneath the legal story, the committee created a melodrama in which love and gallantry filled the vacuum created by a cruel and hopelessly failed marriage that unraveled in a harsh and dangerous frontier setting.[44]

Inasmuch as the villain here was the first husband, the melodrama had an unorthodox twist, pivoting on the irredeemable nature of his depravity. The evil inherent in Lewis Robards, according to the Jacksonians, emanated from a pathological jealousy that so obscured his judgment and inflamed his anger as to render him incapable of sustaining his marriage vows. In the fall of 1788 and in the third year of her marriage, Rachel Donelson Robards "was compelled . . . by her husband" to leave Kentucky and seek a home with her mother, a widow living on the Tennessee frontier. John Overton, who had been boarding with the Robardses, explained that "Capt. Robards and his wife lived very unhappily on account of his being jealous of Mr. Short," an otherwise unidentified attorney also boarding with the Robardses. Lewis Robards, however, alternated between fits of jealousy and periods of contrition, and as he came to regret the expulsion of his wife, he besought Overton to do what he could to restore harmony between them.[45]

This brings the narrative to the Donelson compound on the banks of the Cumberland River, where a group of young lawyers, including John Overton and Andrew Jackson, came to seek their fortunes in the winter of 1788–1789. That winter Overton did arrange a reunion for the Robardses, whereby it was agreed they would live on a preemption on the south side of the Cumberland. Yet the setting at the Donelson compound was more than such a man as Robards could contend with. Overton, who had introduced Jackson into the Donelson household, described the living conditions as "Jackson and myself, our friends and clients &c occupying one cabin, and the family another, a few steps from it."[46] For a brief period in 1789, then, the unstable Lewis Robards, his lovely wife Rachel, and the dashing Andrew Jackson all lived in exceedingly close proximity.

It was only a matter of time before Lewis Robards's uncontrollable jealousy was directed toward Andrew Jackson, whose "character and standing added to his engaging and sprightly manners" were sufficient "to inflame" Robards's obsessively jealous mind. When Overton warned his good friend Andrew Jackson about Robards's suspicions, and Jackson, "conscious of his innocence," remonstrated with Robards on the injustice that he had done his wife, Robards turned "violently angry and abusive." But even though he threatened to whip Jackson, and Jackson replied "that if he insisted on fighting, he would give him gentlemanly satisfaction," no physical violence took place. Instead, Robards declared he was determined not to live with his wife. Yet as he changed his mind once again, Jackson found it prudent to give up boarding with the Donelsons. When Robards finally left for Kentucky in the spring of 1790, it was with "the avowed intention of returning and settling" near the Donelson compound. However, Thomas Crutcher, who rode back to Kentucky with him, insisted he declared on the way home "he would be damned if ever he would be seen in the Cumberland again."[47]

Although the opposition could read the trouble with Short as evidence of another extramarital liaison, the first part of the narrative created a plausible alternative to the Adamsite version of the story. The Jacksonians, after all, did not aim to condone illicit sexual relations; rather they sought to expand the definition of licit sexual relations to incorporate the Jacksons' union by recounting Robards's guilt. If jealousy was not a legal ground for ending a marriage, desertion was, in many jurisdictions, and that implicitly was Robards's conjugal fault. When the members of the Nashville Committee took up the public record, however, their heroic efforts to cast Robards as the villain were less convincing.

In an extraordinary demonstration of loyalty to the general, men with years of legal experience conveniently set aside their knowledge of the law. Consider the letter from James Breckenridge, who had sat in the Virginia legislature and served on the judiciary committee, whose task it was to report on the Robards bill. Sidestepping the fact that Lewis Robards was the petitioner before the legislature and therefore the aggrieved party, Breckenridge avowed that Robards was presented as a man "of vile, wild habits and harsh temper." His wife, by contrast, was "lovely and blameless in her disposition and deportment," and she was so cruelly treated, Breckenridge claimed (suddenly raising the possibility of physical abuse), "as to make a separation necessary to her happiness." Regarding his own affirmative vote on the Robards bill, he averred, "If Mr. Robards alledged incontinency . . . I am very sure that I thought her innocent, and that my vote was intended to liberate her, as the injured party." As for the verdict of the Kentucky jury that found her guilty of adultery, Thomas Allen, one-time clerk of the Kentucky court issuing the decree, noted it was an ex parte proceeding "with nothing shewing that the defendant had any kind of notice of the existence of that suit." Ignoring the widespread acceptance of presumptive service, a procedure whereby publication of the suit in a local paper sufficed as notice, Allen underscored the defendant's inability to present her side of the story. He also observed, as if to undermine the husband's motive in bringing the suit when he did, that Lewis Robards remarried almost immediately after the divorce.[48]

Even more problematic was the sequence of events following Robards's departure from the Donelson compound. The Nashville Committee claimed that after hearing rumors that Lewis Robards was coming to bring her back to Kentucky, Rachel Robards fled downriver to Natchez in January 1791 under the protection of Andrew Jackson. Jackson, it was alleged, left for Nashville as soon as he had safely deposited his charge with family friends and returned to marry her in the summer of that year only after hearing that a legislative decree had been issued. Nonetheless, as the ever-vigilant Charles Hammond observed, "If Jackson and Mrs. Robards had been married at or near Natchez, they would long since have produced some evidence to support their own assertions . . . and published it to the world!"[49]

The final function of the Nashville report was to repair the damage to Rachel Jackson's honor by presenting her as "deserving and enjoying the kindest attentions of her female acquaintances." Underscoring the "free and unreserved intercourse" among a handful of respected Virginia families who first settled along the Cumberland River, these women invested her marriage to Andrew Jackson with the seal of community approval. Elizabeth Craighead, widow of Thomas Craighead, the west Tennessee Presbyterian minister, avowed that "no lady ever conducted herself in a more becoming manner." Sally Smith, widow of Tennessee senator Daniel Smith, claimed Robards "was spoken everywhere as a man of irregular habits and much given to jealous suspicion." Mary Bowen, widow of William Bowen, identified herself by her deceased son, a Tennessee congressman, and by her father, who had married Patrick Henry's sister; she declared, "Not the least censure ought to be thrown upon any person but Mr. Robards." In a revealing rationale for the credibility of her version of the story, she observed that "[t]his was the language of all the country and I never heard until now that there was any person living who had entertained a different opinion, except Mr. Robards himself, in whose weak and childish disposition, I think the whole affair originated."[50]

As for Charles Hammond's accusation that the woman Jackson "took to his bed" was unchaste, and that "he had himself destroyed that chastity, if indeed it existed at the time," the Jacksons' friends responded by privileging the "language of the country" over the stipulations of the law. Rachel Jackson was deemed chaste in the sense of being morally free to enter into a second union, and Andrew Jackson was portrayed as enough of a gentleman to appreciate that fact. Despite the volition implicit in her remarriage, however, her role in the Jacksonian narrative was an altogether passive one. The recognition of her chastity was entirely dependent on the general's chivalry. As Sally Smith noted, her minister husband gave the Jacksons' union his benediction when he observed that "it was a happy change for Mrs. Robards and highly creditable to General Jackson who . . . evinced his own magnanimity as well as the purity and innocence of Mrs. Robards." Commenting in a similar vein on Jackson's remarkable empathy for the helplessness of women, Overton noted that "in his singularly delicate sense of honor, and in what I thought his chivalrous conception of the Female sex, it occurred to me that he was distinguishable from every other person with whom I was acquainted."[51]

Rachel Jackson, the focus of so much political newsprint, bore the public assault on her character with anguished resignation. As she put it to a friend in the summer of 1828, "the Enemyes of the Genls have Dipt their arrows in wormwood & gall & sped them at me." She lived long enough to witness her husband's victory, only to die "A consort True, who shar'd his cares—but could not his honors view." In the prolific effusions of national mourning, she became the pathetic object of an ocean of sentiment. Only in death, it seems, when every vestige of her volition was forever obliterated, could the Jacksonians depict her chastity as a virtue that was her own as opposed to being a gift from the general. "A being so gentle and so virtuous," proclaimed her tombstone, "slander might wound but could not dishonor." "Far from the reach of the venom'd dart," intoned a broadside memorial, "By wretched Malice thrown in vain." The words affirming her honor stand inscribed on a silk broadside designed to decorate a respectable parlor: "She died—in all she held so dear—Unsullied name—unspotted worth."[52]

Although the larger implications of this seemingly narrow focus must remain speculative, the contest over the Robards affair raises a host of compelling questions about the nexus of gender and politics in the second party system. Narrowly construed, the contest crystallized around two specific issues: the definition of marital transgression in the context of Andrew Jackson's sexual behavior and the import of a candidate's sexual behavior in the political life of the nation. It also impinged on a host of related issues, albeit only implicitly. It is not hard to imagine how an antebellum voter might have linked the Adamsites' insistence on an active governmental role in policing the boundaries of marriage to a drive for internal improvements and a strong protective tariff. Nor is it farfetched to tie the Jacksonians' reliance on localism and personalism in defining marital legitimacy to an antipathy to banks, bureaucracies, and an aggressively activist government.

The great promise in a gendered political focus such as this, however, lies not so much in its capacity to illuminate policy goals, which were persistently muted in the campaigns of the second party system, as in its power to reveal the appeals resonating beneath the surface of conscious political discourse. Because marriage by virtue of its universality afforded homely material for thinking analogically about the social order, and because gender by virtue of its alleged naturalness required no thinking at all, the Robards affair could serve as an evocative reference point for deep cultural conflicts that were customarily unexpressed. With hindsight it is possible to see that the vexing tensions between such ideals as responsibility and freedom, social discipline and self-expression, and ecumenicism and pluralism—tensions that embattled politicians could not even comprehend fully themselves, much less articulate clearly for the public— were encapsulated in the narratives of the Robards affair. At a level that defies precise definition and surely merits further analysis, individuals translated competing paradigms for manly men, womanly women, and licit gender relations into divergent visions of the social order. Not only did these paradigms help voters far from the seats of political power choose their party affiliations but they also enabled each party to define itself by sharpening its antagonism to the values of the opposition.[53]

How, then, did these paradigms play out in the election of 1828? In this case, the pious Christian gentleman from Massachusetts was no match for the chivalric hero of New Orleans. But given Jackson's popularity in the election of 1824 and the unpopularity of John Quincy Adams, it is risky to read Jackson's subsequent victory as broad support for the freedom of informal marital arrangements; his popular majority might have been even larger had the scandal never surfaced. Surface it did, however, and it was not sufficient to defeat him. If a majority of the voters was at least willing to tolerate the prospect of "a convicted adulteress and her paramour husband" living together in the White House, it is probably because they refused to characterize the Jacksons' union in those terms and opted to believe instead in their adherence to the spirit of the law. Legislative petitions from the period indicate that numerous men and women tried to put a swift and inexpensive end to their marriages by appealing to extralegal community codes and by demonstrating support from friends and neighbors. Others simply walked away from their marriages and began unions anew.[54] We can hypothesize that the marital difficulties of Andrew Jackson represented an experience that the common men to whom he appealed did not believe disqualified him from serving in the office. Furthermore, as the elaborate defensiveness of the Adamsites indicates, their unremitting assault on Rachel Jackson may very well have "unmanned" them and driven some fence-sitters into the Jackson camp.

A closely related consideration is what the Robards affair can tell us about the political culture. For one thing, it suggests that, by 1828, it was difficult to invest marriage with the same political meaning it had carried in the post–Revolutionary era. Most Americans were no longer predisposed to view seduction, as John Adams once did on reading *Clarissa,* as a political parable or to see the nation, as his generation had, as the family writ large. Metaphorical associations of household with polity would reverberate throughout the nineteenth century and into the twentieth, but the shift in sensibilities that had already occurred at the onset of the second party system had emptied the family of its most overtly political connotations. As a consequence, the Adamsite exposure of the Robards affair was beginning to take on the prurient overtones that mark the political exploitation of sexual scandals in our own day. The ideal marriage could no longer stand as a trope for the ideal republic because the disjunction between public and private life had grown too large, and the differences that inhered in the construction of separate spheres had turned oppositional.[55]

By keeping the separate spheres separate, not only did the Jacksonians incorporate this cultural shift more completely than did the Adamsites but they also put it to the service of their laissez-faire agenda. The defense they created to validate the general's marriage converged with their resistance to an interventionist government driven by the aims of ecumenical reformers. In celebrating the sanctity of privacy, the Jacksonians were upholding the very essence of the negative state. The appeals they made to honor and community should not obscure the fact that they deployed these familiar code words for tradition to support the principle of individual privacy, the ultimate value of the modern liberal state.

It is tempting to conclude that in reading the Robards affair as a political parable, it was the Adamsites who looked backward. The post–presidential years of John Quincy Adams, the preeminent proto-Whig of the 1820s, present striking evidence of how closely he could mirror his father in linking seduction to national ruin. An epic poem he published in 1832 attributes the twelfth-century conquest of Ireland to the sexual incontinence of Dermot MacMorrogh, an Irish king who stole a neighboring king's wife and set the stage for a foreign invasion. Although Adams never made the comparison explicit, it is only too apparent that MacMorrogh's abduction of Dovergilda provided an almost perfect parallel with Jackson's "abduction" of Rachel.[56]

And yet because the meaning of seduction was historically constructed, the metaphor was anything but backward looking as the Adamsites employed it. Starting from the premise of separate spheres, the Adamsites drew on the Robards affair to demonstrate the need for both sexual restraint and legal contractualism, thereby anticipating the large and influential strand of Victorian ideology that assumed that moral and material development were synergistically linked. Their reading of the

Robards affair went to the heart of their reformist agenda because it espoused a narrowing of the double standard and incorporated law into their quest for social discipline. Like temperance, Sabbatarianism, and antislavery, conjugal fidelity provided an issue that connected the electorate to the political ideology of the party. The framing of so morally explosive an issue in a human interest story with salacious overtones not only served to engage the average voter fully; it also introduced him, in deceptively traditional terms, to the modern world view of the Whigs.

As the foregoing observations suggest, one benefit of taking a narrow lens to a canvass of campaign literature is its capacity to illuminate the subtle transformation of familiar political terms. But when we employ the same lens to explore the ramifications of that transformation for women and the social construction of gender, the historical evidence becomes so thin that we are compelled to interpret its exclusions. Because this was a discourse about the boundaries of marriage, a pivotal social institution in the lives of women, its reticence about women is particularly striking. In contrast to the vivid images that clothe the persona of Andrew Jackson, the figure of Rachel Jackson remains a threadbare abstraction, a symbolic woman who was owned by men and whose chastity was contingent on male protection. What was at issue in the two narratives about the Robards affair was the nature of the protection. Whereas the Jacksonians entrusted female virtue (and its definition) to the purview of individual men (husbands, brothers, and fathers), the Adamsites inscribed it in a legal system controlled by male professionals (lawyers and judges).[57] Both models, it would seem, were equally effective in sustaining gender hierarchies and obstructing female empowerment.

Nevertheless, the Adamsite model offered women a few rays of autonomy. In providing a place in the legal system to remedy conjugal lapses, it undermined the traditional corporatism of marriage and provided female divorce plaintiffs with a direct relationship to the state. More important, because the Adamsites' most extravagant censures of Rachel Jackson invested her with responsibility for her own sexuality, they challenged the stereotype of female passivity and opened the door to female self-assertion. If a woman could be "a modern Jezebel," she could be a Joan of Arc as well and exert herself as a force for righteousness. An ambivalent 1838 speech by John Quincy Adams encapsulated both the possibilities and the limits that Whig reform would afford antebellum women. Arguing for the right of his female constituents to petition Congress against the acquisition of Texas, Adams compared the role of these intrepid abolitionists to that of the heroines of the Old Testament, while he justified their right to petition as a feminine act of supplication.[58]

Regardless of its limitations, the Whig ethos opened up political spaces for women. If, as Paula Baker has observed, women developed separate political traditions in the nineteenth century in which they enacted their gender identities, they also participated in and were influenced by the dominant male political traditions.[59] It is not surprising that the reform agenda of the Whigs and later the Republicans would provide white, Protestant, bourgeois women with an ethos congenial to their modest self-assertion, since it assumed an underlying consensus about key moral issues and functioned to render the distinctions between public and private less oppositional.

The insistence of the Jacksonians on the principle of individual privacy provided the men who gravitated toward their party with a buffer against the intrusions of evangelicalism, but it appears to have offered little to women as women. In fact, the Jacksonians' sharp demarcation between the public and the private not only contributed to the depoliticization of all that was private, but it also masked the disparities inherent in the male appropriation of private power. Nevertheless, as the heirs of Enlightenment rationalism and natural rights, the Jacksonians contributed a critical ideological component to the political self-assertion of women. When the demand for individual rights that was so central to the Democratic ethos was appropriated by women, it provided a powerful counterforce to the equation of feminine virtue with self-abnegation. By the late 1830s, when women began to construct their own marital codes by demanding property rights for married women, they did so in the name of their moral superiority in the face of intemperate and irresponsible male spouses (the Whig model), but they did so also in the name of those private islands of self-ownership, derived from the principles of the Enlightenment, that became the hallmarks of the negative state (the Democratic model).[60]

Finally, the competing marital codes delineated in the 1828 campaign prefigure a profound historical shift in gender relations by exposing the underlying instability in the prevailing synthesis about marriage. The debate over the Robards affair probed the gaping contradictions of a society committed to conjugal love on the one hand and lifelong monogamy on the other. In doing so, it confronted the vexing question of what would happen to a society when love broke away from the old moorings of responsibility and moderation, when men and women would not be bound by the constraints of self-discipline or the sanctions of law, and when the romantic self loomed as a wellspring of anarchy. The nineteenth-century construction of the romantic self, as Karen Lystra has notes, pivoted on a distinction in roles in which the inner self was perpetually at odds with the obligations of conjugal duty.[61]

Faced with a choice between love and duty, the Adamsites opted for duty. In a highly limited sense, the Jacksonians did so as well, only they employed a less formal source of authority to define what duty was. In a more fundamental sense, however, they opted for love. Charles Hammond was prescient when he warned voters about the example that would be created by placing an adulterer in the White House. In the end, it was the passionate love story, the subtext of the "real" story the Jacksonians constructed to contest the legal story, that was the long-term legacy of the Robards affair.

NOTES

Research for this essay was funded by an American Antiquarian Society–National Endowment for the Humanities fellowship. Earlier versions were presented at the American Studies Association annual meeting at Costa Mesa in November 1992 and at the New York University Law School Legal History Colloquium in November 1992.

I want to thank Scott Casper, Robert Gross, Annette Igra, Mary Kelley, Jan Lewis, Louis Masur, William Nelson, Elisabeth Perry, Carl Prince, Marylyn Salmon, David Thelen, and the referees of the *Journal of American History* for their insightful comments, and I want to express my indebtedness to Joanne Chaison, Georgia Barnhill, and the staff of the American Antiquarian Society for their generous assistance.

1. *Truth's Advocate and Monthly Anti-Jackson Expositor* (June 1828), 235–36.

2. James Parton, who interviewed the slave in whose arms Rachel Jackson expired, suggests she died of a heart condition aggravated by the stress of the campaign; see James Parton, *Life of Andrew Jackson,* 3 vols. (New York: Mason Brothers, 1860), 3:154. For the influence of her death on Andrew Jackson's subsequent defense of the maligned Peggy Eaton and his enduring enmity toward John Quincy Adams, see James C. Curtis, *Andrew Jackson and the Search for Vindication* (Boston: Little, Brown, 1976).

3. For the definitive pro-Jackson view, see *A Letter from the Jackson Committee of Nashville, in Answer to One from a Similar Committee, at Cincinnati, upon the Subject of Gen. Jackson's Marriage* (Nashville, Tenn.: Hill and Fitzgerald-Republican Office, 1827). All the pamphlets, handbills, broadsides, and election ephemera cited here are, unless otherwise noted, available at the American Antiquarian Society, Worcester, Mass. For a meticulous assessment of the extant evidence related to the Jacksons' first marriage, see Harriet Chappell Owsley, "The Marriages of Rachel Donelson," *Tennessee Historical Quarterly* 36 (Winter 1977): 479–92.

4. [Charles Hammond], *View of General Jackson's Domestic Relations, in Reference to his Fitness for the Presidency* (Cincinnati, 1828), 15. See also *An Appeal to the Moral and Religious of All Denominations; or, An Exposition of Some of the Indiscretions of General Andrew Jackson as Copied from Records and Certified by the Clerk of Mercer County Kentucky* (New York, 1828), 4.

5. On the second party system, see, for example, Ronald P. Formisano, *The Transformation of Political Culture: Massachusetts Parties, 1790s–1840s* (New York: Oxford University Press, 1983); Richard L. McCormick, *The Party Period and Public Policy: American Power From the Age of Jackson to the Progressive Period* (New York: Oxford University Press, 1986); and Harry L. Watson, *Liberty and Power: The Politics of Jacksonian America* (New York: Hill and Wang, 1990). For literacy, literature, and sensationalism, see David S. Reynolds, *Beneath the American Renaissance:*

The Subversive Imagination in the Age of Emerson and Melville (Cambridge, MA: Harvard University Press, 1988); Jane Tompkins, *Sensational Choices: The Cultural Work of American Fiction, 1790–1860* (New York: Oxford University Press, 1985); and Cathy N. Davidson, *Revolution and the Word: The Rise of the Novel in America* (New York: Oxford University Press, 1986). Both the scope and the nature of the Jackson scandal differed from those about Thomas Jefferson and Sally Hemings. Assertions that Hemings, Jefferson's slave, was his mistress were not disseminated with the same efficiency; and Hemmings, as the object of property, had a perilous claim on her own chastity. To the extent that a free white woman was viewed as the property of her husband, however, a further distinction between the two cases inheres in the fact that Sally Hemings was owned by Thomas Jefferson, whereas Rachel Robards, it was claimed, was stolen by Andrew Jackson. Nonetheless, the Jacksonians donned Jefferson's mantle by comparing "the falsehood, abuses, and calumny lavished on Thomas Jefferson" with the slander directed at Andrew Jackson. See *Portland Spirit of '28*, Oct. 29, 1828; see also Robert V. Remini, *Andrew Jackson and the Course of American Democracy, 1833–1835* (New York: Harper and Row, 1985), 256.

6. For the political import of seduction stories, see Jan Lewis, "The Republican Wife: Virtue and Seduction the Early Republic," *William and Mary Quarterly* 44 (Oct. 1987), 689–721. See also Ruth Bloch, "The Gendered Meaning of Virtue in Revolutionary America," *Signs* 13 (Autumn 1987): 37–58.

7. Joan Wallach Scott, *Gender and the Politics of History* (New York: Columbia University Press, 1988), 49.

8. On ethnocultural appeals, see especially Lee Benson, *The Concept of Jacksonian Democracy: New York as a Test Case* (Princeton, N.J.: Princeton University Press, 1961); and Robert Kelley, *The Cultural Pattern in American Politics: The First Century* (New York: Knopf, 1979).

9. Although Walker Howe's distinctions between Whig and Democratic worldviews focus only on the North, they have shaped the contours of this essay. His insights, narrowly tested as they are here, against the political treatment of the Robards affair, seem to transcend sectional differences. See Daniel Walker Howe, "The Evangelical Movement and Political Culture in the North during the Second Party System," *Journal of American History* 77 (March 1991): 1216–39. On the emergent worldviews of the two parties at the onset of the second party system, see also Rubil Morales, "The Cloudy Medium: John Quincy Adams, Andrew Jackson, and the Uses of Republican Language in the 1820s" (master's thesis, Rutgers University, 1993).

10. The influence of evangelicalism was not confined to denominations that held strictly to evangelical doctrines. On the streams of evangelicalism and the varied and secular directions they took, see James Turner, *Without God, Without Creed: The Origins of Unbelief in America* (Baltimore: Johns Hopkins University Press, 1985), 73–113.

11. On feminine weakness as a rhetorical foil for republican manliness, see Linda K. Kerber, "The Paradox of Women's Citizenship in the Early Republic: The Case of *Martin vs. Massachusetts*, 1805," *American Historical Review* 97 (April 1992): 349–78; on decoding the politics of gender in a later marital scandal in France, see Edward Berenson, "The Politics of Divorce in France of the Belle Epoque: The Case of Joseph and Henriette Caillaux," *The American Historical Review* 93 (Feb. 1988): 31–55.

12. *Cincinnati Gazette*, March 23, 1827; *Truth's Advocate and Monthly Anti-Jackson Expositor* (Jan 1828); [Hammond], *General Jackson's Domestic Relations* (March 1828), 117.

13. *Truth's Advocate and Monthly Anti-Jackson Expositor* (March 1828), 117.

14. This impression is based on a canvass of 1828 newspapers and special campaign extras held by the American Antiquarian Society. See Bradford Dunbar, comp., "Campaign Newspapers Published before 1877, Including Holdings at the American Antiquarian Society" (typescript, 1980, reading room, American Antiquarian Society).

15. *Daily National Journal*, March 26, 1827; Thomas Arnold, *To the freeman of the counties of Cocke, Sevier, Blount, Jefferson . . .* (Knoxville, 1827). Arnold's pamphlet went through at least two editions.

16. On the role of gender in social contract theory, see Carole Pateman, *The Sexual Contract* (Stanford: Stanford University Press, 1988).

17. *Daily National Journal*, March 26, 1827. This paper, which began as a semi-weekly in 1823 when John Quincy Adams was secretary of state, was considered the special organ of the president. The other major political organ was the pro-Jackson *United States Telegraph*, also Washington based, edited by Duff Green. The *National Intelligencer*, a pro-administration Washington paper, committed itself primarily to the fortunes of Henry Clay. See Culver Haygood Smith, *The Press, Politics, and Patronage: The American Government's Use of Newspapers, 1789–1875* (Athens: University of Georgia Press, 1977), 57; Parton, *Life of Jackson*, 3:143; John Tebbel and Sarah Miles Watts, *The Press and the Presidency from George Washington to Ronald Reagan* (New York: Oxford University Press, 1985), 74–88; and William Miles, 1828 comp., *The People's Voice: An Annotated Bibliography of American Presidential Campaign Newspapers, 1828–1984* (Westport, CT: Greenwood Press, 1987).

18. Robert V. Remini, *The Election of Andrew Jackson* (Philadelphia: Lippincott, 1963), 152.

19. *Daily National Journal*, April 12, 1827.

20. Michel Foucault, *The History of Sexuality: Volume I*, trans. Robert Hurley (New York: Vintage, 1990), 35.

21. In the four-way contest of 1824, in which Jackson received a plurality of both the popular and electoral votes, the election devolved into the House of Representatives; Clay was accused of throwing his support to Adams in return for his appointment as secretary of state, a traditional stepping-stone to the presidency. Fueled by their outrage over "the corrupt bargain," Jacksonians began the next campaign almost immediately. *Albany Signs of the Times*, Jan. 5, 1828; Sept. 27, 1828.

22. Jane M. Gaines, *Contested Culture: The Image, the Voice, and the Law* (Chapel Hill: University of North Carolina Press, 1991), 179.

23. *Vindication of the Character and Public Services of Andrew Jackson in Reply to the Richmond Address, argued by Chapman Johnson, and to Other Electioneering Calumnies* (Boston, 1828), 3; Dr. Noah J. T. George, *A Biographical Chart, Exhibiting at one View the Principal Events in the Life of General Andrew Jackson* (broadside).

24. *Boston Jackson Republican*, Sept. 3, 1828. For a similar shift in loyalty, see *John Quincy Adams Exposed and Andrew Jackson Vindicated by a Federalist* (n.p., 1828).

25. *Portland Spirit of '28*, Oct. 29, 1828; *Delaware Democrat & Easton Gazette*, Aug. 6, 1827. On Jackson's leadership and involvement despite his stance of being above the fray, see Robert V. Remini, *Andrew Jackson and the Course of American Freedom, 1822–1832* (New York: Harper and Row, 1981), 120–21.

26. *Daily National Journal*, Oct. 14, 1828; [Hammond], *General Jackson's Domestic Relations*, 1; *We the People*, April 12, 1828; April 19, 1828. For a similar statement on Jackson's private life, see also *An Address to the People of the United*

States on the Subject of the Presidential Election: With a Special Reference to the Nomination of Andrew Jackson containing Sketches of his Public and Private Character (Utica, 1828), 37. On character and republicanism, see Karen Halttunen, *Confidence Men and Painted Women: A Study of Middle-Class Culture in America, 1830–1870* (New Haven: Yale University Press, 1982), 9.

27. On the accusations against Adams, see Remini, *American Freedom*, 130, 134; *Weekly Marylander*, Nov 6, 1828.

28. [Hammond], *General Jackson's Domestic Relations*, 20, 18. For a significant debate about the intent and consciousness of antebellum reformers, see the essays by John Ashworth, David Brion Davis, and Thomas L. Haskell in *The Antislavery Debate: Capitalism and Abolitionism as a Problem in Historical Interpretation*, ed. Thomas Bender (Berkeley: University of California Press, 1992), 107–99. For two pivotal older works stressing the social control side of reform, see Paul Johnson, *A Shopkeeper's Millennium: Society and Revivals in Rochester, New York, 1850–1837* (New York: Hill and Wang, 1978); and Anthony Wallace, *Rockdale: The Growth of an American Village in the Early Industrial Revolution* (New York: Knopf, 1978). For a more plastic view of class, especially as it relates to participation in temperance societies, see Mary P. Ryan, *Cradle of the Middle Class: The Family in Oneida County, New York, 1790–1865* (Cambridge: Cambridge University Press, 1981).

29. *Appeal to the Moral and Religious*, 4; [Hammond], *General Jackson's Domestic Relations*, 18.

30. [Hammond], *General Jackson's Domestic Relations*, 2; *Appeal to the Moral and Religious*, 5.

31. See Mary Poovey, *Uneven Developments: The Ideological Work of Gender in Mid-Victorian England* (Chicago: University of Chicago Press, 1988), 12–13. [Hammond], *General Jackson's Domestic Relations*, 9.

32. On the sexual responsibility of women, see Nancy Cott, "Passionlessness," *Signs* 4 (winter 1978): 219–36; and Nancy Cott, "Divorce and the Changing Status of Women in Eighteenth-Century Massachusetts," *William and Mary Quarterly* 33 (Oct. 1976): 586–614. *Appeal to the Moral and Religious*, 8.

33. *Appeal to the Moral and Religious*, 7; Jesse Strung, *The Confession of Jesse Strung, who was convicted of the Murder of John Whipple, At a Special court of Oyer and Terminer, held in and for the County of Albany, on the fourth day of August 1827* (Albany, 1827).

34. *Political Extracts from a Leading Adams Paper, The Massachusetts Journal, Edited and Published in Boston by David L. Child* (Boston, 1828), 10, 13. This pamphlet is available at the Boston Athenaeum.

35. On promise keeping and contracts, see Thomas L. Haskell, "Capitalism and the Origins of Humanitarian Sensibility, Part 2," in *Antislavery Debate*, 141–46.

36. On the new cognitive style, see ibid., 136, 153. Although divorce had been widely available at the end of the eighteenth century, the Adamsite emphasis on the letter of the law with regard to divorce converged with the legislative efforts of many states to refine their divorce statutes; see Roderick Phillips, *Putting Asunder: A History of Divorce in Western Society* (Cambridge: Cambridge University Press, 1988), 154–58, 439–61. [Hammond], *General Jackson's Domestic Relations*, 8.

37. [Hammond], *General Jackson's Domestic Relations*, 11; *Daily National Journal*, June 22, 1827; see also ibid., Oct. 30, 1828.

38. McCormick, *Party Period and Public Policy*, 47. *Weekly Marylander*, Nov. 6, 1828; *Address of the State Convention of Delegates from the Several Counties of the State of New-York to the People on the Subject of the Approaching Presidential Election* (Albany, 1828), 2.

39. *A Brief Inquiry into Some of the Objections urged Against the Election of Andrew Jackson* (n.p., [1828]), *A Plain Truth* (no. 4, [1828]); *Weekly Marylander*, Oct. 30, 1828; *Address to the People*, 37; *A Short Account of some of the Bloody Deeds of Gen. Jackson* (broadside); *A Mirror for Politicians* (broadside). For a list of the indictments against Jackson's violent and illegal public behavior, including his suspension of habeas corpus, his treatment of the Seminoles, and his penchant for dueling, see Remini, *American Freedom*, 118–24.

40. *Daily National Journal*, Oct. 11, 1828; June 7, 1828; *We the People*, April 12, 1828; *Daily National Journal*, June 24, 1824; *A Voice of Warnings! to the Freemen of Steuben* (broadside). I am indebted here, of course, to Halttunen, *Confidence Men and Painted Women*.

41. For an emphasis on Jacksonian traditionalism, see Lawrence Frederick Kohl, *The Politics of Individualism: Parties and the American Character in the Jacksonian Era* (New York: Oxford University Press, 1989). For Andrew Jackson's readiness to defend his honor, see Kenneth S. Greenberg, "The Nose, the Lie, and the Duel in the Antebellum South," *American Historical Review* 95 (Feb. 1990): 57–74. I am not denying the role of honor in antebellum society, but I am suggesting its diminution, even in the South. Jackson, as Greenberg notes, may have been more than willing to assert his manhood through physical combat, but his supporters' efforts to suppress such combative images suggest a shift was already under way. On the diminution of dueling, see Robert H. Wiebe, *The Opening of American Society: From the Adoption of the Constitution to the Eve of Disunion* (New York: Knopf, 1984), 328–29. On the cult of sensibility, see especially Jan Lewis, *The Pursuit of Happiness: Family and Values in Jefferson's Virginia* (Cambridge: Cambridge University Press, 1983).

42. [John Kintzling Kane], *A Candid View of the Presidential Question, by a Pennsylvanian* (Philadelphia, 1828); *Delaware Democrat & Easton Gazette*, March 13, 1828. On Andrew Jackson's appeal to men who worked by the sweat of their brow, see Kohl, *Politics of Individualism*, 26–27. On his adherence to a higher order of justice, see John William Ward, *Andrew Jackson: Symbol for an Age* (New York: Oxford University Press, 1955), 56–57.

43. *Letter from the Jackson Committee of Nashville*, 3. For a more general defense of Jackson's character, see *Eradication of the Character and Public Services of Andrew Jackson, originally published in the Nashville Republican and attributed to Major Henry Lee* (Boston, 1828),

44. Apart from that of James Parton, Andrew Jackson's engaging nineteenth-century biographer, who had the advantage of interviewing many of Jackson's contemporaries, John Overton's affectionate portrait remains the only extended and intimate view we have of the Jacksons' controversial courtship and marriage. Overton, however, destroyed his correspondence with Jackson, citing the confidential nature of their relationship. See Robert O. Rupp and Robert V. Remini, *Andrew Jackson: A Bibliography* (Westport, CT: Greenwood, 1991), 6. On the tensions between a single, authoritative legal story and other varieties of narrative, see Carol Weisbrod, "Divorce Stories: Readings, Comments, and Questions on Law and Narrative," *Brigham Young University Law Review* (part 1, 1991): 143–96.

45. *A Letter from the Jackson Committee of Nashville*, 4, esp. 24–25. Short's identity is unclear; there are four listed on 1790 tax rolls in Kentucky: see Charles B. Heineman, *"First Census" of Kentucky* (Washington, 401, 1940), 86.

46. *Jackson Committee of Nashville*, 26.

47. Ibid., 4–5, 20, 26–27.

48. Ibid., 13–14, 22–23. The committee insisted that Hugh M'Gary, who had served as a witness against Rachel Robards, never saw her with the general until

September 1791, after their first marriage; he had testified against her out of anger against the general, with whom he had had a disagreement while traveling in Indian country.

49. Ibid., 28–29. For an informed account speculating that they first married in February or March 1791, see Owsley, "Marriages of Rachel Donelson," 491; for a popular account that has them marrying in August 1791 at Springfield, Thomas Green's plantation on the banks of the Mississippi River, near Natchez, see Peggy Robbins, "Andrew and Rachel Jackson," *American History Illustrated* 12 (Aug. 1977): 22–28; for Hammond's skepticism, see *Truth's Advocate and Monthly Anti-Jackson Expositor* (March 1828), 117–18. Andrew Jackson's papers include documents relating to the marriage and divorce of Rachel Donelson and Lewis Robards and to the Jacksons' second marriage, but there are no documents for the first marriage. Two alternative scenarios for the Jacksons' first union come to mind: one is that the first marriage took place in Natchez, a foreign jurisdiction, either before the legislative bill was passed or with the knowledge that the bill was not a divorce decree (perhaps they were attempting to create a legal loophole by marrying in a foreign jurisdiction); the other, which Remini espouses and which seems more plausible, is that they did not formally marry. See Harold D. Moser, Sharon Macpherson, and Charles F. Bryan, *The Papers of Andrew Jackson*, 3 vols. (Knoxville: University of Tennessee Press, 1984), 1:423–28; and Robert V. Remini, *Andrew Jackson and the Course of American Empire, 1767– 1821* (New York: Harper and Row, 1977), 65–67.

50. *Jackson Committee of Nashville*, 14–17.

51. Ibid., 17, 28; see also [Hammond], *General Jackson's Domestic Relations*, 19.

52. Rachel Jackson to Elizabeth Watson, July 18, 1828, cited in Owsley, "Marriages of Rachel Donelson," 491; "A Humble Tribute to the Virtues of the Late Hon. Mrs. Jackson," in Margaret Botsford, *Viola: Heiress of St. Valverde . . . to which is Annexed a Variety of Original Poetical Pieces* (Philadelphia, 1829), 197; *Lines Written for the United States' Telegraph, on the Death of Mrs. Jackson* (broadside). On negative reference groups, see Howe, "Evangelical Movement and Political Culture," 1224–25.

53. On negative reference groups, see Howe, "Evangelical Movement and Political Culture," 1224–25.

54. Tennessee divorce petitions, for example, could carry up to seventy or eighty signatures. See Gale W. Badman and Debbie W. Spero, *Tennessee Divorces, 1791–1858* (Nashville, Tenn., 1985). On the alternatives to legal divorce, see Phillips, *Putting Asunder*, 279–313.

55. On John Adams, see Lewis, "Republican Wife," 693; On the oppositional nature of separate spheres, see John Ashworth, "The Relationship between Capitalism and Humanitarianism," in *Antislavery Debate*, 191–98.

56. Jacqueline Kaye, "John Quincy Adams and *The Conquest of Ireland*," *Eire-Ireland* 16, no. 1 (1981): 34–53.

57. I am grateful to Mary Kelley for pointing out this distinction between the two marital codes in an earlier version of this essay. Michael Grossberg has used these two models to describe the shift in family governance during the nineteenth century that culminated in the special family courts of the early twentieth century: Grossberg, *Governing the Hearth: Law and the Family in Nineteenth-Century America* (Chapel Hill: University of North Carolina Press, 1985).

58. On the potential power of women in radical evangelicalism, see Carroll Smith-Rosenberg, *Disorderly Conduct: Visions of Gender in Victorian America*

(New York: Knopf, 1985), 129–64; John Quincy Adams, *Speech of John Quincy Adams, of Massachusetts, upon the Right of the People, Men and Women, to Petition* . . . (Washington, D.C.: Gales and Seaton, 1838), 65.

59. Paula Baker, "The Domestication of Politics: Women and American Political Society, 1780–1920," *American Historical Review* 89 (June 1984): 620–47. On the role of women in male political parties, see Mary P. Ryan, *Women Public: Between Banners and Ballots, 1825–1880* (Baltimore: John Hopkins University Press, 1990).

60. Among the voluminous feminist critiques of liberalism and the depoliticization of what is private, see especially Catherine A. MacKinnon, *Toward a Feminist Theory of the State* (Cambridge, Mass.: Harvard University Press, 1989), 190–91. On the antebellum drive for property rights, see Norma Basch, *In the Eyes of the Law: Women, Marriage, and Property in Nineteenth-Century New York* (Ithaca, N.Y.: Cornell University Press, 1982). For an important effort to historicize liberalism in the history of French women, see Lynn Hunt, *The Family Romance of the French Revolution* (Berkeley: University of California Press, 1992), 200–4.

61. Karen Lystra, *Searching the Heart: Women, Men, and Romantic Love in Nineteenth-Century America* (New York: Oxford University Press, 1989), 30.

5

Wartime Dialogues on Illicit Sex: White Women and Black Men

Martha Hodes

In the wartime and Reconstruction climate of social upheaval in the American South, sex between white women and black men became a highly charged political issue, spurring whites to a level of public violence unknown under slavery. The subject of sex between white women and black men entered the national political arena during the Civil War in the presidential election campaign of 1864. It was then that the Democratic Party coined the pejorative term "miscegenation" (from the Latin *miscere,* to mix; and *genus,* race) and asserted that Lincoln's Republican party advocated sex and marriage across the color line. Posing as Republicans, a group of Democrats distributed an anonymous booklet advocating political and social equality, and specifically the mixture of black and white.[1] The authors wrote that although the "frenzy of love in the Southern woman for the negro" was rarely acted upon, plantation mistresses had a stake in slavery because it permitted them sexual access to black men. Yet until racial prejudice was overcome, the authors maintained, the "full mystery of sex—the sweet, wild dream of a perfect love—can never be generally known," and thus should white women be entitled to black husbands.[2] The Democratic posers also wrote about the desire of black men for white women, contending, "Our police courts give painful evidence that the passion of the colored race for the white is often so uncontrollable as to overcome the terror of the law."[3] Although the publication was ignored or renounced by most Republicans, and viewed with suspicion by most American readers,[4] the fears on which its authors played were very shortly to be expressed with seriousness by white southerners.

Democratic politicians also brought the specter of sex between white women and black men into wartime and Reconstruction congressional debates about such issues as integrated transportation and schools and black suffrage. In an 1864 Senate exchange about the exclusion of blacks from Washington, D.C., railroad cars, for example, one Maryland Democrat introduced the point that a white woman marrying a black man would provoke a "trembling, anxious, depressing, harassing, crushing fear" on the part of the woman's male family members.[5] Republicans commonly countered such Democratic offensives by presuming the absurdity of the conflation of black suffrage with sexual transgressions across the color line. A Pennsylvania Republican, for example, wondered in 1866 how anyone could believe that marriage with a white woman would result "because a colored man is allowed to drop a little bit of paper in a box."[6] Thus did white southern politicians begin to conflate the newly won political power of black men with the issue of black male sexuality. With the advent of emancipation, southern whites who sought to maintain a racial hierarchy began systematically to invoke the idea that black men posed a grave sexual threat to white women.

White communities in the antebellum South that had been forced to contend with sexual liaisons between white women and black men (in the forms of bastardy or adultery, for example) had rarely given the black men a chance to tell their own stories. The men were not always named in legal documents and, if named, were rarely consulted for the public record.[7] During the tremendous social chaos of the Civil War years, however, the voices of black men on the subject of sex with white women entered the historical record in the chronicles of the national government.

"I will tell you a fact that I have never seen alluded to publicly, and I suppose a man would be scouted who should allude to it publicly; but my relations with colored people have led me to believe that there is a large amount of intercourse between white women and colored men." So Captain Richard J. Hinton, an ardent white abolitionist who commanded black troops during the Civil War, testified in Washington, D.C., in 1863.[8] Captain Hinton spoke before the American Freedmen's Inquiry Commission (AFIC) which had been formed under the War Department of Congress to address the incorporation of emancipated slaves into American society. The AFIC, composed of three white antislavery men, would ultimately propose the establishment of the Freedmen's Bureau to assist former slaves in the transition to free labor.[9]

Captain Hinton was not the only witness to tell the wartime commission that white women and black men in the South had sex. The indexer for the commission, in fact, saw fit to make entries under the letter "I" for "Intercourse between white women and colored men common—Instances of," and "Illicit intercourse between white women & black men not uncommon."[10] James Redpath, another white abolitionist and a self-described revolutionary, had traveled through the South during the 1850s to talk with black residents.[11] While Redpath told the commission about sexual liaisons between white women and black men in considerable detail, he had withheld this knowledge from the public just a few significant years earlier. In his collection of dispatches from the South, published in 1859, Redpath "most solemnly" declared "that in no one instance have I sought either to darken or embellish the truth—to add to, subtract from, or pervert a single statement of the slaves." Yet Redpath had in fact omitted information about sexual liaisons between white women and black men from the book, at one point extolling the chastity of southern white women, and sympathizing with them for the immoral sexual conduct of their white husbands, fathers, and brothers.[12] Perhaps Redpath had understood (along with his publisher) how dangerous to the cause of abolition would be any disclosure of sexual liaisons between white women and black men. Four years later, in the middle of the Civil War, James Redpath, Richard Hinton, and others seized upon the historical moment of social and political change to speak up. As it turned out, in deference to their own political agenda, the officers of the AFIC would suppress the testimony they had heard about sex between white women and black men. Thus, it was only in the brief moment of wartime disruption that the voices of black men were given credence in a public, political arena. The narratives offered in these wartime dialogues (mostly, though not entirely, mediated through the words of white northerners) allow us to move a little bit closer to the truth about sexual liaisons between white women and black men in the antebellum South.

Testifying before the AFIC, James Redpath first elaborated on the depravity of white men who sexually exploited slave women, prompting one of the commissioners to ask: "Well sir, among such a universal system of libertinage what is the effect upon white women?" Of his black informants, Redpath said: "I have often heard them talking and laughing about the numerous cases that have occurred in which white women have had colored children." One black man told Redpath that "it was just as common for colored men to have connection with white women, as for white men to have to do with colored women." Another said that "it was an extremely common thing among all the handsome mulattoes in the South to have connection with the white women." Redpath relayed an episode of a white woman "of good family" in Mobile, Alabama, who carried on an affair with a slave, had sex with him on the morning of her wedding, and bore his child nine months later. Redpath concluded: "[T]here is a great deal more of this than the public suspect."[13]

Another white man, Major George Stearnes, told the commissioners: "I have often been amused that the planters here in Tennessee have sometimes to watch their daughters to keep them from intercourse with the negroes. This, though of course exceptional, is yet common enough to be a source of uneasiness to parents."[14] And Samuel Lucille, also white, told the commissioners that in Mississippi the "cross between a white woman and a black man" was "not uncommon," adding: "I knew well a ferry man on the Wachita river, whose mother was a white woman and his father a black man. He was a free voter, but it was notorious in the neighborhood that he was a half-blooded negro."[15]

Richard Hinton told the AFIC in no uncertain terms that white women in the South sought out sex with black men. A black Mississippi River steamboat steward named Patrick H. Miner (he was the son of a white plantation owner in New Orleans, and a graduate of Oberlin College[16]) told Hinton about the women of a particular white family. According to Miner, "the colored men on that river knew that the women of the Ward family of Louisville, Kentucky, were in the habit of having the stewards, or other fine looking fellows, sleep with them when they were on the boats." Miner also relayed a personal anecdote about a Ward woman who, when on Miner's boat, had offered him five dollars and "told him to come to her house at Louisville on a certain day, giving him particular directions as to the door at which he was to knock." Upon arrival, Miner was "shown to the room adjoining her bedroom," where he waited until he had to return to work. Although the rendezvous never took place, Miner "had no doubt that she wanted him to have connection with her."[17] Another story offered by Hinton concerned the Missouri frontier, where white settlers from North Carolina and Tennessee had grown richer; the daughters in these families were envious of their brothers who "got a flashy education, which they completed in the slave quarters and the bar-room." As Hinton understood it: "The girls knew that their brothers were sleeping with the chambermaids, or other servants, and I don't see how it could be otherwise than that they too should give loose to their passions."[18] Redpath had heard similar stories. When pressed on how liaisons with white women came to pass, one black man had told Redpath: "'I will tell you how it is here. I will go up with the towels, and when I go into the room the woman will keep following me with her eyes, until I take notice of it, and one thing leads to another. Others will take hold of me and pull me on to the sofa, and others will stick out their foot and ask one to tie their boot, and I will take hold of their foot, and say 'what a pretty foot.'"[19]

Most antebellum documents regarding liaisons between white women and black men concern women from the servant or yeoman classes, women whose families did not command the social authority to stay out of court for transgressions such as bastardy or adultery.[20] The narratives of the black men as recorded in the wartime testimony, on the other hand, also concern illicit liaisons with planters' daughters or plantation mistresses, and specifically illuminate the phenomenon of the sexual coercion of black men by white women. Again in no uncertain terms, Hinton informed the commission that white women of the planter classes could force black men into having sex with them. In southern slave society, men of the planter classes ruled, but white women of slaveholding families also commanded power over slaves, both female and male.[21] While scholars have documented the sexual exploitation of black women by white men,[22] the voices of black men, recorded during the Civil War years, point to a consequence of slave society that has remained unexplored.

"I have never yet found a bright looking colored man, whose confidence I have won," Hinton said, "who has not told me of instances where he has been compelled, either by his mistress, or by white women of the same class, to have connection with them." Hinton recounted a conversation with a white Kansas doctor who knew "from his experience in Virginia and Missouri, that a very large number of white women, especially the daughters of the smaller planters, who were brought into more direct relations with the negro, had compelled some one of the men to have something to do with them."[23] A former slave likewise told Hinton about his experiences with his forty-year-old widowed mistress. The man, who had been "brought up in the family," said he had "never had anything to do with his mistress until after her husband died," but that almost a year into her widowhood, the woman "ordered him to sleep with her, and he did regularly."[24]

A black underground railroad agent named Captain Matthews told Hinton about another black man who relayed that "a young girl got him out in the woods and told him she would declare he attempted to force her, if he didn't have connection with her." The black steward, Patrick Miner, told Hinton "several cases of the same kind."[25] Although the class status of the women in these last incidents remained unspecified, poorer white women might not have attempted such a threat. Those who held authority in antebellum southern communities were likely to consider white women outside the planter classes to be the depraved agents of their illicit liaisons with black men.[26] White women of the planter classes, however, were protected by an ideology of white female virtue. Redpath asked one black man who had spoken of sexual liaisons with planter-class women: "'Do you dare to make advances?'" to which the man answered, "'No, we know too much for that.'" Of the white daughters on the Missouri frontier, Hinton said: "It was a great deal safer for them to have one of these colored fellows than a white man."[27] This point was corroborated by one of Redpath's informants, who pointed out: "'If I have connection with a white girl she knows that if she takes precautions she is safe, for if I should tell I should be murdered by her father, her brother, or herself.'"[28]

During Hinton's testimony, one of the commissioners prompted him: "But the consequences are terrible to the negro if found out?" When Hinton agreed, the commissioner asked: "What are the consequences to the woman if found out?" to which Hinton replied: "They generally brush it up."[29] This testimony is supported by an antebellum North Carolina case in which a white woman had local justices of the peace record an oath that the father of her bastard child was white, when many people knew that the father had been one of the family's slaves.[30] Planter-class white women were also more likely to have access to effective birth control, as indicated by the words of Redpath's informant about taking precautions. The black man who had been ordered to sleep with his widowed mistress told Hinton that the woman had "procured some of those French articles, that are used to prevent the consequences of sexual intercourse," a reference to condoms.[31] Another black man had told Redpath that white women (of more well-to-do families) and black men had sex "because the thing can be so easily concealed. The woman has only to avoid being impregnated, and it is all safe."[32] While dominant ideas about the depravity of poorer white women could in fact serve to override blame for black men with whom those women entered into sexual liaisons, it was both more dangerous for black men to consort with planter-class white women and more dangerous for them to resist sexual coercion by those women.

Questions about agency and consent are difficult to untangle in a slave society. If a coerced slave man complied with a white woman, that compliance was in some measure strategic; and just as some black women chose to risk fending off white men, some black men who were propositioned also chose to risk refusal.[33] At the same time, the wartime testimony before the AFIC points to well-guarded circles of black men, both free and slave, as one arena in which black men expressed defiance about sex with white women. Recall the words of the steamboat steward Patrick Miner, who said that black men who worked on the Mississippi River shared information among themselves about the desires of certain white women to "sleep with them." Recall Redpath's words about his informants, who were slaves in the 1850s: "I have often heard them talking and laughing about the numerous cases that have occurred in which white women have had colored children." Even if Hinton and Redpath were exaggerating their roles as insiders, there is no reason to doubt that black men traded information and laughed together about their defiance of law and taboo.

Moreover, the possibility of men like Hinton and Redpath having fabricated their testimony before the AFIC is contradicted by more direct, if rarer, records of black voices. In her 1861 autobiography, for example, fugitive slave Harriet Jacobs wrote of planters' daughters: "They know that the women slaves are subject to their father's authority in all things; and in some cases they exercise the same authority over the men slaves. I have myself seen the master of such a household whose head was bowed down in shame; for it was known in the neighborhood that his daughter had selected one of the meanest slaves on his plantation to be the father of his first grandchild." Jacobs pointed out that this white woman "did not make her advances to her equals, nor even to her father's more intelligent servants." Rather, this woman "selected the most brutalized, over whom her authority could be exercised with less fear of exposure."[34] Just after the war, the black press in the South made reference to coercion by white women. An 1866 essay in the Augusta, Georgia, *Colored American* noted that white men feared that white women would marry newly freed black men, and added that the white man "seems to be afraid that some of his daughters may do what a good many of his sons and himself have done time and again."[35] If there were such a thing as a consensual sexual relationship between a black man, either slave or free, and a white woman, black men talking to white abolitionists like Hinton and Redpath may have crafted their narratives as stories of coercion in order to present themselves as innocent participants in such legal and social transgressions. Yet stories of reluctance and resistance, even if crafted for white ears, would not have been fabricated out of imagination alone; rather, their tellers would be drawing upon dynamics that they knew to exist between white women and black men.[36] Although we have no way of knowing how common or uncommon were scenarios such as those the black men described to Hinton and Redpath, their words uncover a ground of coercion in the slave South that lurked as a possibility regardless of how often it was acted upon.

While dominant white southern ideology about female sexuality exempted planter-class women from convictions of depravity, northerners were less convinced of this distinction among the white women of the South. The theme of profligacy among white southerners of all classes was common in northern antislavery thought, and Hinton and other witnesses before the AFIG unmistakably drew upon this tradition in their wartime testimony.[37] Hinton's portrayal of all southern white women was one of total licentiousness. "The complete demoralization of the South is astonishing," he told the commissioners. "I have seen white women who call themselves ladies, stand on the street and call minor officers, as they were passing by, 'sons of bitches,' 'God damn' them, and use all such phrases; and I have never been to any locality where the officers and men, who were so disposed, did not sleep with all the women around."[38]

Another white northern man described the white men and women of the Gulf States, saying that "a more degraded, profligate, ignorant and sinful race cannot easily be imagined."[39] In one printed report, commissioner Samuel Howe wrote: "[I]t is certain that the inevitable tendency of American slavery is not only to bring about promiscuous intercourse among the blacks, and between black women and white men, but also to involve white women in the general depravity, and to lower the standard of female purity." Howe continued: "The subject is repulsive, but whoever examines critically the evidence of the social conditions of the Slave States, sees that the vaunted superior virtue of the Southern women is mere boast and sham."[40] (White southerners, for their part, counteraccused northern white women of promiscuity, fastening particularly upon those who came South to teach in the freedpeople's schools. One southern white man wrote in 1864 about "Yankee 'School marms' who philanthropically miscegenate as well as teach," noting sarcastically "the prolific birth of mongrel babies by these worthy school mistresses."[41])

The wartime testimony also indicates that black convictions about the sexuality of southern white women were in accord with those of white northerners. The sentiments of a black man who had fled the South for Canada were likely shared by others; the town's white mayor reported to the wartime commission: "A colored man ran away with a white girl, and a colored man, speaking of the affair, said 'I always looked upon him as a respectable man. I didn't think he would fall so low as to marry a white girl.'"[42] Even approval on the part of black communities indicates black convictions of the depraved nature of white women. A black bishop from the British Methodist Episcopal Church, who had also left the South for Canada, told the commissioners that when a white woman and a black man got married, "If the man is an upright man, and the woman an upright woman, they treat them as if they were both colored." This man also mentioned two white women married to black men who were both accorded as much respect as "any black woman."[43]

White ideologies about black male sexuality in the slave South were far from straightforward. Black men had been accused and convicted of raping white women, in the context of a racist legal system, since the colonial era, and the castration and lynching of black men for the alleged sexual assault of white women was not unknown in either the antebellum or wartime South.[44] On the other hand, while whites feared slave uprisings during the Civil War, no great tide of sexual alarm engulfed white southerners as white men left white women at home with slave men. One white schoolteacher, for example, wrote in her Tennessee diary about a group of armed black men who were being mustered out of service. "If these corrupted negroes are to be turned loose among us," she commented in a manner that can hardly be characterized as terrified, "I do not know what will follow, but evidently no great amount of good."[45] If anything, white women left alone were inclined to see white Yankee soldiers as sexually threatening.[46]

The wartime testimony indicates as well that white northerners were ambivalent about black male sexuality. Richard Hinton both invoked and contradicted the idea of black men as especially sexual; at the same time that he accepted the idea of black male sexual ardor, Hinton presented black men as reluctant to comply with the sexual aggression of white women. When Hinton spoke about the white woman who took a black man into the woods and threatened to cry rape if he didn't have sex with her, one of the commissioners commented: "He didn't need much persuasion, did he?" Hinton answered: "I have generally found that, unless the woman has treated them kindly, and won their confidence, they have to be threatened, or have their passions roused by actual contact, which a woman who goes as far as that would not hesitate to give." Elsewhere, however, Hinton sustained white ideas about black male potency. For example, he concluded the story of the Missouri frontier daughters who wished to "give loose to their passions" by saying, "and I suppose, as the negro is very strongly amative, that the gratification of passion would be greater with them than with a white man."[47]

In the end, the American Freedmen's Inquiry Commission kept the testimony they had heard about sex between white women and black men a secret from the secretary of war and from Congress. Hinton's testimony had covered thirty-two pages, with the information on white women and black men occupying the last six of those pages. On the cover sheet, someone had penciled: "This paper can be printed as far as this mark x on page 27. The remaining portion should be suppressed." The "x" marked Hinton's disclosure about sex between white women and black men.[48] Neither of the two major reports printed by the AFIC addressed the subject of sex between white women and black men. The commission clearly judged it too detrimental to let the secretary of war and Congress, or any other readers, believe that emancipation would bring sex between white women and black men in its wake, especially if such liaisons could not be written off as the province of the poorer classes of white women.

Ultimately, it was the conflation of politics and sex in the minds of white southerners that would generate so much of the Reconstruction-era violence in the South. With the demise of slavery, the separation of black and white became essential to white southerners who wished to retain racial supremacy. Thus did sex across the color line become a much more severe taboo than it had ever been before. Because it was the men among the former slave population who gained political power, and therefore had the potential to destroy the racial caste system, southern whites focused on the taboo of sex between white women and black men with a new urgency. Sexual transgressions in the form of liaisons between white women and black men that had previously been the province of local communities and courts took on national political dimensions after the war.[49] In testimony about the Ku Klux Klan taken before Congress in 1871, white southerners often charged black men with illicit sexual conduct toward or with white women alongside charges of Republican activism or successful crops, that is, for political or economic independence.[50]

To separate politics and sexuality at this moment in the history of the American South would be to define politics far too narrowly. When a congressional investigating committee asked a North Carolina Klansman about the purpose of his organization, the man said: "It was to keep down the colored un's from mixing with the whites." And by what means would this be accomplished? "To keep them from marrying, and to keep them from voting," he answered.[51] Another white North Carolina man said: "[T]he common white people of the country are at times very much enraged against the negro population. They think that this universal political and civil equality will finally bring about social equality." He added: "[T]here are already instances . . . in which poor white girls are having negro children."[52] After the war, then, with the determination of white southerners to retain dominance through the construction of a rigid color line, whites conflated the new political power of black men with sexual transgressions against white women.

While white ideology about the hypersexuality of all black men developed swiftly from emancipation forward, the twin ideology about the purity of all white women never took on the same ironclad quality. Rather, class distinctions in white ideology about white female sexuality remained.[53] The reputation and character of white women was constantly assessed by white southerners in the 1871 congressional testimony about the Klan, and the investigating committee participated in this discourse, with both sides identifying white female transgressors as "lowdown," as "tramps," and as women of "bad character."[54] The sexual coercion of black men by white women was in fact still understood to be a possibility. In the narrative of freedman Henry Lowther, who survived castration by Klansmen, one white witness said that the white woman with whom Lowther was accused of consorting had followed Lowther into the woods and "solicited him to have intercourse with her." Of this woman, a white judge remarked, "the inference I drew was that she was a very bad, abandoned character."[55] White women judged by the Klansmen to be lacking in virtue were, like black women, also subject to abuse ranging from insulting language to rape and sexual mutilation.[56]

The wartime dialogues on sex between white women and black men got no farther than a government commission composed of three white, northern, abolitionist men. Yet the voices of black men recorded therein now serve to better illuminate both the nature of sexual liaisons between white women and black men in the slave South, and white ideologies of sexuality in the crucial transitional period of war and emancipation. At the same time, the wartime suppression of the testimony, along with southern white's conflation of black male power and black male sexuality, indicate how sex between white women and black men came to be a deeply political issue connected directly to the maintenance of racial hierarchy from emancipation forward.

NOTES

1. [David Croly and George Wakeman], *Miscegenation: The Theory of the Blending of the Races, Applied to the American White Man and Negro* (New York, 1863).

2. Ibid., 43–44, 51. This might well be a parody of free-love language.

3. Ibid., 28.

4. James McPherson, *Battle Cry of Freedom: The Civil War Era* (New York: Ballantine, 1988), 789–91; Sidney Kaplan, "The Miscegenation Issue in the Election of 1864," *Journal of Negro History* 34 (1949): 274–343; Forrest Wood, *Black Scare: The Racist Response to Emancipation and Reconstruction* (Berkeley: University of California Press, 1968), chap. 4.

5. *Congressional Globe*, 38th Cong., 1st sess., pt. 2, March 17,1864, p. 1157. In 1866, a Democratic senator from Kentucky announced that the establishment of the Freedmen's Bureau would mean that black men could marry white women in violation of his state's laws. *Congressional Globe*, 39th Cong., lst sess., pt. 1, Jan. 25, 1866, p. 418.

6. *Congressional Globe*, 39th Cong., 1st sess., pt. 1, Jan. 10, 1866, pp. 179, 180. In 1868, a Michigan Republican asked if those who professed such fears would feel obliged to arrange a social visit "because your ballot and theirs had been mingled in the same box?" And, he elaborated, "should your ballot and that of a black man happen to be placed in juxtaposition, would you for that reason at once deem it incumbent on you to give your daughter in marriage to the 'American citizen of African descent'?" *Congressional Globe*, 40th Cong., 2nd sess., pt. 2, March 18, 1868, p. 1970.

7. Martha Hodes, "Sex across the Color Line: White Women and Black Men in the Nineteenth-Century American South" (Ph.D. diss., Princeton University, 1991), esp. chaps. 2, 3, 4.

8. Testimony of Captain Richard J. Hinton, American Freedmen's Inquiry Commission, Letters Received, Office of the Adjutant General, Main Series, 1861–70, record group 94, M619, reels 199–201 (hereafter cited as AFIC), file 8,

National Archives, Washington, D.C. (hereafter cited as NA); grammar and spelling have been altered slightly for readability in all quotations. Hinton also served as an army correspondent in Kansas, Missouri, and Tennessee; wrote Abraham Lincoln's campaign biography; organized the Kansas Emancipation League in 1862 to aid four thousand former slaves; admired John Brown; and wrote for the *National Anti-Slavery Standard*. See Herbert Gutman, *The Black Family in Slavery and Freedom, 1750–1925* (New York: Pantheon Books, 1976), 613 n. 9; James McPherson, *The Struggle for Equality: Abolitionists and the Negro in the Civil War and Reconstruction* (Princeton, N.J.: Princeton University Press, 1964), 20, 170, 424.

9. The commissioners were Samuel Gridley Howe, a Boston physician and advocate for the blind and deaf; James McKaye, a New York activist against slavery; and Robert Dale Owen, a freethinker and advocate of birth control and sexual equality. On the purposes of the commission, see *War of the Rebellion: A Compilation of the Official Records of the Union and Confederate Armies* (Washington, D.C.: Government Printing Office, 1880–1901), ser. 3, vol. 3, pp. 73–74; and *Congressional Globe*, 38th Cong., 1st sess., 1864, pp. 2799–800. On recommendations of the commission, see: "Preliminary Report of the American Freedmen's Inquiry Commission," *War of the Rebellion*, ser. 3, vol. 3, pp. 430–54; "Final Report of the American Freedmen's Inquiry Commission," *War of the Rebellion*, ser. 3, vol. 4, pp. 289–382; John Sproat, "Blueprint for Radical Reconstruction," *Journal of Southern History* 23 (1957): 25–44; McPherson, *Struggle for Equality*, 182–87; Eric Foner, *Reconstruction: America's Unfinished Revolution, 1863–1877* (New York: Harper and Row, 1988), 68–69.

10. AFIC, General index, file 8 index, file 7 index, NA.

11. James Redpath, *The Roving Editor, or Talks with Slaves in Southern States* (New York: A. A. Burdick, 1859), vi, 2; Charles Homer, *The Life of James Redpath and the Development of the Modern Lyceum* (New York: Barse & Hopkins, 1926), 24, 40; McPherson, *Struggle for Equality*, 6, 127, n. 128, 155, 388–89.

12. Redpath, *Roving Editor*, 2–3, 140–41, 184, 234–35, 257–58.

13. Testimony of James Redpath, AFIC file 9, NA.

14. Testimony of Major George Steamnes, AFIC file 7, NA.

15. Testimony of Samuel B. Lucille, AFIC file 7, NA. Lucille also said: "I believe the instances at the South where a yellow woman breeds with a fullblooded black man are fewer than where a black man has breeded on a white woman." See also testimony of Dr. James H. Richardson, AFIC, file 10, NA; J. P. Litchfield to Samuel Gridley Howe, Sept. 7, 1863, American Freedmen's Inquiry Commission Papers, Houghton Library, Harvard University (hereafter cited as HL).

16. Slaveholders were known to send the children they had fathered by slave women to Oberlin College in the nineteenth century, and records indicate that Colonel Miner was one of them. See Robert Samuel Fletcher, *A History of Oberlin College From Its Foundation through the Civil War* (Oberlin, OH: Oberlin College, 1943), 528, 535–36; James Fairchild, *Oberlin: The Colony and the College, 1833–1883* (Oberlin, OH: Oberlin College, 1883), 111.

17. Testimony of Richard Hinton, AFIC file 8, NA.

18. Ibid.

19. Testimony of James Redpath, AFIC file 9, NA. Incidentally, the confession of the Mobile woman who had intercourse with her slave on her wedding day included the information that the man "came up to tie her boots the morning of her marriage, and had connection with her before the ceremony."

20. According to Bertram Wyatt-Brown and Catherine Clinton, women of the planter class were under too much scrutiny to be able to commit sexual offenses, while poorer women had an easier time of it; see Wyatt-Brown, *Southern Honor:*

Ethics and Behavior in the Old South (New York: Oxford University Press, 1982), 298; Clinton, *The Plantation Mistress: Woman's World in the Old South* (New York: Pantheon, 1982), 72–73. Wyatt-Brown also surmises that white women had heard so much about the ardent sexuality of black men that they were curious to see for themselves if it was true (*Southern Honor,* 316). Of planter-class white women, Elizabeth Fox-Genovese writes: "That some southern white women took black lovers could be freely acknowledged, for it was assumed that the women were lower class and disreputable. But ladies? Through the wall of silence seeped gossip and occasional hard facts. Liaisons between white ladies and black men may have occurred rarely, but they did occur, not only in cities . . . but on the plantations"; and: "a few committed the ultimate rebellion against the dominance of white males by having sexual relations with black men." See Fox-Genovese, *Within the Plantation Household: Black and White Women of the Old South* (Chapel Hill: University of North Carolina Press, 1988), 208, 241.

21. While those white women did suffer from and lament the abuses of the men who ruled their households and plantations, they did not, for the most part, challenge that authority. See Fox-Genovese, *Plantation Household,* 145; also 24, 49, 97–98, 101–2, 192–93, 243, 326, 334, 359; George Rable, *Civil Wars: Women and the Crisis of Southern Nationalism* (Urbana: University of Illinois Press, 1989), chap. 2 and *passim.*

22. On black women and white men in the slave South, see Deborah Gray White, *Ar'n't I a Woman?: Female Slaves in the Plantation South* (New York: Pantheon Books, 1985), 33–46; Wyatt-Brown, *Southern Honor,* 237, 297–98, 307–15, 319–24; Eugene Genovese, *Roll, Jordan, Roll: The World the Slaves Made* (New York: Norton, 1972), 413–31, 461; Gutman, *Black Family,* 83–84, 386–96, 399–402; Clinton, *Plantation Mistress,* 211–20; James Hugo Johnston, *Race Relations in Virginia and Miscegenation in the South, 1776–1860* (Amherst: University of Massachusetts Press, 1970), chap. 9; Richard Steckel, "Miscegenation and the American Slave Schedules," *Journal of Interdisciplinary History* 11 (1980): 251–63; Steven Brown, "Sexuality and the Slave Community," *Phylon* 42 (1981): 7–8; C. Vann Woodward, *American Counterpoint: Slavery and Racism in the North-South Dialogue* (Boston: Little, Brown, 1964), 47–48, 75. For a primary source, see Harriet Jacobs, *Incidents in the Life of a Slave Girl, Written by Herself,* ed. Jean Fagan Yellin (Cambridge, MA: Harvard University Press, 1987).

23. Testimony of Richard Hinton, AFIC file 8, NA.

24. Ibid.

25. Ibid.

26. Poorer white women who attempted to coerce black men could be held responsible for the illicit liaison. In an 1813 Virginia case, for example, a slave was pardoned after he went on a violent rampage in the home of a white family because he had been coerced into "a considerable intimacy" by the daughter over several years. See Letters to Governor James Barbour, Oct. 5, 1813, Executive Papers, Letters Received, Virginia State Library and Archives, Richmond (hereafter cited as VSLA). In an 1825 Virginia case about a married white woman and a neighborhood slave, the man's master testified: "I have good reason for believing this man of mine has been disposed to forsake this woman, which has produced considerable discontent in her, and has been the cause of her often visiting my negro houses and staying all night in the quarters." The woman was censured, while the man suffered no public retribution. See Deposition of John Richardson, Jan. 18, 1825, Lewis Bourne Divorce Petition, Louisa County, Jan. 20, 1825, no. 8305, Legislative Papers, VSLA. See also Hodes, "Sex across the Color Line," chap. 2, 3.

27. Testimony of Richard Hinton, AFIC file 8,, NA.

28. Testimony of James Redpath, AFIC file 9, NA.

29. Testimony of Richard Hinton, AFIC file 8, NA.

30. Benjamin Sherwood to "B. S. Hedrick and family," speech delivered in Iowa, April 7, 1860, Benjamin Sherwood Hedrick Papers, William Perkins Library, Duke University, Durham (hereafter cited as WPL).

31. Testimony of Richard Hinton, AFIC file 8, NA; Linda Gordon, *Woman's Body, Woman's Right: A Social History of Birth Control in America* (New York: Vintage, 1977), 44.

32. Testimony of James Redpath, AFIC file 9, NA. Failing access to effective birth control, planter-class women also resorted to infanticide to protect themselves and their partners. A black man told Hinton about a planter's daughter in Missouri who had given birth to a "black child," and refused to reveal the father's name until the man had escaped to Kansas. "The child was reported to have died," Hinton said, "but the man believes it was killed," AFIC file 8, NA. See also Jacobs, *Incidents,* 52. For an earlier case of planter-class infanticide, see *King vs. Sarah Wiggins,* Secretary of State Court Records, box 3, 12, April–May 1772, Dobbs County, North Carolina Department of Archives and History, Raleigh.

33. It is illuminating here to apply Orlando Patterson's discussion of male slaveholders and female slaves to sexual liaisons between white women and black men. "I know of no slaveholding society in which a master, when so inclined, could not exact sexual services from his female slaves," Patterson writes, later adding: "What masters and slaves do is struggle: sometimes noisily, more often quietly; sometimes violently, more often surreptitiously; infrequently with arms, always with the weapons of the mind and soul." See Patterson, *Slavery and Social Death: A Comparative Study* (Cambridge, MA: Harvard University Press, 1982), 173, 207.

34. Jacobs, *Incidents,* 52.

35. "Equality," in *Colored American* (Augusta, GA), Jan. 6, 1866.

36. Antebellum documents support the phenomenon of coercion by planter-class women less directly. See, for example, Benjamin Sherwood to "B. S. Hedrick and family," April 7, 1860, Hedrick Papers, WPL. For a case regarding a female slaveowner and her male slave, see *Armstrong vs. Hodges,* in Ben Monroe, *Reports of Cases at Common Law and in Equity Decided in the Court of Appeals of Kentucky* (fall 1841), 69–71.

37. See Ronald Walters, *The Anti-Slavery Appeal: American Abolitionism after 1830* (New York: Norton, 1978), chap. 5. Some elite white women joined in the chorus of voices about the depravity of southern white men; see Mary Chesnut, *Mary Chesnut's Civil War,* ed. C. Vann Woodward (New Haven: Yale University Press, 1981), 29, 169; Nell Irvin Painter, "The Journal of Ella Gertrude Clanton Thomas: An Educated White Woman in the Eras of Slavery, War, and Reconstruction," in *The Secret Eye: The Journal of Ella Gertrude Clanton Thomas, 1848–1889,* ed. Virginia Ingraham Burr (Chapel Hill: University of North Carolina Press, 1990), 55–56.

38. Testimony of Richard Hinton, AFIC file 8, NA. Confederate women felt they were responding in kind to insolent Yankee soldiers; see, for example, Laura Lee Diary, Winchester, VA, March 11, April 18, May 15, June 5, 7, 1862, Earl Gregg Swem Library, College of William and Mary, Williamsburg, Va.; Amanda Chappelear Diary, April 19, 1862, Virginia Historical Society, Richmond (hereafter cited as VHS); Mary Rawson Diary, Sept. 6, 1864, Atlanta Historical Society (hereafter cited as AHS); Kate Hester Robson Memoirs (1910), 23, AHS; George Rable, *Civil Wars,* 164; Drew Gilpin Faust, "Altars of Sacrifice: Confederate Women and the Narratives of War," *Journal of American History* 76 (1990): 1213.

39. Letter from L. B. Cotes, Oct. 31, 1863, AFIC Papers, HL.

40. Samuel Howe, *The Refugees from Slavery in Canada West: Report to the Freedmen's Inquiry Commission* (Boston, 1864), 333, 94; for the manuscript version of the report (almost the same), see AFIC, "The Self-Freedmen of Canada West, Supplemental Report A of the AFIC," May 14, 1864, NA.

41. John C. Gorman Diary-Memoir, 1864, p. 55, John C. Gorman Papers, WPL. Southern white women also expressed disgust at the fraternization of white Yankee soldiers and black women; see, for example, Eliza Andrews, *The War-Time Journal of a Georgia Girl, 1864–1865*, ed. Spencer King (Macon, GA: Ardivan Press, 1960), 267, 306.

42. Testimony of Mayor Cross, AFIC file 10, NA; see also testimony of John Kinney, Mr. Sinclair, and Col. W. W. Stephenson, file 10, NA. In the North, black antislavery agitator David Walker said in 1829: "I would not give a *pinch of snuff* to be married to any white person I ever saw in all the days of my life. And I do say it, that the black man, or man of color, who will leave his own color (provided he can get one who is good for any thing) and marry a white woman, to be a double slave to her just because she is *white,* ought to be treated by her as he surely will be, viz; as a NIGER!!!" *David Walker's Appeal, with a Brief Sketch of His Life: By Henry Highland Garnet* (New York, 1848), 19.

43. Testimony of Bishop Green, AFIC file 10, NA; see also testimony of Rev. Dr. McCaul, file 10, NA.

44. See Donna Spindel, *Crime and Society in North Carolina, 1663–1776* (Baton Rouge: Louisiana State University Press, 1989), 109; Philip Schwarz, *Twice Condemned: Slaves and the Criminal Laws of Virginia* (Baton Rouge: Louisiana State University Press, 1988), 21–22, 72, 82–84, 150–52, 155–64, 179–80, 202–10, 291–95. For lynchings of black men for the alleged rape of white women during the war years, see *Daily Sun* (Columbus, Ga.), Feb. 22, March 2, 29, Dec. 5, 1861; *Southern Banner* (Athens, Ga.), July 16, 23, 1862.

45. Abbie M. Brooks Diary, May 9, 1865, AHS. See also Mary T. Hunley Diary, March 19, May 13, 1864, Southern Historical Collection, University of North Carolina, Chapel Hill, N.C. (hereafter cited as SHC); Ann Bridges to Charles E. Bridges, July 17, 1865, Charles E. Bridges Papers, WPL; Grace B. Elmore Diary, Oct. 1, 1865, SHC.

46. See, for example, Emma J. Slade Prescott Reminiscences, 1881, vol. 2, p. 9 , AHS. On sexual violence against southern white women by Yankee soldiers, see, for example, Sydney S. Champion to Matilda Champion, April 4, 1863, Sydney S. Champion Papers, WPL. See also Rable, *Civil Wars,* 161, 341, n. 25. Some white women alluded to fears of a conspiracy between Yankee soldiers and black men; see Amanda Chappelear Diary, Aug. 24, 1862, VHS; Louisa Quitman Lovell to Capt. Joseph Lovell, Feb. 7, 1864, Quitman Family Papers, SHC.

47. Testimony of Richard Hinton, AFIC file 8, NA. Fox-Genovese has noted the contradictory images of the virile "Buck" and the docile "Sambo" attributed to black men by whites in the slave South; see *Plantation Household,* 291. Winthrop Jordan has traced perceptions of black men and women as bestial and lustful to early British accounts of West Africa, and before that to early modern European literature that connected Africans with lasciviousness; see Jordan, *White Over Black: American Attitudes toward the Negro, 1550–1812* (1968; reprint, New York: Oxford University Press, 1977), 579; see also 32–43, 151–62, 398–99. Fox-Genovese and Genovese, however, both correctly point out that the idea of black male hypersexuality fully formed in white minds only after emancipation; see Fox-Genovese, *Plantation Household,* 291; Genovese, *Roll, Jordan, Roll,* 422, 461–62. See also Leon Litwack, *Been*

in the Storm So Long: The Aftermath of Slavery (New York: Knopf, 1979), 265–66; Jacquelyn Dowd Hall, *Revolt against Chivalry: Jessie Daniel Ames and the Women's Campaign against Lynching* (New York: Columbia University Press, 1979), 131–32.

48. Testimony of Richard Hinton, AFIC file 8, NA.

49. Hodes, *Sex across the Color Line,* chaps. 2, 3, 4, 6; see also Nell Irvin Painter, "A Prize-Winning Book Revisited," *Journal of Women's History* 2 (1991): 132–33.

50. Two extremely illuminating cases are those of Jordan Ware and Henry Lowther, both in Georgia. See *Testimony Taken by the Joint Select Committee to Inquire into the Condition of Affairs in the Late Insurrectionary States,* 42nd Cong., 2nd sess., no. 41, 1871 (hereafter cited as *KKK Report*), pt. 6, pp. 21–22, 30–31, 44–46, 74–75, 130 (Ware); and pt. 6, pp. 356–63, 426, 430–31, 443 (Lowther). See also Testimony of John W. Long, Ku Klux Klan Papers, WPL. In the minds of Klansmen and their sympathizers, the rape of white women was the logical extreme to which black men would go without the institution of slavery to restrain them; see, for example, *KKK Report,* pt. 6, p. 124; pt. 7, pp. 833, 835–36, 842–45; pt. 9, p. 1260; pt. 13, pp. 6–7, 14–15. See also Wyatt-Brown, *Southern Honor,* 453–54.

51. *KKK Report,* pt. 2, p. 434; see also pt. 7, pp. 1113–14.

52. Ibid., pt. 2, p. 318.

53. Genovese notes that white convictions about the sexual promiscuity of black women took precedence over ideas about black male sexuality in order to excuse sexual exploitation by male slaveholders could be excused; see *Roll, Jordan, Roll,* 461–62. But whites' focus on the presumed depravity of black women was also crucially accompanied by convictions about the depravity of white women outside the planter classes; it was these beliefs that could overshadow ideas about the hypersexuality of black men in the antebellum South.

54. See, for example, *KKK Report,* pt. 2, pp. 371–72; pt. 6, pp. 108–9, 125, 291–92; pt. 7, pp. 920–21; pt. 10, p. 1854. Black men and women used the same language to describe white women; see, for example, *KKK Report,* pt. 6, p. 362, 407–8, 412, 472; pt. 7, p. 1010.

55. *KKK Report,* pt. 6, p. 431.

56. See, for example, *KKK Report,* pt. 2, pp. 4, 37; pt. 7, pp. 1007, 1022, 1096, 1120; pt. 8, pp. 476, 549–51; pt. 9, pp. 771, 956; pt. 12, pp. 652, 672, 823, 839, 870, 912, 922–23, 1075, 1144, 1165–66; pt. 13, p. 137. On the treatment of black women by Klansmen, see, for example, *KKK Report,* pt. 2, pp. 36–37, 49, 148; pt. 6, pp. 75, 140–41, 375–77, 387; pt. 7, pp. 914, 1004; pt. 8, pp. 79–80, 547, 553; pt. 9, pp. 930, 1188, 1189; pt. 11, pp. 38–39; pt. 12, p. 1084.

6

Free, Indentured, Enslaved: Chinese Prostitutes in Nineteenth-Century America

Lucie Cheng

In societies undergoing rapid industrialization, prostitution serves a double economic function. It helps to maintain the labor force of single young men, which is in the interest of the capitalists who would otherwise have to pay higher wages to laborers with families to support. In addition, prostitution enables entrepreneurs to extract large profits from the work of women under their control and thus accumulate considerable capital for other investments. Further, in multiracial areas, prostitutes of minority or colonized groups can also provide cheap labor themselves. Chinese prostitutes in the nineteenth-century American West performed all three functions as free agents and as enslaved and indentured workers.

After the formal abolition of black slavery, the capitalist mode of production predominated in nineteenth-century America. However, aspects of slavery persisted in varying degrees among racial minorities, for example, in contract labor and in Chinese prostitution in California. White prostitution on the American frontier quickly moved from a precapitalist form of organization to one characterized by either a partnership between madam and prostitutes or a relationship of employer and wageworker. Chinese prostitution, in contrast, remained a semifeudal organization until the twentieth century. While sexual prejudice obscured the exploitative nature of prostitution as a business, a sense of racial superiority at first led whites to condone Chinese female slavery.[1] In addition, the linkages between the emigrant societies in China and the Chinese community in California helped to perpetuate the precapitalist relations in prostitution. Chinese prostitution also provided Chinese entrepreneurs one of the few opportunities to accumulate capital in a hostile society.

This essay will examine the social history of Chinese prostitution within the context of conditions in nineteenth-century China and the economic development of California. It will focus on Chinese prostitution as an economic institution and on the Chinese prostitute as a particular class of labor, earning direct or indirect profits for a complex web of individuals. Furthermore, it will seek to explicate the double oppression by race and sex and the lethal exploitation of Chinese prostitutes both as part of the working class in America and as sacrificial victims for the maintenance of patriarchy in semifeudal China.

CONDITIONS LEADING TO THE IMPORTATION OF WOMEN FOR PROSTITUTION

Victimized by population pressure, landlord oppression, and foreign imperialism, many peasant families in nineteenth-century China lived on the edge of subsistence.[2] In a number of communities, particularly in Fujian and Guangdong, where emigration to distant lands was feasible, a large proportion of the male population left home in search of employment.[3]

In times of natural disaster and war, families often resorted to infanticide, abandonment, mortgaging, or selling of children.[4] Females, whose labor was less valuable than that of males, were frequently the first victims of extreme poverty. Furthermore, in patriarchal and patrilineal Chinese society, the family that raised a girl would not benefit from her labor and she could never carry on the ancestral line.

One remunerative solution for relieving the family of its female members was prostitution: the family did not have to provide for the girl's upkeep and her sale or part of her earnings could help support the family. The importance of this for the survival of the family is seen in the report of a Qing dynasty official, that ten family members were dependent for their sustenance upon every prostitute in Canton.[5]

The discovery of gold in 1848 along the Sacramento River brought thousands of immigrants from many countries to California.[6] Mining was an exclusively male activity; few of the men brought families with them because, among other reasons, mining involved moving from place to place, seeking the most productive site. Among the first female arrivals were prostitutes of varying racial and national origins.[7] In San Francisco, where miners from nearby sites congregated during the winter and where immigrants gathered before they went into the mining

TABLE 6.1 Sex Ratio of Chinese and Total Population in California, 1850–1970

	Chinese*	Total*
1850	39,450†	1,228.6
1860	1,858.1	255.1
1870	1,172.3	165.4
1880	1,832.4	149.3
1890	2,245.4	137.6
1900	1,223.9	123.5
1910	1,017.0	125.4
1920	528.8	112.5
1930	298.6	107.6
1940	223.6	103.7
1950	161.9	100.1
1960	127.8	99.5
1970	107.0	96.9

Sources: – Ratio for Chinese from 1860 to 1960 based on California Department of Industrial Relations. *Californians of Japanese, Chinese, and Filipino Ancestry* (San Francisco: State Office, 1965). 1970 data based on U.S. Bureau of the Census. *Historical Census of the United States*, Bicentennial ed. (Washington, D.C.: Government Printing Office, 1975).

  * Males per 100 females.

  † There were only two Chinese women in 1850.

areas, prostitution became a lucrative business. It was not uncommon for successful prostitutes to use their earnings to finance the miners or to invest in other pursuits.[8] The tremendous sexual imbalance (shown in table 1) and the lack of alternative employment made prostitution a major occupation for women. This relationship between a surplus of males, limited employment opportunities for women, and the demand for prostitution in developing areas is well documented by Boserup.[9]

The demand for prostitution in San Francisco was partially met by Chinese women from Hong Kong, Canton, and its surrounding areas. Canton, opened up as a treaty port under the guns of Western imperialism, and Hong Kong, ceded to the British after the Opium War, were the first cities where a large number of foreigners arrived, and from them the early Chinese prostitutes came.[10]

Only a few women crossed the Pacific on their own in search of better compensation for their labor in prostitution. Usually the family, not the girl, arranged the sale. Girls often accepted their sale, however reluctantly, out of filial loyalty, and most of them were not in a position to oppose their families' decision. In addition, the sheltered and secluded lives that women were forced to live made them particularly vulnerable to manipulation, and many were tricked or lured into prostitution.

An important but unexplored facet of the relationship between patriarchy and prostitution in the Chinese case is its role in perpetuating Chinese sojourning abroad and in its support of the migrant labor system in America. The Chinese patriarchal family system discouraged or even forbade "decent" women from traveling abroad. In addition, the anti-Chinese sentiment and violence in California was often cited by immigrant Chinese merchants as a major reason for not bringing their families.[11] These two factors discouraged the emigration of Chinese women, who would have made possible a stable Chinese community in America. The failure of the Chinese to form families that would reproduce the workforce locally prolonged the use of the Chinese by American employers as a migrant labor force.

Further, the patriarchal system required the preservation of the relationship between the men who went abroad to seek work and the families they left behind. It was common practice for the emigrant male to marry before his departure to insure that a wife be at home to fulfill his filial duties; and with luck to give him a male descendant. These married women in the emigrant communities of China and Hong Kong, as noted by Chen Ta and Watson, were under more watchful eyes than their counterparts in nonemigrant communities.[12] The relatives were charged with the duty of keeping the women of the emigrants "pure," and in return the emigrants were obliged to send their earnings to support their families. This arrangement permitted the preservation of the Chinese family at home and the perpetuation of the Chinese emigrant laborer's sojourning role in America. The emigrants, whenever they could afford it, returned to China to sire a child. If the child was a boy, he eventually joined his father in America. This arrangement recirculated Chinese labor in the migrant labor system; and the home villages of China reproduced the labor force, in terms of procreation and child rearing, for work in America.

Chinese prostitution was an integral part of that arrangement. While patriarchy prohibited the emigration of "decent" women, it did not forbid the emigration of prostitutes. The emigration of Chinese prostitutes helped to stabilize and preserve the family because Chinese emigrant males could thereby avoid liaisons that might lead to permanent relationships with foreign women. On the other hand, the earnings of Chinese prostitutes in America helped to support their families in China. One such prostitute sent back as much as two or three hundred dollars after seven months in San Francisco.[13]

The phenomenon of Chinese sojourning and the use of Chinese as migrant labor could not be attributed to poverty, patriarchy, and prostitution alone. Equally, if not more, important was the racist hostility of white society. In addition, like the European colonists who often made sure that the African laborer's wife and children did not follow the man to his new workplace,[14] American capitalists paid low wages to Chinese men to deter their women from crossing the Pacific. (The same phenomenon is observed in Western Europe today.[15]) Some whites in California advocated the importation of more Chinese laborers and not their women so they would not establish a permanent population here; others advocated the importation of more Chinese prostitutes who could meet the sexual demands of Chinese men and thus lessen the threat they perceived to white womanhood.[16] Similar arguments were later advanced by whites in Australia vis-à-vis Japanese prostitutes.[17]

Despite these mutual economic and social advantages, profit was undoubtedly the major reason for the creation and maintenance of the traffic in prostitution. Two distinct periods of Chinese prostitution in California corresponded with two types of relations in profit making: *(a)* the initial period of free competition, during which the prostitute was also the owner of her body service; and *(b)* a period of organized trade, during which the prostitute was a semislave and other individuals shared the benefits of her exploitation.

THE PERIOD OF FREE COMPETITION: THE SELF-EMPLOYED PROSTITUTES AND SMALL ENTREPRENEURS

The brief period of free competition (ca. 1849–54) was characterized by individual initiative and enterprise. Like their white counterparts, a number of Chinese prostitutes during this period were able to accumulate sufficient capital to leave the profession. Some returned to China as relatively affluent members of the business community. Others remained in America and either continued in prostitution as brothel owners or invested in other businesses.

Among the first Chinese female residents in America allegedly was a twenty-year-old prostitute from Hong Kong who landed in San Francisco late in 1848.[18] A free agent serving a predominantly non-Chinese clientele during a period of affluence, she accumulated enough money to buy a brothel within two years and retired the widow of a wealthy Chinese man.[19]

Other free-agent prostitutes during this initial period emigrated under different circumstances. A popular social novel in the late Qing dynasty period told of a Cantonese prostitute brought to San Francisco by her American paramour when she was eighteen. After seven years, she returned to Hong Kong with approximately $16,300, married a Chinese laborer, and opened a store specializing in foreign goods.[20]

This period of free competition among owner-prostitutes did not last long. Few Chinese prostitutes could afford the transportation expenses or had the business know-how to take advantage of the situation. Still, the affluence of the male residents and the extreme imbalance of the sexes suggested that a considerable sum of money could be made in the business. That prospect attracted Chinese entrepreneurs, who organized various aspects of the business; specialization occurred and a monopoly developed by 1854 under the control of the Chinese secret societies.

THE PERIOD OF ORGANIZED TRADE

In contrast to the first phase, the second period of Chinese prostitution in California (ca. 1854–1925) was characterized by a widespread organization of the trade with a network of specialized functions extending across the Pacific to Canton and Hong Kong. The persons chiefly responsible for this trade were the procurers who kidnapped, enticed, or bought Chinese women; the importers who brought them into America; the brothel owners who lived by their exploitation; the Chinese highbinders who collected fees for protecting them from other highbinders; the police who collected monies for keeping them from being arrested; and the white Chinatown property owners who leased their land and buildings for exorbitant rents.

The process by which brothels in San Francisco obtained their inmates was complex. The owner of a brothel recruited workers either by taking a trip to Canton or Hong Kong or by securing them through an agent or importer. A West Coast newspaper reported that agents of California brothels regularly went about China buying girls and young women. These agents received a regular circular or "price current" from San Francisco giving them information concerning the state of the market and the maximum prices that could be paid to derive an acceptable profit.[21]

Luring and kidnapping were the most frequent methods of procurement, particularly after 1870. When the agents did not find enough females to fill their orders, they sent subagents into rural districts to lure or kidnap girls and young women and forward the victims to them at the shipping ports.[22] Quite frequently those individuals who did the luring were returned emigrants from that community. The baits used included promises of gold, marriage, jobs, or education.[23] Sometimes the victims were invited to see the big American steamer anchored at the docks, and while they were enjoying the tour, the boat would sail off to San Francisco.[24] More often, kidnapping was carried out by force, and the victims were sometimes daughters of relatively well-to-do families.[25]

A number of women came to San Francisco under a contractual arrangement similar to that described in the Chinese contract coolie system.[26] The contract involved body service for a specified time, and if the prostitute succeeded in fulfilling the terms of service, she could, theoretically, get out of the business. Families, rather than the women themselves, participated in these transactions. Most Chinese women, who could not read or write, could easily be duped into affixing their thumbprint to any document by the agent or party who was the beneficiary of the contract.

In the organization of the trade, importation was a separate activity from that of procurement. Importers received the women from the recruiting agents, arranged for their passage, and handed them over to the brothel owners upon arrival in the United States. Although other secret societies were known to have engaged in the traffic of women,[27] the Hip-Yee Tong was clearly the predominant importer during the third quarter of the nineteenth century. It was estimated that between 1852 and 1873, the Hip-Yee Tong alone imported six thousand women,[28] or about 87 percent of the total number of Chinese women who arrived during that period. The Hip-Yee Tong charged a forty-dollar fee to each buyer, ten dollars of which were said to have gone to white policemen.[29] The Hip-Yee netted an estimated two hundred thousand dollars between 1852 and 1873 from the import business.[30]

The traffic in women became more difficult after the passage of the code that allowed the commissioner of immigration to prevent certain classes of people, including "lewd or debauched" women, from immigrating to California,[31] and the enactment of the Page Act of 1875. The immediate effectiveness of these laws in reducing the number of female arrivals is unclear, but the statutes did subject women to close scrutiny both in Hong Kong and San Francisco and eventually made it more expensive to import women. These added expenses took the form of bribes that had to be paid to various U.S. consulate and customs officials.

The American consulate in Hong Kong was charged with the initial examination of Chinese women to determine if they were "lewd or debauched." If the consul's office was convinced of their good character, it would stamp the women's arms and send them to the harbor master, who would do the same. Only then would the women be allowed to purchase tickets and board the steamer.[32] The certificate with the woman's photograph issued by the consulate was mailed to the collector of customs at San Francisco. Women without appropriate documentation were refused landing and often had to wait more than twenty-four hours before they were cleared.[33] This procedure was subject to abuse by corrupt consular officials, who could be convinced of a woman's good character with money or could refuse to certify a woman's good character without money. It was discovered in 1879 that Consul Bailey's office received between ten and fifteen dollars for every woman shipped to the United States during his tenure in Hong Kong.[34]

Americans on this side of the Pacific also benefited materially from these new statutes. As noted by the U.S. Supreme Court, the 1873 code was subject to a variety of abuses: "It is hardly possible to conceive a statute more skillfully framed, to place in the hands of a single man the power to prevent, entirely, the vessels engaged in a foreign trade, say with China, from carrying passengers, or to compel them to submit to systematic extortion of the grossest kind." The commissioner, noted the Court, could arbitrarily designate immigrants as paupers, idiots, convicted criminals, or prostitutes and deny them entrance on that basis.[35]

These regulations benefited white lawyers as well as the customs inspector. Some lawyers colluded with the Chinese importers in obtaining habeas corpus decrees to allow the landing of Chinese women headed for the brothels.[36] Although a number of these women were legal immigrants, some probably sought the help of American lawyers because U.S. customs officers were dissatisfied with their documentation.

The Chinese Exclusion Act of 1882 allowed only women who were native born, married, or born overseas to domiciled merchants to immigrate to the United States. Accordingly, enterprising Chinese developed elaborate arrangements to continue the traffic in women. Chinese agents in the United States instructed agents in China to coach the emigrant women in responding to questions by the immigration authorities. These coaching papers, circulated in Hong Kong and Canton, included eighty-one questions on subjects ranging from standard personal details to the geography of San Francisco.[37]

Each successive law placing additional restrictions on Chinese immigration provided more opportunities for corruption. People soon found that U.S. immigration inspectors and interpreters could easily be persuaded to accept bribes to render favorable decisions and interpretations of the law.[38] As the rules became more severe, the investigation of the immigrants' status took longer to complete, and the immigrants were subjected to greater indignities, pain, and suffering. Beginning in 1891 and particularly after 1910, Chinese men and women were detained at Angel Island while waiting to be cleared. Most stayed at least three or four weeks, while others waited under very austere living conditions for months or even years while their cases were being fought in the courts.[39]

As importation became increasingly complex and expensive, the Hip-Yee Tong gradually lost its monopolistic control over the traffic. Because of the increasing complexity and costs of importing prostitutes, the price for their delivery skyrocketed. After 1870, for example, girls who originally sold for fifty dollars in Canton now brought one thousand dollars in San Francisco.[40] And in the 1890s it was reported that as much as three thousand dollars in gold was paid for a single Chinese female in San Francisco.[41]

Still, the importation of women continued primarily because it provided large profits. In the 1890s a shoe manufacturer and tong leader, Fong Ching, alias Little Pete, was well known for, among other things, his ingenuity in importing women for prostitution. Besides bribing customs officials and paying both white and Chinese men thirty dollars each for bearing false character witnesses, he used fairs and expositions held in Chicago, Atlanta, and San Francisco to import women. For example, during the Midwinter Fair in Golden Gate Park he imported over a hundred women ostensibly to perform at the fair. They ended up in brothels after spending only a brief time at the fair. San Francisco newspapers reported that Little Pete netted fifty thousand dollars through his female imports.[42]

Other methods employed by the tongs to land Chinese women were smuggling in women attired as boys, hiding them in buckets of coal, and concealing them in padded crates billed as dishware.[43] The cost of smuggling a woman into the United States may have been as high as twenty-five hundred dollars.[44] When customs officials at San Francisco began enforcing the law, women were brought in through Portland, Oregon, Canada, or Mexico.[45]

Eventually, however, faced with the dwindling supply of females in China,[46] the nearly prohibitive costs and difficulties of procurement and importation, and the loss of prostitutes from brothels in San Francisco to other cities and mining towns, the tongs were forced to look for their supply locally. Whereas local Chinese women were supplementary to overseas recruitment previously, after 1882 they became the major source of new supply.[47] It was reported that, in just one week in February 1898, eight women were kidnapped for prostitution.[48]

THE LIFE AND ECONOMICS OF PROSTITUTION

After the women had been transported to Chinatown, they were housed in temporary quarters known as "barracoons" to await their distribution. One barracoon reputedly held up to one hundred women.[49] Those who had been imported for specific customers left when their owners paid the passage fare and the forty-dollar fee. The others were carefully dressed and displayed before the bidding.[50] Well-to-do Chinese in San Francisco purchased the cream of this lot as concubines or mistresses. The remainder fell into two categories: the best went into higher-class brothels reserved only for the Chinese, while the rest were sold to inferior dens of prostitution that served a racially mixed clientele.[51]

The distinction between higher- and lower-grade brothels was one of both class and race. Chinese men generally felt that the most degrading thing a Chinese woman could do was to have sexual relations with a white man.[52] However, because of their comparatively low fees of twenty-five to fifty cents, the lower-class prostitutes were visited by whites and Chinese alike, while higher-class prostitutes had an exclusively Chinese clientele. Thus, the lower-grade prostitutes tended to attract the poorest laborers, teenage boys, sailors, and drunkards. They were often mistreated by their owners as well as their customers. A few brothel owners, for example, occasionally even beat some of them to death,[53] and white men often forced them to engage in aberrant sexual acts.[54] Prostitutes in mining camps served both Chinese and white clients and were often more harshly treated than their counterparts in San Francisco.[55]

The lower-grade prostitutes lived in rooms usually not larger than four by six feet, often facing a dimly lit alley.[56] "Bright cotton hangings hung in the doorways leading off from the main room or were sometimes used to break a larger room up into smaller compartments."[57] These rooms were sparsely furnished, usually with only a bamboo chair or two, a washbowl, and hard bunks of shelves covered with matting and set against the wall. The door, normally the only opening to the outside, was invariably covered with bars or a heavy screen, behind which the woman would stand and call to passersby.[58]

The prostitutes who only served Chinese generally lived in upstairs apartments and had more or less long-term, regular customers. Very often the prostitute's client was also her owner. It is not always accurate to characterize them as prostitutes, for some may have been concubines while others may have lived in polyandry.[59] These higher-class prostitutes were often attractive and expensively adorned. Although they may have appeared to be well treated, they were nevertheless chattel, "one day loaded with jewels, the next day to be stripped and sold to the highest bidder, if it were the desire of their masters."[60]

Neither lower- nor higher-class prostitutes received regular wages, but the latter were sometimes asked to entertain at parties given by tong leaders and Chinese merchants, and they were permitted to keep the jewelry, silk, and cash gifts given to them by their customers. This is perhaps how some prostitutes were able to send money to their parents in China.[61]

The exploitative relations between the prostitute-worker and the procurer and brothel owner are clear. The capital outlay—kidnapper's fee, passage, bribes, legal fees—was miniscule compared with the profits from the woman's labor as a prostitute. For example, the cost of her passage would have been around $50 if she traveled in the same manner as the Chinese male laborers, and at the most $150 if she had comfortable accommodations, no doubt extremely rare.[62] The kidnapper's fee was once reported at $185.[63] And although we do not have data on the exact amount of bribes and legal fees, it seems safe to say that these did not usually exceed $100, though they became increasingly large as restrictions on Chinese immigration grew.

The most profitable way of importing a woman, from the procurer's point of view, was to lure the woman into going with him or her voluntarily to America. In one such case, the procurer, after painting a glowing picture of life in California and paying $98, obtained the consent of a girl's mother to permit her daughter to emigrate. Upon arrival, the procurer sold the girl for $1,950, a net profit of at least $1,700. This girl continued to bring in profits for her owner by laboring two years and averaging no less than $290 per month. At the end of the two years she was resold for $2,100.[64] The brothel owner's gross income from her labor as a prostitute and from her resale was about $9,060; even if she was kept at a higher standard of living and if we deduct the cost of her purchase, the brothel owner's net profit was no less than $5,000 in two years.

Besides through kidnapping and luring, Chinese women entered American brothels under a system of contract mentioned before. Although this was on the surface the least exploitative form of Chinese prostitution, it was in fact devised to mask those features that permitted the procurers, importers, and brothel owners to derive considerable profits without any real advantage to the prostitute or indentured worker. The contracts were drawn up in appealing terms: they offered the contractee free passage to America, an advance of over four hundred dollars, and a limited period of labor of about four and a half years. The contract system seemed all the more attractive considering that females were often sold for about four hundred dollars at the time.

In reality, though, the contract system offered very little advantage over the outright sale or slave system and was, in a number of ways, more brutal because it raised false hopes. First, the length of a prostitute's career, as noted before, was about four or five years. Thus, as far as the brothel owner was concerned, a prostitute was useful only for about four years, the period of the contract. Second, the terms of the contract specified that the person must work a minimum of 320 days, failing which the contract period could be extended by one additional year. Third, the contract prostitute would have less incentive to run away because of her limited period of labor. Fourth, her family was discouraged from redeeming her because the repurchase price included an exorbitant interest.[65] And finally, even after a woman had served out her contract, there were cases in which she continued in servitude and was not released.[66] The following is a translation of one such contract:[67]

> The contractee Xin Jin is indebted to her master/mistress for passage from China to San Francisco and will voluntarily work as a prostitute at Tan Fu's place for four and one-half years for an advance of 1,205

yuan ($524) to pay this debt.[68] There shall be no interest on the money, and Xin Jin shall receive no wages. At the expiration of the contract, Xin Jin shall be free to do as she pleases. Until then, she shall first secure the master/mistress's permission if a customer asks to take her out. If she has the four loathsome diseases, she shall be returned within 100 days; beyond that time the procurer has no responsibility. Menstruation disorder is limited to one month's rest only. If Xin Jin becomes sick at any time for more than fifteen days, she shall work one month extra; if she becomes pregnant, she shall work one year extra. Should Xin Jin run away before her term is out, she shall pay whatever expense is incurred in finding and returning her to the brothel. This is a contract to be retained by the master/mistress as evidence of the agreement. Receipt of 1,205 yuan ($524) by Ah Vo. Thumb print of Xin Jin the contractee. Eighth month 11th day of the 12th year of Guang-zu (1886).

Thus far, a total of four such contracts have been discovered, the earliest dated 1873 and the latest 1899.[69]

A fourth way in which Chinese women entered San Francisco brothels was through outright purchase; in this case the women were no more than slaves. Initially, the average capital outlay for a woman brought over in this way amounted to no more than six hundred dollars: the purchase price, the cost of passage, and the expenses associated with importation. But as immigration restrictions became more severe and the complexity of the importation system grew, the cost of buying and importing a prostitute likewise increased. The purchase and importation of a seventeen-year-old prostitute named Tsoi Ye illustrates this process. Tsoi Ye was sold in Hong Kong in the 1880s for a little over four hundred dollars. She was resold by the procuress to a tong man for $882, who in turn entrusted a Chinese sailor to bring her over. After she was landed successfully, she was resold to a brothel for $1,800 in gold.[70] Despite the high cost, it is clear that brothel owners found it profitable to purchase women at such prices due to their potential earnings as computed above.

If the kidnapped woman was sold during the later decades of the nineteenth century, the importer could receive between $1,000 and $3,000. If, however, the importer was also a brothel owner, the kidnapped woman would labor in his or her brothel. From the information on hand, we are able to venture some conservative estimates of her earnings. The lowest grade of prostitutes received twenty-five to fifty cents per customer. According to the literature on prostitution in general, an average full-time prostitute-worker receives four to ten customers per day,[71] and the average career life of such a prostitute is estimated at four to five years.[72] This means that, at an average of thirty-eight cents per

TABLE 6.2 Number and Size of Chinese Brothels in San Francisco, 1860–80

Size	1860	1870	1880
1	3	2	13
2	13	2	19
3	9	4	29
4	20	12	14
5	7	18	7
6	13	13	3
7	6	10	6
8	6	20	1
9	8	15	0
10	3	10	2
11	2	15	1
12	1	12	1
13	0	7	0
14	0	2	0
15	0	5	1
16–20	0	10	3
21–25	1	2	0
26–30	1	0	1
31–35	1	0	0
Total	94	159	101
M size of brothel	5.9	9.0	4.3

Sources: – Computed from unpublished census manuscripts for San Francisco for 1860, 1870, and 1880 (available from the National Archives).

customer and seven customers per day, a lower-grade prostitute would earn about $850 per year and $3,400 after four years.[73] Since women in lower-class brothels were generally kept at subsistence levels,[74] the cost of maintaining them probably did not exceed $8 per month or $96 per person each year.[75] The profits for the owner of a prostitute, then, even one of the lower grade, were considerable.

If a lower-grade prostitute earned an average of $850 a year, and if we assume that the average brothel in 1870 contained nine prostitutes (see table 6.2), the owner's gross annual income would have been about $7,650. In 1873, Chinese owned only 7 percent of the 153 major pieces of property in Chinatown, and as late as 1904, they owned only 8 percent of the 316 major parcels listed.[76] White landlords, many of whom were prominent citizens of San Francisco, owned most of the real estate in Chinatown, and they extracted high rents from brothel owners, often double or treble the rent they received from whites.[77] According to the Bureau of Labor Statistics, the average rental per month of a flat consisting of three to six rooms in San Francisco was $14.[78] The Chinese brothel owners probably had to pay no less than $28 per month or $336 a year. If the rent and maintenance of the women are deducted from the gross income, the owner would still have received an annual profit of no less than $6,000. Even if we add other expenses such as protection fees paid to the police and taxes extorted by the tongs from brothels not owned by their members, the profit the brothel owner received would still compare very favorably with the less than $500 average annual income of other occupations in which he or she might engage.[79] Other commentators' estimates of the income of brothel owners make this look conservative. For instance, Cameron, a contemporary San Francisco reformer, stated that the average Chinese prostitute usually made between five and six dollars per day; one prostitute estimated that she made $278 per month, while another claimed to have made $318 per month.[80]

The exploitation of Chinese prostitutes was not limited to sex alone but also included their labor as semiskilled workers. Many sources indicate that in the daytime, when business was slack, women in the brothels sewed buttonholes and pantaloons and worked on shirts, slippers, men's clothing, and women's underwear.[81] The work was farmed out by sweatshops that subcontracted with the manufacturers. Since these female operatives probably did not receive payment for this extra work, the brothel owners and sweatshop owners reaped a handsome profit.[82]

There were still other forms of exploitation. Besides the tax levied on brothel owners who were not tong members, the tongs imposed a weekly tax of twenty-five cents on every Chinese prostitute. If any woman refused to pay, they promised to use "harsh measures" to collect.[83] These harsh measures included whipping, torture by fire, banishment to brothels in the mining regions, and finally, shooting and killing the victim.[84] Blackmailing Chinese prostitutes was another method employed by the tongs to extort money. Members of a tong, noted one report, "went around among Chinese prostitutes and told them that a new chief of police had come in, and unless he received a handsome present, would shut up the houses. They collected from one and a half to five dollars from each prostitute, and the money was divided among the members of that society."[85]

Owners of brothels sometimes also owned opium dens and gambling joints.[86] A number of prostitutes were addicted to opium and/or gambled excessively.[87] The owners often encouraged these addictions so that the loans needed to feed them would increase the prostitutes' debts.[88] Desperate women committed suicide by swallowing raw opium or drowning themselves in the bay.[89]

The best thing that could happen to these women was to be redeemed and married. Occasionally a white male fell in love with a brothel inmate and married her after having paid the owner.[90] However, most of the men who married prostitutes were Chinese laborers. Chinese working people did not attach the same stigma to prostitution as whites did. One reason might have been that prostitutes in China were generally not seen as "fallen women" but as daughters who obeyed the wishes of the family. Although prostitution was not considered an honorable profession, particularly among the gentry, women who were able to get out of it were usually accepted in working-class society. Furthermore, the fact that there was such a shortage of Chinese women in San Francisco during this period would have tended to relax the sex mores that men might have held.

Apparently, quite a few women in San Francisco were able to leave the brothels, although not without struggle, and often at tremendous risk. Throughout the mid-nineteenth and the early twentieth centuries, reports of such instances abound.[91] Typically, a woman ran away to a mission, the police station, or her lover, with the hired tong soldiers in pursuit. The lengths to which the tongs would go in recapturing a runaway prostitute indicated her value to her owner. The tongs often kidnapped the escaped woman or even used the American courts to get her back by filing a charge of theft, claiming the woman had absconded with some clothes or jewelry. After the police had located the woman, the tongs would hire white lawyers to arrange for her bail and then return her to the brothel.[92] If that tactic failed, they placed public announcements on Chinatown walls, warning others who might assist her escape and offering rewards for her capture.

The tongs also offered rewards for the capture of the prostitute's male accomplice; sometimes such rewards ran into the thousands, depending on the value of the woman. If the male accomplice paid the sum asked for the woman's redemption, then the couple was left alone, but very often the man could not pay the exorbitant amount that the tong required. There are stories which tell of such men and women fleeing the San Francisco area in disguise or hidden in wooden boxes.[93] However, the tong network of informers reached even into rural communities. Telegraphs between Chinese men in Marysville, Downieville, San Francisco, and other places reveal that such a system operated at least during the 1870s.[94]

As further insurance against the escape of a prostitute, tongs gave the local police a retainer fee. Until 1877, a Special Police Force was engaged in a quasi-official capacity as peace officers in Chinatown. They received no set wages but derived their income from the Chinese residents. Normally, the "Chinatown Specials" collected fifty cents a week from each prostitute,[95] and they admitted that whenever there was a crackdown on prostitution, their income was reduced.[96] Tongs also made payments to City Hall to secure its agreement not to interfere.[97]

As mentioned before, a prostitute's work life in the brothels was normally four to five years, not surprising in the absence of sound medical care. The abundance of Chinese advertisements of "secret formulas" for curing syphilis and gonorrhea during the period testifies to the prevalence of such diseases.[98] Although some doctors blamed the Chinese prostitutes for spreading the diseases to the white population, it was pointed out by other physicians that these illnesses were equally, if not more, prevalent among white prostitutes in San Francisco.[99]

When a woman was no longer profitable as a prostitute, she might work as a cook or a laundry woman for the brothel.[100] If she was hopelessly ill, she would be left to die by the brothel owners.[101] Although, in general, the remains of the Chinese male laborers were shipped back to their place of nativity for burial, few cared about the remains of these working women. The *Alta* reported in 1870 that the bodies of Chinese women were discarded and left on the streets of Chinatown.[102]

Chinese prostitutes were mostly young women between the ages of sixteen and twenty-five. The year 1870 stood out as a watershed in that there were proportionately more younger prostitutes in that period than in either 1860 or 1880. Table 6.3 shows that close to 46 percent of the women were under twenty years of age in 1870, which was 12 and 23 percentage points higher than the 1880 and the 1860 aggregates, respectively. Since a great majority of the Chinese prostitutes were of childbearing age, a natural question arose as to the mobility of their children.

The children of prostitutes, particularly female ones, were likewise exploited by the brothel owners. Table 6.4 shows the number, place of nativity, and residence of Chinese children living in San Francisco. The data reveal a significant trend: in the 1860 census, proportionately more children lived in brothels than outside brothels; in 1870, an even number of children lived in brothels and outside; and finally, in 1880, the situation was reversed, with many more children living outside than inside. The overrepresentation of girls over boys in the brothels for all three decades was probably due to the owner's practice of retaining girls to do household chores and his or her intention to recruit them into prostitution. It is probably safe to say that native-born children living in brothels were almost invariably the children of prostitutes. But most of the children of prostitutes somehow managed to escape the clutches of the brothel. In 1880, nearly thirty years after the first large-scale importation of prostitutes, only seven of the 435 prostitutes in San Francisco were native born (table 6.3). In general, children moved away from the brothels and into the wider society (table 6.4).

TABLE **6.3** Age and Nativity of Chinese Prostitiutes in San Francisco, 1860–80

	1860			1870			1880			
	Foreign Born	U.S. Born	%	Foreign Born	U.S. Born	%	Foreign Born	U.S. Born	Total	%
15 and under	8	0	1.4	16	1	1.1	18	4	22	5.0
16–20	122	0	21.9	637	0	44.7	125	2	127	29.2
21–25	165	0	18.9	416	0	29.2	129	1	130	29.9
26–30	165	0	29.7	215	0	15.1	86	0	86	19.8
31–35	64	0	11.5	70	0	4.9	32	0	32	7.4
36–40	64	0	11.5	34	0	2.4	20	0	20	4.6
41–45	19	0	3.4	14	0	1.0	8	0	8	1.8
46–50	6	0	1.1	18	0	1.2	8	0	8	1.8
51 and over	3	0	.6	5	0	.3	2	0	2	.5
Total	616	0	100.0	1,425	1	99.9	428	7	435	100.0

Sources: – See Table 6.2

TABLE **6.4** Chinese Children in San Francisco by Sex, Nativity, and Place of Residence, 1860–80

	Live in Brothels			Live Outside		
	Male	Female	Total	Male	Female	Total
1860:						
U.S. born	5	23	28	0	0	0
Foreign born	3	12	15	7	2	9
Total	8	35	43	7	2	9
1860:						
U.S. born	98	74	172	71	57	128
Foreign born	34	48	82	79	34	113
Total	132	122	254	150	91	241
1860:						
U.S. born	24	26	50	203	198	401
Foreign born	11	27	38	89	114	203
Total	35	53	88	292	312	604

Sources: – See Table 6.2

Some of these children were placed in mission homes and with families of Chinese Christians.[103] Others might have returned to China or moved to the American interior. For those who remained in San Francisco, the occupational distribution of native-born Chinese females in the 1880 manuscript census gives a clue as to their destinations. Of the 250 U.S.-born women who were not classified as prostitutes, 227 were housewives, while the rest were students, apprentices, housekeepers, and seamstresses. Although certainly not all native-born women were offspring of prostitutes, a number of them clearly were. It is not incorrect to say, therefore, that the daughters of some indentured and slave prostitute-workers managed to become wage laborers and housewives.

EXTENT AND DISTRIBUTION OF CHINESE PROSTITUTES IN SAN FRANCISCO

The exact number of Chinese prostitutes in California and San Francisco during the nineteenth century is not known. Although several contemporary estimates are available, their tremendous variation indicates low reliability. Fortunately, we are not solely dependent on impressionistic accounts. The recently released manuscript censuses for 1860, 1870, and 1880 contain social and demographic information on individuals that makes it possible to estimate the numbers and to construct a statistical profile of Chinese prostitutes for these decades.

A tabulation of the census schedules of 1860 revealed that there were 2,693 Chinese residents in San Francisco, 654, or 24 percent, of whom were women. Eight of these were laundry/washerwomen; five, gardeners; five, fisherwomen; three, laborers; four, storekeepers; two, clerks; and one, a tailoress; the remainder had no occupation listed.

Eliminating from the last category (a) those women living in households with a man with or without children, (b) those living in households with more than one man, and (c) girls under twelve years old, we have 556 women whose occupations might be said to have been prostitution. This figure represents 85 percent of the Chinese female population in San Francisco, and it is probably a reasonable estimate.

Since "prostitution" was used as an occupational category in the 1870 and 1880 census manuscripts, we have simply followed the designation of the census taker to identify Chinese women engaged in prostitution during those two decades. Obvious distortions may arise from this procedure. Although the census enumerator was instructed to record what was reported to him or her by the interviewee, a language problem could lead to guessing by the census worker. It is also reasonable to assume that the census taker was probably biased toward designating a woman a prostitute because of popular racist beliefs or an inability to distinguish between concubinage and prostitution. On the other hand, the interviewee was probably inclined not to state that she worked as a prostitute even if she really did. Since these biases run in opposite directions, they tend to neutralize each other.

A tabulation from the 1870 census schedules yielded 2,018 Chinese women in San Francisco, of whom 1,426, or 71 percent, were recorded as prostitutes. From these figures, we can see that while the percentage of women in San Francisco engaged in prostitution declined relative to the total Chinese female population, the actual number of prostitutes more than doubled.

Between 1870 and 1880, Chinese prostitution became one of the salient issues in the anti-Chinese movement in California. During the two legislative hearings on Chinese immigration, one conducted by the California State Senate in April 1876 and the other by the U.S. Congress in October of the same year, numerous individuals testified on the extent of Chinese prostitution in San Francisco.[104] These estimates contradicted one another and revealed the witnesses' political biases and self-interests. Because of those contrasting interests, the estimates of Chinese prostitutes in San Francisco differed widely, ranging from 200 to 2,700. In none of the hearings did witnesses or legislators cite the census figures.

A tabulation of the manuscript census for San Francisco in 1880 yielded 2,058 Chinese women, of whom 435, or 21 percent, were recorded as prostitutes. Although this figure was probably an underestimate, other sources suggest that it was not too far afield. The San Francisco police testified in the congressional hearings of 1876 that, as a result of several raids on Chinese prostitution a few months before the hearings, many prostitutes left the city for inland.[105] Later, in 1885, the San Francisco Board of Supervisors reported that there were 567 professional prostitutes in Chinatown.[106]

From the statistics presented, we see the dramatic increase in the number of prostitutes between 1860 and 1870, and the dramatic decrease in both the number and percentage of prostitutes between 1870 and 1880. These figures suggest that the heyday of Chinese prostitution in San Francisco was around 1870, and its precipitous decline occurred just before 1880.

Although Chinese prostitutes served a racially mixed clientele, they were physically concentrated in a few blocks in Ward Four, where Chinatown was located. Outside of Chinatown, in 1860, some brothels were found in three other wards, but in 1870, Chinese brothels were found in only one other ward. Data on the distribution and size of brothels (table 6.2) clearly confirms that the years around 1870 were the heyday of organized prostitution. There were more prostitutes, more and larger brothels, and a heavier concentration of brothels in a very small area. The data also suggest the idea that this was the period when small businesses were consolidated or liquidated by big enterprises.

DECLINE OF ORGANIZED PROSTITUTION

Several converging factors account for the decline of organized prostitution in San Francisco. First, the female supply in South China dwindled, making families less willing to sell or mortgage their daughters and increasing the difficulty of procuring prostitutes. Second, the Chinese Exclusion Act of 1882 greatly reduced the number of prospective prostitutes and made their importation harder. The decline in the annual number of Chinese women immigrants—from an average of 304.6 between 1854 and 1882 to an average of 107.6 between 1883 and 1904—testifies to the effectiveness of the Exclusion Act,[107] despite the ingenious evasive methods devised by the importers, tongs, and brothel owners. The skyrocketing value of prostitutes in America and the increase in kidnapping in California after the 1880s also reflect the decline in Chinese women entering the United States for the purpose of prostitution.

Local conditions in San Francisco and California after the 1880s similarly led to the decline and eventual demise of this organized phase of prostitution. These included the more balanced sex ratio of the California population (see table 6.1); the availability of other sources of supply; the move of Chinese labor from migrant to stationary industries; the desire of capital to maintain a stable, cheap labor force; the change from sojourning to settlement or return; the increased alternatives for women's labor;[108] intra-tong conflicts and the struggle between the tongs and the allied forces of the Chinese consulate and the Six Companies; the enforcement of codes directed against Chinese prostitution; the arrival of white Victorian women and the establishment of white families in California; and finally, the crusade of the white missionaries for the abolition of Chinese prostitution.

The Six Companies, led by Chinese merchants, had their financial basis in Chinese laborers and trade. They supplied labor, collected membership fees, served as bankers for the immigrants, and sold provisions to the laborers.[109] The secret societies, which controlled the gambling, opium, and prostitution businesses, challenged the traditional authority of the Six Companies and competed with the merchants for the laborers' dollars. Their opposition sharpened during the 1880s, partly because the increase in local kidnapping related to prostitution alienated the Chinatown elites, who had families with them.[110] The more money laborers spent in San Francisco tong-controlled businesses, the less they had to spend in the merchants' shops or to send home to their families.[111] Since many emigrant communities in China depended on remittances, the Chinese consulate and the Qing government were also concerned.[112] In addition, the merchants knew that American families would not patronize the growing number of legitimate restaurants, stores, and curio shops in Chinatown if it was seen as a vice district.[113] The fierce competition among secret societies for the control of gambling, opium, and prostitution during the last few decades of the nineteenth century also contributed to their decline.[114]

Moreover, the heyday of Chinese prostitution in San Francisco corresponded with the period of mounting agitation against Chinese labor in general. And although prostitutes consisted of no more than 6 percent of the Chinese population in California, they were singled out for attack by the politicians. Chinese prostitution not only threatened the health of white men, claimed those politicians, but Chinese prostitutes serving as slave labor took away sewing and other jobs from white women.[115] Between 1866 and 1905, at least eight California codes were passed, all aimed at restricting the importation of Chinese women for prostitution and the suppression of Chinese brothels. Although white prostitution was equally if not more prevalent, these were additional and specific laws directed only against the Chinese. Chinese prostitutes, if caught, were sentenced to a fine of twenty-five to fifty dollars and a jail term of at least five days.[116]

Both the Chinese consulate and the Six Companies saw prostitution as one of the major causes for the anti-Chinese movement in California. Further, both were concerned about the economic loss and image of the Chinese, so they actively collaborated with the American authorities in identifying and deporting Chinese prostitutes.[117] In reality, however, since Chinese prostitution was not the reason for the anti-Chinese movement, their action did not thwart the hostility; but their efforts did bring about a temporary decline in the organized traffic.

The increasing arrival of white women immigrants to San Francisco throughout the second half of the nineteenth century transformed the city from a frontier society with a fluid, predominantly male population to a more stable society with families. Smith accurately points out that the status of prostitutes declined with the advent of the Victorian ladies from the East Coast concerned with the preservation of the family, whose Puritan morality led them to crusade against prostitution in general and Chinese prostitution in particular.[118] In 1873, the interests of the Victorian ladies in San Francisco found expression in the Women's Occidental Board. Reportedly alarmed by the immorality of the traffic in women and the sinfulness of the prostitute's sexual activity, Margaret Culbertson and her successor Donaldina Cameron set out to rescue the

Chinese slaves.[119] Although clergymen like Gibson and Loomis also cru-
saded against prostitution, Cameron was always singled out as the
bravest and cleverest savior of Chinese females. She was said to have rescued approximately three thousand girls during her forty-year career,[120]
although Cameron herself testified in 1898 that, twenty-three years after
the establishment of the Mission Home, about six hundred girls had
been rescued.[121]

Missionaries thought that every slave girl or prostitute would rather
live at 920 Sacramento Street, but Chinese women did not always prefer this alternative, particularly if the brothel owner did not mistreat
them too badly.[122] Most women who ran away from brothels to seek the
protection of the Mission or the police cited cruelty, such as flogging and
beating, as the reason for their escape.[123] The Mission established strict
rules for the activities and behavior of the runaways and trained them in
"motherhood" and "industrial skills." The rule against idle hands
extended to cooking, cleaning, and maintaining the Mission, and even to
the use of the women in hard labor. Cameron was known to have contracted with fruit growers in northern California for the labor of Mission residents. She often sent twenty or thirty Chinese women from the
home to work from four to eight weeks in the fields. It is not difficult to
see why many prostitutes refused to run away to the Mission Home, or
why a number of women who had been "rescued" by the missionaries
later escaped from their saviors.[124]

There can be no doubt, however, that as a result of the efforts of
Cameron and others like her, many prostitutes became wives and lived
normal family lives. A few of these women became Christians and joined
in missionary work. Many white women, perhaps including Cameron
herself, were motivated by a sense of moral superiority. The more they
saw Chinese women as helpless, weak, depraved, and victimized, the
more aroused was their missionary zeal. Saving the Chinese slave girls
seemed to have become the "white woman's burden."[125]

CONCLUSION

Rotenberg observes that "the heavy emphasis on the 'sinful' nature of
the prostitute's sexual activity has obscured her role as a worker."[126] This
essay has argued that prostitution is a form of labor. In the case of the
individual owner-prostitute, she is a free agent, in possession of her own
sexuality, offering it in the market in exchange for a fee from her clients.
But the prostitute can be ruthlessly exploited by others who own her sexuality and/or expropriate her earnings. The institution of Chinese prostitution was characterized by many layers of exploitative relations. Men
and women, Chinese and white, reaped benefits from their oppression.

The development of Chinese prostitution as a large enterprise in nine-teenth-century California was related to both material and ideological conditions in the two countries; to the need for cheap labor in Califor-nia and the economic underdevelopment of China; and to white racism and Chinese patriarchy.

NOTES

This essay is part of a research project on "Asian American Labor before World War II" organized by the Asian-American Studies Center at UCLA. I am indebted to Edna Bonacich, Alex Saxton, Gerald Surh, Peg Strobel, Don Nakanishi, and three anony-mous reviewers for their helpful comments on an earlier draft. Special thanks to Gary Okihiro, who gave editorial assistance; to Paul Nakatsuka, who extracted part of the data from the census manuscripts; and to the Mormon Temple Library in Los Ange-les, the Bancroft Library, the Library of Congress, and the National Archives for per-mission to use their collections. I wish also to acknowledge a grant from the UCLA Academic Senate, which made this research possible. Parts of this essay are summa-rized and incorporated in my "Chinese Immigrant Women in Nineteenth-Century California," in *Women of America,* ed. C. Berkin and M. B. Norton (Boston: Houghton Mifflin Co., 1979).

1. Later on, when anti-Chinese sentiment grew into a widespread movement, the slavery aspect of Chinese prostitution was emphasized in anti-Chinese rhetoric. See, for example, California Senate, *Chinese Immigration* (Sacramento: State Office, 1878) (hereafter cited as California Senate).

2. F. Wakerman, *Strangers at the Gate* (Berkeley: University of California Press, 1966), 117–56; K. Hsiao, *Rural China* (Seattle: University of Washington Press, 1967).

3. T. Chen, *Emigrant Communities in South China* (New York: Institute of Pacific Relations, 1940); Hsiao, *Rural China.*

4. Hsiao, *Rural China,* 311–411; A. Smith, *Village Life in China* (New York: Greenwood Press, 1899), 258–316; P. Ho, *Studies on the Population of China* (Cam-bridge, Mass.: Harvard University Press, 1959), 58–62.

5. D. Chen, *Zhong-guo fu-nü sheng-huo-shi* (Shanghai: Shang-Wu, 1928), 296.

6. J. Borthwick, *The Gold Hunters* (New York: Book League, 1929).

7. D. Smith, *Rocky Mountain Mining Camps* (Lincoln: University of Nebraska Press, 1967).

8. Ibid.

9. E. Boserup, *Women's Role in Economic Development* (London: Allen & Unwin, 1970).

10. V. Wu, *Er-shi-nian mu-du guai-xian-zhuang* (Hong Kong: Guang-zhi, 1903), 238–43; X. Chen. *Dan-min di yan-jiu* (Shanghai: Shang-Wu, 1946), 124–28; U.S. Congress Joint Special Committee to Investigate Chinese Immigration, *Report* (Wash-ington, D.C.: U.S. Government Printing Office, 1877), 286 (hereafter cited as U.S. Congress); O. Gibson, *Chinese in America* (Cincinnati: Hitchcock Printers, 1877), 134.

11. Zhong-guo ko-shang hui-guan, "Letter," *Tung-ngai san-luk* (February 8, 1855).

12. T. Chen and J. Watson, *Emigration and the Chinese Lineage* (Berkeley: University of California Press, 1975).

13. Wang Ah-so's letter to her mother in *Orientals and Their Cultural Adjustment*, ed. Fisk University, Social Science Institute (Nashville, Tenn.: Fisk University Social Science Institute, 1949), 54 (hereafter cited as Fisk University).

14. Boserup, *Women's Role in Economic Development*, 76.

15. S. Castles and G. Kosack, *Immigrant Workers and Class Structure in Western Europe* (London: Oxford University Press, 1973).

16. "Editorial," *Out West* (1911): 355–56; U.S. Congress, 141, 652.

17. R. Evans, "'Soiled Doves': Prostitution and Society in Colonial Queensland," *Hecate* 1 (July 1975): 6–24.

18. C. Gentry, *Madams of San Francisco* (New York: Doubleday & Co., 1964).

19. S. Wu, *Mei-guo Huo-quao bai-nian ji-shi* (Hong Kong: by the author, 1954); Gentry, *Madams*; C. Lee, *Days of the Tong Wars* (New York: Ballantine Books, 1974); Borthwick, *Gold Hunters*.

20. Y. Wu, *Er-shi-nian mu-du guai-xian-zhuang*, 238–43.

21. *Eureka West Coast Signal*, January 6, 1875.

22. C. Holder, "Chinese Slavery in America," *North American Review* 165 (1897): 285–94.

23. C. Shepherd, "Chinese Girl Slavery in America," *Missionary Review* 46 (1923): 893–98; Fisk University, 31–35; U.S. Industrial Commission, *Report*, 21 vols. (Washington, D.C. Government Printing Office, 1901), 15:783–90 (hereafter cited as U.S. Industrial Commission).

24. Shepherd, "Chinese Girl Slavery," 896–97.

25. C. Dobie, *San Francisco's Chinatown* (New York: Appleton-Century Publishers, 1936), 69.

26. Z. Chen, "Shi-jiu shi-ji sheng-xing di qi-yue Hua-gong-zhi," *Li-shi Yan-jiu* 79 (1963): 161–79.

27. R. Park and H. Miller, *Old World Traits Transplanted* (New York: Harper & Bros., 1921), 164; R. Lee, *The Chinese in the United States of America* (Hong Kong: Hong Kong University, 1960).

28. Gibson, *Chinese in America*, n. 10.

29. *Alta California*, December 14, 1869.

30. Gibson, *Chinese in America*.

31. *State of California and Amendments, 1873–74* (Sacramento: State Office, 1875).

32. *Alta California*, August 27, 1873.

33. U.S. Congress, 387–920.

34. M. Coolidge, *Chinese Immigration* (New York: Henry Holt & Co., 1909), 419.

35. U.S. Congress, 1165.

36. U.S. Industrial Commission, 762; Gibson, *Chinese in America*, 146–54.

37. U.S. Senate, *Chinese Exclusion* (Washington, D.C.: Government Printing Office, 1902), 470–72 (hereafter cited as U.S. Senate).

38. H. Lai, "The Chinese Experience at Angel Island," *East/West* 10 (1976): 7–9; R. Dillon, *The Hatchet Men* (New York, 1962), 290.

39. Lai, "Angel Island."

40. A. McLeod, *Pigtails and Gold Dust* (Caldwell, ID: Caxton Printers, 1948), 18.

41. U.S. Industrial Commission, 763.

42. Dillon, *Hatchet Men*, 319–21.

43. U.S. Congress, 599; C. Wilson, *Chinatown Quest* (Stanford: Stanford Uni-

versity Press, 1950), 87; D. Gray, *Women of the West* (Millbrae, CA: Les Femmes Publishing, 1976), 69.

44. U.S. Senate, 124.

45. Holder, "Chinese Slavery in America," n. 22.

46. The establishment of orphanages and children's welfare organizations was partly responsible for the decline; see Ho, *Population of China*, n. 4, 58–62.

47. *Alta California*, January 31, 1875; *San Francisco Bulletin*, March 28, 1876; Y. Zhang, *San-zhou ri-Ji* (n.p., 1896), chap. 5.

48. Dillon, *Hatchet Men*.

49. McLeod, *Pigtails and Gold Dust*, 178.

50. Holder, "Chinese Slavery in America," n. 22, 292.

51. Dobie, *San Francisco's Chinatown*, n. 25, 195.

52. Dobie, *San Francisco's Chinatown*, 242–43; California Senate, 213.

53. Dobie, *San Francisco's Chinatown*, 61; A. Genthe, *Pictures of Old Chinatown* (New York: Moffet, Inc., 1909), 52.

54. California Senate, 28, 99, 176; and Dillon, *Hatchet Men*, 46.

55. *Sacramento Bee* June 5, 1876; S. Lyman, *Chinese Americans* (New York: Random House, 1974), 94.

56. U.S. Congress, 192.

57. Dobie, *San Francisco's Chinatown*, 243.

58. McLeod, *Pigtails and Gold Dust*, 182–83; U.S. Congress, 192.

59. Cases of polyandry among the Chinese in San Francisco and Californian interior towns are reported by Henry K. Sienkiewicz, "The Chinese in California," *California Historical Society Quarterly* 34 (1953): 307.

60. McLeod, *Pigtails and Gold Dust*, 183.

61. Fisk University, 34.

62. J. Kemble, "Andrew Wilson's Jottings on Civil War California," *California Historical Society Quarterly* 32 (1953): 209–24, 303–12.

63. Holder, "Chinese Slavery in America," n. 22, 292.

64. U.S. Industrial Commission, 783; Shepherd, "Chinese Girl Slavery," n. 23, 892–95; Fisk University, 31–35.

65. U.S. Industrial Commission, 783; G. Leong, *Chinatown Inside Out* (New York: Barrows Mussey, 1936), 231; Wilson, *Chinatown Quest*, n. 43.

66. *Alta*, April 14, 1870; California Senate, 99.

67. S. Wu, *Mei-guo Huo-quao bai-nian ji-shi*, n. 19, 92; McLeod, *Pigtails and Gold Dust*, n. 40, 177.

68. Although not specified in the contract, I suspect that the currency used was Mexican silver dollars. One Mexican dollar was equivalent to approximately U.S. $0.48 in the mid-nineteenth century.

69. The other three contracts can be found in California Senate, 1877, 128 and 135; U.S. Industrial Commission, 771.

70. U.S. Senate, 227–28.

71. K. Xie, *Mai-yin zhi-duyu Taz-wan chang-ji wen-ti* (Taipei, 1972), 352.

72. W. Sanger, *The History of Prostitution* (New York: Arno Press, 1939); McLeod, *Pigtails and Gold Dust*, 183.

73. The contracts examined indicate that a prostitute had to work a minimum of 320 days per year. An absence of more than fifteen days would subject her to a penalty of having to work one additional month, and menstruation disorder was limited to one month's rest per year.

74. Dobie, *San Francisco's Chinatown*, n. 25, 243.

75. B. Lloyd, *Lights and Shades of San Francisco* (San Francisco, 1876).
76. Dillon, *Hatchet Men*, n. 38.
77. E. Robbins, "Chinese Slave Girls," *Overland Monthly,* n.s., 51 (1908): 100–102; California Senate, 106, 155, 197.
78. California Bureau of Labor Statistics, *Biennial Reports 1887–1888* (Sacramento: State Office, 1888), 104.
79. U.S. Bureau of the Census, *Historical Statistics of the United States: Colonial Times to 1970* (Washington, D.C.: Government Printing Office, 1975), 165.
80. U.S. Industrial Commission, 786; Leong, *Chinatown Inside Out,* n. 65; Fisk University, 36.
81. California Senate, 146, 154; and U.S. Congress, 211, 1169; Dobie, *San Francisco's Chinatown,* n. 25, 243.
82. U.S. Congress, 1170.
83. *Alta,* March 26, 1873.
84. *Alta,* December 4, 1870; U.S. Congress, 110, 211.
85. California Senate, 213.
86. Ibid., 164–66.
87. M. Stabler, "A Bit of Blue China," *Out West,* n.s., 3 (1911): 256–59; and U.S. Congress, 96.
88. U.S. Congress, 96; and California Senate, 99.
89. California Senate, 99, 180; *Alta,* July 6, 1876; and Y. Fu, *You-li Mei-li-jia guo tu-jing You-ji-lei,* vol. 5 (n.p., 1889).
90. *San Francisco Chronicle,* April 1, 1877.
91. "Bancroft Scraps," an unpublished collection of newspaper clippings (Bancroft Library, University of California, Berkeley), vols. 6–9 (1862–81); Wilson, *Chinatown Quest,* n. 23.
92. Calilornia Senate, 120.
93. *San Francisco Bulletin,* June 11, 1878.
94. *California Chinese Chatter* (San Francisco, 1927).
95. California Senate, 166.
96. Ibid., 158.
97. Ibid., 113.
98. Bancroft Library has in its collection of Chinese immigration pamphlets advertisements for such secret formulae. "Chinese Immigration Miscellaneous," unnumbered boxes, Bancroft Library, University of California, Berkeley.
99. U.S. Congress, 142.
100. U.S. Industrial Commission, 778; Gray, *Women of the West,* n. 45, 69.
101. *San Francisco Chronicle,* December 5, 1869.
102. *Alta,* October 9, 1870.
103. M. Slingerland, *Child Welfare Work in California* (New York, 1915), 98–99.
105. U.S. Congress, 192.
106. San Francisco Board of Supervisors, *Special Committee Report on Chinatown* (San Francisco, 1885), 9; and California Bureau of Labor Statistics, *Biennial Reports, 1887–1888* (Sacramento: State Office, 1888), 108.
107. Coolidge, *Chinese Immigration,* n. 34, 502.
108. V. Nee and B. Nee, *Longtime Californ'* (New York: Pantheon Books, 1973); J. Hooks, *Women's Occupation through Seven Decades* (Washington, D.C.: Women's Bureau, 1947); B. Liu, *Mei-guo Hua-giao shi* (Taipei: Li-ming, 1976).
109. S. Lyman, "Conflict and the Web of Group Affiliation in San Francisco's Chinatown, 1880–1910," *Pacific Historical Review* 43 (1974): 473–99.
110. Dillon, *Hatchet Men,* n. 38; 1. Light, "From Vice District to Tourist Attraction,"

Pacific Historical Review 43 (1974): 367–94; and Liu, *Mei-guo Hua-giao shi*; Lyman, "Web of Group Affiliation."

111. Q. Liang, *Xin-da-lu You-i, jie-lu* (Shanghai, 1936), 110.

112. T. Chen, *Emigrant Communities*, n. 3; Hsiao, *Rural China*, n. 2; G. Li, *Huan-you di-qiu xin-lu* (n.p., 1877); D. Li, "Zao-qi Hua-ren yi-Mei ji An-ji-li tiao-yue qian-ding," *Lien-ho Shu-Yuan Xue-bao* 3 (1964): 1–29; and *Mei-quo Hua-gia shi*.

113. Light, "Vice District."

114. E. Gong and B. Grant, *Tong War!* (New York: Brown, Inc., 1930); Dillon, *Hatchet Men*, n. 38; C. Reynolds, "Chinese Tongs," *American Journal of Sociology* 40 (1935): 610–23; C. Lee, *Days of the Tong Wars*, n. 19.

115. California Senate; U.S. Congress; and U.S. Senate.

116. California Senate, 163.

117. Gibson, *Chinese in America*, n. 10; and Liu, *Mei-guo Hua-giao shi*, n. 108.

118. D. Smith, *Rocky Mountain Mining Camps*, n. 7.

119. Robbins, "Chinese Slave Girls," n. 77; Wilson, *Chinatown Quest*, n. 23; Gray, *Women of the West*, n. 43, 67–74.

120. Gray, *Women of the West*, 74.

121. U.S. Industrial Commission, 788.

122. Wilson, *Chinatown Quest*.

123. *Alto,* July 31, 1873.

124. Wilson, *Chinatown Quest*, 85, 125; *Alta*, May 28, 1876.

125. Gray, *Women of the West*, n. 43.

126. L. Rotenberg, "The Wayward Worker: Toronto's Prostitute at the Turn of the Century," in *Women at Work,* ed. J. Acton, P. Goldsmith, and R. Shepherd (Toronto: Canadian Women's Ediucational Press, 1974), 33–69.

part three

Modernization and A New Century

MODERNIZATION AND A NEW CENTURY

Identity

We have opened this section with a discussion of identity. In this we allow the voices of their time the lead in setting the agenda. The confusion that reigned over "who was what and how to tell" dominated the public discussion. This borderland—between the known and the unknown, the seen and the unseen, the homosexual and the heterosexual—produced a powerful driving force to twentieth century sexual development. While the obsession hardly disappeared after this early moment, the heightened focus in the early twentieth century clearly reminds us of our own fascinations in the early twenty-first century.

The stories told here reinforce a sense of the past and the future colliding in a present that reveals itself to be a mixture of both. For example, as George Chauncey Jr. discusses in his classic and influential essay "Christian Brotherhood or Sexual Perversion? Homosexual Identities and the Construction of Sexual Boundaries in the World War I Era," Navy officials grappling with the conduct of sailors engaged in homosexual activity had to operate within longstanding categories of behavior. It is precisely their familiarity with what suddenly seemed like radically different behavior that forced a reevaluation of everything they thought they knew. As sailors testified to homosexual encounters, they, and their official interrogators, came to a fundamental recognition that the borders marking gender no longer denoted sexual knowledge as well.

Lisa Duggan's fascinating lesbian murderess Alice Mitchell brought out all the leading experts of her day as they sought to explain and "fix" her within a web of certainty. Yet Mitchell eluded classification and Duggan uses the attempt to call attention to not only Mitchell's indeterminacy but also the fraught and tendentious nature of the process itself. Through a story of "madness and murder," Duggan reminds us that "self presentation" in the borderlands trumps the expert testimony with its "determination to dissent."

From these struggles, heterosexuality was born.

Sex and the State

As noted in the introduction, state attempts to regulate sexuality have a long history in America. From Puritan punishment for crimes against reproduction to miscegenation laws that determined the limitations of racial definitions, lawmakers have often eagerly interfered with the bodies of Americans and the sexual practices in which they engaged.

The change in the twentieth century reflected the expanded state itself. As the country grew so too did the call for an enhanced civil authority. We often celebrate the modern state which cares for its citizens with pension plans and health care for the sick. Yet this shift to seeing the individual as someone in whom the state has a personal interest carries with it the inevitable likelihood that sexuality too will engage the state's attention.

Unsurprisingly, when that moment comes in the twentieth century, it carried with it the burdens of past struggles. From the nineteenth century, the state brought forward the racial fears which had so defined citizenship. Peggy Pascoe looks at the effort to construct a supposedly race-blind legal theory in "Miscegenation Law, Court Cases, and Ideologies of Race in Twentieth Century America." In Pascoe's examples, those using the courts to express racial fears in the twentieth century offered a more subtle but no less effective modern radicalized discourse. Pascoe's complex reading of these ideologies uncovers their racist potential and requires us to reevaluate our assumptions about law and race.

Class stands as a constant in these discussions and Ruth Alexander's research points to the serious fate awaiting working-class women under the regulatory eye of early-twentieth-century reformers in New York. In "The 'Girl Problem:' Female Sexual Delinquency in New York, 1900–1930," Alexander highlights an old sexual problem made new again—how the middle class needed to police appropriate heterosexual conduct in the industrial economy. As the border between the traditions of community and the realities of urban life broke down, young single working women began their own adventures in self-definition—to the consternation of social reformers.

Organizing a challenge to middle-class sexuality proved difficult even for political groups committed to a revolutionary critique of American capitalism. Kathleen Brown and Elizabeth Faue examine the complex and often contradictory sexual ideologies and practices of members of the left in the 1920s and 30s. Believing themselves alienated from American society, the left retreated from pre-war discussions of sexual emancipation and gender equality. Despite the official return to sexual conservatism, however, members of the left explored a variety of sexual arrangements and practices such as nonmonogamy, interracial relationships, and homosexuality. They note the difficulty that members of the left in applying basic beliefs about sexual equality and self-ownership to their sexual practices. Their article further reinforces the disjuncture between ideology and practice and encourages us to look beyond official pronouncements to understand how individuals negotiated the borderlands of changing sexualities and political ideals.

Consumption, Popular Culture, and a Visual Society

If the twentieth century can be said to truly contribute something new to this story, then it is in the vast expansion of consumer culture and the collateral explosion of visual technologies. Sex became currency in the consumer world and, as might be expected, a significant component of that which appeared in the visual society. These elements presented sexuality as it was, revealed more of what might be hidden, and ultimately helped transform our relationship to sexuality more profoundly than any previous historical development.

While some progressive reformers were interested in controlling the sexual geography of the city and young women's sexual behavior, others explored how the sexual practices of non-European cultures could liberate their sexuality. The move towards cultural relativism and the anti-modernist sentiment held by some prominent social scientists led white men and women to look for more "natural" and consequently uninhibited sexual practices among Native American societies. This interest in controlling and appropriating the cultures of non-Western people also spilled over to the emergent consumer culture. Midori Takagi examines how images of the Orient entered into advertising initially to support imperialism. She argues that the images of the "oriental" as the exotic other strengthened European Americans' images of themselves as civilizers. Closer to home, American women saw Asian womanhood as an exotic commodity which they could purchase through consumer goods. Like Cheng, Takagi underscores the importance of international politics and economic developments in how Americans view their sexual identities.

The growing importance of consumer culture played a key role in modern constructions of sexuality. It became a space in which Americans acted out and debated changes in sexual behaviors and identities. Joanne Meyerowitz's essay examines the proliferation of cheesecake images of women in popular magazines and the conflicts that those images engendered. Essential to the modernization of sexuality, these images came to represent "our primary public symbol of eroticism." With an eye to current feminist debates over pornography, Meyerowitz is hesitant to dismiss these images as solely degrading to women. Instead her interest is in examining the debates between women over the meaning of these images. For some women these images represented the objectification of women, but for others, these images allowed them to explore sexual desire.

Meyerowitz examines these debates in both magazines geared to a white audience and those directed towards African Americans. As did white readers, African Americans were concerned about the appropriateness of sexual images; but unlike white readers, African Americans had to take account of a historical tradition that defined African American women as sexually available. For some readers, these images reinforced these racist assumptions; for others, however, they provided African American women with images of beauty. As in the white community, these debates illustrate that the line demarking older Victorian values and sexual modernity was not a hard and fast one. Instead, that line was a malleable frontier in which competing images of womanhood shaped women's participation in a modern sexual culture.

7

The Trials of Alice Mitchell: Sensationalism, Sexology, and the Lesbian Subject in Turn-of-the-Century America

Lisa Duggan

The years 1880 to 1920 were a crucible of change in gender and sexual relations in the United States. This long transition was neither even nor easy; it was deeply marked by conflict and tragedy as well as by erotic excitements. As Victorian certainties faded and the possibilities of the modern slowly materialized, new sexualities took shape and the modern desiring subject emerged.

Historians writing about this transition now generally agree that the modern lesbian was one such new desiring subject appearing at the turn of the century in Europe and Anglo-America.[1] They argue not that sexual relations or love between women were new then, but that the subjectivity this lesbian embodied was a radical innovation. She came to see herself as an erotic subject—as a woman whose desire for women was felt as a fundamental component of her sense of self, marking her as erotically different from most other women. As the period progressed, this new subjective sense of self interacted in a complex way with the emergence of public lesbian identities and communities.

The new lesbian relationships that formed in the midst of these changes significantly modified earlier forms of women's partnerships, which have been described by historians as falling within two broadly defined class-bound types—the romantic friendship in which bourgeois girls and women made passionate commitments to each other within a gender-segregated female world, and the "marriage" between a "female husband" who passed and worked as a man among workingmen and her "wife."[2] The historical picture of the transition from these earlier forms of relationship to modern lesbianism—the emergence of lesbian subjectivity into public visibility at the end of the nineteenth century—exists only in broad outline and mostly with respect to white women, both working class and bourgeois. The long historical process through which a new identity was constructed remains relatively obscure. At the heart of this obscurity lies the problematic relationship between the cultural representations (or texts) that historians use as sources and the living historical subjects who produced, consumed, and reproduced them.

The difficulty for historians is illustrated in the debate over the meaning of the figure of the "mannish lesbian"—a figure ubiquitous in published sources of many kinds by the early twentieth century.[3] Was this figure a distorted representation produced by antifeminist sexologists, intent on discrediting and stigmatizing the relationships of newly independent New Women? Or was the mannish lesbian in part a strategically deployed self-representation, used by some sexually active New Women to carve out a new identity? Underlying this debate are questions about the nature of the relationship between the representations of mannish lesbians in various texts and the subjectivities and identities of living women: Did hostile sexologists construct the mannish lesbian, or did she, in any meaningful way, construct herself?

Early in the nineteenth century, for instance, aristocratic British diarist Anne Lister represented herself as erotically interested in women exclusively and associated this interest with her appropriations of various aspects of masculinity.[4] But women such as Lister were relatively isolated and did not form socially visible networks or forge connections linking their sexual subjectivity to public representations of lesbianism, as began to happen later in the century. Nonetheless, the manner in which they linked masculine traits, economic independence, and the erotic love of women drew on and reproduced tropes of sexual difference in combinations that presaged modern lesbian identities. The interrelations of their early representations with those of the first sexologists present historians with a polyvocal cultural dialogue not reducible to any single site of historical invention.

In these pages, I want to examine this complex dialogue in a new way. I want to look at the project of constructing identities as a historical process of contested narration, a process in which contrasting "stories" of the self and others—stories of difference—are told, appropriated, and retold as stories of location in the social world of structured inequalities. Looked at in this way, individual and collective subjectivities are interactively linked to representations (including self-representations) through historically and materially specific stories of identity. In illustration, I will show here how mass-circulation newspapers fashioned stories out of living women's relationships, how sexologists then reappropriated those stories as "cases," and how women themselves reworked them as "identities" in an extended battle over the meaning of women's erotic partnerships at the turn of the century. Out of this battle, the first publicly visible forms of modern lesbianism were born; as we shall see, it was a terrifyingly difficult birth.

Identity is defined in these pages as a narrative of a subject's location within social structure. As stories rather than mere labels, identities traverse the space between the social world and subjective experience, constituting a central organizing principle connecting self and world. Individual identities, usually multiple and often contradictory, structure and give meaning to personal experience. Collective identities—of gender, race, class, or nation—forge connections among individuals and provide links between past and present, becoming the basis for cultural representation and political action.

In an extended discussion of the problems facing feminists addressing such theoretical problems, Teresa de Lauretis modifies the poststructuralist rejection of the notion of unmediated experience by redefining experience "in the general sense of a process by which, for all social beings, subjectivity is constructed. Through that process one places oneself or is placed in social reality, and so perceives and comprehends as subjective (referring to, even originating in, oneself) those relations— material, economic, and interpersonal—which are in fact social, and, in a larger perspective, historical."[5] I use the term *experience* in de Lauretis's sense. Identity, I argue, is the story or narrative structure that gives meaning to experience.

Stories of identity are never static, monolithic, or politically innocent. By situating people within shifting structures of social power and inequality, they become contested sources of authority and legitimation. This is especially true during moments of radical social transformation. Old stories assume new narrative meanings; new stories emerge, patched together from cultural fragments appropriated for new purposes.[6] Never created out of whole cloth, never uniquely individual, each narrative is a retelling, an act of social interaction, a positioned intervention in the shared, contested narratives of a given culture.[7]

"Lesbian" was just such a bitterly contested identity at the turn of the century, as new stories of lesbian life and experience developed at the changing nexus of gender identity and sexuality. The content of the identities "man" and "woman" shifted from their Victorian to their modern configurations, and the heterosexual/homosexual polarity emerged as a newly central preoccupation of gendered stories of identity.[8] Lesbianism in particular emerged as an issue in debates about female sexuality, aggression, economic independence, education, reform efforts, and feminism. Contests over the meanings of stories of lesbian identity expressed profound social anxiety over the boundary masculine/feminine itself. By tracing new stories of lesbian identity as they developed out of the earlier stories of romantic friends and female husbands, and by examining how they were reworked and retold by different agents to different audiences for different and often conflicting social ends, we can observe the process of contested narration in motion.

One of the most sensational early accounts of a relationship perceived as of a new type was contained in the news reports of the 1892 murder of seventeen-year-old Freda Ward by nineteen-year-old Alice Mitchell in Memphis, Tennessee. Headlines nationwide announced that this was "A Very Unnatural Crime" in which the murderess claimed to have loved her victim so much that she killed her rather than live estranged from her. Though the murders of spouses and sweethearts—commonly called *love-murders*—were frequent fare of sensational news, this one was treated as nearly incomprehensible and as unique on American soil. The *New York World,* for instance, reported that because of Mitchell's act,

> a sober American community and an unimaginative American court must deal in a matter-of-fact fashion with matters which have been discussed hitherto by French writers of fiction only. Gen. Luke E. Wright and Col. George Gantt, of Tennessee, find themselves compelled to do in open court the work that Balzac did in tracing to physical sources mental perversion. In the Criminal Court of Memphis, Shelby County, Adolphe Belot's *Mlle.[Giraud] J Ma Femme* will be the only text-book at hand. Judge DuBose, of Tennessee, will have cited to him, as bearing on the case of an American girl, the creations of French writers whom he and all his associates have looked upon as perverted creatures, dealing with matters outside of real life, or at least outside of American life.
>
> In all the long history of crime and insanity there is no such case recorded.[9]

Other such cases were in fact recorded. By 1892, there was a developing medical literature on same-sex love and its relation to crime and insanity produced by American doctors who adapted the theories of Krafft-Ebing and other Europeans. These doctors were captivated by Alice Mitchell's love-murder, which seemed a perfect illustration of their theories. Innumerable articles were published applying the new theories to this case, which was added in turn to later editions of Krafft-Ebing's *Psychopathia Sexualis.*[10] By 1901 the first American edition of Havelock Ellis's *Sexual Inversion* stated that Alice Mitchell was "a typical invert of a very pronounced kind" and that "there have been numerous cases in America more recently."[11]

The story of Alice Mitchell's murder of Freda Ward persisted as a topic of newspaper sensationalism and of scientific sexology well into the twentieth century. The case also served as the partial basis for at least three works of fiction, a folk ballad that survived in oral tradition into the 1960s, and a proposed play for Sarah Bernhardt to be written by famed librettist Victorian Sardou (Bernhardt visited Mitchell in jail and kept a scrapbook on the case).[12]

Alice was not tried in criminal court for the murder. Instead, she appeared at a lunacy inquisition. The plan of the attorneys hired by her father was to have her declared "presently insane" and incompetent to stand trial, then confined to the state lunatic asylum as dangerous to the community. They brought physicians into the courtroom to testify as experts that Alice was insane. The prosecution countered that she was rational but vicious, degraded, and "fast."

To make their case, the defense attorneys constructed Alice's life as a case history and presented it to expert witnesses as the basis for their opinions. The case history read, in part, as follows:

HYPOTHETICAL CASE[13]

Alice was a nervous, excitable child, somewhat undersize. As she grew she did not manifest interest in those childish amusements and toys that girls are fond of.

When only 4 or 5 years old she spent much time at a swing in the yard of the family, in performing such feats upon it as skinning the cat and hanging by an arm or leg. She was fond of climbing, and expert at it.

She delighted in marbles and tops, in base ball and foot ball. . . . She spent much time with her brother Frank. . . . She preferred him and his sports to her sisters. He practiced with her at target shooting with a small rifle, to her great delight. She excelled this brother . . . at feats of activity. She was fond of horses. . . . To the family she seemed a regular tomboy.

. . . She disliked sewing and needle work. . . . To most persons, even her relatives, she seemed distant and indifferent. She was wholly without that fondness for boys that girls usually manifest.

She had no intimates or child sweethearts among the boys, and when approaching womanhood . . . she had no beaux and took no pleasure in the society of young men. She was regarded as mentally wrong by young men toward whom she had thus acted. . . .

For Fred Ward, a girl about her own age, she had an extraordinary fondness. . . . The attachment seemed to be mutual, but was far stronger in Alice Mitchell than in Fred.

They were very different in disposition. Fred was girl-like and took no pleasure in the boyish sports that Alice delighted in. Her instincts and amusements were feminine. She was tender and affectionate. Time strengthened the intimacy between them. They became lovers in the sense of that relation between persons of different sexes. . . .

In Feb. 1891, Alice proposed marriage. She repeated the offer in three separate letters. To each Fred replied, agreeing to become her wife. Alice wrote her upon the third promise that she would hold her to the engagement, and that she would kill her if she broke the promise. . . .

It was agreed that Alice should be known as Alvin J. Ward, so that Fred could still call her by pet name Allie, and Fred was to be known as Mrs. A. J. Ward. The particulars of formal marriage and elopement were agreed upon. Alice was to put on man's apparel, and have her hair trimmed by a barber like a man; was to get the license to marry, and Fred was to procure the Rev. . . . [or] a justice of the peace to marry them. The ceremony performed, they intended to leave for St. Louis. Alice was to continue to wear man's apparel, and meant to try and have a mustache, if it would please Fred. She was going out to work for Fred in men's clothes.

In the latter part of June, 1891, Ashley Roselle . . . began to pay court to Fred, who gave him one of her photographs. The watchful vigilance of Alice got track of this affair, and she remonstrated warmly with Fred, and charged her with deception and infidelity. Fred acknowledged she had done wrong, vowed unshaken fidelity to Alice, and promised never more to offend.

The scheme of marrying and eloping seemed almost ready for execution in the latter part of July. . . . By chance, Mrs. Volkmar, the married sister . . . with whom Fred was living, saw part of the correspondence of the girls, which disclosed the relations between them, and the plans to elope and marry. . . . An exciting scene ensued. Mrs. Volkmar wrote to Mrs. Mitchell, the mother of Alice, and at the same time wrote to Alice, returning the engagement ring, and other love tokens, and declaring that all intercourse between the girls must at once cease. . . .

The effect on Alice of the return of the engagement ring and the inhibition of all communication with Fred was almost crushing. She wept, passed sleepless nights, lost her appetite, frequently declined even to come to the table. . . .

. . . In her language she more than loved Fred. She took her life because she had told her she would, and because it was her duty to do it. The best thing would have been the marriage, the next best thing was to kill Fred. That would make sure that no one else could get her.

This account was, of course, a strategic construction, a case history designed to procure a particular medical opinion and a desired legal outcome. But unlike the medical case histories published in journals and texts, this one was corroborated by the testimony of witnesses and contested in court through cross-examination and the testimony of opposing witnesses. Family members and neighbors, as well as Alice herself, recounted their version of events, and Alice and Freda's letters were read aloud and printed in the papers. The newspaper reports of this hypothetical case, the testimony, and the trial summarized the many tellings and retellings of the story of love and murder from multiple points of view.

The relations of Alice and Freda emerged in these stories as a hybrid form developed from different class contexts. At first, their love was perceived as an ordinary, if excessive, schoolgirls' romantic friendship—in Memphis, such relations were called "chumming."[14] But their plans for cross-dressing and marriage pushed them beyond the bounds of that category. They had adopted a classic "passing" strategy—a strategy so rare among bourgeois white women that their plan was perceived as so radically inappropriate as to be insane. Though the local papers regularly noted cases of workingmen and farm laborers who turned out to be "passing" women, their lives and partnerships with other women were reported as simply eccentric or remarkable—not sexual, deviant, or insane. But at the trial, Alice's belief that she could marry Freda while disguised as "Alvin" was portrayed by her attorneys and their medical experts, and reported in the press, as a "morbid" or "imperative delusion" and a sign of sexual "perversion."

The descriptions of witnesses and experts at trial also reveal an emerging belief that Alice's plan to pass as Alvin was not merely a disguise but an expression of some deep and partially hidden truth—that Alice was masculine and that her masculinity and her desire for Freda were linked. For medical writers, this link was the basis for the construction of female sexual "inversion."[15] But the link was also made by Alice before the interventions following the murder; it shaped her relations with Freda.

The "story" of Alice and Freda up to the time of the murder, as it was presented and reworked in the mass-circulation press during 1892, was composed of three essential structural elements. First, the contrast drawn between Alice's "masculine" characteristics and Freda's "feminine" manner was universally agreed on—repeated not only by doctors but also by Alice's best friend Lillie, by the girls' school principal, and by neighbors. It also ran clearly through Alice's and Freda's published letters.

Second, conflict between Alice and Freda over the nature of their relationship was presented as the first and possibly the most important foundation for the later violence. Alice wanted Freda to commit herself totally to their love; Freda vacillated, making and breaking engagements with at least two young men. Alice was certain that she wanted to marry Freda and that she herself had no interest in men; Freda was full of doubt and treated Alice as one among several suitors. This conflict led Alice to threats of violence and a suicide attempt. The plan to elope was a sign of, and a means to ensure, Alice's ultimate success in securing the relationship and in ensuring that Freda would not betray Alice by marrying a man.

The third structural element of the story is conflict between the engaged couple and their female relatives. Although Freda's older sister and Alice's mother did not object to the intensity of their attachment or the continual displays of physical affection, nor even to their exchange of engagement rings, the plan to elope with Alice posing as Alvin led the older women to end all contact between the lovers. Male relatives and the world of male authority were not brought into the affair until after the murder; only then did Alice come into direct conflict with the male-dominated institutions of law and medicine.

Running through all three elements of the story are themes of cross-gender identification and cross-dressing. Though there was no evidence reported of any sexual contact between Alice and Freda (and both those who claimed they were pure and those who claimed they indulged in unnatural practices had ulterior motives), there were indications in the news accounts that they recognized, played with, and eroticized a masculine/feminine difference between them. In her most affectionate letters, Freda referred to Alice as "Alvin" and included lines such as "If you chew tobacco, love, I won't let you kiss me."[16] In their conflict over the nature of their relationship, Alice used the plan to cross-dress and marry as a strategy to define their love as a serious commitment equivalent to any of Freda's potential connections to a man. In their conflict with female relatives, the gender-crossing and elopement plans were a red flag signaling that these young women had gone too far and that their relationship had to be viewed as dangerous and possibly sexual rather than as foolishly but harmlessly romantic.

Overall, the cumulative newspaper story of Alice and Freda constituted one version of a new narrative-in-formation—a cultural marker of the emergence of a partially cross-gender-identified lesbian and her separation from and conflict with the family-based female world of the nineteenth century and, in this version of the story, from the bourgeois values of sexual purity and motherhood. In this story, I interpret Alice's "masculinity" as a paradoxical strategy, moving her both away from and closer to a life with other women. Her cross-gender identification worked as an expression of difference from other women, as a rejection of the pastimes and the conventional family-based relations of the female world, and as a mark of her commitment to the lasting erotic love of women. As part of her conflict with Alice, Freda expressed another kind of ambivalence toward the world of women represented by her sisters; she was ultimately reintegrated into its conventions through obedience to female authority. Her attachment to Alice might have been an interlude in an otherwise traditionally feminine life. But Alice's wish to leave the female world and to escape its conventions was so profound and unshakable that its frustration led her to destroy Freda and eventually herself as well. Alice, committed to the Tennessee State Insane Asylum at Bolivar in 1892, died in 1898; her death was reported as due to tuberculosis, but in a later interview one of the attorneys involved in the case claimed that she had killed herself by jumping into the water tower.[17]

This narrative-in-formation appeared in various permutations in newspapers throughout the period 1880–1920. But such narratives were not merely the lurid, sensational productions of prosperous, white, male editors and reporters. Though the newspaper stories did stress the element of violence for shock value, they were nonetheless based on the stories women told about their own relationships. The newspaper retellings, altered to fit the worldview and assumptions of reporters and editors and the expectations, fears, and fantasies of readers, were not free of the shaping influence of women like Alice Mitchell and of the story she told her family, lawyers, trial experts, and court. They were, that is, not simply impositions but appropriations.

The press coverage of the Mitchell-Ward murder in 1892 stimulated especially intense attention to many similar cases. Some were cast as memories of cases past.[18] Others were accounts of rumors, denied by the principals.[19] The story of Alice and Freda as it appeared in the mainstream daily press also had precursors in the disreputable crime and police papers of earlier decades.[20] Some of these older accounts were picked up and circulated in the mainstream press and in the medical literature after the Mitchell-Ward murder. The newspaper stories that resulted varied somewhat, especially with regard to the class and racial contexts within which they were situated, but all shared one or more of the three structural elements of the Mitchell-Ward tale.

On February 11, 1892, for instance, the *Memphis Public Ledger*[21] appended to an article on the Mitchell-Ward case a short report headlined "The Case of Male Impersonator Marie Hindle, Who Beaued the Girls at Broome's Variety Theater. Almost a Parallel Case." It read:

Discussion of the Mitchell-Ward murder has brought to light a number of similar cases of abnormal affection existing between persons of the same sex, differing only in that they did not end in the death of one "lover" at the hands of the other. But there was a case of the kind located in Memphis, which narrowly missed being a prototype of that which is now engaging so much attention all over the country. It dates back nearly twenty-three years, but is still fresh in the memory of citizens who were familiar with the local life after dark of that period.

In 1869–70 the bright particular star of Broome's Variety Theater, on Jefferson Street, was Marie Hindle, a very attractive woman, who played male parts. Nature had especially fitted her for that line of the business. Her features and voice were masculine, and her tastes in accord with her physical peculiarities. Though by no means chary of accepting the admiration of the other sex, she cared nothing for men as such. Her inclination was altogether toward women, and she inspired in them a like feeling toward herself. It was remarked by the stage hands and those among the habitues who were admitted to the inner circle of the performers that Marie was a reigning beau among the petticoat brigade, from the well-paid high kicker to the humblest "chair warmer."

Two of the former class were special favorites of hers. The girls were named Ione and Lizette, both pretty and clever and both madly in love with Marie. She distributed her favor with so much tact that each considered herself the queen bee in the Hindle hive, and neither had any eyes for the male creatures in their train when she was present. They were jealous of each other in a way, but Marie always managed to prevent active hostilities occurring between them. But the fires of rivalry were kindled and only needed occasion to break forth in flame.

The time came toward the close of the season when Marie had made ready to go on to New York to fill an engagement at the Bowery Theater. Ione and Lizette were wild with grief at the thought of parting from her, and would scarcely let her out of their sight. Naturally, each grudged the other a moment of their common idol's time, and jealousy gave place to hatred. When the day of separation came they were wrought up to a pitch that made them reckless of consequences. Both had laid on their war paint and got ready for action.

The night of Marie's departure found them in a state bordering on frenzy. Each had resolved to act as Marie's special escort from the Overton Hotel, where she was stopping, to the train that was to bear her away; and neither was aware of the other's intention. They chanced to meet at the ladies' entrance to the hotel. It was a match to the magazine. Instantly there came an explosion which attracted the attention of several men standing near, one of whom was Dick English, the river editor of the *Appeal*. He knew of the enmity existing between the two girls, and fearing lest they should do something desperate he ran toward them. By the time he reached the spot they had clinched and were struggling around in the alley.

He kept on after them and reached them just as they pulled out knives and began carving each other. He seized them, and with the assistance of another man, who had followed him, succeeded in separating them and wresting their weapons from their hands, but not until both had received ugly slashes on the face and bosom. But for his timely arrival and prompt action there would have been murder done.

Marie Hindle repeated in New York the professional conquests of her Memphis career. Again she became a successful rival of the gilded youth in the affections of the girls of the company and not a few among her audience. One of the latter she singled out for a favorite and they lived together up to the time of her death, which occurred not long ago. After this it was reported, and published in the papers, that she had actually married the girl.

"Mrs. Hindle" was interviewed by a New York paper soon after her partner passed away. She seemed overcome with grief at her loss and said that Marie had been "a dear, good husband."

This little story, both comic and contemptuous (and, of course, featuring male heroism), drew on and reframed various stock nineteenth-century narrative conventions. It was anything but "factual," and was full of gross errors as well as predictable distortions. Marie was actually Annie Hindle, the first male impersonator to make a name for herself on the American stage.[22] She did in fact marry a woman, Annie Ryan, with female impersonator Gilbert Saroney at her side. But it was Ryan who died in 1891. The story, both the apocryphal and the real, had little in common with the Mitchell-Ward case except for one important element—the masculine/feminine contrast between Hindle and her admirers, with only the manly Hindle believed to be inclined exclusively toward women in her affections. This difference was clearly eroticized, and the Variety Theater, on the very margins of respectability, provided a rare setting for its expression. Another 1892 article in a Lincoln, Nebraska, entertainment paper, *Vanity Fair*, also linked the Mitchell-Ward case with the story of Hindle, getting more of the facts right and commenting that "it is a fact that this dashing singer was the recipient of as many 'mash' notes as ever went to a stage favorite of this country. Once she compared notes with H. J. Montague, that carelessly handsome actor at whose

shrine so many silly women had worshiped; but Hindle's admirers out-
numbered his, and they were all women, strange as it may seem."[23]

The tragic conflicts that led to the Memphis murder never appeared
in tales of Hindle's life and career (though she did have a brief and mis-
erable marriage to the man who founded the Elks Lodge). Such good
fortune was no doubt due to the theater's serving as an institution where
collectivities of those with unconventional gender identifications and
sexual lives could congregate relatively free from censure. For this reason Hindle's story also did not include isolation within the white bourgeois family, as did Alice Mitchell's. (Interestingly, both Alice and Freda
were themselves "stage struck" and had fantasies of running off to join
the theater.)

Another article, published in the *Memphis Weekly Commercial*,[24] told
a story of Addie Phillips, whose mother worried that her love for Minnie Hubbard would develop into a "Mitchell-Ward affair," and who was
thrown into despair when Addie, after swearing never to marry a man,
ran away from home and was found in a brothel. Male impersonation
was associated in this era with the demimonde and, geographically if not
literally, with prostitution.[25] This story focused on young women from
the barely respectable working class, at some social distance from Alice
Mitchell's wealthy family. But the newspaper story drew many comparisons between them, finding some marked similarities across class lines
and stressing the third element of the Mitchell-Ward "story"—the conflict between mother and daughter. The first element, the masculine/fem-
inine contrast, was absent in this version, while the second element of
conflict between the young women was only suggested: Addie was
reported to have wished to marry Minnie, but when they ran away
together, Minnie changed her mind and returned, to Addie's chagrin.

The mass circulation daily newspapers deliberately crossed class lines
in their reporting as part and parcel of their marketing strategy—but the
papers were controlled by local elites, and the stories of working-class
life were (re)told from the elite perspective. The newspapers were explicitly racist, however. Comparisons across racial lines were much rarer
and were laced with overt hostility or condescension. The *Memphis
Commercial* ran a series of stories under the heading "Similar Cases
Recalled"[26] on February 24, 1892 one of which follows:

> Mobile, Ala.—Eleanora Richardson is now lying at her home in this
> city, between the borders of life and death from seven stab wounds,
> the most severe being through the lower rib. She will die. She is a
> handsome and well-formed mulatto, 17 years of age. Emma Williams,
> a black but comely woman of 23, is in jail, awaiting the results of the
> wounds she inflicted upon her friend. . . . The motive was a paroxysm

of jealousy resulting from an unnatural passion similar to that case in Memphis, which has caused the world to wonder. The two women have been living in the same house for nearly a year. Eleanor says the past six months Emma Williams has been taking the most unusual interest in her. She has been showering caresses upon her daily and hourly, and though both were seen, the Williams girl went to work, and her wages supported and clothed her and the girl. If the Richardson girl spoke to a male acquaintance, the woman would upbraid her, and beg her not to allow any man to ever separate them. If any males called at the house the Williams woman would see them alone, invent excuses and resort to all artifices to prevent any interview with her companion. Last week Eleanora Richardson left the house where the Williams woman was and took up her residence with a married sister in another part of town. Her companion, wretched almost to the point of madness, yesterday afternoon was told by someone who knew of her unnatural infatuation, that Eleanora had left her because she was going to be married. This the Williams woman answered, "Never mind; I'll get her." She went immediately to the girl's house and . . . asked when . . . [she] was coming home. Her companion replied she would be back when her sister tired of her. Bursting into a fury of rage, the Williams woman said: "You are lying and trying to deceive me; you shall never marry that——," and rushing upon her she drew the murderous knife from her stocking and attacked her, plunging the knife into her body repeatedly, saying with each stab "Oh, you darling." The girl's screams finally brought her sister's husband on the scene, and the furious woman was seized and disarmed, but not until she had inflicted wounds which the physicians declare dangerous and possibly fatal.

This tale deploys the second element of the Mitchell-Ward narrative, the conflict between the two women over the nature of the relationship. Few of the many stories in the newspapers during 1892 had all of the structural elements of the Alice and Freda case. All such elements were most likely to appear in stories about bourgeois white women and girls. Given that these narratives appeared in daily newspapers produced primarily by and for privileged white people, it is not surprising that most of them were "about" the gender and sexual disputes of this limited population. The stories of developing lesbian identity among working women and prostitutes or among African-American, Chicana, or Asian women were not entirely absent from the newspapers, but they were not developed at length there. Research into other sources of these narratives may show them to have been structured differently.

A typical account of love and conflict between young white bourgeois women appeared in a long article published in the *New York Sun* and reprinted in the *Memphis Commercial*,[27] a cautionary tale written by a girls' boarding school principal.

LIKE MISS MITCHELL

. . . When Blanche's parents brought her to our school and confided her to my care she had just passed her sixteenth birthday. She was of a vivacious disposition and of a will rather inclined to be imperious. . . . Blanche was a very high-minded girl. Her ideals were all lofty. Though strangely ignorant of the real significance of love, courtship and marriage, she was very free with her criticisms of the attitude of men toward women. Her ideas on this subject were plainly derived from the literature of chivalry. . . .

Blanche lost no time in cultivating the friendship of Mary, the sweetest and most angelic of our flock. In disposition Mary was to Blanche as the soft spring rain is to the electricity which explodes and precipitates it to earth. She was of about the same age as Blanche, and equally innocent and ignorant. She seemed to yield with passive happiness to the new friendship held out to her. In a few weeks the individuality of Blanche seemed to have absorbed her individuality completely. They were constantly together, and both were supremely happy.

. . . Mary, like the ideal lady love, was softly and yieldingly affectionate. She leaned upon Blanche, looked up to her and trusted her as one whose strength and courage were wholly to be relied upon. Blanche on the other hand, exhibited the spirit, dash, and valor with the deferential devotion of the knight, the record of whose glorious career rested beneath her pillow. . . .

And when in a gayer mood I have seen her seize Mary unawares in the darkened hall or behind a door to steal a kiss, as is the fashion of more modern lovers. Neither made any attempt to conceal her infatuation from other pupils of the school, and as there were other cases of a similar kind, their behavior occasioned no particular comment. . . .

[Mary goes home to tend her sick mother and returns after several weeks, a changed girl.]

Mary had been playing a medley of gay dance music while Blanche stood regarding her gloomily from a corner of the room. Presently she approached the piano, and seizing Mary's hand to hers, exclaimed passionately: "Mary, Mary, don't you love me anymore?"

"Yes, my dicky bird—passionately," answered Mary gayily. "But not as you used to," broke in the poor girl.

"Well, if you were a nice young man now, for instance," said Mary, smilingly, "the case would be—"

"Ah, you are false," broke in Blanche, wringing her hands. "You who promised to be true till death! What is it you have in that locket?" she demanded angrily. And while the rest of us looked on too astonished to move, Blanche snatched the gold ornament hanging at Mary's throat, opened it, and with a cry of rage dashed it on the floor.

. . . A miniature photograph and a lock of dark hair were broken loose from their frame and lay on the carpet. Blanche stamped upon them and fled, weeping, to her room.

The photograph was that of a handsome, manly-looking young fellow, such as almost any girl might be pardoned for falling in love with. He was Mary's cousin, and it was their growing attachment for each other that had so long delayed Mary's return to school, after her mother had been pronounced convalescent.

Mary's compassion soon overcame her anger. She went to her friend's room and on the following day I noticed that their reconciliation seemed complete. But I was not at all pleased to see that Mary was again apparently under the influence of her irresistible girl friend. Day after day Blanche's attitude toward her grew more and more loverlike. They were constantly together. It was plain that the handsome dark-haired cousin was forgotten. . . . I noticed the sparkle of a little diamond on the third finger of Blanche's left hand.

"Why, what does this mean?" I asked.

"It means that we are engaged," said Blanche innocently. "I am so happy."

"Engaged! To whom?" I demanded.

"Why, to my darling Mary, of course. To whom else?"

I glanced at Mary's left hand. The third finger bore the duplicate of Blanche's diamond. At first I was very much alarmed but gradually, as nothing further happened out of the ordinary, I concluded that my anxiety was groundless. . . .

In later years, when experience had burdened my knowledge of such matters, I would have acted on the warning which was now given in the actions of Blanche. She could not bear to have Mary out of her sight. . . .

[Blanche and Mary then make two attempted escapes from the school. On the first they are quickly caught, on the second they make it off the school grounds, leaving a note for the principal: "DEAR MISS LAGRANGE: It is useless for you to follow us. We have gone away, Mary and I, to be married, for we love each other, and have sworn never to be separated. Farewell, BLANCHE." But the girls are caught in the town and brought back.]

As Dr. Greene [from the town] came quite close, I saw beside him in his carriage the muffled-up figures of Blanche and Mary, while at their feet was the bundle which the eloping couple had taken with them. Mary was pale and frightened. Blanche was perfectly calm. Neither said a word.

When Dr. Greene drove back to the village he carried two telegrams. They were addressed to the parents of Blanche and Mary respectively, and urged their immediate presence at the school. Mary's parents arrived the next day, much alarmed. They agreed that it was best that Mary be taken home at once.

"Have you any objection to her cousin," I asked, "The manly-looking fellow with the dark hair?" They had not the slightest objection to him.

"Then," I said, "invite him to your house and Mary will be herself again in less than a week."

It was arranged that Mary's departure should be unknown to Blanche—at least, I supposed I had so arranged it. But the carriage had hardly passed the great gate when the sound of a pistol shot in the north dormitory created a panic in the house.

It was true. Poor Blanche had proven faithful to her ideal of lover, even to the extent of providing herself with the means of self-destruction. I had forgotten that her window commanded a view of the highway. She lay at full length on the floor. In one hand was the smoking pistol, and in the other a photograph of Mary.

The wound was not serious—the shock was even beneficial, for when Blanche was restored to consciousness after the lapse of several hours, she wept copiously, begged forgiveness for her rash act, and willingly accompanied her parents to her home. I learned afterward that a year of travel abroad not only restored her to a proper condition of mind, but supplied in the place of Mary a young gentleman who was in every way worthy of her, and to whom two years later she was happily married.

If the foregoing shall point a moral that will remain fixed in the memories of parents who read it, I am persuaded that they need never bewail such a misfortune as has plunged two Tennessee families into despair.

The narrative arrangement of this story suggests a clear motive—the principal is concerned to argue that schoolgirl friendships, even extremely intense ones, are not morbid or pathological, as medical writers were beginning to argue, but simply based on ignorance and excessively romantic notions. Regulation of them could safely be left to vigilant female authority. She is therefore at considerable pains to portray the students as innocent of sexuality and to provide a suitably happy ending.

It thus contrasts sharply with the more hostile, sensational newspaper stories, though it has all the elements of the masculine/feminine contrast, the conflict between the young women, and the conflict with female authority. This contrast shows how the narrative fragments could be recombined for a variety of purposes, as they continued to be over the next several decades.

During the 1890s, however, nearly all the newspaper stories had tragic endings. They were stories of struggle and failure; they ended with violence or loss. Only a very few, about women in exceptional circumstances like those of Anne Hindle, had happier endings. When successful partnerships between women were mentioned in the news columns, they almost always appeared in desexualized form only. The suggestion of sexuality, however subtle or implicit, was generally paired with bloodletting.

This focus on violence was partly an artifact of the moralizing sensationalism of the press. The late-nineteenth-century newspaper narratives of lesbian love featured violence as a boundary marker; murders or suicides served to abort the forward progress of the tale, signaling that such erotic love between women was not only tragic but ultimately hopeless. The selective nature of the reports made the exceptional cases of violent conflict among women seem characteristic of female sexual passion. The stories were thus structured to emphasize, ultimately, that no real love story was possible.

But the emphasis on conflict and violence in the newspaper stories must also have reflected the stories of overwhelming opposition and social isolation told by women whose erotic partnerships transgressed the boundaries of gender-appropriate, spiritual, romantic friendship. Young women like Alice, Emma, and Blanche faced hostility and opposition not only from pathologizing sexologists and patriarchal social institutions but also from their closest female relatives and friends. In addition, they all struggled to establish a reciprocal love relationship with another woman who did not fully share their commitment to live outside the traditional heterosexual family.

Such structural analysis of the newspaper narratives suggests that modern lesbian identity may have been constructed from an amalgam of elements drawn from the stories of romantic friendship and passing women. In 1892, Alice Mitchell did not present herself, nor was she perceived, as a "lesbian"—no such clear category yet existed. Rather, she combined her unremarkable story of schoolgirl "chumming" with a plan to cross-dress and marry Freda, and it was this combination and not either element by itself that signaled something new and incited opposition. It was Alice Mitchell's attempt to forge a new way of life— new in both material and social terms, a life outside the white bourgeois family and its hierarchical gender arrangements—that marked her as different and dangerous. Her love for other women was neither temporary nor complementary to heterosexual marriage; her appropriation of "masculinity" and her determination to marry Freda were not for the purpose of a temporary or superficial disguise but were the seeds of a new identity.

The relative powerlessness of lesbians (as of other marginalized groups) has been enforced historically by limiting their means of direct public self-representation, leaving lesbian historians few of women's own representations of their developing lesbian identities to use as sources. Instead, historians must make the most of mediated sources contaminated by hostility, like the turn-of-the-century newspaper narratives, by reading them "against the grain."[28] Not until the 1920s do we begin to have a body of self-representations, such as African-American blues songs outlining the exploits of masculine "bulldaggers" or *The Well of Loneliness,* Radclyffe Hall's widely circulated British novel featuring the "masculine" heroine Stephen Gordon.[29]

Both the hostile representations and the self-representations of lesbians at the turn of the century, however, suggest that for newly visible lesbians gender-crossing or cross-dressing became a term of address in several simultaneous dialogues. Through masculine identification they separated themselves from the family-based female world, defined their desire for other women as erotic, and declared their unyielding commitment to a new way of life. The feminine partners in developing lesbian relationships, from Freda Ward to *The Well*'s Mary, along with the feminine pairs joined in romantic friendships, were not perceived as lesbian until the mid-twentieth century and later.[30]

Analysis of the newspaper narratives discussed here also shows that turn-of-the-century sexologists, far from creating or producing new lesbian identities, drew their "cases" from women's own stories and newspaper retellings of them as well as from French fiction and pornography as "empirical" bases for their theories.[31] They did not initiate or control the social conversation from which lesbian identity developed but, rather, entered into it. Basing their descriptions on relationships like that of Alice and Freda, the sexologists took as their task the definition of deviance, the drawing of a line between acceptable romantic friends or simply eccentric passing women and intolerable lesbian lovers. In this they were not unique but, rather, like women such as Freda's sister, who had drawn such a line in forbidding Freda any further contact with Alice. Sexologists' point of departure from all these other narratives of lesbian identity was their determination to interpret behaviors rooted in changing and contested social relations as biologically based and properly subject to medical regulation.

Sexologists decidedly did influence the conversations they entered.

Many commentators have noted, for instance, the appropriation of medical language and biological assumptions in many lesbian self-representations, particularly in *The Well of Loneliness*.[32] But in tracing the roots of Hall's narrative, it is equally important to note that *The Well* also shares the structure of the Mitchell-Ward newspaper stories—the masculine/feminine contrast, the conflict between the female partners, and the conflict with female authority (it is Stephen Gordon's mother who is most hostile to her, not her father). In Hall's version there is no violence, however—the conflict is experienced internally by Stephen Gordon, who releases the "normal" Mary rather than murdering her or killing herself. This narrative structure, imbricated with the difficult, conflict-laden history of the emergence of lesbian identities in the twentieth century, may help explain the book's widespread, enduring popularity despite its medicalized portrait of "inversion."

Thus, we can look back now at the figure of the turn-of-the-century mannish lesbian and see her as at least a double-edged construction—a representation used by sexologists and others to attack the independence and achievements of New Women, yet at the same time a self-represented historical subject who was attacked (sometimes even by feminists) for what she embodied: her rejection of the feminine body and the maternal body for herself. Her self-presentation took her outside the boundaries of the female world; for her, feminine dress and gestures were unnatural. She therefore existed largely beyond the categories of thought that, wedded to a fixed dualistic view of gender, can comprehend her only as a dupe of pathologizing sexologists who accepted the overvaluation of the masculine or as simply male identified.[33] Yet her history also defies any attempt to represent her as simply a hero of lesbian resistance, as Alice Mitchell's story, with its horrific act of murder, clearly shows.

The emerging new narratives of lesbian identity shaped new ways of living for some women, as new material possibilities and social positions outside the kin-based family also came into being at the turn of the century. These narratives both reproduced aspects of conventional gender hierarchy and were subversive of them. They suggest that it is useful to relinquish the fixed opposition of oppression versus resistance and to modify our own often too simple historical tales of lesbian innocence, romance, or heroism. Lesbians do not come from outside culture, outside history, or outside class, race, and gender to raise the flag for a self-evident version of freedom, justice, and equality. Rather, lesbian resistance consists instead of our determination to dissent—to retell our culture's dominant stories with an eye to reorganizing its distribution of cultural and material resources. With these new stories we re-present and re-make the world from the interaction of our own points of view and those of others in an ongoing process of re-vision.

NOTES

1. For overviews of this historical argument, see Jeffrey Weeks, *Sex, Politics and Society: The Regulation of Sexuality since 1800* (London: Longman, 1981), esp. "The Construction of Homosexuality," 96–121; and Michel Foucault, *The History of Sexuality, Vol. 1: An Introduction,* trans. Robert Hurley (New York: Vintage, 1978). For a discussion of the emergence of the "lesbian" and "homosexual" in the American context, see Jonathan Ned Katz, *Gay/Lesbian Almanac: A New Documentary.* (New York: Harper and Row, 1983), esp. "The Invention of the Homosexual, 1880–1950," 137–74; and John D'Emilio and Estelle Freedman, *Intimate Matters: A Social History of Sexuality In America* (New York: New York, 1988), esp. "Toward a New Sexual Order, 1880–1930," 171–235.

2. For studies of romantic friendship, see Carroll Smith-Rosenberg, "The Female World of Love and Ritual: Relations between Women in Nineteenth Century America," *Signs: Journal of Women in Culture and Society* 1, no. 1 (1975): 1-29; and Lillian Faderman, *Surpassing the Love of Men: Romantic Friendship and Love between Women from the Renaissance to the Present* (New York: Morrow, 1981). For discussions of "passing women," see Jonathan Ned Katz, *Gay American History: Lesbians and Gay Men in the U.S.A.* (New York: Crowell, 1976); and San Francisco Lesbian and Gay History Project 1989.

3. See Esther Newton, "The Myth of the Mannish Lesbian: Radclyffe Hall and the New Woman." Also Carroll Smith-Rosenberg, "Discourses of Sexuality and Subjectivity: The New Woman 1870–1936." Both found in *Hidden From History: Reclaiming the Lesbian and Gay Past,* ed. Martin Duberman, Martha Vicinus, and George Chauncey Jr. (New York: Meridian Books, 1989), 281–93 and 264–80, respectively.

4. Anne Lister [1891–1840]. *I Know My Own Heart: The Diaries of Anne Lister,* ed. Helena Whitbread (London: Virago, 1988).

5. Teresa de Lauretis, *Alice Doesn't: Feminism, Semiotics, Cinema* (Bloomington: University of Indiana Press, 1984), 159.

6. These contents do not take place solely within various types of texts but are produced within and circulate through the material social world, both shaping and reflecting structured social antagonisms. For a particularly lucid discussion of this process, see Judith R. Walkowitz, "Patrolling the Borders: Feminist Historiography and the New Historicism.," *Radical History Review* 4 (1989): 25–31. Walkowitz stakes out a materialist grounding for her appropriation of poststructuralist theories of meaning production. See also Mary Poovey, *Uneven Developments: The Ideological Work of Gender in Mid-Victorian England* (Chicago: University of Chicago Press, 1988), where Poovey makes a specifically historical argument for the interdependence of material conditions and representations.

7. This notion somewhat parallels Judith Butler's metaphor of "performance," or the set of repetitive practices through which identity is constituted. See Butler, *Gender Trouble: Feminism and the Subversion of Identity* (New York, 1990). My version of this argument was also influenced by Barbara Herrnstein Smith's interesting analysis of narrative construction as a purposeful act. See Herrnstein Smith, "Narrative Versions, Narrative Theories," in *On Narrative,* ed. W. J. T. Mitchell (Chicago, 1981), 209–32.

8. For a provocative and influential argument placing the heterosexual/homosexual dyad at the center of cultural life in the modern West, see Eve Kosofsky Sedgwick, *Epistemology of the Closet* (Berkeley: University of California Press, 1990).

9. "Alice Mitchell's Crime," *New York World,* January 31, 1892, 6.

10. Richard Von Krafft-Ebing, *Psychopathia Sexualis, With Special Reference to Antipathic Sexual Instinct: A Medico-Forensic Study* (London: Rebam, 1899), 550.

11. Havelock Ellis, *Sexual Inversion* (Philadelphia: F. A. Davis, 1901), 121.

12. Sensationalism: Paul Coppock, "Memphis' Strangest Love Murder Had All Girl Cast," *Memphis Commercial*, September 7, 1930, sec. 4, p. 5. Sexology: D. O. Cauldwell, M.D., "Lesbian Love Murder," *Sexology* 16, no. 12 (1950): 773–79. Fiction: Mary P. Hatch, *The Strange Disappearance of Eugene Comstock.* (New York: G. W. Dillingham, 1895); Mary Wilkins Freeman, "The Long Arm," in *American Detective Stories,* ed. Carolyn Wells (1895; reprint, New York: Oxford University Press, 1927), 135–78; J. W. Carhart, M.D., *Norma Trist: A Story of the Invention of the Sexes* (Austin, TX: Eugene von Boekman, 1895). Ballad: Edwin Howard, "Resurrected Ballad Recalls a Strange Memphis Killing," *Memphis Press Scimitar,* November 13, 1961. Bernhardt: "Bernhardt At The Jail: The Great Actress Wanted to See Miss Alice Mitchell," *Memphis Appeal Avalanche,* February 17, 1892, 4.

13. The defense team's "hypothetical case" was reprinted in "Sane or Insane? Is She Cruel Murderess or irresponsible Lunatic?" *Memphis Commercial,* July 19, 1892, 1; and in F. L. Sim, M.D., "Forensic Psychiatry: Alice Mitchell Adjudged Insane," *Memphis Medical Monthly* 12, no. 8 (1892): 377–428. Freda Ward was referred to throughout by her nickname, Fred.

14. For an account of this common phenomenon, also called "smashing" in a northern college setting, see Nancy Sahli, "Smashing: Women's Relationships before the Fall," *Chrysalis* 8, (1979): 17–27.

15. George Chauncey Jr., "From Inversion to Homosexuality: Medicine and the Changing Conceptualization of Female Deviance," *Salamagundi* 58–59 (1982–83): 114–46.

16. "Still in Doubt, Alice Mitchell's Sanity Not Yet Determined," *Memphis Commercial,* July 20, 1892, 1.

17. Coppock, "Memphis' Strangest Love Murder."

18. See, for example, "United in Death: A Tragedy Almost Identical with That of Monday: A Girl's Love for a Girl: How It Caused a Murder and a Suicide Twenty years Ago," *Memphis Public Ledger,* January 27, 1892, 1.

19. See, for example, "Like The Memphis Case: Another Story Which Furnishes Rich Food for The Gossips," *Memphis Commercial,* February 19, 1892, 5.

20. See, for example, "A Female Romeo: Her Terrible Love for a Chosen Friend of Her Own Sex Assumes a Passionate Character that Blazes into Jealousy of so Fierce a Quality that it Fires Her to the Sacrifice of the Object of Her Unnatural Passion: A Queer Psychological Study," *National Police Gazette,* June 7, 1879, 6.

21. "The Plea for Bail," *Memphis Public Ledger,* February 11, 1892, 2.

22. For a discussion of Annie Hindle's career, see Laurence Senelick, "The Evolution of the Male Impersonator on the Nineteenth-Century Stage," *Essays In Theatre* 1, no. 1 (1982): 31–46.

23. "Marrying a Maiden! Can a Woman Legally Marry a Woman?" *Vanity Fair,* February 13, 1892, 1.

24. "A Strange Affection, Addie Phillips Shows Traces of Alice Mitchell-Fondness, Another Case Partially Paralleling the Famous One," *Memphis Weekly Commercial,* March 23, 1892, 12.

25. The proximity of theatrical and prostitution districts in England is discussed in Tracy Davis's fascinating study, *Actresses As Working Women: Their Social Identity in Victorian Culture* (London: Routledge, 1991). The theatre's role as a haven for the unconventional is also examined in Benjamin McArthur, *Actors and American Culture, 1880–1920* (Philadelphia: Temple University Press, 1984).

26. "Unfolded, Revelation of Facts Surrounding Freda Ward's Death . . . Similar Cases Recalled," *Memphis Commercial*, February 24, 1892, 1–3.

27. "Like Miss Mitchell . . . An Infatuation Which Existed between Two School Girls," *Memphis Commercial*, February 14, 1892, 13.

28. For an exploration of the possibilities for reading "against the grain" for the history of lesbians, see Jennifer Terry, "Theorizing Deviant Historiography," *differences* 3, no. 2 (1991): 55–74, which draws from the work of Gayatri Spivak and Michel Foucault to construct such a method.

29. On representations of "bulldaggers" in blues songs, see Hazel Carby, "It Jus' Be's Dat Way Sometime: The Sexual Politics of Women's Blues," in *Unequal Sisters: A Multicultural Reader in U.S. Women's History*, ed. Ellen duBois and Vicki Ruiz (New York: Routledge, 1990), 238–49; and Eric Garber, "A Spectacle in Color: The Lesbian and Gay Subculture of Jazz Age Harlem," in *Hidden From History*, 318–31.

30. Research by Elizabeth Kennedy and Madeline Davis suggests that, even after World War II, this issue of whether "fems" were really "lesbians" was still open to dispute. Elizabeth Kennedy and Madeline Davis, "The Reproduction of Butch-Fem Roles: A Social Constructionist Approach," in *Passion and Power: Sexuality In History*, ed. Kathy Peiss and Christina Simmons (Philadelphia: Temple University Press, 1989), 241–56.

31. I discuss at length this process of constructing a supposedly "empirical" basis for the typical lesbian case history of turn-of-the-century sexology in Lisa Duggan, "The Trials of Alice Mitchell: Sexual Science and Sexual Identity in Turn of the Century America," (Ph.D. diss., University of Pennsylvania, 1992), esp. chap. 6, "Sapphic Slashers, or, the Scientific Construction of Lesbian Desire."

32. See Newton, "Myth of the Mannish Lesbian"; and Smith-Rosenberg, "Discourses of Sexuality and Subjectivity."

33. Such oversimple thought is represented in the work of Sheila Jeffreys, whose *The Spinster and Her Enemies: Feminism and Sexuality, 1800–1930* (London: Pandora, 1985) is structured as a stark melodrama with male villains and female victims and heroines appearing almost as cartoon characters. Jeffreys cannot conceive of the male-authored medical literature as any kind of resource for subversive appropriation but only as pure evil opposed to the pure good of woman's true nature. Paradoxically, such paradigms only end up reproducing the very gendered categories they are meant to attack.

8

Christian Brotherhood or Sexual Perversion? Homosexual Identities and the Construction of Sexual Boundaries in the World War I Era[1]

George Chauncey

In the spring of 1919, officers at the Newport, Rhode Island, Naval Training Station dispatched a squad of young enlisted men into the community to investigate the "immoral conditions" obtaining there. The decoys sought out and associated with suspected "sexual perverts," had sex with them, and learned all they could about homosexual activity in Newport. On the basis of the evidence they gathered, naval and municipal authorities arrested more than twenty sailors in April and sixteen civilians in July, and the decoys testified against them at a naval court of inquiry and several civilian trials. The entire investigation received little attention before the navy accused a prominent Episcopal clergyman who worked at the Y.M.C.A. of soliciting homosexual contacts there. But when civilian and then naval officials took the minister to trial on charges of being a "lewd and wanton person," a major controversy developed. Protests by the Newport Ministerial Union and the Episcopal bishop of Rhode Island, and a vigorous editorial campaign by the *Providence Journal,* forced the navy to conduct a second inquiry in 1920 into the methods used in the first investigation. When that inquiry criticized the methods but essentially exonerated the senior naval officials who had instituted them, the ministers asked the Republican-controlled Senate Naval Affairs Committee to conduct its own investigation. The committee agreed and issued a report in 1921 that vindicated the ministers' original charges and condemned the conduct of the highest naval officials involved, including Franklin D. Roosevelt, President Wilson's assistant secretary of the navy and the 1920 Democratic vice presidential candidate.[2]

The legacy of this controversy is a rich collection of evidence about the organization and phenomenology of homosexual relations among white working-class and middle-class men and about the changing nature of sexual discourse in the World War I era. The two naval courts of inquiry and the minister's second civilian trial produced some thirty-five hundred pages of testimony from the decoys, suspected "perverts," ministers, and town and naval officials about their relations with men, their often conflicting understandings of sexuality, and their reactions to the investigation itself.[3] On the basis of this evidence it is possible to reconstruct the organization of a homosexual subculture during this period, how its participants understood their behavior, and how they were viewed by the larger community, thus providing a benchmark for generalizations about the historical development of homosexual identities and communities. The evidence also enables us to reassess current hypotheses concerning the relative significance of medical discourse, religious doctrine, and folk tradition in the shaping of popular understandings of sexual behavior and character. Most importantly, analysis of the testimony of the government's witnesses and the accused churchmen and sailors offers new insights into the relationship between homosexual behavior and identity in the cultural construction of sexuality. Even when witnesses agreed that two men had engaged in homosexual relations with each other, they disagreed about whether both men or only the one playing the "woman's part" should be labeled as "queer." More profoundly, they disagreed about how to distinguish between a "sexual" and a "nonsexual" relationship; the navy defined certain relationships as homosexual and perverted which the ministers claimed were merely brotherly and Christian. Because disagreement over the boundary between homosexuality and homosociality lay at the heart of the Newport controversy, its records allow us to explore the cultural construction of sexual categories in unusual depth.

THE SOCIAL ORGANIZATION OF HOMOSEXUAL RELATIONS

The investigation found evidence of a highly developed and varied gay subculture in this small seaport community, and a strong sense of collective identity on the part of many of its participants. Cruising areas, where gay men and "straight" sailors[4] alike knew that sexual encounters were to be had, included the beach during the summer and the fashionable Bellevue Avenue close to it, the area along Cliff Walk, a cemetery, and a bridge. Many men's homosexual experiences consisted entirely (and irregularly) of visits to such areas for anonymous sexual encounters, but some men organized a group life with others who shared their inclinations. The navy's witnesses alluded to groups of servants who worked in the exclusive "cottages" on Bellevue Avenue and of civilians who met at places such as Jim's Restaurant on Long Wharf.[5] But they focused on a tightly knit group of sailors who referred to themselves as "the gang,"[6] and it is this group whose social organization the first section of this paper will analyze.

The best-known rendezvous of gang members and of other gay sailors was neither dark nor secret: "The Army and Navy Y.M.C.A. was the headquarters of all cocksuckers [in] the early part of the evening," commented one investigator, and, added another, "everybody who sat around there in the evening . . . knew it."[7] The Y.M.C.A. was one of the central institutions of gay male life; some gay sailors lived there, others occasionally rented its rooms for the evening so that they would have a place to entertain men, and the black elevator operators were said to direct interested sailors to the gay men's rooms.[8] Moreover, the Y.M.C.A. was a social center, where gay men often had dinner together before moving to the lobby to continue conversation and meet the sailors visiting the Y.M.C.A. in the evening.[9] The ties which they maintained through such daily interactions were reinforced by a dizzying array of parties; within the space of three weeks, investigators were invited to four "fagott part[ies]" and heard of others.[10]

Moreover, the men who had developed a collective life in Newport recognized themselves as part of a subculture extending beyond a single town; they knew of places in New York and other cities "where the 'queens' hung out"; made frequent visits to New York, Providence, and Fall River; and were visited by gay men from those cities. An apprentice machinist working in Providence, for instance, spent "week-ends in Newport for the purpose of associating with his 'dear friends,' the 'girls,'" and a third of the civilians arrested during the raids conducted in the summer were New York City residents working as servants in the grand houses of Newport. Only two of the arrested civilians were local residents.[11]

Within and sustained by this community, a complex system of personal identities and structured relationships took shape, in which homosexual behavior per se did not play a determining part. Relatively few of the men who engaged in homosexual activity, whether as casual participants in anonymous encounters or as partners in ongoing relationships, identified themselves or were labeled by others as sexually different from other men on that basis alone. Most observers recognized that many "straight" sailors (their term) had sex with members of the gang, but, as

I will explain below, few believed that this alone meant such sailors were homosexual. The determining criterion in labeling a man as "straight" or "queer" was not the extent of his homosexual activity, but the gender role he assumed. The only men who sharply differentiated themselves from other men, labeling themselves as "queer," were those who assumed the sexual and other cultural roles ascribed to women; they might have been termed "inverts" in the early twentieth-century medical literature, because they not only expressed homosexual desire but "inverted" (or reversed) their gender role.[12]

The most prominent queers in Newport were effeminate men who sometimes donned women's clothes—when not in uniform—including some who became locally famous female impersonators. Sometimes referred to as "queens," these men dominated the social activities of the gang and frequently organized parties at their off-base apartments to which gay and "straight" sailors alike were invited. At these "drags" gang members could relax, be openly gay, and entertain "straight" sailors from the base with their theatrics and their sexual favors. One gay man described a party held in honor of some men from the USS *Baltimore* in the following terms:

> I went in and they were singing and playing. Some were coked up that wasn't drunk. And there was two of the fellows, 'Beckie' Goldstein and Richard that was in drags, they call it, in costume. They had on some kind of ball gowns, dancing costumes. They had on some ladies' underwear and ladies' drawers and everything and wigs. . . . I saw them playing and singing and dancing and somebody was playing the piano. . . . Every once in a while 'Beckie' (Goldstein) would go out of the room with a fellow and . . . some would come back buttoning up their pants.[13]

Female impersonation was an unexceptional part of navy culture during the World War I years, sufficiently legitimate—if curious—for the *Providence Journal* and the navy's own magazine, *Newport Recruit,* to run lengthy stories and photo essays about the many theatrical productions at the navy base in which men took the female roles.[14] The ubiquity of such drag shows and the fact that numerous "straight"-identified men took part in them sometimes served to protect gay female impersonators from suspicion. The landlord of one of the gay men arrested by the navy cited the sailor's stage roles in order to explain why he hadn't regarded the man's wearing women's clothes as "peculiar," and presumably the wife of the training station's commandant, who loaned the man "corsets, stockings, shirt waists, [and] women's pumps" for his use in *H.M.S. Pinafore,* did not realize that he also wore them at private parties.[15]

But if in some circles the men's stage roles served to legitimate their wearing drag, for most sailors such roles only confirmed the impersonators' identities as queer. Many sailors, after all, had seen or heard of the queens' appearing in drag at parties where its homosexual significance was inescapable. According to the navy's investigators, for instance, numerous sailors in uniform and "three prize fighters in civilian clothes" attended one "fagott party" given in honor of a female impersonator visiting Newport to perform at the Opera House. Not only were some of the men at the party—and presumably the guest of honor—in drag, but two men made out on a bed in full view of the others, who "remarked about their affection for each other."[16] Moreover, while sailors commonly gave each other nicknames indicating ethnic origin (e.g., "Wop" Bianchia and "Frenchman" La Favor) or other personal characteristics (e.g., "Lucky" and "Pick-axe"), many of them knew the most prominent queers *only* by their "ladies' names," camp nicknames they had adopted from the opera such as "Salome," "Theda Bara," and "Galli Curci."[17]

Female impersonation was only the most extreme form of the effeminacy that queers and straights alike considered to be the basis for labeling a man as an invert. Several of the navy's witnesses described other signs of effeminacy one might look for in a queer. A straight investigator explained that "it was common knowledge that if a man was walking along the street in an effeminate manner, with his lips rouged, his face powered and his eye-brows pencilled, that in the majority of cases you could form a pretty good opinion of what kind of a man he was, . . . a 'fairy.'"[18]

One gay man, when pressed by the court to explain how he identified someone as "queer," pointed to more subtle indicators: "He acted sort of peculiar; walking around with his hands on his hips. . . . [H]is manner was not masculine. . . . The expression with the eyes and the gestures. . . . If a man was walking around and did not act real masculine, I would think he was a cocksucker."[19] A sailor, who later agreed to be a decoy, recalled that upon noticing "a number of fellows . . . of effeminate characters" shortly after his arrival at Newport, he decided to look "into the crowd to see what kind of fellows they were and found they were perverts."[20] Effeminacy had been the first sign of a deeper perversion.

Although a man's effeminacy was regarded as the outward sign of his being queer, his distinctively *sexual* tastes were equally important in the construction of his social role and identity. The inverts grouped themselves together as "queers" on the basis of their effeminate gender behavior,[21] and they all played roles culturally defined as feminine in sexual contacts. But they distinguished among themselves on the basis of the "feminine" sexual behavior they preferred, categorizing themselves as "fairies" (also called "cocksuckers"), "pogues" (men who liked to be "browned," or anally penetrated), and "two-way artists" (who enjoyed both). The ubiquity of these distinctions and their importance to personal self-identification cannot be overemphasized. Witnesses at the naval inquiries explicitly drew the distinctions as a matter of course and incorporated them into their descriptions of the gay subculture. One "pogue" who cooperated with the investigation, for instance, used such categories to label his friends in the gang with no prompting from the court: "Hughes said he was a pogue; Richard said he was a cocksucker; Fred Hoage said he was a two-way artist. . . ." While there were some men about whom he "had to draw my own conclusions; they never said directly what they was or wasn't," his remarks made it clear he was sure they fit into one category or another.[22]

A second group of sailors who engaged in homosexual relations and participated in the group life of the gang nonetheless occupied a more ambiguous sexual category because they, unlike the queers, conformed to masculine gender norms. Some of them were heterosexually married. None of them behaved effeminately or took the "woman's part" in sexual relations, they took no feminine nicknames, and they did not label themselves—nor were they labeled by others—as queer. Instead, gang members, who reproduced the highly genderized sexual relations of their culture, described the second group of men as playing the "husbands" to the "ladies" of the "inverted set." Some husbands entered into steady, loving relationships with individual men known as queer; witnesses spoke of couples who took trips together and maintained monogomous relationships.[23] It was on the basis of the husbands' sexual—and sometimes explicitly romantic—interest in men that the queers distinguished them from other men: one gay man explained to the court that he believed the rumor about one man being the husband of another must have "some truth in it because [the first man] seems to be very fond of him, more so than the average man would be for a boy."[24] But the ambiguity of the sexual category such men occupied was reflected in the difficulty observers found in labeling them. The navy, which sometimes grouped such men with the queers as "perverts," found it could only satisfactorily identify them by describing what they *did*, rather than naming what they were. One investigator, for instance, provided the navy with a list of suspects in which he carefully labeled some men as "pogues" and others as "fairies," but he could only identify one man by noting that he "went out with all the above named men at various times and had himself sucked off or screwed them through the rectum."[25] Even the queers' terms for such men—"friends" and "husbands"—identified the men only *in relation to* the queers, rather than according them an autonomous sexual identity. Despite the uncertain definition of their sexual identity, however, most observers recognized these men as regular—if relatively marginal—members of the gang.

The social organization of the gang was deeply embedded in that of the larger culture; as we have seen, its members reproduced many of the social forms of genderized heterosexuality, with some men playing "the woman's part" in relationships with conventionally masculine "husbands." But the gang also helped men depart from the social roles ascribed to them as biological males by that larger culture. Many of the "queers" interrogated by the navy recalled having felt effeminate or otherwise "different" most of their lives. But it was the existence of sexual subcultures—of which the gang was one—that provided them a means of structuring their vague feelings of sexual and gender difference into distinctive personal identities. Such groups facilitated people's exploration and organization of their homosexuality by offering them support in the face of social opprobrium and providing them with guidelines for how to organize their feelings of difference into a particular social form of homosexuality, a coherent identity and way of life. The gang offered men a means of assuming social roles which they perceived to be more congruent with their inner natures than those prescribed by the dominant culture, and sometimes gave them remarkable strength to publicly defy social convention.

At the same time, the weight of social disapprobation led people within the gang to insist on a form of solidarity that required conformity to its own standards even as it offered release from the behavioral imperatives of the dominant culture. To be accepted by the gang, for instance, one had to assume the role of pogue, fairy, two-way artist, or husband, and present oneself publicly in a manner consistent with that labeling. But while men chose to assume one or another role on the basis of which most closely approximated their sexual preferences, they appear to have maintained a critical perspective on the significance of the role for their personal identities. Even while assuming one role for the purpose of interaction in the gang, at least some continued to explore their sexual interests when the full range of those interests was not expressed in the norms for that role. Frederick Hoage, for instance, was known as a "brilliant woman" and a "French artist" (or "fairy"), but he was also reported surreptitiously to have tried to "brown" another member of the gang—behavior inappropriate to a "queer" as defined by the gang.[26]

Gang members, who believed they could identify men as pogues or fairies even if the men themselves had not yet recognized their true natures, sometimes intervened to accelerate the process of self-discovery. The gang scrutinized newly arrived recruits at the Y.M.C.A. for likely sexual partners and "queers," and at least one case is recorded of their approaching an effeminate but straight-identified man named Rogers in order to bring him out as a pogue. While he recalled always having been somewhat effeminate, after he joined the gang Rogers began using make-up "because the others did," assumed the name "Kitty Gordon," and developed a steady relationship with another man (his "husband").[27] What is striking to the contemporary reader is not only that gang members were so confident of their ability to detect Rogers's homosexual interests that they were willing to intervene in the normal pattern of his life, but that they believed they could identify him so precisely as a "latent" (not their word) pogue.

Many witnesses indicated they had at least heard of "fairies" before joining the service, but military mobilization, by removing men like Rogers from family and neighborhood supervision and placing them in a single-sex environment, increased the chances that they would encounter gay-identified men and be able to explore new sexual possibilities. Both the opportunities offered by military mobilization and the constraints of hometown family supervision were poignantly reflected in Rogers's plea to the court of inquiry after his arrest. After claiming that he had met gay men and had homosexual experiences only after joining the navy, he added:

> I got in their company. I don't know why; but I used to go out with them. I would like to say here that these people were doing this all their lives. I never met one until I came in the Navy. . . . I would like to add that I would not care for my folks to learn anything about this; that I would suffer everything, because I want them to know me as they think I am. This is something that I never did until I came in the Navy.[28]

Straight witnesses at the naval inquiry demonstrated remarkable familiarity with homosexual activity in Newport; like gay men, they believed that "queers" constituted a distinct group of people, "a certain class of people called 'fairies.'"[29] Furthermore, almost all of them agreed that one could identify certain men as queer by their mannerisms and carriage. At the second court of inquiry, a naval official ridiculed the bishop of Rhode Island's assertions that it was impossible to recognize "fairies" and that he had never even heard of the term:

> Then you don't know whether or not it is common to hear in any hotel lobby the remark, when a certain man will go by, and somebody will say, 'There goes a fairy.' You have *never* heard that expression used in that way?[30]

Not only did most people recognize the existence of individual "fairies," but they knew that such men had organized a collective life, even if they were unfamiliar with its details. As we have seen, many sailors at the naval training station knew that the Y.M.C.A. was a "headquarters" for such people, and Newport's mayor recalled that "it was information that was common . . . in times gone by, summer after summer," that men called "floaters" who appeared in town "had followed the fleet up from Norfolk."[31] In a comment that reveals more about straight perceptions than gay realities, a navy officer described gay men to the Newport chief of police as "a gang who were stronger than the Masons . . . [and who] had signals and a lot of other stuff. . . . [T]hey were perverts and well organized."[32]

Straight people's familiarity with the homosexual subculture resulted from the openness with which some gay men rejected the cultural norms of heterosexuality. Several servicemen, for instance, mentioned having encountered openly homosexual men at the naval hospital, where they saw patients and staff wear make-up and publicly discuss their romances and homosexual experiences.[33] The story of two gang members assigned to the Melville coaling station near Newport indicates the extent to which individual "queers," with the support of the gang, were willing to make their presence known by defying social convention, even at the cost of hostile reactions. "From the time that they arrived at the station they were both the topic of conversation because of their effeminate habits," testified several sailors stationed at Melville. Because the men refused to conform to masculine norms they suffered constant harassment; many sailors refused to associate with them or abused them physically and verbally, while their officers assigned them especially heavy work loads and ordered their subordinates to "try to get [one of them] with the goods."[34] Straight sailors reacted with such vigor because the gay men flaunted their difference rather than trying to conceal it, addressing each other with "feminine names," witnesses complained, and "publish[ing] the fact that they were prostitutes and such stuff as that."[35] At times they were deliberately provocative; one astounded sailor reported that he had "seen Richard lying in his bunk take one leg and, putting it up in the air, ask everyone within range of his voice and within range of this place how they would like to take it in this position."[36]

Even before the naval inquiry began, Newport's servicemen and civilians alike were well aware of the queers in their midst. They tolerated them in many settings and brutalized them in others, but they thought they knew what they were dealing with: perverts were men who behaved like women. But as the inquiry progressed, it inadvertently brought the neat boundaries separating queers from the rest of men into question.

DISPUTING THE BOUNDARIES OF THE "SEXUAL"

The testimony generated by the navy investigation provided unusually detailed information about the social organization of men who identified themselves as queer. But it also revealed that many more men than the queers were regularly engaging in some form of homosexual activity. Initially the navy expressed little concern about such men's behavior, for it did not believe that straight sailors' occasional liaisons with queers raised any questions about their sexual character. But the authorities' decision to prosecute men not normally labeled as queer ignited a controversy which ultimately forced the navy and its opponents to define more precisely what they believed constituted a homosexual act and to defend the basis upon which they categorized people participating in such acts. Because the controversy brought so many groups of people— working- and middle-class gay- and straight-identified enlisted men, middle-class naval officers, ministers, and town officials—into conflict, it revealed how differently those groups interpreted sexuality. A multiplicity of sexual discourses coexisted at a single moment in the civilian and naval seaport communities.

The gang itself loosely described the male population beyond the borders of its inner circle of "queers" and "husbands" as "straight," but its members further divided the straight population into two different groups: those who would reject their sexual advances, and those who would accept them. A man was "trade," according to one fairy, if he "would stand to have 'queer' persons fool around [with] him in any way, shape or manner."[37] Even among "trade," gay men realized that some men would participate more actively than others in sexual encounters. Once they had confirmed a straight sailor's sexual availability, gay men who were so inclined felt free to indicate their own interests, even though the sailor clearly set the limits. Most gay men were said to prefer men who were strictly "straight and [would] not reciprocate in any way," but at least one fairy, as a decoy recorded, "wanted to kiss me and love me [and] . . . insisted and begged for it."[38] The etymology of the term, which was widely used by gay men in the United States from the turn of the century until the 1960s, is unclear, but "trade" accurately described a common pattern of interaction between gay men and their straight sexual partners. In Newport, a gay man might take a sailor to a show or to dinner, offer him small gifts, or provide him with a place to stay when he was on overnight leave; in exchange, the sailor allowed his host to have sex with him that night, within whatever limits the sailor cared to set. The exchange was not always so elaborate: the navy's detectives reported several instances of gay men meeting and sexually servicing numerous sailors at the Y.M.C.A. in a single evening. Men who were "trade" normally did not expect or demand direct payment for their services, although gay men did sometimes lend their partners small amounts of money without expecting it to be returned, and they used "trade" to refer to some civilians who, in contrast to the sailors, paid *them* for sexual services. "Trade" normally referred to straight-identified men who played the "masculine" role in sexual encounters solicited by "queers."[39]

The boundary separating trade from the rest of men was easy to cross. As we have seen, there were locations in Newport, such as the Y.M.C.A., a bridge, and sections of Bellevue Avenue, where straight men knew they could present themselves in order to be solicited. One decoy testified that to infiltrate the gang he merely sat with its members in the Y.M.C.A. lobby one evening. As the decoy had already been in Newport for some time, presumably without expressing any interest in the gang, a gang member named Kreisberg said:

> he was surprised to see me in such company. I finally told him that I belonged to the gang and very soon after that Kreisberg . . . said "So we can consider you trade?" I replied that he could. Very soon Kreisberg requested that I remove my gloves as he, Kreisberg, wanted to hold my hands. Kreisberg acknowledged that he was abnormal and wanted to spend the night with me.[40]

Almost all straight sailors agreed that the effeminate members of the gang should be labeled "queer," but they disagreed about the sexual character of a straight man who accepted the sexual advances of a queer. Many straight men accepted it as a matter of course that young recruits would accept the sexual solicitations of the perverts. "It was a shame to let these kids come in and run in to that kind of stuff," remarked one decoy; but his remarks indicate he did not think a boy was "queer" just because he let a queer have sex with him.[41] The nonchalance with which many sailors regarded such sexual encounters was strikingly revealed by the ways in which they defined "queers" to the court of inquiry. Most pogues defined themselves as "men who like to be browned," but straight men casually defined pogues as "[people] *that you can 'brown'*" and as men who "offered themselves in the same manner which women do."[42] Both remarks imply that "normal" men could take advantage of the pogues' availability without questioning their own identities as "straight"; the fact that the sailors made such potentially incriminating statements before the naval court indicates that this was an assumption they fully expected the board to share (as in fact it did). That lonesome men could unreservedly take advantage of a fairy's availability is perhaps also the implication, no matter how veiled in humor, of the remark made by a sailor stationed at the Melville coaling station near Newport: "it was common talk around that the Navy Department was getting good. They were sending a couple of 'fairies' up there for the 'sailors in Siberia.' As we used to call ourselves . . . meaning that we were all alone."[43] The strongest evidence of the social acceptability of trade was that the enlisted men who served as decoys volunteered to take on the role of trade for the purpose of infiltrating the gang, but were never even asked to consider assuming the role of queer. Becoming trade, unlike becoming a queer, posed no threat to the decoys' self-image or social status.

While many straight men took the sexual advances of gay men in stride, most engaged in certain ritual behavior designed to reinforce the distinction between themselves and the "queers." Most importantly, they played only the "masculine" sex role in their encounters with gay men—or at least claimed that they did—and observed the norms of masculinity in their own demeanor. They also ridiculed gay men and sometimes beat them up after sexual encounters in order to distance themselves from them. Other men, who feared it brought their manhood into question simply to be approached by a "pervert," were even more likely to attack gay men. Gang members recognized that they had to be careful about whom they approached: some men might respond violently to the mere suggestion of a sexual encounter, and others to the fact of its consummation. They all knew friends who had received severe beatings upon approaching the wrong man.[44] The more militant of the queers even played on straight men's fears in order to taunt them. One of the queers at the Melville coaling station "made a remark that 'half the world is queer and the other half trade,'" recalled a straight sailor, who then described the harassment the queer suffered in retribution.[45]

It is now impossible to determine how many straight sailors had such sexual experiences with the queers, although Alfred Kinsey's research suggests the number might have been large. Kinsey found that 37 percent of the men he interviewed in the 1930s and 1940s had engaged in some homosexual activity, and that a quarter of them had had "more than incidental homosexual experience or reactions" for at least three years between the ages sixteen and fifty-five, even though only 4 percent were exclusively homosexual throughout their lives.[46] Whatever the precise figures at Newport, naval officials and queers alike believed that very many men were involved. Members of the court of inquiry never challenged the veracity of the numerous reports given them of straight sailors having sex with the queers; their chief investigator informed them on the first day of testimony that one suspected pervert had fellated "something like fifteen or twenty young recruits from the Naval Training Station" in a single night. As the investigation progressed, however, even the court of inquiry became concerned about the extent of homosexual activity uncovered. The chief investigator later claimed that the chairman of the first court had ordered him to curtail the investigation because "'If your men [the decoys] do not knock off, they will hang the whole state of Rhode Island.'"[47]

While straight sailors disagreed about the boundaries between "friends," "trade," and "straights," naval officials sought to distinguish the actively "perverted" from the merely complicit in their own way. As we have seen, they were aware of the number of sailors who engaged in occasional homosexual activity at Newport. But they never considered prosecuting the many sailors who they fully realized were being serviced by the fairies each year, because they did not believe that the sailors' willingness to allow such acts "to be performed upon them" in any way implicated their sexual character as homosexual.

Instead, the navy chose to prosecute only those men who were intimately involved in the gang, or otherwise demonstrated (as the navy tried to prove in court) that homosexual desire was a persistent, constituent element of their personalities, whether or not it manifested itself in effeminate behavior. The fact that naval and civilian authorities could prosecute men only for the commission of specific acts of sodomy should not be construed to mean that they viewed homosexuality simply as an act rather than as a condition characteristic of certain individuals; the whole organization of their investigation suggests otherwise. At the January 1920 trial of Reverend Kent the prosecution contended that

> we may offer evidence of other occurrences similar to the ones the indictment is based on for the purpose of proving the disposition on the part of this man. I submit that it is a well-known principle of evidence that in a crime of this nature where disposition, inclination, is an element, that we are not confined to the specific conduct which we have complained of in the indictment, that the other incidents are gone into for their corroborative value as to intent, as to disposition, inclination.[48]

As the investigation and trials proceeded, however, the men prosecuted by the navy made it increasingly difficult for the navy to maintain standards that categorized certain men as "straight" even though they had engaged in homosexual acts with the defendants. This was doubtless particularly troubling to the navy because, while its opponents focused their questions on the character of the decoys in particular, by doing so they implicitly questioned the character of *any* man who had sex with a "pervert." The decoys testified that they had submitted to the queers' sexual advances only in order to rid the navy of their presence, and the navy, initially at least, guaranteed their legal immunity. But the defendants readily charged that the decoys themselves were tainted by homosexual interest and had taken abnormal pleasure in their work. Reverend Kent's lawyers were particularly forceful in questioning the character of any man who would volunteer to work as a decoy. As one decoy after another helplessly answered each question with a quiescent "Yes, sir," the lawyers pressed them:

Q. You volunteered for this work?
A. Yes, sir.
Q. You knew what kind of work it was before you volunteered, didn't you?
A. Yes, sir.
Q. You knew it involved sucking and that sort of thing, didn't you?
A. I knew that we had to deal with that, yes, sir.
Q. You knew it included sodomy and that sort of thing, didn't you?
A. Yes, sir.
Q. And you were quite willing to get into that sort of work?
A. I was willing to do it, yes, sir.
Q. And so willing that you volunteered for it, is that right?
A. Yes, sir. I volunteered for it, yes, sir.
Q. You knew it included buggering fellows, didn't you?[49]

Such questions about the decoys' character were reinforced when members of the gang claimed that the decoys had sometimes taken the initiative in sexual encounters.

The defendants raised questions about the character not only of men who volunteered to be decoys but of any man capable of responding to the advances of a pervert. Such questions forced the navy to reexamine its standards for distinguishing "straight" from "perverted" sexuality. At the second naval court of inquiry, even the navy's judge advocate asked the men about how much sexual pleasure they had experienced during their contacts with the suspects. As the boundaries distinguishing acceptable from perverted sexual response began to crumble, the decoys recognized their vulnerability and tried to protect themselves. Some simply refused to answer any further questions about the sexual encounters they had described in graphic detail to the first court. One decoy protested that he had never responded to a pervert's advances: "I am a man. . . . The thing was so horrible in my sight that naturally I could not become passionate and there was no erection," but was immediately asked, "Weren't [the other decoys] men, too?" Another, less fortunate decoy had to plead:

Of course, a great deal of that was involuntary inasmuch as a man placing his hand on my penis would cause an erection and subsequent emission. That was uncontrollable on my part. . . .

Probably I would have had it [the emission] when I got back in bed anyway. . . . It is a physiological fact.[50]

But if a decoy could be suspected of perversion simply because he had a certain physiological response to a pervert's sexual advances, then the character of countless other sailors came under question. Many more men than the inner circle of queers and husbands would have to be investigated. In 1920, the navy was unprepared to take that step. The decision of the Dunn Inquiry to condemn the original investigation and the navy's decision to offer clemency to some of the men imprisoned as a result of it may be interpreted, in part, as a quiet retreat from that prospect.

CHRISTIAN BROTHERHOOD UNDER SUSPICION

The navy investigation revealed that even when two men engaged in what was generally regarded as a "sexual" relationship, whether both or only one of them should be labeled a sexual pervert was still disputed. But the investigation raised even more fundamental questions—concerning the definition of a "sexual relationship" itself—when it reached beyond the largely working-class milieu of the military to label a prominent local Episcopal clergyman, Samuel Kent, and a Y.M.C.A. volunteer and churchman, Arthur Leslie Green, as homosexual. When Kent fled the city, the navy tracked him down and brought him to trial on sodomy charges. Two courts acquitted him despite the fact that five decoys claimed to have had sex with him, because the denials of the respected minister and of the numerous clergymen and educators who defended him seemed more credible. Soon after Kent's second acquittal in early 1920, the bishop of Rhode Island and the Newport Ministerial Union went on the offensive against the navy. The clergymen charged that the navy had used immoral methods in its investigation, by instructing young enlisted men "in the details of a nameless vice" and sending them into the community to entrap innocent citizens. They wrote letters of protest to the secretary of the navy and the president, condemned the investigation in the press, and forced the navy to convene a second court of inquiry into the methods used in the first inquiry. When it exculpated senior naval officials and failed to endorse all of the ministers' criticisms, the ministers persuaded the Republican-controlled Senate Naval Affairs Committee to undertake its own investigation, which eventually endorsed all of the ministers' charges.[51]

The simple fact that one of their own had been attacked did not provoke the fervor of the ministers' response to the navy investigation, nor did they oppose the investigation simply because of its "immoral" methods. Close examination of the navy's allegations and of the ministers' countercharges suggests that the ministers feared that the navy's charges against the two churchmen threatened to implicate them all.

Both Green and Kent were highly regarded local churchmen; Kent had been asked to preach weekly during Lent, had received praise for his work at the Naval Hospital during the influenza epidemic, and at the time of the investigation was expected to be named superintendant of a planned Seaman's Church Institute.[52] Their behavior had not differed markedly from that of the many other men who ministered to the needs of the thousands of boys brought to Newport by the war. When the navy charged that Kent's and Green's behavior and motives were perverted, many ministers feared that they too could be accused of perversion, and, more broadly, that the inquiry had questioned the ideology of nonsexual Christian brotherhood that had heretofore explained their devotion to other men. The confrontation between the two groups represented fundamentally a dispute over the norms for masculine gender behavior and over the boundaries between homosociality and homosexuality in the relations of men.

The investigation threatened Newport's ministers precisely because it repudiated those conventions that had justified and institutionalized a mode of behavior for men of the cloth or of the upper class that would have been perceived as effeminate in other men. The ministers' perception of this threat is reflected in their repeated criticism of the navy operatives' claim that they could detect perverts by their "looks and actions."[53] Almost all sailors and townspeople, as we have seen, endorsed this claim, but it put the ministers as a group in an extremely awkward position, for the major sign of a man's perversion according to most sailors was his being effeminate. As the ministers' consternation indicated, there was no single norm for masculine behavior at Newport; many forms of behavior considered effeminate on the part of working-class men were regarded as appropriate to the status of upper-class men or to the ministerial duties of the clergy. Perhaps if the navy had accused only working-class sailors, among whom "effeminacy" was more clearly deviant from group norms, of perversion, the ministers might have been content to let this claim stand. But when the naval inquiry also identified churchmen associated with such an upper-class institution as the Episcopal Church of Newport as perverted because of their perceived effeminacy, it challenged the norms that had heretofore shielded men of their background from such suspicions.

One witness tried to defend Kent's "peculiar" behavior on the basis of the conventional norms when he contended that "I don't know whether you would call it abnormal. He was a minister."[54] But the navy refused to accept this as a defense, and witnesses repeatedly described Kent and Green to the court as "peculiar," "sissyfied," and "effeminate." During his daily visits to patients at the hospital, according to a witness named Brunelle, Green held the patients' hands and "didn't talk like a man—he

talk[ed] like a woman to me."[55] Since there is no evidence that Green had
a high-pitched or otherwise "effeminate" *voice*, Brunelle probably meant
Green addressed men with greater affection than he expected of a man.
But all ministers visited with patients and spoke quiet, healing words to
them; their position as ministers had permitted them to engage in such
conventionally "feminine" behavior. When the navy and ordinary sailors
labeled this behavior "effeminate" in the cases of Green and Kent, and
further claimed that such effeminacy was a sign of sexual perversion, they
challenged the legitimacy of many Christian social workers' behavior.

Even more disturbing to the ministers was the navy's charge that perverted sexual interest had motivated Kent's and Green's ministry to
young enlisted men. During the war, Newport's clergymen had done all
they could to minister to the needs of the thousands of boys brought to
the Naval Training Station. They believed they had acted in the spirit of
Christian brotherhood, but the naval inquiry seemed to suggest that less
lofty motives were at work. Ministers had loaned sailors money, but
during the inquiry they heard Green accused of buying sex. They had
visited boys in the hospital and now heard witnesses insinuate that this
was abnormal: "I don't know what [Kent's] duties were, but he was
always talking to some boys. It seems though he would have special
boys to talk to. He would go to certain fellows [patients] and probably
spend the afternoon with them."[56] They had given boys drives and taken
them out to dinner and to the theater, and now heard Kent accused of
lavishing such favors on young men in order to further his salacious purposes. They had opened their homes to the young enlisted men but now
heard Kent accused of inviting boys home in order to seduce them.[57]
When one witness at the first court of inquiry tried to argue that Green's
work at the Y.M.C.A. was inspired by purely "charitable" motives, the
court repudiated his interpretation and questioned the motives of *any*
man who engaged in such work:

> Do you think a normal active man would peddle stamps and paper
> around a Hospital and at the Y.M.C.A.? . . .
> Do you think that a man who had no interest in young boys would
> voluntarily offer his services and work in the Y.M.C.A. where he is
> constantly associated with young boys?[58]

To question the motives of Green in this manner was to raise questions
about the motives of all the men who had worked with him during the
war, and this posed personal and professional dangers of the greatest
magnitude. Reverend Deming of the Ministerial Union reported that
numerous ministers shared the fear of one man who was "frantic after
all he had done for the Navy":

When this thing [the investigation] occurred, it threw some of my personal friends into a panic. For they knew that in the course of their
work they had had relations with boys in various ways; they had been
alone with them in some cases. As one boy [a friend] said, frequently
boys had slept in the room with him. But he had never thought of the
impropriety of sleeping alone with a navy boy. He thought probably
he would be accused.[59]

The ministers sought to defend Kent—and themselves—from the navy's
insinuations by reaffirming the cultural interpretation of ministerial
behavior as Christian and praiseworthy. While they denied the navy's
charge that Kent had had genital contact with sailors, they did not deny
his devotion to young men, for to have done so would have implicitly
conceded the navy's interpretation of such behavior as salacious—thus
have left all ministers who had demonstrated similar devotion open to
suspicion. Rather than deny the government's claim that Kent had
sought intimate relationships with sailors and devoted unusual attention
to them, therefore, Kent and his supporters depicted such behavior as an
honorable part of the man's ministry. Indeed, demonstrating just how
much attention Kent had lavished on boys became as central to the strategy of the ministers as it was to that of the government, but the ministers offered a radically different interpretation of it. Their preoccupation
with validating ministerial behavior turned Kent's trial and the second
naval inquiry into an implicit public debate over the cultural definition
of the boundaries between homosociality and homosexuality in the relations of men. The navy had defined Kent's behavior as sexual and perverted; the ministers sought to reaffirm that it was brotherly and
Christian.

Kent himself interpreted his relations with sailors as "[t]rying to be
friends with them, urging them to come to my quarters and see me if
they wanted to, telling them—I think, perhaps, I can best express it by
saying 'Big Brotherhood.'" He quoted a letter from another minister
commending his "brotherly assistance" during the influenza epidemic,
and he pointed out that the Episcopal War Commission provided him
with funds with which to take servicemen to the theater "at least once a
week" and to maintain his automobile in order to give boys drives "and
get acquainted with them."[60] He described in detail his efforts to minister to the men who had testified against him, explaining that he had
offered them counsel, a place to sleep, and other services just as he had
to hundreds of other enlisted men. But he denied that any genital contact
had taken place, and in some cases claimed he had broken off the relationships when he realized that the decoys wanted sexual contact.

Kent's lawyers produced a succession of defense witnesses—respected clergymen, educators, and businesspeople who had known Kent at every stage of his career—to testify to his obvious affection for boys, even though by emphasizing this aspect of his character they risked substantiating the navy's case. The main point of their testimony was that Kent was devoted to boys and young men and had demonstrated such talent in working with them that they had encouraged him to focus his ministry on them. Kent's lawyers prompted a former employer from Kent's hometown of Lynn, Massachusetts, to recall that Kent, a "friend of [his] family, and especially [his] sons and sons' associates," had "[taken] charge of twelve or fourteen boys [from Lynn] and [taken] them down to Sebago Lake," where they camped for several weeks "under his charge."[61] The bishop of Pennsylvania recalled that, as Kent's teacher at the Episcopal Theological School in Cambridge in 1908, he had asked Kent to help him develop a ministry to Harvard men, "because [Kent] seemed peculiarly fitted for it in temperament and in experience, and in general knowledge of how to approach young men and influence them for good."[62] The rector of the Holy Church of the Communion in New York, where Kent had served as assistant minister from 1913 to1915, testified that he had also assigned Kent to youth work because of his obvious talents and called Kent "a perfectly splendid manly man among men and boys."[63] The sentiments of Kent's character witnesses were perhaps best summarized by a judge who sat on the Episcopal War Commission that employed Kent. The judge assured the court that Kent's reputation was "excellent; I think he was looked upon as an earnest Christian man [who] was much interested in young men."[64]

The extent to which Kent's supporters were willing to interpret his intimacy with young men as brotherly rather than sexual is perhaps best illustrated by the effort of Kent's defense lawyer to show how Kent's inviting a decoy named Charles Zipf to sleep with him was only another aspect of his ministering to the boy's needs. Hadn't the decoy told Kent he was "lonesome" and had no place to sleep that night, the defense attorney pressed Zipf in cross-examination, before Kent invited him to spend the night in his parish house? And after Kent had set up a cot for Zipf in the living room, hadn't Zipf told Kent that he was cold before Kent pulled back the covers and invited him to join him in his bed?[65] The attorney counted on the presumption of Christian brotherhood to protect the minister's behavior from the suspicion of homosexual perversion, even though the same evidence would have seemed irrefutably incriminating in the case of another man.

Kent's defense strategy worked. Arguments based on assumptions about ministerial conduct persuaded the jury to acquit Kent of the government's charges. But Newport's ministers launched their campaign against the navy probe as soon as Kent was acquitted because they recognized that it had succeeded in putting their devotion to men under suspicion. It had raised questions about the cultural boundaries distinguishing homosexuality from homosociality that the ministers were determined to lay to rest.

But while it is evident that Newport's ministers feared the consequences of the investigation for their public reputations, two of their charges against the navy suggest that they may also have feared that its allegations contained some element of truth. The charges reflect the difference between the ministers' and the navy's understanding of sexuality and human sinfulness, but the very difference may have made the navy's accusations seem plausible in a way that the navy could not have foreseen. First, the ministers condemned the navy for having instructed young enlisted men—the decoys—"in the details of a nameless vice," and having ordered them to use that knowledge. The naval authorities had been willing to let their agents engage in sexual acts with the "queers" because they were primarily concerned about people manifesting a homosexual disposition rather than those engaging occasionally in homosexual acts. The navy asserted that the decoys' investigative purpose rendered them immune from criminal prosecution even though they had committed illegal sexual acts. But the ministers viewed the decoys' culpability as "a moral question . . . not a technical question at all"; when the decoys had sex with other men, they had "scars placed on their souls," because, inescapably, "having immoral relations with men is an immoral act."[66] The sin was in the act, not the motive or the disposition. In addition, the ministers charged that the navy had directed the decoys to entrap designated individuals and that no one, no matter how innocent, could avoid entrapment by a skillful decoy. According to Bishop Perry, the decoys operated by putting men "into compromising positions, where they might be suspected of guilt, [even though they were] guiltless persons." Anyone could be entrapped because an "innocent advance might be made by the person operated upon and he might be ensnared against his will."[67] Implicitly, any clergyman could have done what Kent was accused of doing. Anyone's defenses could fall.

The ministers' preoccupation with the moral significance of genital sexual activity and their fear that anyone could be entrapped may reflect the continued saliency for them of the Christian precept that *all* people, including the clergy, were sinners subject to a variety of sexual temptations, including those of homosexual desire.[68] According to this tradition, Christians had to resist homosexual temptations, as they resisted others, but simply to desire a homosexual liaison was neither a singular failing nor an indication of perverted character. The fact that the ministers never clearly elucidated this perspective and were forced increasingly to use the navy's own terms while contesting the navy's conclusions may reflect both the ministers' uncertainty about it and their recognition that such a perspective was no longer shared by the public whose opinion they wished to influence.

In any case, making the commission of specified physical acts the distinguishing characteristic of a moral pervert made it definitionally impossible to interpret the ministers' relationships with sailors—no matter how intimate and emotionally moving—as having a "sexual" element, so long as they involved no such acts. Defining the sexual element in men's relationships in this narrow manner enabled the ministers to develop a bipartite defense of Kent, which simultaneously denied he had had sexual relationships with other men and celebrated his profound emotional devotion to them. It legitimized (nonphysical) intimacy between men by precluding the possibility that such intimacy could be defined as sexual. Reaffirming the boundaries between Christian brotherhood and perverted sexuality in this manner was a central objective of the ministers' very public debate with the navy. But it may also have been of private significance to churchmen forced by the navy investigation to reflect on the nature of their brotherhood with other men.

CONCLUSION

The richly textured evidence provided by the Newport controversy makes it possible to reexamine certain tenets of recent work in the history of sexuality, especially the history interactionism and the labeling theory of deviance, has argued that the end of the nineteenth century witnessed a major reconceptualization of homosexuality. Before the last century, homosexual-as-person; they regarded homosexuality as simply another form of sinful behavior in which anyone might choose to engage. The turn of the century witnessed the "invention of the homosexual," that is, the new determination that homosexual desire was limited to certain identifiable individuals for whom it was an involuntary sexual orientation of some biological or psychological origin. The most prominent advocates of this thesis have argued that the medical discourse on homosexuality that emerged in the late nineteenth century played the determinative role in this process, by creating and popularizing this new model of homosexual behavior (which, in order to emphasize the centrality of medical discourse in its development, they have termed the "medical model" of homosexuality). It was on the basis of the new medical model, they argue, that homosexually active individuals came to be labeled in popular culture—and to assume an identity—as sexual deviants different in nature from other people, rather than as sinners whose sinful nature was the common lot of humanity.[69]

The Newport evidence indicates that the role of medical discourse has been exaggerated in this thesis, and it also suggests how we might begin to refine our analysis of the relationship between homosexual behavior and identity. First, and most clearly, the Newport evidence indicates that medical discourse still played little or no role in the shaping of working-class homosexual identities and categories by World War I, more than thirty years after the discourse had begun. There would be no logical reason to expect that discussions carried on in elite journals whose distribution was limited to members of the medical and legal professions would have had any immediate effect on the larger culture, particularly the working class. In the Newport evidence, only one fairy even mentioned the favored medical term "invert," using it as a synonym for the already existing and widely recognized popular term "queer." Moreover, while "invert" was commonly used in the medical literature there is no reason to assume that it originated there, and the Newport witness specified that he had first heard it in theater circles and not through reading any "literature." The culture of the sexual underground, always in a complex relationship with the dominant culture, played a more important role in the shaping and sustaining of sexual identities.

More remarkably, medical discourse appears to have had as little influence on the military hierarchy as on the people of Newport.[70] Throughout the two years of navy investigations related to Newport, which involved the highest naval officials, not a single medical expert was invited to present the medical perspective on the issues at stake. The only member of the original board of inquiry who even alluded to the published literature (and this on only one occasion during the Foster hearings, and once more at the second inquiry) was Dr. E. M. Hudson, the welfare officer at the naval hospital and one of the decoys' supervisors. Hudson played a prominent role in the original investigation not because of his medical expertise, but because it was the flagrantly displayed (and normally tolerated) effeminacy and homosexuality of hospital staff and patients that first made naval officials consider undertaking an investigation. As the decoys' supervisor, Hudson drew on his training in fingerprinting and detective work considerably more than his medical background. Only after he became concerned that the decoys might be held legally culpable for their homosexual activity did he "read several medical books on the subject and read everything that I could find out as to what legal decisions there were on these cases."[71] But he never became very familiar with the medical discourse on sexual nonconformity; after his reading he still thought that the term "invert," which had first appeared in U.S. medical journals almost forty years earlier, was "practically a new term," less than two years old.[72]

Moreover, Hudson only accepted those aspects of the medical analysis of homosexuality that confirmed the common beliefs about "queers" he already shared with other, nonmedical naval officials. Thus he accepted as authoritative the distinction that medical writers drew between "congenital perverts" (called "queers" in common parlance) and "normal people submitting to acts of perversion, as a great many normal people do, [who] do not become perverts themselves," such as men isolated from women at a military base. He accepted this "scientific" distinction because it only confirmed what he and other naval officials already believed: that many sailors had sex with the queers without being "queer" themselves. But when the medical literature differed from the assumptions he shared with most navy men, he ignored it. Rather than adopting the medical viewpoint that homosexuals were biological anomalies who should be treated medically rather than willful criminals who should be deterred from homosexuality by severe legal penalties, for instance, he agreed with his colleagues that "these conditions existed and should be eradicated and the men guilty of offenses should be rounded up and punished."[73] In the course of 109 days of hearings, Dr. Hudson referred to medical authorities only twice, and then only when they confirmed the assumptions of popular culture.

It thus appears more plausible to describe the medical discourse as a "reverse discourse," to use Michel Foucault's term, rather than as the central force in the creation of new sexual categories around which individuals shaped their personal identities. Rather than creating such categories as "the invert" and "the homosexual," the turn-of-the-century medical investigators whom Hudson read were trying to describe, classify, and explain a preexisting sexual underground whose outlines they only vaguely perceived. Their scientific categories largely reproduced those of popular culture, with "queers" becoming "inverts" in medical parlance but retaining the characteristic cross-gender behavior already attributed to them in popular culture. Doctors developed generalizations about homosexuals based on their idiosyncratic observations of particular individuals and admitted from the beginning that they were responding to the existence of communities of such people whose mysterious behavior and social organization they wished to explore. As one of the first American medical commentators observed in 1889, in explaining the need to study sexual perversion, "[t]here is in every community of any size a colony of male sexual perverts; they are usually known to each other, and are likely to congregate together."[74] By the time of the Newport investigation, medical researchers had developed an elaborate system of sexual classification and numerous explanations for individual cases of homosexuality, but they still had little comprehension of the complex social and cultural structure of gay life. One of the country's most prominent and best-informed medical investigators asserted in 1916 that

> Chicago has not developed a euphemism yet for these male perverts. In New York they are known as 'fairies' and wear a red necktie (inverts are generally said to prefer green). In Philadelphia they are known as 'Brownies.'[75]

That gay men in a single city might use the terms "fairy" and "Brownie" (or "pogue") to refer to two different kinds of "inverts" had not even occurred to him.

The Newport evidence helps put the significance of the medical discourse in perspective; it also offers new insights into the relationship between homosexual behavior and identity. Recent studies that have established the need to distinguish between homosexual behavior (presumably a transhistorically evident phenomenon) and the historically specific concept of homosexual identity have tended to focus on the evolution of people whose *primary* personal and political "ethnic" identification is as gay, and who have organized a multidimensional way of life on the basis of their homosexuality. The high visibility of such people in contemporary Western societies and their growing political significance make analysis of the historical development of their community of particular scholarly interest and importance.[76] But the Newport evidence indicates that we need to begin paying more attention to *other* social forms of homosexuality—other ways in which homosexual relations have been organized and understood, differentiated, named, and left deliberately unnamed. We need to specify the *particularity* of various modes of homosexual behavior and the relationships between those modes and particular configurations of sexual identity.

For even when we find evidence that a culture has labeled people who were homosexually active as sexually deviant, we should not assume *a priori* that their homosexual activity was the determinative criterion in the labeling process. As in Newport, where many men engaged in certain kinds of homosexual behavior yet continued to be regarded as "normal," the assumption of particular sexual roles and deviance from gender norms may have been more important than the coincidence of male or female sexual partners in the classification of sexual character. "Fairies," "pogues," "husbands," and "trade" might all be labeled "homosexuals" in our own time, but they were labeled—and understood themselves—as fundamentally different kinds of people in World War I–era Newport. They all engaged in what we would define as homosexual behavior, but they and the people who observed them were more careful than we to draw distinctions between different modes of such behavior. To classify their behavior and character using the simple polarities of "homosexual" and "heterosexual" would be to misunderstand the complexity of their sexual system. Indeed, the very terms "homosexual behavior" and " identity," because of their tendency to conflate phenomena that other cultures may have regarded as quite distinct, appear to be insufficiently precise to denote the variety of social forms of sexuality we wish to analyze.[77]

The problems that arise when different forms of homosexual activity and identity are conflated are evidenced in the current debate over the consequences of the development of a medical model of homosexuality. Recent studies, especially in lesbian history, have argued that the creation and stigmatization of the public image of the homosexual at the turn of the century served to restrict the possibilities for intimacy between all women and all men, by making it possible to associate such intimacy with the despised social category of the homosexual. This thesis rightly observes that the definition of deviance serves to establish behavioral norms for everyone, not just for the deviant. But it overlooks the corollary of this observation, that the definition of deviance serves to legitimize some social relations even as it stigmatizes others; and it assumes that the turn-of-the-century definition of "sexual inversion" codified the same configuration of sexual and gender phenomena which "homosexuality" does today. But many early-twentieth-century romantic friendships between women, for instance, appear to have been unaffected by the development of a public lesbian persona, in part because that image characterized the lesbian primarily as a "mannish woman," which had the effect of excluding from its stigmatizing purview all conventionally feminine women, no matter how intimate their friendships.[78]

Similarly, even though Newport residents were familiar with a particular image of "queers," they did not classify ministers who were intimate as Christian brothers with other men or sailors who had sex with effeminate men as "queer," because the character of neither group fully corresponded to the public's image of what a queer should be like. Moreover, both the sailors and clergymen defined sexual behavior and perversion in ways that excluded their own behavior from being labeled as either, no matter how suspect their behavior might seem from another perspective. The sailors legitimized their physical sexual contact with the queers by restricting the form of that contact and by proscribing effeminate behavior and emotional intimacy with their partners. The ministers interpreted the boundaries between acceptable and unacceptable male relations in precisely the opposite manner: for they defended their apparent effeminacy and emotional intimacy with men by defining sexuality as physical contact, which their moral code proscribed.

At the heart of the controversy provoked and revealed by the Newport investigation was a confrontation between several such definitional systems, a series of disputes over the boundaries between
homosociality and homosexuality in the relations of men and over the
standards by which their masculinity would be judged. The investigation
became controversial when it verged on suggesting that the homosocial
world of the navy and the relationships between sailors and their Christian brothers in the Newport ministry were permeated by homosexual
desire. Newport's ministers and leading citizens, the Senate Naval Affairs
Committee, and to some extent even the navy itself repudiated the Newport inquiry because they found such a suggestion intolerable. Although
numerous cultural interpretations of sexuality were allowed to confront
each other at the inquiry, ultimately certain cultural boundaries had to
be reaffirmed in order to protect certain relations as "nonsexual," even
as the sexual nature of others was declared and condemned. The Newport evidence reveals much about the social organization and self-
understanding of men who identified themselves as "queer." But it also
provides a remarkable illustration of the social nature of the boundaries
established between the "sexual" and the "nonsexual" in human relations and reminds us that cultural struggles over the demarcation of
those boundaries are a central aspect of the history of sexuality.

NOTES

1. This is a revised version of a paper originally presented at the conference
"Among Men, Among Women: Sociological and Historical Recognition of Homosocial Arrangements," held at the University of Amsterdam, June 22–26, 1983. I am
grateful to Allan Berube, John Boswell, Nancy Cott, Steven Dubin, James Schultz,
Anthony Stellato, James Taylor, and my colleagues at the Amsterdam conference for
their comments on earlier versions.

2. The Newport investigation was brought to the attention of historians by
Frank Freidel, *Franklin D. Roosevelt: The Ordeal* (Boston: Little, Brown, 1954), 41,
46–47, 96–97; and Jonathan Katz, *Gay American History: A Documentary* (New
York: Crowall, 1976), 579 n. Katz reprinted the Senate report in *Government Versus Homosexuals* (New York: Arno Press, 1975), a volume in the Arno Press series
on homosexuality he edited. A useful narrative account of the naval investigation is
provided by Lawrence R. Murphy, "Cleaning Up Newport: The U.S. Navy's Prosecution of Homosexuals After World War I," *Journal of American Culture* 7 (fall
1984): 57–64.

3. Murphy J. Foster presided over the first Court of Inquiry, which began its
work in Newport on March 13, 1919, and heard 406 pages of testimony in the
course of twenty-three days (its records are hereafter cited as *Foster Testimony*). The
second court of inquiry, convened in 1920 "to inquire into the methods
employed . . . in the investigation of moral and other conditions existing in the
Naval Service; [and] to ascertain and inquire into the scope of and authority for said

investigation," was presided over by Rear Admiral Herbert O. Dunn and heard 2,500 pages of testimony in the course of eighty-six days (hereafter cited as *Dunn Testimony*). The second trial of Reverend Kent, *U.S. v. Samuel Neal Kent,* heard in Rhode Island District Court in Providence beginning January 20, 1920, heard 532 pages of evidence (hereafter cited as *Kent Trial*). The records are held at the National Archives, Modern Military Field Branch, Suitland, Maryland, record group 125.

4. I have used "gay" in this essay to refer to men who identified themselves as sexually different from other men—and who labeled themselves and were labeled by others as "queer"—because of their assumption of "feminine" sexual and other social roles. As I explain below, not all men who were homosexually active labeled themselves in this manner, including men, known as "husbands," who were involved in long-term homosexual relationships but nonetheless maintained a masculine identity.

5. *Foster Testimony,* Ervin Arnold, 5; F. T. Brittain, 12; Thomas Brunelle, 21. *Dunn Testimony,* Albert Viehl, 307; Dudley Marriott, 1737.

6. Frederick Hoage, using a somewhat different construction than most, referred to them as "the inverted gang" (*Foster Testimony,* 255).

7. *Foster Testimony,* Arnold, 5; *Dunn Testimony,* Clyde Rudy, 1783. For a few of the many other comments by "straight" sailors on the presence of gay men at the Y.M.C.A., see *Dunn Testimony,* Claude McQuillin, 1759, and Preston Paul, 1836.

8. A man named Temple, for instance, had a room at the Y.M.C.A. where he frequently took pick-ups (*Foster Testimony,* Brunelle, 207–8); on the role of the elevator operators, see *Foster Testimony,* William McCoy, 20, and Samuel Rogers, 61.

9. *Foster Testimony,* Arnold, 27; Frederick Hoage, 271; Harrison Rideout, 292.

10. Ibid., Hoage, 267; Rogers, 50; Brunelle, 185.

11. Ibid., Gregory A. Cunningham, 30; Arnold, 6. *Dunn Testimony,* John S. Tobin, 720–21.

12. For an elaboration of the conceptual distinction between "inversion" and "homosexuality" in the contemporary medical literature, see my article, "From Sexual Inversion to Homosexuality: Medicine and the Changing Conceptualization of Female Deviance," *Salmagundi* 58–59 (fall 1982–winter 1983): 114–46.

13. *Foster Testimony,* Rogers, 50–51.

14. For example, an article included the following caption beneath a photograph of Hughes dressed in women's clothes: "This is Billy Hughes, Yeo. 2c. It's a shame to break the news like that, but enough of the men who saw 'Pinafore' fell in love with Bill, without adding to their number. 'Little Highesy,' as he is affectionately known, dances like a Ziegfeld chorus girl. . . . " ("We Sail the Ocean Blue: 'H.M.S. Pinafore' as Produced by the Navy," *Newport Recruit,* 6 [August 1918]: 9). See also, e.g., "Mayor Will Greet Navy Show Troupe: Official Welcome Arranged for 'Jack and Beanstalk' Boys," which quotes an admiral saying, "'It is a corker. I have never in my life seen a prettier 'girl' [a man] than 'Princess Mary.' She is the daintiest little thing I ever laid eyes on." (*Providence Journal* [26 May 1919]: 9). I am grateful to Lawrence Murphy for supplying me with copies of these articles.

15. *Dunn Testimony,* John S. Tobin, 716; *Foster Testimony,* Charles Zipf, 377; confirmed by Hoage, 289, and Arnold (*Dunn Testimony,* 1405). The man who received the women's clothes was the Billy Hughes mentioned in the newspaper article cited in the previous note. I am grateful to Allan Berube for informing me of the regularity with which female impersonators appeared in navy shows during and immediately following World War I.

16. Ibid., Hoage called it a "faggot party" and "a general congregation of inverts" (267); Brunelle, who claimed to have attended the party for only fifteen minutes,

noted the presence of the sailors and fighters; he also said only one person was in drag, but mentioned at least two (194, 206); John E. McCormick observed the lovers (332).

17. For the straight sailors' nicknames, see *Foster Testimony*, William Nelson Gorham, 349. On the ubiquity of nicknames and the origins of some of them, see Hoage, 253, 271; Whitney Delmore Rosensszweig, 397.

18. *Dunn Testimony*, Hudson, 1663.

19. *Foster Testimony*, Rideout, 76–77.

20. Ibid., Cunningham, 29. For other examples, see Wade Stuart Harvey, 366; and *Dunn Testimony*, Tobin, 715.

21. *Foster Testimony*, George Richard, 143; Hoage, 298.

22. Ibid., Rideout, 69; see also Rogers, 63; Viehl, 175; Arnold, 3; and passim.

23. An investigator told the navy that one gay man had declined to make a date with him because "he did not like to 'play with fire' . . . [and] was afraid Chief Brugs would beat him up" (*Foster Testimony*, Arnold, 36); the same gay man told the court he had traveled to Providence with Brugs two weekends in a row and gone to shows with him (Rogers, 53–54). Speaking of another couple, Hoage admitted he had heard "that Hughes has traveled with Brunelle separately for two months or so" and that "they were lovers." He added that "of course that does not indicate anything but friendship," but that "naturally I would suspect that something else was taking place" (Hoage, 268).

24. *Foster Testimony*, Hoage, 313.

25. Ibid., Arnold, 5.

26. Ibid., Viehl, 175; Brunelle, 235; Rideout, 93. Hoage, when cross-examined by Rosensszweig, denied another witness's charge that he, Hoage, had *boasted* of browning Rosensszweig, but he did not deny the act itself—nor did Rosensszweig ask him to do so (396).

27. Ibid., Hoage, 271; Rogers, 131–36.

28. Ibid., Rogers, 39–40; other evidence tends to confirm Rogers's contention that he had not known openly gay men or women before joining the navy. For other examples of the role of the war in introducing men to gays, see Brunelle, 211; and in the *Dunn Testimony*, Rudy, 1764. For extended discussions of the similar impact of military mobilization on many people's lives during World War II, see Allan Berube, "Marching to a Different Drummer," in *Powers of Desire: The Politics of Sexuality*, ed. Ann Snitow, Christine Stansell, and Sharon Thompson (New York: Monthly Review Press, 1983), 88–99; and John D'Emilio, *Sexual Politics, Sexual Communities: The Making of a Homosexual Minority in the United States, 1940–1970* (Chicago: University of Chicago Press, 1983), 23–39.

29. *Foster Testimony*, Rideout, 78.

30. *Dunn Testimony*, E. M. Hudson questioning Bishop James De Wolf Perry, 609 (my emphasis).

31. Ibid., Jeremiah Mahoney, 698.

32. Ibid., Tobin, 717.

33. Witnesses who encountered gay men at the hospital or commented on the presence of homosexuals there included Gregory Cunningham, *Foster Testimony*, 29; Brunelle, 210; John McCormick, *Dunn Testimony*, 1780; and Paul, 1841. Paul also described some of the open homosexual joking engaged in by patients, *Foster Testimony*, 393–94.

34. *Foster Testimony*, Hervey, 366; Johnson, 153, 155, 165, 167; Smith, 221.

35. Ibid., Johnson, 153; Smith, 169.

36. Ibid., Smith, 171.

37. Ibid., Hoage, 272. Hoage added that "[t]rade is a word that is only used among people temperamental [i.e., gay]," although this does not appear to have been entirely the case.

38. Ibid., Hoage, 269, 314; Rudy, 14. The decoy further noted that, despite the fairy's pleas, "I insisted that he do his work below my chest."

39. Frederick Hoage provided an example of this pattern when he described how a gay civilian had taken him to a show and dinner, let him stay in his room, and then "attempted to do what they call 'browning.'" But he devoted much of his testimony to *denying* that his "tak[ing] boys to dinner and to a show," offering to share his bed with sailors who had nowhere else to stay, and giving them small gifts and loans had the sexual implications that the court obviously suspected (*Foster Testimony*, Hoage, 261, 256, 262, 281–82). For other examples of solicitation patterns, see Maurice Kreisberg, 12; Arnold, 26; *Dunn Testimony*, Paul, 1843. Edward Stevenson describes the "trade" involved in military prostitution in *The Intersexes: A History of Semi-sexualism* (privately printed, 1908), 214. For an early sociological description of "trade," see Albert Reiss Jr., "The Social Integration of Queers and Peers," *Social Problems* 9 (1961): 102–20. It is possible that "trade" originally took on sexual connotations because of the frequency with which boys and young men who were engaged in "street trades" such as newspaper hawking earned extra money by having sex with older men. See Helen Kitchen Branson, "'Street Trades' and Their Sex Knowledge," *Sexology* (April 1949): 568–71.

40. *Foster Testimony*, Rudy, 13.

41. *Dunn Testimony*, Paul, 1836; see also, e.g., Mayor Mahoney's comments, 703.

42. *Foster Testimony*, James Daniel Chase, 119 (my emphasis); Zipf, 375.

43. Ibid., Walter F. Smith, 169.

44. See, e.g., the accounts of Hoage, *Foster Testimony*, 271–72, and Rideout, 87.

45. *Foster Testimony*, Smith, 169.

46. Alfred Kinsey, Wardell Pomeroy, and Clyde Martin, *Sexual Behavior in the Human Male* (Philadelphia: W. B. Saunders, Co., 1948), 650–51.

47. *Foster Testimony*, Arnold, 6; *Dunn Testimony*, Arnold, 1495.

48. *Kent Trial*, 21.

49. Ibid., defense attorney's interrogation of Charles McKinney, 66–67. See also, e.g., the examination of Zipf, esp. 27–28.

50. Ibid., Zipf, 2113, 2131 (the court repeatedly turned to the subject). The "manly" decoy was Clyde Rudy, 1793.

51. The ministers' efforts are reviewed and their charges affirmed in the Senate report, 67th Congress, 1st session, Committee on Naval Affairs, *Alleged Immoral Conditions of Newport (R.I.) Naval Training Station* (Washington, D.C.: Government Printing Office, 1921), and in the testimony of Bishop Perry and Reverend Hughes before the Dunn Inquiry.

52. *Dunn Testimony*, Rev. Deming, 30; Rev. Forster, 303.

53. Hudson quoted in the Senate report, *Alleged Immoral Conditions*, 8; see also *Dunn Testimony*, Tobin, 723, cf. Arnold, 1712. For the ministers' criticism, see, e.g., Bishop Perry, 529, 607.

54. *Foster Testimony*, Hoage, 319.

55. Ibid., Brunelle, 216. He says the same of Kent on p. 217.

56. *Kent Trial*, cross-examination of Howard Rider, 296.

57. Ibid., Malcolm C. Crawford, 220–23; Dostalik, 57–71.

58. *Foster Testimony*, interrogation of Hoage, 315, 318.

59. *Dunn Testimony*, Deming, 43.

60. *Kent Trial,* Kent, 396, 419, 403.

61. Ibid., Herbert Walker, 318–20.

62. Ibid., Bishop Philip Rhinelander, 261–62.

63. Ibid., Rev. Henry Motett, 145–49, 151.

64. Ibid., Judge Darius Baker, 277.

65. Ibid., interrogation of C. B. Zipf, 37–38.

66. *Dunn Testimony,* Rev. Deming, 42; Bishop Perry, 507.

67. Ibid., Perry, 678.

68. Jonathan Katz argues that such a perspective was central to Puritan concepts of homosexuality, "The Age of Sodomitical Sin, 1607–1740," in his *Gay/Lesbian Almanac* (New York: Harper and Row, 1983), 23–65. But see also John Boswell, "Revolutions, Universals and Sexual Categories," *Salmagundi* 58–59 (fall 1982–winter 1983): 89–113.

69. This argument was first introduced by Mary McIntosh, "The Homosexual Role," *Social Problems* 16 (1968): 182–92, and has been developed and modified by Jeffrey Weeks, *Coming Out: Homosexual Politics in Britain from the Nineteenth Century to the Present* (London: Quartet Books, 1977); Michel Foucault, *The History of Sexuality: An Introduction,* trans. Robert Hurley (New York: Vintage, 1978); Lillian Faderman, *Surpassing the Love of Men: Romantic Friendships and Love between Women From the Renaissance to the Present* (New York: Morrow, 1981); Kenneth Plummer, ed., *The Making of the Modern Homosexual* (London: Hutchinson, 1981); and Katz, *Gay/Lesbian Almanac.* Although these historians and sociologists subscribe to the same general model, they disagree over the timing and details of the emergence of a homosexual role, and McIntosh's original essay did not attribute a key role in that process to medical discourse.

70. The situation had changed considerably by World War II, when psychiatrists occupied a more influential position in the military, which used them to help select and manage the more than fifteen million men and women it mobilized for the war. See, for instance, the role of psychiatrists in the records of courts-martial conducted from 1941 to 1943, held at the National Archives (Army A.G. 250.1) and the 1944 investigation of lesbianism at the Third WAC Training Center, Fort Oglethorpe, Georgia (National Archives, Modern Military Field Branch, Suitland, Maryland, record group 159, entry 26F). Allan Berube's important study, *Coming Out Under Fire: The History of Gay Men and Women in World War Two* (New York: Plume, 1991), studies at length the role of psychiatrists in the development and implementation of World War II–era military policies.

71. *Dunn Testimony,* Hudson, 1630.

72. Ibid., 300. The transcript does not identify the speaker, but the context strongly suggests it was Hudson.

73. Ibid., 1514, 1628.

74. George Frank Lydston, "Sexual Perversion, Satyriasis, and Nymphomania," *Medical and Surgical Reporter* 61 (1889): 254. See also Chauncey, "From Sexual Inversion to Homosexuality," 142–43.

75. James Kiernan, "Classification of Homosexuality," *Urologic and Cutaneous Review* 20 (1916): 350.

76. John D'Emilio has provided the most sophisticated analysis of this process in *Sexual Politics, Sexual Communities: The Making of a Homosexual Minority in the United States, 1940–1970* (Chicago: University of Chicago Press, 1983). See also Toby Moratta, *The Politics of Homosexuality* (Boston: Houghton Mifflin, 1981), and the pioneering studies by Jeffrey Weeks and Lillian Faderman cited above.

77. One would also hesitate to assert that a single definition of homosexuality obtains in our own culture. Jonathan Katz has made a similar argument about the need to specify the meaning of homosexual behavior and identity in his *Gay/Lesbian Almanac*, although our analyses differ in a number of respects (see my review in *The Body Politic*, no. 97 (1983): 33–34.

78. Lillian Faderman, in "The Mordification of Love between Women by 19th-Century Sexologists," *Journal of Homosexuality* 4 (1978): 73–90, and *Surpassing the Love of Men*, is the major proponent of the argument that the medical discourse stigmatized romantic friendships. Alternative analyses of the role of the medical literature and of the timing and nature of the process of stigmatization having been proposed by Martha Vicinus, "Distance and Desire: English Boarding-School Friendships," *Signs* 9 (1984): 600–22; Carroll Smith-Rosenberg, "The New Woman as Androgyne: Social Disorder and Gender Crisis, 1870–1936," in *Disorderly Conduct: Visions of Gender in Victorian America* (New York: Knopf, 1985), 245–96; and Chauncey, "From Sexual Inversion to Homosexuality." On the apparent ubiquity of the early-twentieth-century public image of the lesbian as a "mannish woman," see Esther Newton, "The Mythic Mannish Lesbian: Radclyffe Hall and the New Woman," *Signs* 9 (1984): 557–75. Nineteenth-century medical articles and newspaper accounts of lesbian couples stigmatized only the partner who played "the man's part" by dressing like a man and seeking male employment, but found the "womanly" partner unremarkable, as if it did not matter that her "husband" was another female so along as she played the conventional wifely role (see Chauncey, l25ff). The medical reconceptualization of female deviance as homosexual object choice rather than gender role inversion was underway by the 1920s, but it is difficult to date any such transition in popular images, in part because they remained so inconsistent.

9

Miscegenation Law, Court Cases, and Ideologies of "Race" in Twentieth-Century America

Peggy Pascoe

On March 21, 1921, Joe Kirby took his wife, Mayellen, to court. The Kirbys had been married for seven years, and Joe wanted out. Ignoring the usual option of divorce, he asked for an annulment, charging that his marriage had been invalid from its very beginning because Arizona law prohibited marriages between "persons of Caucasian blood, or their descendants" and "negroes, Mongolians or Indians, and their descendants." Joe Kirby claimed that while he was "a person of the Caucasian blood," his wife, Mayellen, was "a person of negro blood."[1]

Although Joe Kirby's charges were rooted in a well-established—and tragic—tradition of American miscegenation law, his court case quickly disintegrated into a definitional dispute that bordered on the ridiculous. The first witness in the case was Joe's mother, Tula Kirby, who gave her testimony in Spanish through an interpreter. Joe's lawyer laid out the case by asking Tula Kirby a few seemingly simple questions:

> *Joe's lawyer:* To what race do you belong?
> *Tula Kirby:* Mexican.
> *Joe's lawyer:* Are you white or have you Indian blood?
> *Kirby:* I have no Indian blood.
> *Joe's lawyer:* Do you know the defendant [Mayellen] Kirby?
> *Kirby:* Yes.
> *Joe's lawyer:* To what race does she belong?
> *Kirby:* Negro.

Then the cross-examination began.

Mayellen's lawyer: Who was your father?
Kirby: Jose Romero.
Mayellen's lawyer: Was he a Spaniard?
Kirby: Yes, a Mexican.
Mayellen's lawyer: Was he born in Spain?
Kirby: No, he was born in Sonora.
Mayellen's lawyer: And who was your mother?
Kirby: Also in Sonora.
Mayellen's lawyer: Was she a Spaniard?
Kirby: She was on her father's side.
Mayellen's lawyer: And what on her mother's side?
Kirby: Mexican.
Mayellen's lawyer: What do you mean by Mexican, Indian, a native[?]
Kirby: I don't know what is meant by Mexican.
Mayellen's lawyer: A native of Mexico?
Kirby: Yes, Sonora, all of us.
Mayellen's lawyer: Who was your grandfather on your father's side?
Kirby: He was a Spaniard.
Mayellen's lawyer: Who was he?
Kirby: His name was Ignacio Quevas.
Mayellen's lawyer: Where was he born?
Kirby: That I don't know. He was my grandfather.
Mayellen's lawyer: How do you know he was a [S]paniard then?
Kirby: Because he told me ever since I had knowledge that he was a Spaniard.

Next the questioning turned to Tula's opinion about Mayellen Kirby's racial identity.

Mayellen's lawyer: You said Mrs. [Mayellen] Kirby was a negress. What do you know about Mrs. Kirby's family?
Kirby: I distinguish her by her color and the hair; that is all I do know.[2]

The second witness in the trial was Joe Kirby, and by the time he took the stand, the people in the courtroom knew they were in murky waters. When Joe's lawyer opened with the question "What race do *you* belong to?" Joe answered "Well . . . " and paused, while Mayellen's lawyer objected to the question on the ground that it called for a conclusion by the witness. "Oh, no," said the judge, "it is a matter of pedigree." Eventually allowed to answer the question, Joe said, "I belong to the white race, I suppose." Under cross-examination, he described his father as having been of the "Irish race," although he admitted, "I never knew any one of his people."[3]

Stopping at the brink of this morass, Joe's lawyer rested his case. He told the judge he had established that Joe was "Caucasian." Mayellen's lawyer scoffed, claiming that Joe had "failed utterly to prove his case" and arguing that "[Joe's] mother has admitted that. She has [testified] that she only claims a quarter Spanish blood; the rest of it is native blood." At this point the court intervened. "I know," said the judge, "but that does not signify anything."[4]

FROM THE DECLINE AND FALL OF SCIENTIFIC RACISM TO AN UNDERSTANDING OF MODERNIST RACIAL IDEOLOGY

The Kirbys' case offers a fine illustration of Evelyn Brooks Higginbotham's observation that, although most Americans are sure they know "race" when they see it, very few can offer a definition of the term. Partly for this reason, the questions of what "race" signifies and what signifies "race" are as important for scholars today as they were for the participants in *Kirby v. Kirby* seventy-five years ago.[5] Historians have a long—and recently a distinguished—record of exploring this question.[6] Beginning in the 1960s, one notable group charted the rise and fall of scientific racism among American intellectuals. Today, their successors, more likely to be schooled in social than intellectual history, trace the social construction of racial ideologies, including the idea of "whiteness," in a steadily expanding range of contexts.[7]

Their work has taught us a great deal about racial thinking in American history. We can trace the growth of racism among antebellum immigrant workers and free-soil northern Republicans; we can measure its breadth in late-nineteenth-century segregation and the immigration policies of the 1920s. We can follow the rise of Anglo-Saxonism from Manifest Destiny through the Spanish-American War and expose the appeals to white supremacy in woman suffrage speeches. We can relate all these developments (and more) to the growth and elaboration of scientific racist attempts to use biological characteristics to scout for racial hierarchies in social life, levels of civilization, even language.

Yet the range and richness of these studies all but end with the 1920s. In contrast to historians of the nineteenth- and early-twentieth-century United States, historians of the nation in the mid- to late-twentieth century seem to focus on racial ideologies only when they are advanced by the far Right (as in the Ku Klux Klan) or by racialized groups themselves (as in the Harlem Renaissance or black nationalist movements). To the extent that there is a framework for surveying mainstream twentieth-century American racial ideologies, it is inherited from the classic histories that tell of the post–1920s decline and fall of scientific racism. Their final pages link the demise of scientific racism to the rise of a vanguard of social scientists led by the cultural anthropologist Franz Boas: when modern social science emerges, racism runs out of intellectual steam. In the absence of any other narrative, this forms the basis for a commonly held but rarely examined intellectual trickle-down theory in which the attack on scientific racism emerges in universities in the 1920s and eventually, if belatedly, spreads to courts in the 1940s and 1950s and to government policy in the 1960s and 1970s.

A close look at such incidents as the *Kirby* case, however, suggests a rather different historical trajectory, one that recognizes that the legal system does more than just reflect social or scientific ideas about race; it also produces and reproduces them.[8] By following a trail marked by four miscegenation cases—the seemingly ordinary *Kirby v. Kirby* (1922) and *Estate of Monks* (1941) and the path-breaking *Perez v. Lippold* (1948) and *Loving v. Virginia* (1967)—this essay will examine the relation between modern social science, miscegenation law, and twentieth-century American racial ideologies, focusing less on the decline of scientific racism and more on the emergence of new racial ideologies.

In exploring these issues, it helps to understand that the range of nineteenth-century racial ideologies was much broader than scientific racism. Accordingly, I have chosen to use the term *racialism* to designate an ideological complex that other historians often describe with the terms "race" or "racist." I intend the term *racialism* to be broad enough to cover a wide range of nineteenth-century ideas, from the biologically marked categories scientific racists employed to the more amorphous ideas George M. Fredrickson has so aptly called "romantic racialism."[9] Used in this way, "racialism" helps counter the tendency of twentieth-century observers to perceive nineteenth-century ideas as biologically "determinist" in some simple sense. To racialists (including scientific racists), the important point was not that biology determined culture (indeed, the split between the two was only dimly perceived), but that race, understood as an indivisible essence that included not only biology but also culture, morality, and intelligence, was a compellingly significant factor in history and society.

My argument is this: During the 1920s, American racialism was challenged by several emerging ideologies, all of which depended on a modern split between biology and culture. Between the 1920s and the 1960s, those competing ideologies were winnowed down to the single, powerfully persuasive belief that the eradication of racism depends on the deliberate nonrecognition of race. I will call that belief *modernist racial ideology* to echo the self-conscious "modernism" of social scientists, writers, artists, and cultural rebels of the early twentieth century. When historians mention this phenomenon, they usually label it "antiracist" or "egalitarian" and describe it as in stark contrast to the "racism" of its predecessors. But in the new legal scholarship called "critical race theory," this same ideology, usually referred to as "color blindness," is criticized by those who recognize that it, like other racial ideologies, can be turned to the service of oppression.[10]

Modernist racial ideology has been widely accepted; indeed, it compelled nearly as much adherence in the late-twentieth-century United States as racialism did in the late nineteenth century. It is therefore important to see it not as what it claims to be—the nonideological end of racism—but as a racial ideology of its own, whose history shapes many of today's arguments about the meaning of race in American society.

THE LEGACY OF RACIALISM AND THE *KIRBY* CASE

Although it is probably less familiar to historians than, say, school segregation law, miscegenation law is an ideal place to study both the legacy of nineteenth-century racialism and the emergence of modern racial ideologies.[11] Miscegenation laws, in force from the 1660s through the 1960s, were among the longest lasting of American racial restrictions. They both reflected and produced significant shifts in American racial thinking. Although the first miscegenation laws had been passed in the colonial period, it was not until after the demise of slavery that they began to function as the ultimate sanction of the American system of white supremacy. They burgeoned along with the rise of segregation and the early-twentieth-century devotion to "white purity." At one time or another, forty-one American colonies and states enacted them; they blanketed western as well as southern states.[12]

By the early twentieth century, miscegenation laws were so widespread that they formed a virtual road map to American legal conceptions of race. Laws that had originally prohibited marriages between whites and African Americans (and, very occasionally, American Indians) were extended to cover a much wider range of groups. Eventually, twelve states targeted American Indians; fourteen, Asian Americans (Chinese, Japanese, and Koreans); and nine, "Malays" (or Filipinos). In Arizona, the *Kirby* case was decided under categories first adopted in a 1901 law that prohibited whites from marrying "negroes, Mongolians or Indians"; in 1931, "Malays" and "Hindus" were added to this list.[13]

Although many historians assume that miscegenation laws enforced American taboos against interracial sex, marriage, more than sex, was the legal focus.[14] Some states did forbid both interracial sex and interracial marriage, but nearly twice as many targeted only marriage. Because marriage carried with it social respectability and economic benefits that were routinely denied to couples engaged in illicit sex, appeals courts adjudicated the legal issue of miscegenation at least as frequently in civil cases about marriage and divorce, inheritance, or child legitimacy as in criminal cases about sexual misconduct.[15]

By the time the *Kirby* case was heard, lawyers and judges approached miscegenation cases with working assumptions built on decades of experience. There had been a flurry of challenges to the laws during Reconstruction, but courts quickly fended off arguments that miscegenation laws violated the Fourteenth Amendment guarantee of "equal protection." Beginning in the late 1870s, judges declared that the laws were constitutional because they covered all racial groups "equally."[16] Judicial justifications reflected the momentum toward racial categorization built into the nineteenth-century legal system and buttressed by the racialist conviction that everything from culture, morality, and intelligence to heredity could be understood in terms of race.

From the 1880s until the 1920s, lawyers whose clients had been caught in the snare of miscegenation laws knew better than to challenge the constitutionality of the laws or to dispute the perceived necessity for racial categorization; these were all but guaranteed to be losing arguments. A defender's best bet was to do what Mayellen Kirby's lawyer tried to do: to persuade a judge (or jury) that one particular individual's racial classification was in error. Lawyers who defined their task in these limited terms occasionally succeeded, but even then the deck was stacked against them. Wielded by judges and juries who believed that setting racial boundaries was crucial to the maintenance of ordered society, the criteria used to determine who fit in which category were more notable for their malleability than for their logical consistency. Genealogy, appearance, claims to identity, or that mystical quality, "blood"— any of these would do.[17]

In Arizona, Judge Samuel L. Pattee demonstrated that malleability in deciding the *Kirby* case. Although Mayellen Kirby's lawyer maintained that Joe Kirby "appeared" to be an Indian, the judge insisted that parentage, not appearance, was the key to Joe's racial classification:

> Mexicans are classed as of the Caucasian Race. They are descendants, supposed to be, at least of the Spanish conquerors of that country, and unless it can be shown that they are mixed up with some other races, why the presumption is that they are descendants of the Caucasian race.[18]

While the judge decided that ancestry determined that Joe Kirby was "Caucasian," he simply assumed that Mayellen Kirby was "Negro." Mayellen Kirby sat silent through the entire trial; she was spoken about and spoken for but never allowed to speak herself. There was no testimony about her ancestry; her race was assumed to rest in her visible physical characteristics. Neither of the lawyers bothered to argue over Mayellen's racial designation. As Joe's lawyer later explained,

> The learned and discriminating judge . . . had the opportunity to gaze upon the dusky countenance of the appellant [Mayellen Kirby] and could not and did not fail to observe the distinguishing characteristics of the African race and blood.[19]

In the end, the judge accepted the claim that Joe Kirby was "Caucasian" and Mayellen Kirby "Negro" and held that the marriage violated Arizona miscegenation law; he granted Joe Kirby his annulment. In so doing, the judge resolved the miscegenation drama by adding a patriarchal moral to the white supremacist plot. As long as miscegenation laws regulated marriage more than sex, it proved easy for white men involved with women of color to avoid the social and economic responsibilities they would have carried in legally sanctioned marriages with white women. By granting Joe Kirby an annulment, rather than a divorce, the judge not only denied the validity of the marriage while it had lasted but also in effect excused Joe Kirby from his obligation to provide economic support to a divorced wife.[20]

For her part, Mayellen Kirby had nothing left to lose. She and her lawyer appealed to the Arizona Supreme Court. This time they threw caution to the winds. Taking a first step toward the development of modern racial ideologies, they moved beyond their carefully limited argument about Joe's individual racial classification to challenge the entire racial logic of miscegenation law. The Arizona statute provided a tempting target for their attack, for under its "descendants" provision, a person of "mixed blood" could not legally marry anyone. Pointing this out, Mayellen Kirby's lawyer argued that the law must therefore be unconstitutional. He failed to convince the court. The appeals court judge brushed aside such objections. The argument that the law was unconstitutional, the judge held:

> is an attack . . . [Mayellen Kirby] is not entitled to make for the reason that there is no evidence that she is other than of the black race. . . . It will be time enough to pass on the question she raises . . . when it is presented by some one whose rights are involved or affected.[21]

THE CULTURALIST CHALLENGE TO RACIALISM

By the 1920s, refusals to recognize the rights of African American women had become conventional in American law. So had refusals to recognize obvious inconsistencies in legal racial classification schemes. Minions of racialism, judges, juries, and experts sometimes quarreled over specifics, but they agreed on the overriding importance of making and enforcing racial classifications.

Lawyers in miscegenation cases therefore neither needed nor received much courtroom assistance from experts. In another legal arena, citizenship and naturalization law, the use of experts, nearly all of whom advocated some version of scientific racism, was much more common. Ever since the 1870s, naturalization lawyers had relied on scientific racists to help them decide which racial and ethnic groups met the United States naturalization requirement of being "white" persons. But in a series of cases heard in the first two decades of the twentieth century, this strategy backfired. When judges found themselves drawn into a heated scientific debate on the question of whether "Caucasian" was the same as "white," the United States Supreme Court settled the question by discarding the experts and reverting to what the justices called the opinion of the "common man."[22]

In both naturalization and miscegenation cases, judges relied on the basic agreement between popular and expert (scientific racist) versions of the racialism that permeated turn-of-the-century American society. But even as judges promulgated the common sense of racialism, the ground was shifting beneath their feet. By the 1920s, lawyers in miscegenation cases were beginning to glimpse the courtroom potential of arguments put forth by a pioneering group of self-consciously "modern" social scientists willing to challenge racialism head on.

Led by cultural anthropologist Franz Boas, these emerging experts have long stood as the heroes of histories of the decline of scientific racism (which is often taken to stand for racism as a whole). But for modern social scientists, the attack on racialism was not so much an end in itself as a function of the larger goal of establishing "culture" as a central social science paradigm. Intellectually and institutionally, Boas and his followers staked their claim to academic authority on their conviction that human difference and human history were best explained by culture. Because they interpreted character, morality, and social organization as cultural, rather than racial, phenomena and because they were determined to explore, name, and claim the field of cultural analysis for social scientists, particularly cultural anthropologists, sociologists, and social psychologists, they are perhaps best described as culturalists.[23]

To consolidate their power, culturalists had to challenge the scientific racist paradigms they hoped to displace. Two of the arguments they made were of particular significance for the emergence of modern racial ideologies. The first was the argument that the key notion of racialism—race—made no biological sense. This argument allowed culturalists to take aim at a very vulnerable target. For most of the nineteenth century, scientific racists had solved disputes about who fit into which racial categories by subdividing the categories. As a result, the number of scientifically recognized races had increased so steadily that by 1911, when the anthropologist Daniel Folkmar compiled the intentionally definitive *Dictionary of Races and Peoples,* he recognized "45 races or peoples among immigrants coming to the United States." Folkmar's was only one of several competing schemes, and culturalists delighted in pointing out the discrepancies between them, showing that scientific racists could not agree on such seemingly simple matters as how many races there were or what criteria—blood, skin color, hair type—best indicated race.[24]

In their most dramatic mode, culturalists went so far as to insist that physical characteristics were completely unreliable indicators of race; in biological terms, they insisted, race must be considered indeterminable. Thus, in an influential encyclopedia article on "race" published in the early 1930s, Boas insisted that "it is not possible to assign with certainty any one individual to a definite group." Perhaps the strongest statement of this kind came from Julian Huxley and A. C. Haddon, British scientists who maintained that "the term *race* as applied to human groups should be dropped from the vocabulary of science." Since Huxley was one of the first culturalists trained as a biologist, his credentials added luster to his opinion. In this and other forms, the culturalist argument that race was biologically indeterminable captured the attention of both contemporaries and later historians.[25]

Historians have paid much less attention to a second and apparently incompatible argument put forth by culturalists. It started from the other end of the spectrum, maintaining not that there was no such thing as biological race, but that race was nothing more than biology. Since culturalists considered biology of remarkably little importance, consigning race to the realm of biology pushed it out of the picture. Thus Boas ended his article on race by concluding that although it remained "likely" enough that scientific study of the "anatomical differences between the races" might reveal biological influences on the formation of personality, "the study of cultural forms shows that such differences are altogether irrelevant as compared with the powerful influence of the cultural environment in which the group lives."[26]

Following this logic, the contrast between important and wide-reaching culture and unimportant (but biological) race stood as the cornerstone of many culturalist arguments. Thus the cultural anthropologist Ruth Benedict began her influential 1940 book, *Race: Science and Politics,* with an analysis of "what race is *not,*" including language, customs, intelligence, character, and civilization. In a 1943 pamphlet coauthored with Gene Weltfish and addressed to the general public, she explained that real "racial differences" occurred only in "nonessentials such as texture of head hair, amount of body hair, shape of the nose or head, or color of the eyes and the skin." Drawing on these distinctions, Benedict argued that race was a scientific "fact," but that racism, which she defined as "the dogma that the hope of civilization depends upon eliminating some races and keeping others pure," was no more than a "modern superstition."[27]

Culturalists set these two seemingly contradictory depictions of race—the argument that biological race was nonsense and the argument that race was merely biology—right beside each other. The contradiction mattered little to them. Both arguments effectively contracted the range of racialist thinking, and both helped break conceptual links between race and character, morality, psychology, and language. By showing that one after another of these phenomena depended more on environment and training than on biology, culturalists moved each one out of the realm of race and into the province of culture, widening the modern split between culture and biology. Boas opened his article on race by staking out this position. "The term race is often used loosely to indicate groups of men differing in appearance, language, or culture," he wrote, but in his analysis, it would apply "solely to the biological grouping of human types."[28]

In adopting this position, culturalist intellectuals took a giant step away from popular common sense on the issue of race. Recognizing— even at times celebrating—this gap between themselves and the public, they devoted much of their work to dislodging popular racial assumptions. They saw the public as lamentably behind the times and sadly prone to race "prejudice," and they used their academic credentials to insist that racial categories not only did not rest on common sense, but made little sense at all.[29]

THE *MONKS* CASE AND THE MAKING OF MODERN RACIAL IDEOLOGIES

This, of course, was just what lawyers challenging miscegenation laws wanted to hear. Because culturalist social scientists could offer their arguments with an air of scientific and academic authority that might persuade judges, attorneys began to invite them to appear as expert witnesses. But when culturalists appeared in court, they entered an arena where their argument for the biological indeterminacy of race was shaped in ways neither they nor the lawyers who recruited them could control.

Take, for example, the seemingly curious trial of Marie Antoinette Monks of San Diego, California, decided in the Superior Court of San Diego County in 1939. By all accounts, Marie Antoinette Monks was a woman with a clear eye for her main chance. In the early 1930s, she had entranced and married a man named Allan Monks, potential heir to a Boston fortune. Shortly after the marriage, which took place in Arizona, Allan Monks declined into insanity. Whether his mental condition resulted from injuries he had suffered in a motorcycle crash or from drugs administered under the undue influence of Marie Antoinette, the court would debate at great length. Allan Monks died. He left two wills: an old one in favor of a friend named Ida Lee and a newer one in favor of his wife, Marie Antoinette. Ida Lee submitted her version of the will for probate, Marie Antoinette challenged her claim, and Lee fought back. Lee's lawyers contended that the Monks' marriage was illegal. They charged that Marie Antoinette Monks, who had told her husband she was a "French" countess, was actually "a Negro" and therefore prohibited by Arizona law from marrying Allan Monks, whom the court presumed to be Caucasian.[30]

Much of the ensuing six-week-long trial was devoted to determining the "race" of Marie Antoinette Monks. To prove that she was "a Negro," her opponents called five people to the witness stand: a disgruntled friend of her husband, a local labor commissioner, and three expert witnesses, all of whom offered arguments that emphasized biological indicators of race. The first so-called expert, Monks's hairdresser, claimed that she could tell that Monks was of mixed blood from looking at the size of the moons of her fingernails, the color of the "ring" around the palms of her hands, and the "kink" in her hair. The second, a physical anthropologist from the nearby San Diego Museum, claimed to be able to tell that Monks was "at least one-eighth negroid" from the shape of her face, the color of her hands, and her "protruding heels," all of which he had observed casually while a spectator in the courtroom. The third expert witness, a surgeon, had grown up and practiced medicine in the South and later served at a Southern Baptist mission in Africa. Having once walked alongside Monks when entering the courthouse (at which time he tried, he said, to make a close observation of her), he testified that he could tell that she was of "one-eighth negro blood" from the contour of her calves and heels, from the "peculiar pallor" on the back of her neck, from the shape of her face, and from the wave of her hair.[31]

To defend Monks, her lawyers called a friend, a relative, and two expert witnesses of their own, an anthropologist and a biologist. The experts both started out by testifying to the culturalist position that it was impossible to tell a person's race from physical characteristics, especially if that person was, as they put it, "of mixed blood." This was the argument culturalists used whenever they were cornered into talking about biology, a phenomenon they tended to regard as so insignificant a factor in social life that they preferred to avoid talking about it at all.

But because this argument replaced certainty with uncertainty, it did not play very well in the *Monks* courtroom. Seeking to find the definitiveness they needed to offset the experts who had already testified, the lawyers for Monks paraded their own client in front of the witness stand, asking her to show the anthropologist her fingernails and to remove her shoes so that he could see her heels. They lingered over the biologist's testimony that Monks's physical features resembled those of the people of southern France. In the end, Monks's lawyers backed both experts into a corner; when pressed repeatedly for a definite answer, both reluctantly admitted that it was their opinion that Monks was a "white" woman.[32]

The experts' dilemma reveals the limitations of the argument for racial indeterminacy in the courtroom. Faced with a conflict between culturalist experts, who offered uncertainty and indeterminacy, and their opponents, who offered concrete biological answers to racial questions, judges were predisposed to favor the latter. To judges, culturalists appeared frustratingly vague and uncooperative (in other words, lousy witnesses), while their opponents seemed to be good witnesses willing to answer direct questions.

In the *Monks* case, the judge admitted that his own "inexpert" opinion—that Marie Antoinette "did have many characteristics that I would say . . . [showed] mixed negro and some other blood"—was not enough to justify a ruling. Turning to the experts before him, he dismissed the hairdresser (whose experience he was willing to grant, but whose scientific credentials he considered dubious); he passed over the biologist (whose testimony, he thought, could go either way); and he dismissed the two anthropologists, whose testimonies, he said, more or less canceled each other out. The only expert the judge was willing to rely on was the surgeon, because the surgeon "seemed . . . to hold a very unique and peculiar position as an expert on the question involved from his work in life."[33]

Relying on the surgeon's testimony, the judge declared that Marie Antoinette Monks was "the descendant of a negro" who had "one-eighth negro blood . . . and 7/8 caucasian blood"; he said that her "race" prohibited her from marrying Allan Monks and from inheriting his estate. The racial categorization served to invalidate the marriage in two overlapping ways. First, as a "negro," Marie Antoinette could not marry a white under Arizona miscegenation law; and second, by telling her husband-to-be that she was "French," Marie Antoinette had committed a "fraud" serious enough to render the marriage legally void. The court's decision that she had also exerted "undue influence" over Monks was hardly necessary to the outcome.[34]

As the *Monks* case suggests, we should be careful not to overestimate the influence culturalists had on the legal system. And, while in courtrooms culturalist experts were trying—and failing—to convince judges that biological racial questions were unanswerable, outside the courts their contention that biological racial answers were insignificant was faring little better. During the first three decades of the twentieth century, scientists on the "racial" side of the split between race and culture reconstituted themselves into a rough alliance of their own. Mirroring the modern dividing line between biology and culture, its ranks swelled with those who claimed special expertise on biological questions. There were biologists and physicians; leftover racialists such as physical anthropologists, increasingly shorn of their claims to expertise in every arena *except* that of physical characteristics; and, finally, the newly emerging eugenicists.[35]

Eugenicists provided the glue that held this coalition together. Narrowing the sweep of nineteenth-century racialist thought to focus on biology, these modern biological experts then expanded their range by offering physical characteristics, heredity, and reproductive imperatives as variations on the biological theme. They were particularly drawn to arenas in which all these biological motifs came into play; accordingly, they placed special emphasis on reforming marriage laws. Perhaps the best-known American eugenicist, Charles B. Davenport of the Eugenics Record Office, financed by the Carnegie Institution, outlined their position in a 1913 pamphlet, *State Laws Limiting Marriage Selection Examined in the Light of Eugenics,* which proposed strengthening state control over the marriages of the physically and racially unfit. Davenport's plan was no mere pipe dream. According to the historian Michael Grossberg, by the 1930s, forty-one states used eugenic categories to restrict the marriage of "lunatics," "imbeciles," "idiots," and the "feebleminded"; twenty-six states restricted the marriages of those infected with syphilis and gonorrhea; and twenty-seven states passed sterilization laws. By midcentury, blood tests had become a standard legal prerequisite for marriage.[36]

Historians have rather quickly passed over the racial aspects of American eugenics, seeing its proponents as advocates of outmoded ideas soon to be beached by the culturalist sea change. Yet until at least

World War II, eugenicists reproduced a modern racism that was biological in a particularly virulent sense. For them, unlike their racialist predecessors (who tended to regard biology as an indicator of a much more expansive racial phenomenon), biology really was the essence of race. And unlike nineteenth-century scientific racists (whose belief in discrete racial dividing lines was rarely shaken by evidence of racial intermixture), twentieth-century eugenicists and culturalists alike seemed obsessed with the subject of mixed-race individuals.[37]

In their determination to protect "white purity," eugenicists believed that even the tightest definitions of race by blood proportion were too loose. Setting their sights on Virginia, in 1924 they secured passage of the most draconian miscegenation law in American history. The act, entitled "an Act to preserve racial integrity," replaced the legal provision that a person must have one-sixteenth of "negro blood" to fall within the state's definition of "colored" with a provision that:

> It shall hereafter be unlawful for any white person in this State to marry any save a white person, or a person with no other admixture of blood than white and American Indian. For the purpose of this act, the term "white person" shall apply only to the person who has no trace whatsoever of any blood other than Caucasian; but persons who have one-sixteenth or less of the blood of the American Indian and have no other non-Caucasic blood shall be deemed to be white persons.

Another section of the Virginia law (which provided for the issuance of supposedly voluntary racial registration certificates for Virginia citizens) spelled out the "races" the legislature had in mind. The list, which specified "Caucasian, Negro, Mongolian, American Indian, Asiatic Indian, Malay, or any mixture thereof, or any other non-Caucasic strains," showed the lengths to which lawmakers would go to pin down racial categories. Within the decade, the Virginia law was copied by Georgia and echoed in Alabama. Thereafter, while supporters worked without much success to extend such laws to other states, defenders of miscegenation statutes added eugenic arguments to their rhetorical arsenal.[38]

Having been pinned to the modern biological wall and labeled as "mixed race," Marie Antoinette Monks would seem to have been in the perfect position to challenge the constitutionality of the widely drawn Arizona miscegenation law. She took her case to the California Court of Appeals, Fourth District, where she made an argument that echoed that of Mayellen Kirby two decades earlier. Reminding the court of the wording of the Arizona statute, her lawyers pointed out that "on the set of facts found by the trial judge, [Marie Antoinette Monks] is concededly

of Caucasian blood as well as negro blood, and therefore a descendant
of a Caucasian." Spelling it out, they explained:

> As such, she is prohibited from marrying a negro or any descendant
> of a negro, a Mongolian or an Indian, a Malay or a Hindu, or any of
> the descendants of any of them. Likewise . . . as a descendant of a
> negro she is prohibited from marrying a Caucasian or descendant of
> a Caucasian, which of course would include any person who had any
> degree of Caucasian blood in them.

Because this meant that she was "absolutely prohibited from contracting
valid marriages in Arizona," her lawyers argued that the Arizona law
was an unconstitutional constraint on her liberty.[39]

The court, however, dismissed this argument as "interesting but in
our opinion not tenable." In a choice that speaks volumes about the
depth of attachment to racial categories, the court narrowed the force of
the argument by asserting that "the constitutional problem would be
squarely presented" only if one mixed-race person were seeking to
marry another mixed-race person, then used this constructed hypothetical to dodge the issue:

> While it is true that there was evidence that appellant [Marie
> Antoinette Monks] is a descendant of the Caucasian race, as well as
> of the Negro race, the other contracting party [Allan Monks] was of
> unmixed blood and therefore the hypothetical situation involving an
> attempted alliance between two persons of mixed blood is no more
> present in the instant case than in the Kirby case. . . . The situations
> conjured up by respondent are not here involved. . . . Under the facts
> presented the appellant does not have the benefit of assailing the
> validity of the statute.

This decision was taken as authoritative. Both the United States Supreme
Court and the Supreme Judicial Court of Massachusetts (in which
Monks had also filed suit) refused to reopen the issue.[40]

Perhaps the most interesting thing about the Monks case is that there
is no reason to believe that the public found it either remarkable or
objectionable. Local reporters who covered the trial in 1939 played up
the themes of forgery, drugs, and insanity; their summaries of the racial
categories of the Arizona law and the opinions of the expert witnesses
were largely matter-of-fact.[41]

In this seeming acceptability to the public lies a clue to the development of modern racial ideologies. Even as judges narrowed their conception of race, transforming an all-encompassing phenomenon into a

simple fact to be determined, they remained bound by the provisions of miscegenation law to determine who fit in which racial categories. For this purpose, the second culturalist argument, that race was merely biology, had far more to offer than the first, that race was biologically indeterminable. The conception of race as merely biological seemed consonant with the racial categories built into the laws, seemed supportable by clear and unequivocal expert testimony, and fit comfortably within popular notions of race.

THE DISTILLATION OF MODERNIST RACIAL IDEOLOGY: FROM *PEREZ* TO *LOVING*

In the *Monks* case we can see several modern racial ideologies—ranging from the argument that race was biological nonsense to the reply that race was essentially biological to the possibility that race was merely biology—all grounded in the split between culture and biology. To distill these variants into a unified modernist racial ideology, another element had to be added to the mix, the remarkable (in American law, nearly unprecedented) proposal that the legal system abandon its traditional responsibility for determining and defining racial categories. In miscegenation law, this possibility emerged in a case that also, and not coincidentally, featured the culturalist argument for biological racial indeterminacy.

The case was *Perez v. Lippold*. It involved a young Los Angeles couple, Andrea Perez and Sylvester Davis, who sought a marriage license. Turned down by the Los Angeles County clerk, they challenged the constitutionality of the California miscegenation law directly to the California Supreme Court, which heard their case in October 1947.[42]

It was not immediately apparent that the *Perez* case would play a role in the development of modernist racial ideology. Perhaps because both sides agreed that Perez was "a white female" and Davis "a Negro male," the lawyer who defended the couple, Daniel Marshall, did not initially see the case as turning on race categorization. In 1947, Marshall had few civil rights decisions to build on, so he tried an end-run strategy: he based his challenge to miscegenation laws on the argument that, because both Perez and Davis were Catholics and the Catholic Church did not prohibit interracial marriage, California miscegenation law was an arbitrary and unreasonable restraint on their freedom of religion.

The freedom-of-religion argument made some strategic sense, since several courts had held that states had to meet a high standard to justify restrictions on religious expression. Accordingly, Marshall laid out the religion argument in a lengthy petition to the California Supreme Court.

In response, the state offered an even lengthier defense of miscegenation laws. The state's lawyers had at their fingertips a long list of precedents upholding such laws, including the *Kirby* and *Monks* cases. They added eugenic arguments about racial biology, including evidence of declining birth rates among "hybrids" and statistics that showed high mortality, short life expectancies, and particular diseases among African Americans. They polished off their case with the comments of a seemingly sympathetic Roman Catholic priest.[43]

Here the matter stood until the California Supreme Court heard oral arguments in the case. At that session, the court listened in silence to Marshall's opening sally that miscegenation laws were based on prejudice and to his argument that they violated constitutional guarantees of freedom of religion. But as soon as the state's lawyer began to challenge the religious freedom argument, one of the court's associate justices, Roger Traynor, impatiently interrupted the proceedings. "What," he asked, "about equal protection of the law?"

> *Mr. Justice Traynor:* . . . it might help to explain the statute, what it means. What is a negro?
>
> *Mr. Stanley:* We have not the benefit of any judicial interpretation. The statute states that a negro [Stanley evidently meant to say, as the law did, "a white"] cannot marry a negro, which can be construed to mean a full-blooded negro, since the statute also says mulatto, Mongolian, or Malay.
>
> *Mr. Justice Traynor:* What is a mulatto? One-sixteenth blood?
>
> *Mr. Stanley:* Certainly certain states have seen fit to state what a mulatto is.
>
> *Mr. Justice Traynor:* If there is $1/8$ blood, can they marry? If you can marry with $1/8$, why not with $1/16$, $1/32$, $1/64$? And then don't you get in the ridiculous position where a negro cannot marry anybody? If he is white, he cannot marry black, or if he is black, he cannot marry white.
>
> *Mr. Stanley:* I agree that it would be better for the Legislature to lay down an exact amount of blood, but I do not think that the statute should be declared unconstitutional as indefinite on this ground.
>
> *Mr. Justice Traynor:* That is something anthropologists have not been able to furnish, although they say generally that there is no such thing as race.
>
> *Mr. Stanley:* I would not say that anthropologists have said that generally, except such statements for sensational purposes.
>
> *Mr. Justice Traynor:* Would you say that Professor Wooten of Harvard was a sensationalist? The crucial question is how can a county clerk determine who are negroes and who are whites.[44]

Although he addressed his questions to the lawyers for the state, Justice Traynor had given Marshall a gift no lawyer had ever before received in a miscegenation case: judicial willingness to believe in the biological indeterminacy of race. It was no accident that this argument came from Roger Traynor. A former professor at Boalt Hall, the law school of the University of California, Berkeley, Traynor had been appointed to the court for his academic expertise rather than his legal experience; unlike his more pragmatic colleagues, he kept up with developments in modern social science.[45]

Marshall responded to the opening Traynor had provided by making sure that his next brief included the culturalist argument that race was biological nonsense. In it, he asserted that experts had determined that "race, as popularly understood, is a myth"; he played on the gap between expert opinion and laws based on irrational "prejudice" rooted in "myth, folk belief, and superstition"; and he dismissed his opponents' reliance on the "grotesque reasoning of eugenicists" by comparing their statements to excerpts from Adolf Hitler's *Mein Kampf*.[46]

Marshall won his case. The 1948 decision in the *Perez* case was remarkable for many reasons. It marked the first time since Reconstruction that a state court had declared a state miscegenation law unconstitutional. It went far beyond existing appeals cases in that the California Supreme Court had taken the very step the judges in the *Kirby* and *Monks* cases had avoided—going beyond the issue of the race of an individual to consider the issue of racial classification in general. Even more remarkable, the court did so in a case in which neither side had challenged the racial classification of the parties. But despite these accomplishments, the *Perez* case was no victory for the culturalist argument about the biological indeterminacy of race. Only the outcome of the case—that California's miscegenation law was unconstitutional—was clear. The rationale for this outcome was a matter of considerable dispute.

Four justices on the California Supreme Court condemned the law and three supported it; altogether, they issued four separate opinions. A four-justice majority agreed that the law should be declared unconstitutional but disagreed about why. Two justices, led by Traynor, issued a lengthy opinion that pointed out the irrationality of racial categories, citing as authorities a virtual who's who of culturalist social scientists, from Boas, Huxley, and Haddon to Gunnar Myrdal. A third justice issued a concurring opinion that pointedly ignored the rationality or irrationality of race classifications to criticize miscegenation laws on equality grounds, contending that laws based on "race, color, or creed" were—and always had been—contrary to the Declaration of Independence, the Constitution, and the Fourteenth Amendment; as this justice saw it, the Constitution was color-blind. A fourth justice, who reported that he

wanted his decision to "rest upon a broader ground than that the challenged statutes are discriminatory and irrational," based his decision
solely on the religious freedom issue that had been the basis of Marshall's original argument.[47]

In contrast, a three-justice minority argued that the law should be
upheld. They cited legal precedent, offered biological arguments about
racial categories, and mentioned a handful of social policy considerations. Although the decision went against them, their agreement with
each other ironically formed the closest thing to a majority in the case.
In sum, although the *Perez* decision foreshadowed the day when American courts would abandon their defense of racial categories, its variety
of judicial rationales tells us more about the range of modern racial ideologies than it does about the power of any one of them.[48]

Between the *Perez* case in 1948 and the next milestone miscegenation
case, *Loving v. Virginia,* decided in 1967, judges would search for a
common denominator among this contentious variety, trying to find a
position of principled decisiveness persuasive enough to mold both public and expert opinion. One way to do this was to back away from the
culturalist argument that race made no biological sense, adopting the
other culturalist argument that race was biological fact and thus shifting
the debate to the question of how much biological race should matter in
determining social and legal policy.

In such a debate, white supremacists tried to extend the reach of biological race as far as possible. Thus one scientist bolstered his devotion
to white supremacy by calling Boas "that appalling disaster to American
social anthropology whose influence in the end has divorced the social
studies of man from their scientific base in physical biology."[49] Following the lead of eugenicists, he and his sympathizers tried to place every
social and legal superstructure on a biological racial base.

In contrast, their egalitarian opponents set limits. In their minds, biological race (or "skin color," as they often called it) was significant only
because its visibility made it easy for racists to identify those they subjected to racial oppression. As Myrdal, the best-known of the mid-twentieth-
century culturalist social scientists, noted in 1944 in his monumental
work, *An American Dilemma*:

> In spite of all heterogeneity, the average white man's unmistakable
> observation is that *most Negroes in America have dark skin and
> woolly hair,* and he is, of course, right. . . . [The African American's]
> African ancestry and physical characteristics are fixed to his person
> much more ineffaceably than the yellow star is fixed to the Jew dur-
> ing the Nazi regime in Germany.[50]

To Myrdal's generation of egalitarians, the translation of visible physical characteristics into social hierarchies formed the tragic foundation of American racism.

The egalitarians won this debate, and their victory paved the way for the emergence of a modernist racial ideology persuasive enough to command the kind of widespread adherence once commanded by late-nineteenth-century racialism. Such a position was formulated by the United States Supreme Court in 1967 in *Loving v. Virginia*, the most important miscegenation case ever heard and the only one now widely remembered.

The *Loving* case involved what was, even for miscegenation law, an extreme example. Richard Perry Loving and Mildred Delores Jeter were residents of the small town of Central Point, Virginia, and family friends who had dated each other since he was seventeen and she was eleven. When they learned that their plans to marry were illegal in Virginia, they traveled to Washington, D.C., which did not have a miscegenation law, for the ceremony, returning in June 1958 with a marriage license, which they framed and placed proudly on their wall. In July 1958, they were awakened in the middle of the night by the county sheriff and two deputies, who had walked through their unlocked front door and right into their bedroom to arrest them for violating Virginia's miscegenation law. Under that law, an amalgam of criminal provisions enacted in 1878 and Virginia's 1924 "Act to preserve racial integrity," the Lovings, who were identified in court records as a "white" man and a "colored" woman, pleaded guilty and were promptly convicted and sentenced to a year in jail. The judge suspended their sentence on the condition that "both accused leave . . . the state of Virginia at once and do not return together or at the same time to said county and state for a period of twenty-five years."[51]

In 1963, the Lovings, then the parents of three children, grew tired of living with relatives in Washington, D.C., and decided to appeal this judgment. Their first attempts ended in defeat. In 1965, the judge who heard their original case not only refused to reconsider his decision but raised the rhetorical stakes by opining:

> Almighty God created the races white, black, yellow, malay and red, and he placed them on separate continents. And but for the interference with his arrangement there would be no cause for such marriages. The fact that he separated the races shows that he did not intend for the races to mix.

But by the time their argument had been processed by the Supreme Court of Appeals of Virginia (which invalidated the original sentence but upheld the miscegenation law), the case had attracted enough attention that the United States Supreme Court, which had previously avoided taking miscegenation cases, agreed to hear an appeal.[52]

On the side of the Lovings stood not only their own attorneys, but also the National Association for the Advancement of Colored People (NAACP), the NAACP Legal Defense and Education Fund, the Japanese American Citizens League (JACL), and a coalition of Catholic bishops. The briefs they submitted offered the whole arsenal of arguments developed in previous miscegenation cases. The bishops offered the religious freedom argument that had been the original basis of the *Perez* case. The NAACP and the JACL stood on the opinions of culturalist experts, whose numbers now reached beyond social scientists well into the ranks of biologists. Offering both versions of the culturalist line on race, NAACP lawyers argued on one page, "The idea of 'pure' racial groups, either past or present, has long been abandoned by modern biological and social sciences," and on another, "Race, in its scientific dimension, refers only to the biogenetic and physical attributes manifest by a specified population. It does not, under any circumstances, refer to culture (learned behavior), language, nationality, or religion." The Lovings' lawyers emphasized two central points: Miscegenation laws violated both the constitutional guarantee of equal protection under the laws and the constitutional protection of the fundamental right to marry.[53]

In response, the lawyers for the state of Virginia tried hard to find some ground on which to stand. Their string of court precedents upholding miscegenation laws had been broken by the *Perez* decision. Their argument that Congress never intended the Fourteenth Amendment to apply to interracial marriage was offset by the Supreme Court's stated position that congressional intentions were inconclusive. In an attempt to distance the state from the "white purity" aspects of Virginia's 1924 law, Virginia's lawyers argued that since the Lovings admitted that they were a "white" person and a "colored" person and had been tried under a section of the law that mentioned only those categories, the elaborate definition of "white" offered in other sections of Virginia law was irrelevant.[54]

On only one point did the lawyers for both parties and the Court seem to agree: None of them wanted to let expert opinion determine the outcome. The lawyers for Virginia knew only too well that during the twentieth century, the scientific foundations of the eugenic biological argument in favor of miscegenation laws had crumbled, so they tried to warn the Court away by predicting that experts would mire the Court in "a veritable Serbonian bog of conflicting scientific opinion." Yet the Lovings' lawyers, who seemed to have the experts on their side, agreed that "the Court should not go into the morass of sociological evidence that is available on both sides of the question." "We strongly urge," they told the justices, "that it is not necessary." And the Court, still reeling from widespread criticism that its decision in the famous 1954 case *Brown v. Board of Education* was illegitimate "sociological jurisprudence," was not about to offer its opponents any more such ammunition.[55]

The decision the Court issued was, in fact, carefully shorn of all reference to expert opinion; it spoke in language that both reflected and contributed to a new popular common sense on the issue of race. Recycling earlier pronouncements that "distinctions between citizens solely because of their ancestry" were "odious to a free people whose institutions are founded upon the doctrine of equality" and that the Court "cannot conceive of a valid legislative purpose . . . which makes the color of a person's skin the test of whether his conduct is a criminal offense," the justices reached a new and broader conclusion. Claiming (quite inaccurately) that "We have consistently denied the constitutionality of measures which restrict the rights of citizens on account of race," the Court concluded that the racial classifications embedded in Virginia miscegenation laws were "so directly subversive of the principle of equality at the heart of the Fourteenth Amendment" that they were "unsupportable." Proclaiming that it violated both the equal protection and the due process clauses of the Fourteenth Amendment, the Court declared the Virginia miscegenation law unconstitutional.[56]

LEGACIES OF MODERNIST RACIAL IDEOLOGY

The decision in the *Loving* case shows the distance twentieth-century American courts had traveled. The accumulated effect of several decades of culturalist attacks on racialism certainly shaped their thinking. The justices were no longer willing to accept the notion that race was the all-encompassing phenomenon nineteenth-century racialist thinkers had assumed it to be; they accepted the divisions between culture and biology and culture and race established by modern social scientists. But neither were they willing to declare popular identification of race with physical characteristics (like "the color of a person's skin") a figment of the imagination. In their minds, the scope of the term "race" had shrunk to a point where biology was all that was left; "race" referred to visible physical characteristics significant only because racists used them to erect spurious racial hierarchies. The Virginia miscegenation law was a case in point; the Court recognized and condemned it as a statute clearly "designed to maintain White Supremacy."[57]

Given the dependence of miscegenation laws on legal categories of race, the Court concluded that ending white supremacy required abandoning the categories. In de-emphasizing racial categories, they joined mainstream mid-twentieth-century social scientists, who argued that because culture, rather than race, shaped meaningful human difference, race was nothing more than a subdivision of the broader phenomenon of ethnicity. In a society newly determined to be "color-blind," granting public recognition to racial categories seemed to be synonymous with racism itself.[58]

And so the Supreme Court promulgated a modernist racial ideology that maintained that the best way to eradicate racism was the deliberate nonrecognition of race. Its effects reached well beyond miscegenation law. Elements of modernist racial ideology marked many of the major mid-twentieth-century Supreme Court decisions, including *Brown v. Board of Education*. Its effects on state law codes were equally substantial; during the 1960s and 1970s, most American states repealed statutes that had defined "race" (usually by blood proportion) and set out to erase racial terminology from their laws.[59]

Perhaps the best indication of the pervasiveness of modernist racial ideology is how quickly late-twentieth-century conservatives learned to shape their arguments to fit its contours. Attaching themselves to the modernist narrowing of the definition of race to biology and biology alone, conservative thinkers began to contend that, unless their ideas rested solely and explicitly on a belief in biological inferiority, they should not be considered racist. They began to advance "cultural" arguments of their very own, insisting that their proposals were based on factors such as social analysis, business practicality, or merit—on anything, in other words, except biological race. In their hands, modernist racial ideology supports an Alice-in-Wonderland interpretation of racism in which even those who argue for racially oppressive policies can adamantly deny being racists.

This conservative turnabout is perhaps the most striking, but not the only, indication of the contradictions inherent in modernist racial ideology. Others run the gamut from administrative law to popular culture. So while the United States Supreme Court tries to hold to its twentieth-century legacy of limiting, when it cannot eradicate, racial categories, United States government policies remain deeply dependent on them. In the absence of statutory definitions of race, racial categories are now set by the United States Office of Management and Budget, which in 1977 issued a "Statistical Directive" that divided Americans into five major groups—American Indian or Alaskan Native, Asian or Pacific Islander, Black, White, and Hispanic. The statistics derived from these categories help determine everything from census counts to eligibility for inclusion in affirmative action programs to the drawing of voting districts.[60] Meanwhile, in one popular culture flash-point after another—from the Anita Hill/Clarence Thomas hearings to the *O.J. Simpson* case, mainstream commentators insist that "race" should not be a consideration even as they explore detail after detail that reveals its social pervasiveness.[61]

These gaps between the (very narrow) modernist conception of race and the (very wide) range of racial identities and racial oppressions bedevil today's egalitarians. In the political arena, some radicals have begun to argue that the legal system's deliberate nonrecognition of race erodes the ability to recognize and name racism and to argue for such policies as affirmative action, which rely on racial categories to overturn rather than to enforce oppression. Meanwhile, in the universities, a growing chorus of scholars is revitalizing the argument for the biological indeterminacy of race and using that argument to explore the myriad ways in which socially constructed notions of race remain powerfully salient. Both groups hope to do better than their culturalist predecessors at eradicating racism.[62] Attaining that goal may depend on how well we understand the tortured history of mid-twentieth-century American ideologies of race.

NOTES

This essay was originally presented at the Organization of American Historians' annual meeting in 1992, and it has benefited considerably from the responses of audiences there and at half a dozen universities. For especially helpful readings, suggestions, and assistance, I would like to thank Nancy Cott, Karen Engle, Estelle Freedman, Jeff Garcilazo, Dave Gutierrez, Ramon Gutierrez, Eric Hinderaker, Marcia Klotz, Dorothee Kocks, Waverly Lowell, Valerie Matsumoto, Robyn Muncy, David Roediger, Richard White, the Brown University women's history reading group, and the editors and anonymous reviewers of the *Journal of American History*.

1. Ariz. Rev. Stat. Ann. sec. 3837 (1913); "Appellant's Abstract of Record," Aug. 8, 1921, pp. 1–2, *Kirby v. Kirby*, docket 1970 (microfilm: file 36.1.134), Arizona Supreme Court Civil Cases (Arizona State Law Library, Phoenix).

2. "Appellant's Abstract of Record," 12–13, 13–15, 15, *Kirby v. Kirby.*

3. Ibid., 16–18.

4. Ibid., 19.

5. Evelyn Brooks Higginbotham, "African-American Women's History and the Metalanguage of Race," *Signs* 17 (Winter 1992): 253. See Michael Omi and Howard Winant, *Racial Formation in the United States: From the 1960s to the 1990s* (New York: Routledge and Kegan Paul, 1994); David Theo Goldberg, ed., *Anatomy of Racism* (Minneapolis: University of Minnesota Press, 1990); Henry Louis Gates Jr., ed., *"Race," Writing, and Difference* (Chicago: University of Chicago Press, 1986); Dominick LaCapra, ed., *The Bounds of Race: Perspectives on Hegemony and Resistance* (Ithaca: Cornell University Press, 1991); F. James Davis, *Who Is Black? One Nation's Definition* (University Park: Penn State University Press, 1991); Sandra Harding, ed., *The "Racial" Economy of Science: Toward a Democratic Future* (Bloomington: Indiana University Press, 1993); Maria P. P. Root, ed., *Racially Mixed People in America* (Newbury Park, CA: Safe Publications, 1992); and Ruth Frankenberg, *White Women, Race Matters: The*

Social Construction of Whiteness (Minneapolis: University of Minnesota Press, 1993).

6. Among the most provocative recent works are Higginbotham, "African-American Women's History"; Barbara J. Fields, "Ideology and Race in American History," in *Region, Race, and Reconstruction: Essays in Honor of C. Vann Woodward,* ed. J. Morgan Kousser and James M. McPherson (New York: Oxford University Press, 1982), 143–78; Thomas C. Holt, "Marking: Race, Race-Making, and the Writing of History," *American Historical Review,* 100 (Feb. 1995): 1–20; and David R. Roediger, *Towards the Abolition of Whiteness: Essays on Race, Politics, and Working Class History* (London: Verso, 1994).

7. On scientific racism, see Thomas F. Gossett, *Race: The History of an Idea in America* (Dallas: Southern Methodist University Press, 1963); George W. Stocking Jr., *Race, Culture, and Evolution: Essays in the History of Anthropology* (1968; reprint, Chicago: University of Chicago Press, 1982); John S. Haller Jr., *Outcasts from Evolution: Scientific Attitudes to Racial Inferiority, 1859–1900* (Urbana: University of Illinois Press, 1971); George M. Fredrickson, *The Black Image in the White Mind: The Debate on Afro-American Character and Destiny, 1817–1914* (New York: Harper and Row, 1971); Thomas G. Dyer, *Theodore Roosevelt and the Idea of Race* (Baton Rouge: Louisiana State University Press., 1980); Carl N. Degler, *In Search of Human Nature: The Decline and Revival of Darwinism in American Social Thought* (New York: Oxford University Press, 1991); and Elazar Barkan, *Retreat of Scientific Racism: Changing Concepts of Race in Britain and the United Sties between the World Wars* (Cambridge: Cambridge University Press, 1992). On the social construction of racial ideologies, see the works cited in note 6, above, and Ronald T. Takaki, *Iron Cages: Race and Culture in Nineteenth-Century America* (New York: Knopf, 1979); Reginald Horsman, *Race and Manifest Destiny: The Origins of American Racial Anglo-Saxonism* (Cambridge, Mass.: Harvard University Press, 1981); Alexander Saxton, *The Rise and Fall of the White Republic: Class Politics and Mass Culture in Nineteenth-Century America* (London: Verso, 1990); David R. Roediger, *The Wages of Whiteness: Race and the Making of the American Working Class* (London: Verso, 1991); Audrey Smedley, *Race in North America: Origin and Evolution of a Worldview* (Boulder, CO: Westview Press, 1993); and Tomas Almaguer, *Racial Fault Lines: The Historical Origins of White Supremacy in California* (Berkeley: University of California Press, 1994).

8. On law as a producer of racial ideologies, see Barbara J. Fields, "Slavery, Race, and Ideology in the United States of America," *New Left Review* 181 (May–June 1990): 7; Eva Saks, "Representing Miscegenation Law," *Raritan* 8 (Fall 1988): 56–60; and Collette Guillaumin, "Race and Nature: The System of Marks," *Feminist Issues* 8 (fall 1988): 25–44.

9. See especially Fredrickson, *Black Image in the White Mind.*

10. For intriguing attempts to define American modernism, see Daniel J. Singal, ed., *Modernist Culture in America* (Belmont CA: Wadsworth Publications, 1991); and Dorothy Ross, ed., *Modernist Impulses in the Human Sciences, 1870–1930* (Baltimore: Johns Hopkins University Press, 1994). For the view from critical race theory, see Brian K. Fair, "Foreword: Rethinking the Color Blindness Model," *National Black Law Journal* 13 (Spring 1993): 1–82; Neil Gotanda, "A Critique of 'Our Constitution Is Color-Blind,'" *Stanford Law Review* 44 (Nov. 1991): 1–68; Gary Peller, "Race Consciousness," *Duke Law Journal* (Sept. 1990): 758–847; and Peter Fitzpatrick, "Racism and the Innocence of Law," in *Anatomy of Racism,* 247–62.

11. Many scholars avoid using the word "miscegenation," which dates to the 1860s, means race mixing, and has, to twentieth-century minds, embarrassingly

biological connotations; they speak of laws against "interracial" or "cross-cultural" relationships. Contemporaries usually referred to "anti-miscegenation" laws. Neither alternative seems satisfactory, since the first avoids naming the ugliness that was so much a part of the laws and the second implies that "miscegenation" was a distinct racial phenomenon rather than a categorization imposed on certain relationships. I retain the term "miscegenation" when speaking of the laws and court cases that relied on the concept, but not when speaking of people or particular relationships. On the emergence of the term, see Sidney Kaplan, "The Miscegenation Issue in the Election of 1864," *Journal of Negro History* 24 (July 1949): 274–343.

12. Most histories of interracial sex and marriage in America focus on demographic patterns, rather than legal constraints. See, for example, Joel Williamson, *New People: Miscegenation and Mulattoes in the United States* (New York: Free Press, 1980); Paul R. Spickard, *Mixed Blood: Intermarriage and Ethnic Identity in Twentieth-Century America* (Madison: University of Wisconsin Press, 1989); and Deborah Lynn Kitchen, "Interracial Marriage in the United States, 1900–1980" (Ph.D. diss., University of Minnesota, 1993). The only historical overview is Byron Curti Martyn, "Racism in the United States: A History of the Anti-Miscegenation Legislation and Litigation" (Ph.D. diss., University of Southern California, 1979). On the colonial period, see A. Leon Higginbotham Jr. and Barbara K. Kopytoff, "Racial Purity and Interracial Sex in the Law of Colonial and Antebellum Virginia," *Georgetown Law Journal* 77 (Aug. 1989): 1967–2029; George M. Fredrickson, *White Supremacy: A Comparative Study in American and South African History* (New York: Oxford University Press, 1981), 99–108; and James Hugo Johnston, *Race Relations in Virginia & Miscegenation in the South, 1776–1860* (Amherst: University of Massachusetts Press, 1970), 165–90. For later periods, see Peter Bardaglio, "Families, Sex, and the Law: The Legal Transformation of the Nineteenth-Century Southern Household" (Ph.D. diss., Stanford University, 1987), 37–106, 345–49; Peter Wallenstein, "Race, Marriage, and the Law of Freedom: Alabama and Virginia, 1860s–1960s," *Chicago-Kent Law Review* 70, no. 2 (1994): 371–437; David H. Fowler, *Northern Attitudes towards Interracial Marriage: Legislation and Public Opinion in the Middle Atlantic and the States of the Old Northwest, 1780–1930* (New York: Garland Publications, 1987); Megumi Dick Osumi, "Asians and California's Anti-Miscegenation Laws," in *Asian and Pacific American Experiences: Women's Perspectives*, ed. Nobuya Tsuchida (Minneapolis: University of Minnesota Press, 1982), 2–8; and Peggy Pascoe, "Race, Gender, and Intercultural Relations: The Case of Interracial Marriage," *Frontiers* 12, no. 1 (1991): 5–18. The count of states is from the most complete list in Fowler, *Northern Attitudes,* 336–439.

13. Ariz. Rev. Stat. Ann. sec. 3092 (1901); 1931 Ariz. Sess. Laws, chap. 17. Arizona, Idaho, Maine, Massachusetts, Nevada, North Carolina, Oregon, Rhode Island, South Carolina, Tennessee, Virginia, and Washington passed laws that mentioned American Indians. Arizona, California, Georgia, Idaho, Mississippi, Missouri, Montana, Nebraska, Nevada, Oregon, South Dakota, Utah, Virginia, and Wyoming passed laws that mentioned Asian Americans. Arizona, California, Georgia, Maryland, Nevada, South Dakota, Utah, Virginia, and Wyoming passed laws that mentioned "Malays." In addition, Oregon law targeted "Kanakas" (native Hawaiians), Virginia "Asiatic Indians," and Georgia both "Asiatic Indians" and "West Indians." See Fowler, *Northern Attitudes,* 336–439; 1924 Va. Acts, chap. 371; 1927 Ga. Laws no. 317; 1931 Ariz. Sess. Laws, chap. 17; 1933 Cal. Stat., chap. 104; 1935 Md. Laws chap. 60; and 1939 Utah Laws, chap. 50.

14. The most insightful social and legal histories have focused on sexual relations rather than marriage. See, for example, Higginbotham and Kopytoff, "Racial Purity

and Interracial Sex"; Karen Getman, "Sexual Control in the Slaveholding South: The Implementation and Maintenance of a Racial Caste System," *Harvard Women's Law Journal* 7 (spring 1984): 125–34; Martha Hodes, "Sex across the Color Line: White Women and Black Men in the Nineteenth-Century American South" (Ph.D. diss., Princeton University, 1991); and Martha Hodes, "The Sexualization of Reconstruction Politics: White Women and Black Men in the South after the Civil War," in *American Sexual Politics: Sex, Gender, and Race since the Civil War,* ed. John C. Fout and Maura Shaw Tantillo (Chicago: University of Chicago Press, 1993), 59–74; Robyn Weigman, "The Anatomy of Lynching," ibid., 223–45; Jacquelyn Dowd Hall, "'The Mind That Burns in Each Body': Women, Rape, and Racial Violence," in *Powers of Desire: The Politics of Sexuality,* ed. Ann Snitow, Christine Stansell, and Sharon Thompson (New York: Monthly Review Press, 1983), 328–49; Kenneth James Lay, "Sexual Racism: A Legacy of Slavery," *National Black Law Journal* 13 (spring 1993): 165–83; and Kevin J. Mumford, "From Vice to Vogue: Black/White Sexuality and the 1920s" (Ph.D. diss., Stanford University, 1993). One of the first works to note the predominance of marriage in miscegenation laws was Mary Frances Berry, "Judging Morality: Sexual Behavior and Legal Consequences in the Late Nineteenth-Century South," *Journal of American History* 78 (Dec. 1991): 838–39. On the historical connections among race, marriage, property, and the state, see Saks, "Representing Miscegenation Law," 39–69; Nancy F. Cott, "Giving Character to Our Whole Civil Polity: Marriage and the Public Order in the Late Nineteenth Century," in *U.S. History as Women's History: New Feminist Essays,* ed. Linda K. Kerber, Alice Kessler-Harris, and Kathryn Kish Sklar (Chapel Hill: University of North Carolina Press, 1995), 107–21; Ramon A. Gutierrez, *When Jesus Came, the Corn Mothers Went Away: Marriage, Sexuality, and Power in New Mexico, 1500–1846* (Stanford: Stanford University Press, 1991); Verena Martinez-Alier, *Marriage, Class, and Colour in Nineteenth-Century Cuba: A Study of Racial Attitudes and Sexual Values in a Slave Society* (Ann Arbor: University of Michigan Press, 1989); Patricia J. Williams, "Fetal Fictions: An Exploration of Property Archetypes in Racial and Gendered Contexts," in *Race in America: The Struggle for Equality,* ed. Herbert Hill and James E. Jones Jr. (Madison: University of Wisconsin Press, 1993), 425–37; and Virginia R. Dominguez, *White by Definition: Social Classification in Creole Louisiana* (New Brunswick, NJ: Rutgers University Press, 1986).

15. Of the forty-one colonies and states that prohibited interracial marriage, twenty-two also prohibited some form of interracial sex. One additional jurisdiction (New York) prohibited interracial sex but not interracial marriage; it is not clear how long this 1638 statute was in effect, See Fowler, *Northern Attitudes,* 336–439. My database consists of every appeals court case I could identify in which miscegenation law played a role: 227 cases heard between 1850 and 1970, 132 civil and 95 criminal. Although cases that reach appeals courts are by definition atypical, they are significant because the decisions reached in them set policies later followed in more routine cases and because the texts of the decisions hint at how judges conceptualized particular legal problems. I have relied on them because of these interpretive advantages and for two more practical reasons. First, because appeals court decisions are published and indexed, it is possible to compile a comprehensive list of them. Second, because making an appeal requires the preservation of documents that might otherwise be discarded (such as legal briefs and court reporters' trial notes), they permit the historian to go beyond the judge's decision.

16. Decisions striking down the laws include *Burns v. State,* 48 Ala. 195 (1872); *Bonds v. Foster,* 36 Tex. 68 (1871–72); *Honey v. Clark,* 37 Tex. 686 (1873); *Hart v. Hoss,* 26 La. Ann. 90 (1874); *State v. Webb,* 4 Cent. L. J. 588 (1877); and *Ex parte*

Brown, 5 Cent. L. J. 149 (1877). Decisions upholding the laws include *Scott v. State*, 39 Ga. 321 (1869); *State v. Hairston*, 63 N.C. 451 (1869); *State v. Reinhardt*, 63 N.C. 547 (1869); *In re Hobbs*, 12 F. Cas. 262 (1871) (No. 6550); *Lonas v. State*, 50 Tenn. 287 (1871); *State v. Gibson*, 36 Ind. 389 (1871); *Ford v. State*, 53 Ala. 150 (1875); *Green v. State*, 58 Ala. 190 (1877); *Frasher v. State*, 3 Tex. Ct. App. R. 263 (1877); *Ex parte Kinney*, 14 F. Cas. 602 (1879) (no. 7825); *Ex parte Francois*, 9 F. Cas. 699 (1879) (no. 5047); *Francois v. State*, 9 Tex. Ct. App. R. 144 (1880); *Pace v. State*, 69 Ala. 231 (1881); *Pace v. Alabama*, 106 U.S. 583 (1882); *State v. Jackson*, 80 Mo. 175 (1883); *State v. Tutty*, 41 F. 753 (1890); *Dodson v. State*, 31 S.W. 977 (1895); *Strauss v. State*, 173 S.W. 663 (1915); *State v. Daniel*, 75 So. 836 (1917); *Succession of Mingo*, 78 So. 565 (1917–18); and *In re Paquet's Estate*, 200 P. 911 (1921).

17. Individual racial classifications were successfully challenged in *Moore v. State*, 7 Tex. Ct. App. R. 608 (1880); *Jones v. Commonwealth*, 80 Va. 213 (1884); *Jones v. Commonwealth*, 80 Va. 538 (1885); *State v. Treadway*, 52 So. 500 (1910); *Flores v. State*, 129 S.W. 1111 (1910); *Ferrall v. Ferrall*, 69 S.E. 60 (1910); *Marre v. Marre*, 168 S.W. 636 (1914); *Neuberger v. Gueldner*, 72 So. 220 (1916); and *Reed v. State*, 92 So. 511 (1922).

18. "Appellant's Abstract of Record," 19, *Kirby v. Kirby*.

19. "Appellee's Brief," Oct. 3, 1921, p. 6, *ibid*.

20. On the theoretical problems involved in exploring how miscegenation laws were gendered, see Pascoe, "Race, Gender, and Intercultural Relations"; and Peggy Pascoe, "Race, Gender, and the Privileges of Property: On the Significance of Miscegenation Law in United States History," in *New Viewpoints in Women's History: Working Papers from the Schlesinger Library 50th Anniversary Conference, March 4–5, 1994*, ed. Susan Ware (Cambridge, MA: Harvard University Press, 1994), 99–122. For an excellent account of the gendering of early miscegenation laws, see Kathleen M. Brown, *Good Wives and Nasty Wenches: Gender, Race, and Power in Colonial Virginia* (Chapel Hill: University of North Carolina Press, 1996).

21. "Appellant's Brief," Sept. 8, 1921, *Kirby v. Kirby*; *Kirby v. Kirby*, 206 P. 405, 406 (1922). On *Kirby*, see Roger Hardaway, "Unlawful Love: A History of Arizona's Miscegenation Law," *Journal of Arizona History* 27 (Winter 1986): 377–90.

22. For examples of reliance on experts, see *In re Ah Yup*, 1 F. Cas. 223 (1878) (no. 104); *In re Kanaka Nian*, 21 P. 993 (1889); *In re Saito*, 62 F. 126 (1894). On these cases, see Ian F. Haney Lopez, *White by Law: The Legal Construction of Race* (New York: New York University Press, 1996). For reliance on the "common man," see *U.S. v. Bhagat Singh Thind*, 261 U.S. 204 (1923). On *Thind*, see Sucheta Mazumdar, "Racist Responses to Racism: The Aryan Myth and South Asians in the United States," *South Asia Bulletin* 9, no. 1 (1989): 47–55; Joan M. Jensen, *Passage from India: Asian Indian Immigrants in North America* (New Haven: Yale University Press, 1988), 247–69; and Roediger, *Towards the Abolition of Whiteness*, 181–84.

23. "The rise of Boasian anthropology has attracted much attention among intellectual historians, most of whom seem to agree with the 1963 comment that "it is possible that Boas did more to combat race prejudice than any other person in history"; see Gossett, *Race*, 418. In addition to the works cited in note 7, see I. A. Newby, *Jim Crow's Defense: Anti-Negro Thought in America, 1900–1930* (Baton Rouge: Louisiana State University Press, 1965), 21; and John S. Gilkeson Jr., "The Domestication of 'Culture' in Interwar America, 1919–1941," in *The Estate of Social Knowledge*, ed. JoAnna Brown and David K. van Keuren (Baltimore: Johns Hopkins University Press, 1991), 153–74. For more critical appraisals, see Robert Proctor, "Eugenics among the Social Sciences: Hereditarian Thought in Germany and the

United States," *ibid.*, 175–208; Hamilton Cravens, *The Triumph of Evolution: The Heredity-Environment Controversy, 1900–1941* (Baltimore: Johns Hopkins University Press, 1988); and Donna Haraway, *Primate Visions: Gender, Race, and Nature in the World of Modern Science* (New York: Routledge, 1989), 127–203. The classic—and still the best—account of the rise of cultural anthropology is Stocking, *Race, Culture, and Evolution.* See also George W. Stocking Jr., *Victorian Anthropology* (New York: Free Press, 1987), 284–329.

24. U.S. Immigration Commission, *Dictionary of Races or Peoples* (Washington, 1911), 2. For other scientific racist classification schemes, see *Encyclopedia Britannica,* 11th ed., s.v. "Anthropology"; and *Encyclopedia Americana: A Library of Universal Knowledge* (New York: The author, 1923), s.v. "Ethnography" and "Ethnology."

25. Franz Boas, "Race," in *Encyclopedia of the Social Sciences,* 15 vols., ed. Edwin R. A. Seligman (New York, 1930–35), 13:27; Julian S. Huxley and A. C. Haddon, *We Europeans: A Survey of "Racial" Problems* (London: J. Cape, 1935), 107.

26. Boas, "Race," 34. For one of the few instances in which a historian has noted this argument, see Smedley, *Race in North America,* 275–82.

27. Ruth Benedict, *Race: Science and Politics* (New York: Morgan Ass, Books, 1940), 12; Ruth Benedict and Gene Weltfish, *The Races of Mankind* (New York: Public Affairs Committee, 1943), 5; Benedict, *Race,* 12.

28. Boas, "Race," 25–26.

29. See, for example, Huxley and Haddon, *We Europeans,* 107, 269–73; Benedict and Weltfish, *Races of Mankind*; Benedict, *Race*; and Gunnar Myrdal, *An American Dilemma: The Negro Problem and Modern Democracy* (New York: Harper & Brothers, 1944), 91–115.

30. The Monks trial can be followed in *Estate of Monks,* 4 Civ. 2835, Records of California Court of Appeals, Fourth District (California State Archives, Roseville); and *Gunn v. Giraudo,* 4 Civ. 2832, ibid. (Gunn represented another claimant to the estate.) The two cases were tried together. For the seven-volume "Reporter's Transcript," see *Estate of Monks,* 4 Civ. 2835, ibid.

31. Reporter's Transcript," vol. 2, pp. 660–67, vol. 3, pp. 965–76, 976–98, *Estate of Monks.*

32. Ibid., vol. 5, pp. 1501–49, vol. 6, pp. 1889–1923.

33. Ibid., vol. 7, pp. 2543, 2548.

34. "Findings of Fact and Conclusions of Law," in "Clerk's Transcript," Dec. 2, 1940, *Gunn v. Giraudo,* 4 Civ. 2832, p. 81. One intriguing aspect of the *Monks* case is that the seeming exactness was unnecessary. The status of the marriage hinged on the Arizona miscegenation law, which would have denied validity to the marriage whether the proportion of "blood" in question was "one-eighth" or "one drop."

35. For descriptions of those interested in biological aspects of race, see Stocking, *Race, Culture, and Evolution,* 271–307; I. A. Newby, *Challenge to the Court: Social Scientists and the Defense of Segregation, 1954–1966* (Baton Rouge: Louisiana State University Press, 1969); and Cravens, *Triumph of Evolution,* 15–55. On eugenics, see Proctor, "Eugenics among the Social Sciences," 175–208; Daniel J. Kevles, *In the Name of Eugenics: Genetics and the Uses of Human Heredity* (New York: Knopf, 1985); Mark H. Hailer, *Eugenics: Hereditarian Attitudes in American Thought* (New Brunswick, N.J.: Rutgers University Press, 1963); and William H. Tucker, *The Science and Politics of Racial Research* (Urbana: University of Illinois Press, 1994), 54–137.

36. Charles B. Davenport, *Eugenics Record Office Bulletin No. 9: State Laws Limiting Marriage Selection Examined in the Light of Eugenics* (Cold Spring Harbor, NY, 1913); Michael Grossberg, "Guarding the Altar: Physiological Restrictions and

the Rise of State Intervention in Matrimony," *American Journal of Legal History* 26 (July 1982): 221–24.

37. See, for example, C[harles] B[enedict] Davenport and Morris Steggerda, *Race Crossing in Jamaica* (1929; Westport, CT: Negro University Press, 1970); Edward Byron Reuter, *Race Mixture: Studies in Intermarriage and Miscegenation* (New York: McGraw-Hill, 1931); and Emory S. Bogardus, "What Race Are Filipinos?" *Sociology and Social Research* 16 (1931–32): 274–79.

38. 1924 Va. Acts chap. 371; 1927 Ga. Laws no. 317; 1927 Ala. Acts no. 626. The 1924 Virginia act replaced 1910 Va. Acts chap. 357, which classified as "colored" persons with one-sixteenth or more "negro blood." The retention of an allowance for American Indian "blood" in persons classed as white was forced on the bill's sponsors by Virginia aristocrats who traced their ancestry to Pocahontas and John Rolfe. See Paul A. Lombardo, "Miscegenation, Eugenics, and Racism: Historical Footnotes to *Loving v. Virginia, U.C. Davis Law Review* 21 (Winter 1988): 431–52; and Richard B. Sherman, "'The Last Stand': The Fight for Racial Integrity in Virginia in the 1920s," *Journal of Southern History* 54 (Feb. 1988): 69–92.

39. "Appellant's Opening Brief," *Gunn v. Giraudo,* 12–13. This brief appears to have been prepared for the California Supreme Court but used in the California Court of Appeals, Fourth District. On February 14, 1942, the California Supreme Court refused to review the Court of Appeals decision. See *Estate of Monks,* 48 C.A. 2d 603, 621 (1941).

40. *Estate of Monks,* 48 C.A. 2d 603, 612–15 (1941); *Monks v. Lee,* 317 U.S. 590 *(appeal dismissed,* 1942), 711 *(reh'g denied,* 1942); *Lee v. Monks,* 62 N.E. 2d 657 (1945); *Lee v. Monks,* 326 U.S. 696 *(cert. denied,* 1946).

41. On the case, see *San Diego Union,* July 21, 1939–Jan. 6, 1940. On the testimony of expert witnesses on race, see ibid., Sept. 21, 1939, p. 4A; ibid., Sept. 29, 1939, p. 10A; and ibid., Oct. 5, 1939, p. 8A.

42. *Perez v. Lippold,* L.A. 20305, Supreme Court Case Files (California State Archives). The case was also known as *Perez v. Moroney* and *Perez v. Sharp* (the names reflect changes of personnel in the Los Angeles County clerk's office). I have used the title given in the *Pacific Law Reporter,* the most easily available version of the final decision: *Perez v. Lippold,* 198 P. 2d 17 (1948).

43. "Petition for Writ of Mandamus, Memorandum of Points and Authorities and Proof of Service," Aug. 8, 1947, *Perez v. Lippold;* "Points and Authorities in Opposition to Issuance of Alternative Writ of Mandate," Aug. 13, 1947, ibid.; "Return by Way of Demurrer," Oct. 6, 1947, ibid.; "Return by Way of Answer," Oct. 6, 1947, ibid.; "Respondent's Brief in Opposition to Writ of Mandate," Oct. 6, 1947, ibid.

44. "[Oral Argument] On Behalf of Respondent," Oct. 6, 1947, 3–4, ibid.

45. Stanley Mosk, "A Retrospective," *California Law Review* 71 (July 1983): 1045; Peter Anderson, "A Remembrance," ibid., 1066–71.

46. "Petitioners' Reply Brief," Nov. 8, 1947, 4, 44, 23–24, *Perez v. Lippold.*

47. *Perez v. Lippold,* 198 P. 2d at 17–35, esp. 29, 34.

48. Ibid., 35–47.

49. For the characterization of Franz Boas by Robert Gayres, editor of the Scottish journal *Mankind Quarterly,* see Newby, *Challenge to the Court,* 323. On *Mankind Quarterly* and on mid-twentieth-century white supremacist scientists, see Tucker, *Science and Politics of Racial Research.*

50. Myrdal, *American Dilemma,* 116–17.

51. *Loving v. Commonwealth,* 147 S.E. 2d 78, 79 (1966). For the *Loving* briefs and oral arguments, see Philip B. Kurland and Gerhard Casper, eds., *Landmark*

Briefs and Arguments of the Supreme Court of the United States: Constitutional Law,
vol. 64 (Arlington, VA: University Publications of America, 1975), 687–1007. Edited cassette tapes of the oral argument are included with Peter Irons and Stephanie
Guitton, ed., *May It Please the Court: The Most Significant Oral Arguments Made
before the Supreme Court since 1955* (New York: W. W. Norton, 1993). For scholarly assessments, see Wallenstein, "Race, Marriage, and the Law of Freedom"; Walter Wadlington, "The Loving Case: Virginia's Antimiscegenation Statute in Historical
Perspective," in *Race Relations and the Law in American History: Major Historical
Interpretations,* ed. Kermit L. Hall (New York: Garland Publishing, 1987), 600–634;
and Robert J. Sickels, *Race, Marriage, and the Law* (Albuquerque: University of New
Mexico Press, 1972).

52. *Loving v. Virginia* 388 U.S.1, 3 (1967); Wallenstein, "Race, Marriage, and
the Law of Freedom," 423–25, esp. 424; *New York Times,* June 12, 1992, p. B7. By
the mid-1960s some legal scholars had questioned the constitutionality of miscegenation laws, including C. D. Shokes, "The Serbonian Bog of Miscegenation,"
Rocky Mountain Law Review 21 (1948–1949): 425–33; Wayne A. Melton, "Constitutionality of State Anti-Miscegenation Statutes," *Southwestern Law Journal* 5
(1951): 451–61; Andrew D. Weinberger, "A Reappraisal of the Constitutionality of
Miscegenation Statutes," *Cornell Law Quarterly* 42 (Winter 1957): 208–22; Jerold
D. Cummins and John L. Kane Jr., "Miscegenation, the Constitution, and Science,"
Dicta 38 (Jan.–Feb. 1961), 24–54; William D. Zabel, "Interracial Marriage and the
Law," *Atlantic Monthly* 216 (Oct. 1965): 75–79; and Cyrus E. Phillips IV, "Miscegenation; The Courts and the Constitution," *William and Mary Law Review* 8 (Fall
1966): 133–42.

53. Kurland and Casper, eds., *Landmark Briefs,* 741–88; 847–950, 960–72, esp.
898–99, 901.

54. Ibid., 789–845, 976–1003.

55. Ibid., 834, 1007.

56. *Loving v. Virginia,* 388 U.S. at 12.

57. Ibid., 11.

58. The notion that American courts should be "color-blind" is usually traced to
Supreme Court Justice John Harlan. Dissenting from the Court's endorsement of the
principle of "separate but equal" in *Plessy v. Ferguson,* Harlan insisted that "[o]ur
Constitution is color-blind, and neither knows nor tolerates classes among citizens."
Plessy v. Ferguson, 163 U.S. 537, 559 (1896). But only after *Brown v. Board of Education,* widely interpreted as a belated endorsement of Harlan's position, did courts
begin to adopt color blindness as a goal. *Brown v. Board of Education,* 347 U.S. 483
(1954). On the history of the color blindness ideal, see Andrew Kull, *The Color-Blind
Constitution* (Cambridge, MA: Harvard University Press, 1992). On developments in
social science, see Omi and Winant, *Racial Formation in the United States,* 14–23.

59. *Brown v. Board of Education,* 347 U.S. 483 (1954). The Court declared distinctions based "solely on ancestry" "odious" even while upholding curfews imposed
on Japanese Americans during World War II; see *Hirabayashi v. United States,* 320
U.S. 81 (1943). It declared race a "suspect" legal category while upholding the intern-
ment of Japanese Americans; see *Korematsu v. United States,* 323 U.S. 214 (1944). By
1983, no American state had a formal race-definition statute still on its books. See
Chris Ballentine, "'Who Is a Negro?' Revisited: Determining Individual Racial Status
for Purposes of Affirmative Action," *University of Florida Law Review* 35 (fall 1983):
692. The repeal of state race-definition statutes often accompanied repeal of miscegenation laws. See, for example, 1953 Mont. Laws chap. 4; 1959 Or. Laws chap. 531;
1965 Ind. Acts chap. 15; 1969 Fla. Laws 69–195; and 1979 Ga. Laws no. 543.

60. The fifth of these categories, "Hispanic," is sometimes described as "ethnic," rather than "racial." For very different views of the current debates, see Lawrence Wright, "One Drop of Blood," *New Yorker,* July 25, 1994, 46–55; and Michael Lind, *The Next American Nation: The New Nationalism and the Fourth American Revolution* (New York: Free Press, 1995), 97–137.

61. *People v. O. J. Simpson,* Case no. BA 097211, California Superior Court, L.A. County (1994).

62. See, for example, Kimberle Williams Crenshaw, "Race, Reform, and Retrenchment: Transformation and Legitimation in Antidiscrimination Law," *Harvard Law Review* 101 (May 1988): 1331–87; Dana Y. Takagi, *The Retreat from Race: Asian-American Admissions and Racial Politics* (New Brunswick, NJ: Rutgers University Press, 1992), 181–94; and Girardeau A. Spann, *Race against the Court: The Supreme Court and Minorities in Contemporary America* (New York: New York University Press, 1993): 119–49. See note 5, above. On recent work in the humanities, see Tessie Liu, "Race," in *A Companion to American Thought,* ed. Richard Wightman Fox and James T. Kloppenberg (Cambridge, MA: Harvard University Press, 1995), 564–67. On legal studies, see Richard Delgado and Jean Stefancic, "Critical Race Theory: An Annotated Bibliography," *Virginia Law Review* 79 (March 1993): 461–516.

10

"The Only Thing I Wanted Was Freedom": Wayward Girls in New York, 1900–1930

Ruth M. Alexander

In the summer of 1916 sixteen-year-old Ella Waldstein started "going around with a bad crowd of girls," often staying away from her Brooklyn home until one or two o'clock in the morning. Ella, the daughter of Russian Orthodox Jews, had never before given her parents any trouble; in fact, since the age of fourteen she had worked without complaint as a factory operative, helping to support a family of six. But apparently the girl had changed, and, fearing for her safety and sexual virtue, Ella's mother and father "talked to her and begged and pleaded with her to come home earlier." Ella listened to their pleas in stony silence: "When they asked her where she had been she would say she had been with a girlfriend or simply would not answer. No matter how they scolded her she never talked back."

Throughout the following year, tension within the Waldstein home mounted, peaking in the summer of 1917, when Ella's relatives learned that she was spending her evenings on Coney Island, usually in the company of a handsome married Irishman who "was not of our kind . . . and not very respectable." The man gave Ella expensive gifts and the young woman's parents suspected that she was prostituting herself for him. Mrs. Waldstein approached Ella and "threatened to send [her] away if she would not stay at home in the evenings." Ella would not listen and finally her desperate parents took her to court; she was convicted of "wilful disobedience" and committed to the New York State Reformatory for Women at Bedford Hills. Her three-year sentence was the standard term meted out to all female reformatory inmates.[1]

Ella was committed to Bedford Hills at a time of rapid and disconcerting change in the cultural and experiential construction of female adolescence, particularly within the working class. With the vast expansion of the nation's industrial economy in the late nineteenth and early twentieth centuries, millions of immigrant and native-born young women and girls were drawn into the urban workforce as unskilled factory workers, retail clerks, and waitresses. Most adolescent girls took up wage labor to help their struggling families, but employment also exposed them to a new world of experience and values. At work, previously sheltered teenage girls met young people who shared modern ideas about fashion, recreation, and sex. At night, putting these ideas into practice, working girls flocked to commercial dance halls, nickelodeon theaters, amusement parks, and other "cheap amusements," engaging in social rituals that celebrated feminine allure and heterosexual romance, the autonomy of youth, and the purchase of fun. Substituting an "up-to-date" lifestyle for Victorian and old-world standards of girlhood decorum, the daughters of the working class produced a distinctly modern rendering of female adolescence, one that was enthusiastically taken up by middle-class young women during and after World War I.[2]

Surely we can appreciate the Waldsteins' astonishment and alarm as they witnessed the social transformation of their formerly dutiful daughter. Yet most early-twentieth-century working-class parents did not take their daughters to court and ask for a reformatory commitment.[3] Why, in this instance, were communication and compromise so elusive, and why was New York State so willing to uphold the Waldsteins' right to filial obedience? Just as important, what became of Ella during her incarceration and after her release from Bedford Hills? Did Bedford succeed in "reforming" her and, if so, in a manner agreeable to her family? Or did Ella reject the reformative efforts of family and state, convinced even after her incarceration that self-assertion was a valid and productive path?

Drawing on the inmate case files of two New York State reformatories, I have analyzed the experience of twenty-two young women whose attempts to participate in the remaking of female adolescence met with bitter family opposition and severe legal sanction.[4] All of the "wayward girls" were the daughters of immigrant or working-class parents, committed at the request of family members either to the New York State Reformatory for Women at Bedford Hills or to the Western House of Refuge for Women in Albion, New York.[5] With only three exceptions, the girls served standard three-year sentences, usually spending one or two years of that time on parole.[6]

The experience of New York's wayward girls simultaneously affirms and departs from recent work on early-twentieth-century working women. The splendid scholarship of Kathy Peiss and Joanne Meyerowitz generally emphasizes the agency and inventiveness of America's early-twentieth-century working women, acclaiming their break with social and sexual convention. According to these historians, working-class young women "pioneered new manners and mores," displacing traditional models of female adolescence and young womanhood as they participated in the construction of modern heterosocial culture. Certainly, as both Peiss and Meyerowitz recognize, low wages, a persistent sexual double standard, and a new ethic of material consumption prevented young women from translating sexualized values and behavior into real social autonomy. Nonetheless, through their lively use of leisure and bold explorations of individuality and heterosexuality, America's working women and girls "helped forge the modern sexual expression that replaced Victorian reticence."[7]

Although not denying the agency of young working women or the newness of their lifestyle, I shall shift the focus away from the cultural values they helped to invent and look instead at their sometimes pained and thwarted efforts to construct a new sense of self. This essay is an investigation of the subjective experiences and emerging social identities of young women who, in embracing the "modern," collided with tradition and with the limits of cultural and familial change. In contending with the coercive tactics of reformatories, wayward girls were atypical adolescent females. Their unique ordeal was only a variation on a common theme, however. Just as other working- and middle-class young women in early-twentieth-century America, wayward girls struggled to construct social identities from competing models and ideals of female adolescence. We shall examine how they fared in the contest between modernity and tradition.

The wayward girls at Bedford Hills and Albion came from working-class families that were unusually precarious, economically and socially. Insecurity and hardship tended to make the homes of the wayward girls depressing and unpleasant; misfortune also precluded parents from reacting to cultural change with favor or goodwill. Indeed, the wayward girls' mothers and fathers experienced female adolescent rebellion as a threat to their own survival, and they resorted to legal action to protect their families from further peril.

Although only a few of the wayward girls lived in truly destitute circumstances, nearly all came from families that struggled to remain economically stable. Twenty of the wayward girls were the daughters of men of very modest economic standing; their fathers were factory workers, carpenters, machinists, drivers, house painters, and janitors.[8] Often the incomes of the girls' fathers were inadequate to meet family expenses, and five of the wayward girls had mothers who worked for wages. In addition, all but three of the girls had themselves worked to add to their families' meager earnings, usually leaving school by the age of fourteen to do so.[9]

Economic insecurity was not all that troubled these families. Eighteen of the twenty-two wayward girls came from homes impaired by daunting tragedy or dysfunction: the death of one or both parents, desertion, separation, divorce, alcoholism, disabling illness, pronounced marital discord, wife and child battering, or incest. Moreover, only seven of the young women had American parents; the rest were the daughters of immigrants who daily confronted the trials of cultural dislocation and assimilation. Finally, four of the wayward girls were black and thus came from families forced to contend with racism as well as with economic insecurity and domestic calamity.[10]

Struggle as they must to withstand economic and social adversity, the parents, guardians, and older siblings of New York's wayward girls were unprepared to tolerate the rebellion and sexual experimentation of their daughters or young sisters. These adults depended on their girls to support and uphold the good name of their families; traditional forms of filial obedience and girlhood virtue provided a semblance of security, assuring them of their ability to endure in a difficult world. In this context, a young woman's assertion of self was far more than the ingenuous proclamation of a modern sensibility; it represented an unbearable threat to the survival of an already precarious family unit.

Self-assertion was equally meaningful to the wayward girls, yet to them it represented not danger but an essential route to happiness. The dispiriting atmosphere in the wayward girls' homes compared unfavorably with the buoyant mood and lively companions to be found in city streets, dance halls, and amusement parks. And feeling helpless to change their families, the young women sought friends and recreation that offered respite, hope, and entertainment. They longed for a life different from the one their families could offer, and many saw in New York's urban youth and "cheap amusements" the means to attain it.

Invariably, the wayward girls' explorations of autonomy led to bitter familial conflict; when the strain of generational controversy became unbearable, parents and guardians turned to the courts for assistance and relief. Conflict usually began well before the girls evinced an interest in heterosexual romance, first arising instead over their attraction to the dress, manners, and companionship of urban youth. Few mothers or fathers actually went to court because of their daughters' efforts to find friends or recreation outside of the family setting; rather, parents waited until they saw evidence of sexual misconduct. However, there were exceptions. For example, Louisa Parsons, the daughter of a Utica, New York, insurance agent, wanted to choose and enjoy her friends without paternal interference and occasionally resorted to subterfuge to gain what she desired. Mr. Parsons, a strict disciplinarian with a drinking problem, responded with threats and verbal abuse. When he became convinced that Louisa could be taught to respect his authority in no other way, Mr. Parsons asked for her commitment to Albion.[11]

In other cases, conflict reached intolerable levels when wayward girls tried to avoid (or expose) physical abuse or sexual assault within the family. As with the girls' quests for social independence, attempts to escape severe or violent chastisement produced intense controversy because they signaled adolescent females' unwillingness to shape themselves to the needs and values of an unstable family unit. Rae Rabinowitz was the target of frequent beatings by an older brother who had fashioned himself the family patriarch after Mr. Rabinowitz deserted the household. When Rae tried to make friends on her own and complained that her siblings and mother were "'sticks' [who] want to sit in the house [all evening while] the neighbors sit on their front stoops and visit," her brother responded with insults and physical assaults. Resolving to escape her brother's brutal treatment, Rae ran away from home; but at her family's request, she was pursued, arrested, and committed to Bedford Hills.[12]

Still, for the great majority of the wayward girls, adolescent sexual expression paved the most direct route to court. Sexual virtue was a critical symbol of feminine selflessness and, for the parents of wayward girls, its absence signified disorder and dangerous individualism. Mothers and fathers worried that sexually active daughters had ruined their chances of finding good husbands and becoming respectable wives and mothers. Just as important, parents worried that girls with sexual experience might damage the reputation of their fragile families. Familial distress and humiliation were particularly acute when the sexual relations of adolescent girls resulted in pregnancy or violated racial, religious, or ethnic boundaries.[13]

Thus when twenty-year-old Evelyn Blackwell became pregnant in 1926, "after running out nights with different men," her father, a well-respected black mechanic, "absolutely refused to have the girl at home." Relations between Evelyn and her parents had been severely strained by two earlier pregnancies, and the girl had been pushed into a hasty and disastrous marriage while awaiting the birth of her second child. Now, Evelyn's father, a recent widower, could not stand the dishonor of yet a third illegitimate child. If Evelyn's mother had been alive, the matter might have been handled differently, but Evelyn's father took his daughter to court and "asked to have the girl sent away."[14]

In a similar case, Lena Meyerhoff stunned her Russian immigrant parents by keeping company with a "colored man," sometimes staying out late at night, some nights "not [coming] home at all," and finally leaving her parents' home to live with her lover. Mr. and Mrs. Meyerhoff initially reacted to their daughter's conduct with incomprehension and ineffectual protests, but when Lena gave birth, apparently to a mulatto infant, her mother decided that she must act to protect her daughter and her family from utter ruin. Mrs. Meyerhoff turned to the Jewish Board of Guardians, a social agency that worked with unmarried mothers and, following the board's advice, took Lena to court. There she asked for a reformatory sentence on the grounds that the girl "habitually associates with dissolute persons . . . left her home in Woodbridge [N.Y.] . . . and came to New York City where she lived with J. Smith to whom she is not married and bore an illegitimate child to him."[15]

Undoubtedly the wayward girls were a spirited lot, eager to be free of restraint and fascinated with the youth culture and amusements beyond their doors. Lena stood up to her parents, playing the confusion and hesitation of her mother against that of her father to win the sexual and social autonomy she desired. Rae Rabinowitz ran away from home, heading straight for Coney Island, after deciding that she had had enough of her brother's abuse. In another case, Sophie Polentz left home to take an apartment with a girlfriend after growing impatient with her father's demand that the "first time she met a fellow to bring him up to the house."[16]

The wayward girls' mettle pales next to their vulnerability, however. Some of these young women had been physically abused by members of their family; others had experienced distress over their parents' distrust and withdrawal of affection. Moreover, despite their bold manner, most of the wayward girls were unsophisticated and susceptible to sexual exploitation and abuse. When Rae Rabinowitz ran away to Coney Island, she was raped by two soldiers who had generously paid for a night's entertainment and lodging. Rae allowed the men to pay for a hotel room for her, not understanding that they expected sexual favors in return. As she later told Bedford's psychiatrist, Dr. Cornelia Shorer, "I will never forget that day. . . . You never want to do such a thing only I did not want to stay on the street all night. . . . [The sailor said] 'If you don't let us do it you won't have no place to sleep tonight.' . . . That's when I gave myself away. . . . I didn't think they would do such a thing. You know some fellows have pity." Ella Waldstein also had to cope with sexual exploitation and manipulation, although of a less overt sort. When the young woman gave up trying to communicate with her parents, she was left on her own to decipher her Irish boyfriend's intentions. Most important, she did not know if he was telling the truth when he said that he would someday divorce his wife to marry her.[17]

In addition, sexually active (or exploited) wayward girls risked contracting venereal disease or becoming pregnant. A young woman with knowledgeable friends might find a doctor without too much difficulty who was willing to treat her for VD, although payment of the doctor was another problem. Pregnancy could not be concealed from family members as easily as illness; wayward girls who became pregnant were at once dependent on their families for care and helpless to resist their families' reproof.

Finally, the wayward girls' status as legal dependents made them vulnerable to state coercion. In requesting reformatory commitments, the working-class parents and guardians of wayward girls took advantage of a novel provision of New York's criminal law, one that permitted a partnership between the criminal-justice system and the parents of disobedient or "immoral" adolescent girls. That partnership began in 1886 when New York City amended a statute concerning the reform of prostitutes so that parents or the police might request a reformatory commitment for any girl over the age of twelve "[who] is found in a reputed house of prostitution or assignation; or is willfully disobedient to parent or guardian and is in danger of becoming morally depraved."[18]

The 1886 law was amended several times, and under the so-called incorrigible girl statutes, many working-class young women were sent to Bedford Hills. The laws did not apply to adolescent females beyond the boundaries of New York City, but by the late nineteenth and early twentieth centuries, upstate parents were making creative use of the state's vagrancy and disorderly conduct statutes to secure the commitment of rebellious daughters to the Western House of Refuge for Women in Albion. Thus Millicent Potter was committed to Albion in 1900 after her father went to court complaining that "for six months past, [she] has been frequenting disorderly houses against the wishes of her parents and becoming an inmate of such houses."[19]

In 1923 New York passed the Wayward Minor Act, giving formal recognition to the legal rights of upstate parents. Under the Wayward Minor Law, the main provisions of the old "incorrigible girl" statutes were extended statewide to aid in the control of adolescent females.[20] By this time mental health professionals were beginning to protest the punitive treatment of young delinquents, arguing that juvenile or adolescent misconduct was usually the outcome of improper parenting and should be treated in a clinical setting. Mental health professionals also had begun to abandon Victorian thinking about girlhood, asserting that adolescent girls must have social autonomy and sexual freedom if they were to achieve psychosexual maturity.[21] However, the clinicians' challenges to parental authority and Victorian ideology had little effect on the state's partnership with desperate working-class mothers and fathers. Both the criminal court system and the working-class parents continued to hold disadvantaged young women and girls to Victorian standards of sexual morality, not trusting their ability to explore heterosexuality without drifting into immorality and prostitution. Targeting young women in late adolescence, the Wayward Minor Law affirmed that disobedient or immoral females between the ages of sixteen and twenty-one could be convicted solely on the testimony of their parents or guardians. It gave parents the option of having their daughters remain at home under the supervision of a probation officer but allowed them to request institutional commitment for any girl who "is not a fit subject for probation."[22]

The wayward girls who were sent to Bedford Hills and Albion were viewed by their parents and the courts as self-conscious rebels in need of reform. These adults did not realize that few of the girls demonstrated genuine loyalty either to immoral behavior or to the values of urban youth subcultures. True, the wayward girls had been defiant at home and often sexually active on the streets, but frequently their defiance was closely bound up with "ill treatment" or some other family crisis. Similarly, the pleasures of sex had often been clouded by sexual ignorance, physical danger, and economic need. The wayward girls had confronted hazards and obstacles to their safety, autonomy, and happiness whether they were with their families or with their peers. When they entered the gates of the reformatories, most of these young women were still searching for a satisfying lifestyle or social identity and had yet to find it.

Bedford Hills and Albion did little to ease the difficulty of their search, although over time the reformatories profoundly affected the wayward girls' sense of self. Presenting the matter of female adolescent identity in stark moral terms, Albion and Bedford Hills demanded that the wayward girls adopt a Victorian model of girlhood virtue, abandoning social and sexual expression for deference and sexual control. To hasten the wayward girls' compliance, the reformatories presented them with both positive and negative inducements to reform. Under the watchful eye of morally upright matrons and female teachers, the girls were offered rich opportunities for "self-improvement." Housed separately from the institutions' older and more hardened inmates (usually prostitutes), they were given comfortable rooms in homelike cottages. In addition, the wayward girls were afforded academic and vocational training, recreational activities in a campus setting, and religious instruction. These "opportunities" had been incorporated into the reformatories' programs at the turn of the century by middle-class female reformers who wanted the state to "rescue" impoverished and ignorant young women from lives of immorality and crime.[23]

Thus afforded a wide range of opportunities and privileges, Bedford and Albion expected "their girls" to be ready for lives of honest employment, sexual virtue, and deference to the family claim by the time they were paroled. However, if kindness, education, and moral suasion proved to be working too slowly, coercion could be relied on as an additional prod. Strict surveillance, the censoring of mail, and a formidable array of punishments, including the postponement of parole, made resistance to reform difficult and unpleasant.

There is little evidence to suggest that while they remained inmates the wayward girls found much appeal in the social identity their female keepers held before them. Instead, acutely sensitive to their lack of freedom and privacy, the wayward girls spent much of their time engaged in struggle with reformatory officers, matrons, and teachers. True, nearly half of the young women in my sample were generally well behaved, knowing that to be otherwise was to risk punishment and postponement of parole. Still, even among this "good" group, it is possible to detect signs of discontent and resentment. Althea Davies, an eighteen-year-old West Indian who was committed to Bedford after becoming pregnant, was generally reliable but often "sulky or noisy." Deborah Herman, another young black woman committed because of an illegitimate pregnancy, was an "excellent" worker, and yet she threw occasional temper tantrums.[24]

Moreover, twelve of the wayward girls were openly defiant. Their acts of misconduct included "lewd" talk, smoking, insolence, attempted escape, and innumerable other offenses. Often the troublesome girls acted as individuals, but they also misbehaved together. Acting in pairs or groups, wayward girls revealed something more than a rejection of authority or a willingness to risk punishment; they announced their identification with a distinctive inmate subculture, one that legitimated the right of young women to define their own values and to oppose as irrelevant the genteel model of young womanhood upheld by their keepers.

The lesbian relationships between inmates are a particularly significant example of this inmate subculture. Although no record exists of lesbian attachments at Albion, they were a well-recognized problem at Bedford; among the wayward girls in my sample were two young women who had engaged in homoerotic relationships.[25] Rae Rabinowitz, the seventeen year-old who was sent to Bedford as an "incorrigible girl" after being beaten by her brother and raped by two sailors, was "more or less trouble about colored girls all the time." Similarly, Melanie Burkis, a wayward minor who began her sentence at Bedford in 1924, was much criticized for her "distasteful and demoralizing . . . obsession" with a "colored inmate."[26]

These homoerotic relationships were a form of behavior through which young inmates tried to give evidence of their own power; that is, they used sexual desire and the capacity to shock as ways to deny their defenselessness against the demands of the reformatory staff. Melanie Burkis deliberately made her "obsession" for Valerie Revere obvious, causing one Bedford teacher to remark, "If thwarted in any undesirable action toward Valerie Revere she showed plainly that her affection for her teacher or desire to improve was assumed in order to continue her obsession for the colored pupil."[27]

In addition, the homosexual or homoerotic relationships between inmates at Bedford Hills reveal young women's interest in bending and testing the normative meanings of gender and race that dominated conventional society and urban youth subcultures. The wayward girls in these relationships did not altogether reject the gender roles that were part of contemporary youth cultures, but they insisted on manipulating the meanings of both masculinity and femininity. Similarly, by crossing racial boundaries and playing with race as though it were entirely a social construct, young women defied the deep-seated segregationist sentiments of both their keepers and of the society beyond the institution's gates.

Thus when Jewel Foster, one of Rae's black girlfriends, wrote Rae a love letter, she adopted the persona of a white woman and became "Mama Blondie." Rae was addressed as "my own loving Daddy," and "Mama Blondie" devoted much of her letter to showing that she was worthy of her "Daddy's" love and intended "to be a good true mama to you now and out in the big world." As "Mama Blondie" Jewel emphasized the seductive and aggressive masculinity of her lover and reveled in fantasies of her "beautiful daddy . . . teasing and trying to fuck me and do everything that goes with." Yet she also slipped into speaking of Rae (five feet, two inches tall, 101 pounds) as a "pretty doll" with "cute little arms."[28]

Despite their obvious contempt for the reformatories, even some of the most defiant wayward girls were eventually persuaded to modify their conduct. Although the reformatories' preferred model of young womanhood may have had little appeal, severe and frequent punishment compelled defiant inmates to question the merit of their conduct and to acknowledge the dangers of self-assertion and sexual expression. For example, Ella Waldstein was "childish" and difficult, but only during her first year at Bedford; after that her behavior showed "marked improvement." Numerous minor punishments and confinement for eight days in the reformatory's dilapidated "prison building" were unpleasant enough to cure Ella of her disobedient outbursts. Rae Rabinowitz also showed a definite improvement in behavior. Rae was at various times punished for passing love letters, "being impertinent," and calling others "vile names." She lost recreational privileges, had her parole date postponed, and was at least once placed for two weeks in Bedford's "disciplinary building," a cell block with triple doors on every cell that was used to house the reformatory's most disturbed or troublesome inmates. The weight of these punishments may have eventually induced Rae to heed the reformatory's rules, for when she came up for parole consideration she was judged a good and obedient inmate. She had even "given up colored girls."[29]

Other quite defiant wayward girls made some effort to improve, but not fully understanding or accepting what their keepers were asking of them, they continued to display an unacceptable lack of deference. Melanie Burkis, for example, wrote frequent notes to Bedford's superintendent, trying to persuade him that she was not as bad as others thought her to be:

> I am writing in reference to a little trouble which occurred a few days ago in the cottage. Most likely you have already heard about me doing some thing. Tuesday when Miss Furniss was on duty I Thought I'd be doing myself some Good by behaving myself but it seems as though things have gone against me. While in my room reading Miss Furniss heard someone whistle to another girl on campus and immediately thought I was guilty . . . then a note was thrown out of my window (but not by me) and Miss Furniss figured I was guilty again which I was not. then when Miss Mace spoke to me I tried to defend myself. . . . Of course she thought I was trying to be impudent by defending myself. Now Dr. Baker, I wish you would kindly look into this matter as it means quite alot to me for I am trying my level best to do what is right and no wrong. If you think it best to speak to Miss Furniss about this kindly do so at your earliest convenience as I think it high time for me to be getting affair chance on going out soon.[30]

Of course, there were a few wayward girls who willingly risked punishment throughout their stay at the reformatories, refusing to bow to their keepers and exhibiting delight when they fooled the system. Sophie Polentz apparently boasted within earshot of Bedford's parole officer to the effect that "no girl had been more disorderly than she and that she had been given her parole in eight months. Even though she ran away, was impudent and saucy to the matrons and never hesitated to tell an officer just what she thought of her in impolite language."[31]

We can assume in Sophie's case that the reformatory had given her no reason to be good; the same thing is probably true of her family. Bedford and Albion often turned to parents and guardians for help in securing the inmates' reform, urging them, for example, to write encouraging letters to their daughters.[32] However, not wanting family members to take a free hand in the reform process, Bedford and Albion strictly controlled all contact between the wayward girls and their families, opening and censoring all correspondence, chastising parents who wrote highly critical letters to their girls, and permitting family visitors at infrequent intervals.[33]

These measures ensured the reformatories of the control they desired but ironically also subverted their reformist goals. Prevented from communicating openly, the wayward girls and their relatives could not easily resolve their conflicts or modify their expectations of one another. If inmates and their families managed to reconstruct the ties that bound them, they got little aid from Albion or Bedford Hills.[34]

Moreover, though parents might be prevented from conveying openly hostile or intolerant attitudes to their daughters, by reading between the lines or contemplating a dearth of mail, the wayward girls probably sensed how their parents felt. Sophie, for example, received frequent missives from her father and probably realized that he felt victimized by his troublesome daughter. Mr. Polentz was disabled and had depended on his daughter's income until she became so disobedient that he was forced to send her to Bedford. In one letter, written from the sanatorium where he had been sent by a Jewish charity, Sophie's father wrote, "the Doctor of the Society has forbidden me to think too much and to worry, but I cannot help it. So I want you to pray to God that I will be home again soon, but there is a strong doubt in my mind whether I will be able ever to feed my wife and children again. . . . remain with best greetings as ever, your suffering father." In another letter, Mr. Polentz wrote of his sorrow that Bedford's parole board had refused to grant Sophie her parole, noting that Bedford's superintendent understood how badly Sophie's misconduct hurt her father, even if she did not. "I can write you that Dr. Baker is one of the finest men that I ever met in my life, a true Gentleman. He feels sorry for you, and he also feels more bad for me than my own children. . . . Your Parole come up before the Parole of Manager [again] next month, and I hope that next month you surely will come home." Mr. Polentz wanted his daughter to recognize that she was partially responsible for his suffering, but instead of prompting her reform his attitude may well have annoyed Sophie and redoubled her rebellious intent.[35]

Exceptions like Sophie notwithstanding, by the time of their release on parole most of the wayward girls well understood the hazards of individualism and self-assertion. However, while teaching the wayward girls to cultivate caution, the reformatories had not offered them a convincing role model or given them the tools with which to repair troubled relations with their families. Young women who begged to be forgiven by their families or who swore that they had learned their lesson took the chance of being reunited with parents who themselves had not made any attempt to reform and were still ill prepared to understand or to cope with their daugters.[36] Thus even as they faced the real world many of the wayward girls must have been uncertain of who they were and wary of their ability to steer a beneficial course between the rules of parole, the demands of their families or employers, and the lure of urban youth and city streets.

As parolees, most wayward girls were sent home to their families with the understanding that they would take jobs or do housework as their parents or guardians required. Those who were not sent home were usually placed in domestic positions with reputable middle-class families, although a few wayward girls were paroled to kitchen or laundry positions in hospitals with dormitory facilities.[37] Regardless of where they lived and worked, the parolees were expected to be obedient and dependable young women. They were not permitted to make friends, take any recreation, or go out at night without the explicit approval of their parents or employers. In addition, in monthly letters to the superintendent of Bedford or Albion, parolees were supposed to describe their work, account for their free time, and mention any efforts they might have made to save money or to plan for the future.

Neither reformatory could be entirely certain that the wayward girls were fulfilling their directives. Throughout the period from 1900 to 1930, Bedford and Albion struggled along with fewer parole officers than they needed; and although Bedford was assisted by social workers from Catholic Charities, the Jewish Board of Guardians, and the (Episcopal) Church Mission of Help, the wayward girls were visited by parole officers or social workers on an irregular and infrequent basis.[38] Still, most of the girls who violated parole found it impossible to escape oversight or to avoid punishment altogether. Complaints from parents or employers often came later than the reformatory superintendents would have liked, but nonetheless they provided a critical link between parolees and the reformatories. The New York City Police Department also took a hand in locating Bedford parole violators.

More important, the records of wayward girls on parole demonstrate that most of these young women were persuaded to make truly conservative choices about their lives and identities. In the confinement of the reformatories, the wayward girls' limited powers of resistance had been outweighed by the authority of their keepers, and they had learned to value obedience as an expedient. In the world beyond the gates, the authority of the reformatories was relatively diffuse; wayward girls were exposed simultaneously to the values and expectations of reformatory, family, and urban youth. Peer friendships, heterosexual expression, and urban amusements were once again within reach. As they struggled to situate themselves amid these competing social claims, however, the wayward girls discovered that, pleasure notwithstanding, urban youth subcultures lacked social authority and were unable to shield them from the power of family and reformatory. More consequential still, they learned that conformity to convention offered its own kind of freedom, lessening their vulnerability to familial rejection, social ostracism, and state surveillance. There were, of course, exceptions among the parolees. But as the final phase of a reformatory sentence, parole generally had a conservative and inhibiting impact on working-class wayward girls.

The lessons of parole were surely decisive; surprisingly, for some girls they were relatively uncomplicated. Fully half of the wayward girls realized rather quickly that the protection and approval offered by reformatory or family were worth more than the company of their peers. Three of the young women in this group found socially conservative choices particularly easy to make. Each of the three girls had been badly abused or mistreated by their own kin (sometimes by male lovers as well), and instead of being sent home to their families they were paroled to domestic positions. Ilene Sterling's background, for example, included verbal abuse by an alcoholic stepfather, sexual exploitation by an older boyfriend, and an illegitimate pregnancy. Susanna Nedersen, another Bedford girl, had been committed to the reformatory after being sexually assaulted by her father and raped by a neighbor. The illegitimate infant born as a consequence of the rape was taken from Susanna by her mother and probably killed, for Susanna never saw it again. Although Susanna's parents escaped legal action, their daughter was convicted of perjury (and sent to Bedford) after bringing charges against her father for assault and then, under considerable pressure from her family, dropping them.[39]

Good behavior on parole and deference to a genteel model of female adolescence seemed an obvious choice for these young women, determined largely by the severity of their former mistreatment and unhappiness. Wanting protection and security more than anything else, they looked to reformatory superintendents, parole officers, or domestic employers as surrogate mothers and did all in their power to please them. Thus, after being paroled as a domestic to the home of a middle-class couple in Tuckahoe, New York, Susanna wrote to Bedford's parole officer, "I will never forget what you have done for me and want to now thank you. I could not find anyone so good to me as Mr. and Mrs. Jackson. . . . Mrs. Jackson is my . . . guiding angle [sic] for she tells me all the things that I want to know & she is teaching me how to read the newspaper & to talk better than I did." Similarly, Ilene wrote to Bedford's superintendent, Alice Cobb, to tell her how pleased she was with her new domestic position and with the guidance the reformatory had provided. "I am so happy where I am. . . . Please Miss Cobb give my regards to all the Cowdin [cottage] girls and tell them it pays to be good, if they only knew how happy I am they would realize what I am saying is true."[40]

For the other wayward girls who quickly accepted conservative social values, familial reconciliation was the key to reform. Welcomed

and forgiven by their parents, eight young women reasoned that conformity to working-class family and gender-role expectations was preferable to the excitement, independence, and danger they had previously
found on the streets. Yet the wayward girls in this group were not always
fully content with their new lives. As a parolee, Ella Waldstein was thankful for her family's affection but regretted that life was not as interesting
as it had been when she spent every spare moment on Coney Island. In
one parole letter she remarked, "I would write you more often but there
is really nothing to write it is the same thing over and over again. I'm
always home and go out very little so you can see Bedford has changed
me quite a bit."⁴¹ Nonetheless Ella and the others like her were convinced
that security and long-term happiness lay with conventional family life.

In contrast, other wayward girls found the lessons of parole difficult
and painful. Most of these young women had been "troublesome" as
reformatory inmates, and they were not particularly anxious to be
"good girls" on parole. Some were eager to rejoin urban youth subcultures, and the likelihood of their succeeding on parole was also diminished by the inflexibility of their parents. Eventually, however, the
majority of the women in that group decided that it paid to be good.

In several cases, all involving single mothers, eventual success on
parole was achieved only after the wayward girls recognized that they
could not survive without the support and approval of their kin. Reconciliation with family members was often difficult, but it seemed their
only choice, socially and economically. For example, Althea Davies was
at odds with the married sister and aunt to whom she was paroled for
nearly two years. She complained that they treated her as an "outcast";
they, on the other hand, complained that Althea was "pert and saucy,"
did not take proper care of her baby, and stayed out late at night with
unknown men. But after voluntarily returning to Bedford three times to
escape their criticism and enduring over and over again the constraints
and deprivations of reformatory life, Althea finally returned to her family and, relying on her sister for childcare, settled into a regular job and
a conventional hardworking life.⁴²

In other cases, success on parole was achieved in spite of the wayward
girls' steadfast refusal to reconcile themselves to the demands of their
kin. Nanette Wilkins, after being sent to a domestic position, was
returned to Bedford for impertinence and staying out all night. When
Bedford's superintendent asked her if she would be willing to go to her
family when she was again paroled, Nanette refused: "Do you think it
any pleasure for a girl to go to ther pople when there will never be any
peice in the Home? [sic]" However, by this time Nanette knew that "the
only thing I wanted was freedom," and when she was once again sent to
a domestic position she willingly conformed to the demands of both

Bedford and her employer. After her final discharge, Nanette took another job as a domestic servant.[43]

Only five wayward girls showed evidence of long-term reinvolvement or identification with urban youth or delinquent subcultures. The young women in this group had often been among the most unruly inmates at the reformatory, and they were certainly Bedford's and Albion's worst parole violators. To the historian they appear as iconoclasts, unwilling to compromise their individuality or independence as other inmates and parolees did. They proved unwilling to bow to the demands or expectations of their families and had little interest in or regard for conventional notions of female sexual morality. Nor did they display any respect for or fear of the authority and power of the reformatories. Although some of these women were punished for violating parole, they still refused to "learn a lesson."

All but one of these young women were paroled to their parents, and usually they made an effort to keep to the terms of their parole, at least for a while. Thus, despite Sophie Polentz's boast that she had been one of the worst girls at the reformatory, the new parolee lost no time in finding employment as a factory worker, writing to Superintendent Baker that she was "doing all in my will power to keep my parole." However, Sophie's resolve did not last. Three months after her parole began the young woman "left her home and employment. . . . It is suspected that she went away with a young man who was interested in her." Sophie's file only hints at what may have caused her to run away; the young man may have tempted her to violate her parole. It is likely, however, that relations in Sophie's home were extremely strained. Her immigrant father expected absolute obedience and he was capable of laying a heavy burden of guilt on his children. In a letter sent to Sophie after she was returned to Bedford as a parole violator, Mr. Polentz wrote, "Yes dear Daughter I am still in a Sanatarium and I am very sick. God knows if I shall be able to stand so much suffering, you children make me sick and you will also be responsible for my dying soon. you are ungrateful children who have no feelings for my heart and thoughts. You don't know what the word Father means. you have disgraced me at every step and I am paying for it now with my life."[44]

Janine Rosen, another Bedford parolee, also tried to do well for the first several months on parole, but she could not satisfy her father. Mr. Rosen complained about her "secretive ways" and the "snappy answers" she gave when asked about how she spent her time in the evenings after work. Janine, in turn, insisted that she was maintaining high standards of behavior despite the oppressive conditions in her father's house. Eventually, eager to escape the petty restrictions and confining moral codes of her family, Janine ran away from home.[45]

There is lilttle likelihood that any of the women in this group ever achieved the independence they so evidently wanted. Four of the young women disappeared while they were still on parole, but as parole violators they had good reason to be afraid of the law. They also had good reason to stay away from their families, who might have reported them. However, having little education, few job skills, and small hope of being able to support themselves on the income earned from legal employment, these young women had little choice but to allow prostitution and the risk of arrest to define their lives. Indeed, three of the parole violators eventually were arrested for earning money illegally and were taken back to Bedford.[46]

Sophie Polentz returned to Bedford once but disappeared again when she was reparoled. Although she was never retaken, the institution did hear occasional reports of her, and her experience may be similar to that of others in this group. Sophie became a streetwalker, and once having taken refuge from her family and the reformatory in New York City's street life, the young woman found it difficult to disengage herself from her underworld associates. She married after working for nearly two years as a prostitute and was forced to pay hush money to the couple she had worked for lest her husband be told of her past life. When Sophie missed a few payments her husband was confronted with information about her former career, and as her marriage fell apart Sophie discovered just how relentlessly her "immorality" could haunt her.[47]

Although urban America offered working-class young women opportunity for social invention and heterosexual experimentation during the early twentieth century, it could not protect adolescent females from parental denunciation or legal sanction. Of course, most assertive and sexually active adolescent girls did not become wayward girls. Some defiant young women undoubtedly came from families that found ways to cope with adolescent rebellion. Others may have deliberately (and successfully) concealed their self-expression, knowing that New York's law enforcement system was prepared to work with working-class parents to limit the rebellion of adolescent daughters. Using a variety of strategies, the great majority of adolescent girls and young women must have negotiated America's urban terrain in relative safety, enjoying and inventing sexualized lifestyles while acknowledging the limits of their freedom and acting to protect themselves from social stigma or state action.

New York's wayward girls had a different experience; they were unable to avoid getting into trouble. Domestic misfortune prompted these young women to attach particular importance to the social and cultural landscape beyond their own front doors; they viewed sexualized urban youth cultures as a critical source of amusement, companionship, and relief from family turmoil. Unfortunately, modern youth cultures also exposed them to new forms of sexual exploitation and manipulation. Moreover, adverse conditions at home made it difficult for their parents to tolerate cultural change and filial disobedience. When New York's wayward girls failed to be the daughters their families wanted or needed, the reformatories at Albion and Bedford Hills attempted to remold their character and social identity, urging them to abandon their interest in lively peer groups and cleave once again to old-fashioned values.

As the history of the wayward girls so clearly shows, to a large extent the reformatories succeeded in their goals. Inside the walls of the reformatories and on parole most wayward girls became convinced that self-assertion was a dangerous enterprise: it did not guarantee independence from unhappy or oppressive home conditions, and it made them vulnerable to sexual exploitation, social ostracism, and state control. Having been caught in their attempts at independence, the wayward girls learned to attach new value to safety and to social acceptability, and they worked hard to remove the stigma on their names. By becoming cautious and conventional the wayward girls may not have found comfort or contentment. However, having experienced grief, abuse, and disappointment as wayward girls, these young women reasoned that conformity was the best option they had.

NOTES

1. Ella Waldstein, inmate case file, New York State Reformatory for Women, Bedford Hills, 00018, 1917, Records of the Department of Correctional Services, New York State Archives and Records Administration, State Education Department, Albany, New York 12230. Inmate case file numbers and the names of wayward girls, family members, and friends have been changed in compliance with New York State regulations governing researchers' access to restricted documents.

2. For further examination of the impact of wage work on working-class young women in the early-twentieth-century United States, see Kathy Peiss, *Cheap Amusements: Working Women and Leisure in Turn-of-the-Century New York* (Philadelphia: Temple University Press, 1985); Leslie Tentler, *Wage-Earning Women: Industrial Work and Family Life in the United States, 1900–1930* (New York: Oxford University Press, 1979); Elizabeth Ewen, *Immigrant Women in the Land of Dollars: Life and Culture on the Lower East Side, 1890–1925* (New York: Monthly Review Press, 1985); Alice Kessler-Harris, "Independence and Virtue in the Lives of Wage-Earning Women: The United States, 1870–1930," in *Women and Culture in Politics: A Century of Change*, ed. Judith Friedlander, Blanche Wiesen Cook, Alice Kessler-Harris, and Carroll Smith Rosenberg (Bloomington: Indiana University Press, 1986), 3–17. The transformation of female adolescence in the middle class is discussed in Ruth M. Alexander, "'The Girl Problem': Class Inequity and Psychology in the Remaking of Female Adolescence, 1900–1930" (Ph.D. diss., Cornell University, 1990); John

Modell, *Into One's Own: From Youth to Adulthood in the United States, 1920–1975* (Berkeley: University of California Press, 1989); Paula S. Fass, *The Damned and the Beautiful: American Youth in the 1920s* (New York: Oxford University Press, 1977).

3. For further discussion of parent-daughter conflict and the compromises attained in working-class households see Tentler, *Wage-Earning Women*, 107–14; Ewen, *Immigrant Women in the Land of Dollars*, 208–14; Peiss, *Cheap Amusements*, 67–72.

4. Nineteen of the twenty-two young women were convicted of summary or conduct offenses. Just three were convicted of minor criminal offenses. The twenty-two cases are part of a larger study of one hundred reformatory women, most committed to Bedford Hills or Albion following a police arrest (usually for solicitation) and without evidence of direct intervention by family members. My sample of twenty-two cases includes five young women committed to Albion and seventeen committed to Bedford Hills, all between the ages of sixteen and twenty-one at the time of sentencing. The sample used in this study is admittedly small and does not claim to be statistically representative. I deliberately selected cases that were richly documented, revealing the values and concerns of working-class female adolescents and their families. The files include official reports documenting the inmates' families and criminal histories and their conduct at the reformatories and on parole. Many of the files also include correspondence to, from, and about individual inmates, including letters that did not pass the reformatory censors.

5. I have found no cases of young women from white, middle-class, native-born families who were committed to the reformatories at the request of family members. Such families were undoubtedly unwilling to suffer the stigma of having a daughter in a reformatory and relied on methods of control that did less to disturb their social status and privacy. By the 1920s social workers and psychologists were urging both working- and middle-class parents to turn to outpatient mental hygiene clinics for help with their adolescent daughters. See Alexander, "'Girl Problem,'" chap. 4. One recent study suggests that mental hygiene clinics were used by working-class parents more often than by middle-class parents (for treating problems of all kinds in children of all ages and both sexes), but the wayward girls are proof that working-class families also continued to make use of the criminal court system. See Margo Horn, *Before It's Too Late: The Child Guidance Movement in the United States, 1922–45* (Philadelphia: Temple University Press, 1989). For a study that emphasizes middle-class use of mental hygiene clinics, see Kathleen W. Jones, "As the Twig Is Bent: American Psychiatry and the Troublesome Child, 1890–1940," (Ph.D. diss., Rutgers University, 1988).

6. The wayward girls who did not serve three-year sentences were recommitted from the regular reformatory at Bedford to its Division for Mentally Defective Delinquents. The young women in this division usually had IQs of less than sixty-five and their sentences were indefinite. Bedford had legal authority to keep the "mentally defective" inmates in the institution for life if necessary; however, the case files show that these young women followed the basic reformatory program, although at a slower pace than the other inmates. The "mentally defective" wayward girls in my sample served four-, five-, and seven-year sentences, including time spent on parole.

7. Peiss, *Cheap Amusements*, 8; Joanne J. Meyerowitz, *Women Adrift: Independent Wage Earners in Chicago, 1880–1930* (Chicago: University of Chicago Press, 1988), 141.

8. One of the fathers in this subgroup was an insurance agent and thus a white-collar rather than a manual worker. However, circumstantial evidence suggests that the man had been unable to achieve the social or economic stability that permitted

entry into the middle class; he had a serious drinking problem and his wife supplemented the family income by doing piecework at home. Both of his adolescent daughters were factory workers. Only two young women in the larger group of twenty-two had fathers whose jobs placed them above the typical working-class man: one was a rabbi, the other an owner of a silk goods store.

9. The high percentage of working mothers in this group (23 percent) was well above the national average. In 1900 only 5.6 percent of all married women were in the labor force. That figure rose to 10.7 in 1910, dropped to 9.0 by 1920, and rose again to 11.7 by 1930. Nancy Woloch, *Women and the American Experience* (New York, 1984), 544. New York's Compulsory Education Law of 1903 required all children between the ages of eight and fourteen to attend school during the months from October to June. Children between the ages of fourteen and sixteen were permitted to work as long as they obtained working papers that showed proof of their age and level of schooling. Sol Cohen, *Progressives and Urban School Reform: The Public Education Association of New York City, 1895–1954* (New York: Teacher's College, 1964), 67–68.

10. Two young white women had emigrated to the United States with their parents as small children, one from Austria, the other from the West Indies. Two of the young black women were orphans who had been raised by relatives; one of these orphans was an immigrant from the West Indies. The third black woman lived with her mother, the father having deserted the family when the woman was very young. The fourth lived with a recently widowed father.

11. Louisa Parsons, Albion 00076, 1924.

12. Rae Rabinowitz, Bedford 00052, 1917.

13. In my sample, eighteen of twenty-two young women were taken to court over sexual misconduct. Of the eighteen, five were pregnant and two had just given birth at the time of their commitment to the reformatory. At least two of the wayward girls had been involved with men "outside of their faith"; one girl was involved in an interracial relationship.

14. Evelyn Blackwell, Bedford 00088, 1926.

15. Lena Meyerhoff, Bedford 00084, 1924.

16. Lena Meyerhoff, Bedford 00018, 1917; Rae Rabinowitz, Bedford 00052, 1917; Sophie Polentz, Bedford 00059, 1924.

17. Rae Rabinowitz, Bedford 00052, 1917; Ella Waldstein, Bedford 00018, 1917.

18. New York, *Laws of 1882*, chap. 410, sec. 1466; *Laws of 1886*, chap. 353; *Laws of 1903*, chap. 436; *Laws of 1914*, chap. 445. For a brief discussion of the laws see Paul W. Tappan, *Delinquent Girls in Court: A Study of the Wayward Minor Court of New York* (New York: Columbia University Press, 1947), 44–47.

19. Millicent Potter, Albion 00101, 1900.

20. Two years later the Wayward Minor Act was extended to apply to males as well as to females. New York, *Laws of 1925*, chap. 389.

21. Jessie Taft, "Mental Hygiene Problems of Normal Adolescence," *Mental Hygiene* 5 (Oct. 1921): 741–51; Gerald Pearson, "What the Adolescent Girl Needs in Her Home," *Mental Hygiene* 14 (Jan. 1930): 40–53; Winifred Richmond, *The Adolescent Girl* (New York: Macmillan, 1926); Miriam Van Waters, *Youth in Conflict* (New York: Republic Publishing Company, 1926), chap. 2; Phyllis Blanchard, *New Girls for Old* (New York: Macaulay, 1930), chap. 9; Helen Williston Brown, "The Deforming Influences of the Home," *Journal of Abnormal Psychology* 12 (April 1917): 49–57; Frankwood E. Williams, *Adolescence: Studies in Mental Hygiene* (New York: Farrar and Rinehart, Inc., 1930), chap. 3; E. Van Norman

Emery, "Revising Our Attitude toward Sex," *Mental Hygiene* 11 (April 1927): 324–38; Ruth Kimball Gardiner, "Your Daughter's Mother," *Journal of Social Hygiene* 6 (Oct. 1920): 542; Alexander, "'Girl Problem,'" chap. 4; Jones, "As the Twig Is Bent," 163–66, 215–47.

22. New York, *Laws of 1923*, chap. 868. The passage of the Wayward Minor Act led to a dramatic increase in the number of young women committed to the reformatories at Bedford Hills and Albion for "wilful disobedience" or immorality. In the year ending June 30, 1921, only 7.69 percent of Bedford Hills' new inmates were "incorrigible girls," having been convicted of violating the New York City statute. However, by 1925, 23.6 percent of Bedford's new inmates were wayward minors; in 1928 the percentage was 26.6. Commitments to Albion under the new law were slow at first: In 1925 only 7.8 percent of the inmates admitted that year were wayward minors, yet in 1928, 28.6 percent were. Although these statistics do not tell us who testified against the girls in court, it is probably safe to assume that parents, not police, acted as complainants in the majority of cases. New York State Reformatory for Women at Bedford Hills, *Twenty-first Annual Report* (Albany, N.Y., 1921), 16; New York State Reformatory for Women at Bedford Hills, *Twenty-fifth Annual Report* (Albany, N.Y., 1925), 14; Albion State Training School, *Annual Report* (Albany, N.Y., 1925), 16; State Commission of Correction, *Second Annual Report* (Albany, N.Y., 1928), 519.

23. As Albion's board of managers wrote in its annual report to the New York State legislature in 1919, the various "lines of training" at the reformatory were "intended to make the girl self-supporting, while the one thought which is kept in mind all the time is that she may be surrounded with influences that will tend to strengthen her character and awaken within her the desire to go back out into the world and live a good and useful life." Western House of Refuge for Women at Albion, New York, *Twenty-fifth Annual Report* (1919), 4. In the years from 1900 to 1930 Albion and Bedford responded to new trends in women's employment and popular amusements by making small modifications in their programs—Bedford, for example, showed movies and offered limited training in clerical skills during the 1920s. However, the basic goals and methods of the reformatories remained unchanged. For additional discussion of "protection and rescue" as a mission of the women's reformatories see Estelle Freedman, *Their Sisters' Keepers: Women's Prison Reform in America, 1830–1930* (Ann Arbor: University of Michigan Press, 1981), chap. 3.

24. Althea Davies, Bedford 00083, 1924; Deborah Herman, Mentally Defective Delinquent (MDD), Bedford 00093, 1926.

25. The reformatory was especially offended by cross-race lesbian relationships, which raised fears among staff members that the white girls involved would lose all respect for racial and sexual conventions. In 1915 staff members speculated that the white girls involved in lesbian relationships might "take up living in colored neighborhoods" once they were discharged from the reformatory. Believing that the "most undesirable sex relations grow out of [the] mingling of the two races," Bedford ended its experimentation with integrated housing and established segregated cottages in 1916. State Board of Charities, *Report of the Special Committee . . . to Investigate Charges Made against the New York State Reformatory for Women at Bedford Hills, N.Y.* (Albany, 1915), 18–19, 26–27. For additional discussion of homosexuality among female prison and reformatory inmates see Margaret Otis, "A Perversion Not Commonly Noted," *Journal of Abnormal Psychology* 8 (1913): 113–16; Charles A. Ford, "Homosexual Practices of Institutionalized Females," *Journal of Abnormal Psychology* 23 (1929): 442–48.

26. Rae Rabinowitz, Bedford 00052, 1917, 7; Melanie Burkis, Bedford 00087, 1928, 3.

27. Melanie Burkis, Bedford 00087, 1928, 3.

28. Rae Rabinowitz, Bedford 00052, 1917.

29. Ella Waldstein, Bedford 00018, 1917; Rae Rabinowitz, Bedford 00052, 1917.

30. Melanie Burkis, Bedford 00087, 1928.

31. Sophie Polentz, Bedford 00059, 1924.

32. For example in 1923 Bedford's superintendent Amos Baker wrote to ask Nanette Wilkins's aunt, the individual responsible for the wayward minor charge against the sixteen-year-old black girl, to correspond with her niece. Baker did not mention Nanette's frequent misconduct, but he did point out that "your niece, Nanette Wilkins, tells me that she has not heard from any of her people in some time and she is somewhat discouraged and anxious. I think a line from you would cheer her up and encourage her." Nanette Wilkins, Bedford 00017, 1923, 6.

33. A good example of the reformatories' chastisement of parents is in the file of Lena Meyerhoff, the young Jewish woman committed to Bedford as a wayward minor after giving birth to an illegitimate (mulatto) child. After reading a letter that Mrs. Meyerhoff sent to Lena, Bedford's Superintendent Baker wrote to her, saying, "the statements which you made in your letter are true; nevertheless they were so upsetting to Lena that I doubt the wisdom of writing letters of this kind to her in her present situation. I know it is very difficult to decide just what course to pursue in regard to her, but I think encouraging letters would be better than those that tend to depress and discourage." Lena Meyerhoff, Bedford 00084, 1924, 5.

34. Many families were in fact acutely aware of the reformatories' efforts to limit their involvement in the reform process. It was not uncommon for parents or other relatives to write to the reformatory superintendents to give advice or to make special requests regarding the care of their girls. Requests for the early discharge or parole of a girl were especially frequent. Often, the request for early release was combined with or eventually evolved into a debate over the conditions of parole: Was the inmate to be sent to her families' home or to a domestic position, was the infant of an inmate to be adopted or sent home with the young woman, and so forth. Some families tried to add weight to their requests by hiring lawyers or by soliciting assistance from politicians, ministers, or community leaders. Families rarely succeeded in winning the early release of an inmate; their frustrating and often bitter campaigns offer further proof of the institutions' substantial authority. There were fifteen cases in my sample in which family members challenged the reformatory authorities or intervened in the handling of their daughters.

35. Sophie's father wrote frequently to his daughter and to Bedford's superintendent, Amos Baker. Most of his letters were not censored, but because they were written in German, translations were always made before the letters were passed, and those translations remain in Sophie's file. Sophie Polentz, Bedford 00059, 1924, 6, 7.

36. Althea Davies was one wayward girl who, while still an inmate, apparently promised her family that her "bad" days were behind her. In a letter to Bedford's superintendent, Amos Baker, Althea's aunt noted, "Althea has promised me with eyes of tears that she will amend her ways. She is very sorry of her deeds and promised me that she will not be found in any such trouble again." Althea Davies, Bedford 00083, 1924.

37. Of the twenty-two young women in my sample, thirteen were initially sent home, six were placed in domestic positions, and three were placed in hospital positions. Often, employment changed several times over the course of parole, some

women changing jobs while they remained at home, other young women leaving a hospital position to live at home and take a factory job.

38. Amos Baker, Bedford's superintendent from 1921 to 1927, noted that the lack of adequate parole supervision made it "very difficult, well nigh impossible, to follow each girl a sufficient length of time to determine with absolute certainty what the institution has accomplished." New York State Reformatory for Women, *Twenty-fourth Annual Report* (Albany, N.Y., 1925), 9.

39. Ilene Sterling, Bedford 00024, 1917; Susanna Nedersen, Bedford 00029, 1917.

40. Susanna Nedersen, Bedford 00029, 1917; Ilene Sterling, Bedford 00024, 1917.

41. Ella Waldstein, Bedford 00018, 1917.

42. Althea Davies, Bedford 00083, 1924.

43. Nanette Wilkins, Bedford 00017, 1923.

44. Sophie Polentz, Bedford 00059, 1924.

45. In a letter to Bedford she wrote: "Upon the slightest provocation reference to Bedford is made with much threatening, etc. I am trying to redeem myself and do the right thing. Let me assure you that the inclination to do or be otherwise never enters my mind. All I want is a fair chance; in other words an 'even break.' If I were to say my parents are all wrong and I am in the right I don't doubt that I would sound like every girl that is guilty of breaking parole, but my parent's attitude makes life well nigh impossible at times." Janine Rosen, Bedford 00025, 1926.

46. Janine Rosen, Melanie Burkis, and Sophie Polentz were all returned to Bedford for violating parole. Before being retaken, Janine Rosen had worked in a speakeasy and as a dance hall teacher; the two others had worked as prostitutes. Janine Rosen, Bedford 00025, 1926; Melanie Burkis, Bedford 00087, 1928; Sophie Polentz, Bedford 00059, 1924.

47. Sophie Polentz, Bedford 00059, 1924.

11

Revolutionary Desire: Redefining the Politics of Sexuality of American Radicals, 1919–1945

Kathleen A. Brown and Elizabeth Faue

Writing to a friend about a recent discussion she had with a young Swedish philosopher, black writer and labor activist Thyra Edwards explained that they had spoken of "those who preach sexual liberty but carefully adhere to orthodoxy. We were agreed that one must have a super sense of physical security and sureness in his partner to condone outside relations."[1] Covering the gamut of sexual relations, from courtship and marriage to free love, Edwards commented that it was a "relief to really talk to another" as "most people haven't the courage to face themselves, much less others and speak of the things that occupy much of all our thinking."[2] In her life, Thyra Edwards considered sexuality and intimate relationships central to politics and community; but she also viewed sexuality as fundamentally private. Like many American radicals between the wars, Edwards did not consider the advocacy of sexual freedom as politically viable and lacked a public language and space in which to pursue her sexual politics.

This disjuncture between sex and politics is a common theme in Left and labor history[3] as both historical and historiographical silences have obscured the importance of sexual politics in shaping American radicalism. This essay is an attempt to consider the messy connections between sex radicalism and Left politics, sexual theory and sexual practice, Left feminism and sexual freedom, in the United States between 1919 and 1945. The American Left faced persecution and had to reorganize politically. In common with many cultural critics, radicals strongly supported reworking the boundaries of intimate relationships by sanctioning serial monogamy, birth control, companionate marriage, and divorce. Some argued for and experimented with nonmonogamy; others, such as anarchist Emma Goldman, defended an increasingly visible homosexual minority. For many on the Left, however, wartime charges of corruption, immorality, and sexual perversion were an alarming sign of how far radicals were removed from "American" culture. Across the radical spectrum, organizers, writers, and activists struggled to harness cultural changes to a new politics. In doing so, not all sexual positions, as it were, were equal in the debates over sex, marriage, and family. Much of the experimental thought and coalitional work of the prewar and 1920s Left disappeared and with it the pressure for gender equality and sexual freedom.

By the Great Depression, most radical social theory had delegitimated and dislodged sexual politics as a appropriate topic for discussion.[4] This silence regarding sexual practice was a public one. Privately, leftists grappled with how they organized their own sexual lives and relationships. While the economic crisis arguably took primacy over debates on the Sex Question,[5] the struggle for power in sexual relationships, the linkage between monogamy and women's oppression, and the place in an emancipatory social movement for alternative sexual identities and practices remained contested. These dilemmas were worked out in the daily practice of sexuality and in personal correspondence, shared reading, and private discussions of sex and marriage. While some historians have argued that the interwar Left instilled a political silence on nonmarital sex and alternative sexualities, the evidence remaining from radical lives reminds us that sexual politics was worked out in practical as well as theoretical realms.

The themes this essay addresses are the ideas and sources of Left sexual politics, the individual and social practices of sexuality among American radicals, and the forces that shaped Left sexual politics in both theory and practice. Sexual practice and sexual theory on the Left existed in tension with one another and only rarely in harmony. At the same time, public sexual reticence had real consequences. Rejecting the Sex Question led radicals to deny, neglect, and devalue the contribution of social communities, personal relationships, and intimate lives to their politics. It undercut their social imagination and their ability to explore alternate and oppositional sexual identities and alternative social relations on which a new political movement and a new society could be built. Finally, the rejection of female sexual subjectivity and the politics of sexuality truncated the possibilities of a new radical politics in the interwar years.

Conservative social commentators from the turn of the century through the 1940s reflected a common perception that radicals of any stripe—anarchist, communist, socialist, or pacifist—were not merely politically subversive, but immoral, corrupt, degenerate, and sexually obsessed.[6] Many believed that the lure of socialism was in part its promise "to those pulsating with sex love, who ever hunger after forbidden sex fruits, that along with the new economic conditions, socialism will cause the fruition of their fondest sex hopes, and they will be permitted to satisfy their sexual cravings to satiety."[7] Echoing accusations that the Bolshevik Revolution outlawed celibacy and nationalized women,[8] conservative Elizabeth Dilling argued that American Communists pursued the same social agenda by offering women "sex equality with men through free love, state orphanages, and collectivized factory kitchens. . . ."[9] and by offering men unrestricted sexuality with women of all races and social standing.[10]

In part, what such commentators were reacting to was the "revolution of manners and morals" that had taken place even before World War I. "Jazz Age Morality," V. F. Calverton argued in *The Bankruptcy of Marriage* (1929), was the product of changes in American society. Economic shifts toward a more corporate and more monied society and the corrosive effect of the World War helped alter the sexual landscape. The wider acceptance of premarital sex, increase in divorce, and greater range of sexual expression challenged traditional morality and created a new sexual order. Many observers held the flapper personally responsible for jettisoning the baggage of monogamy and leading a new form of revolution which went beyond the "sex playboyism" of the Left. New dating and courtship patterns, divorce laws, and birth control methods reconfigured the heterosexual terrain, new gay and lesbian subcultures flourished in urban areas. Sexual frankness attained new value in American society, even as nonmarital sexuality was more publicly visible.[11]

One of the most important forces in reshaping politics on the Left was the Russian Revolution. Its impact on sexual politics was felt both in terms of revisiting classic socialist texts on the Woman Question and the influence of the new Soviet culture. Lenin's ideas about gender and sexuality were taken seriously by an American Left searching for models.[12] Alexandra Kollontai was another important voice on gender and sexuality whose views were in wide circulation on the Left.[13] In her autobiography, Communist organizer Dorothy Healey provided examples of how the new Soviet society offered sexual models for the American Left. Having read Krupskaya's *Memories of Lenin* (1930), Healey was impressed by "how Lenin had decried promiscuity, using the example of the glass of water that just as [one] wouldn't want your lips to be on a glass that was muddied by other people's lips, the same was true in a sexual relationship." Using Lenin's analogy, Healey chided her friend Archie Brown, a young Communist newsboy who was "having a lot of interesting sexual relationships at the time." She was stunned when Archie responded that Lenin "'knew nuttin' about sex. . . . I'm not taking my leadership from him!'"[14] Archie and Dorothy recapitulated some of Lenin's arguments with Alexandra Kollontai over her advocacy of "comrade love" as a sexual ideal. She believed that sexual freedom was a necessary condition for revolution, because individual possessiveness, even in intimate relationships, undermined collective solidarity.[15]

In forums in *The Nation, The New Masses,* and *Modern Quarterly,* the "sex boys," as Malcolm Cowley crowned them, debated each other on the necessity, character, and form of sexual politics for radicals. They rarely incorporated women in the debate. Instead, anarchist John Collier, neo-monogamist Floyd Dell, and sexual rebel V. F. Calverton argued with monogamist Upton Sinclair, sexual puritan H. M. Wicks, and critic Malcolm Cowley over the rationality and instrumentality of sexual unions, without a thought to the relations between the sexes. John Collier's "revolutionary proletarian" confronted and rejected the "Christian manhood" of both Eugene Debs and Upton Sinclair. He expressed instead the brawniness, lustiness, and muscularity of a revolutionary class warrior. True revolutionaries, Collier argued, rebelled against middle-class morality in both productive and reproductive terms. This vision did not acknowledge female reproductive labor as part of the double exploitation of capitalism. Rather, the focus was on the proletarian who

> [went] "home" . . . to spend his "leisure time" in rest and "recreation," the most of which is taken up in *procreation* of more wageslaves and in working them up into fit products for the labor market. His recreative night-work (on his own time!) is just as important and necessary to society as his underpaid labor in the day-factory. And it is just as monotonous and degrading.[16]

The "sex boys" accepted the dubious proposition that, whatever the revolutionary sexual order would be, it would benefit women as much as men. From their point of view, sex did not entail relations of exploitation of and power over the opposite sex. Certainly they did not even imagine that same-sex bonds would enter into the equation. Rather, sexual and gender equality remained unproblematized as writers granted a dense interrelationship between revolutionary politics and social-sexual order, one in which men always came out on top.[17]

Despite women's formal absence from the debate, the "sex wars" of the 1920s brought to the forefront of cultural radicalism the conjoined questions of sexuality and women's equality. If *The Daily Worker* and *The New Masses* were loath to consider women's interests with regard to sex, the private relationships between men and women were the subject of study by women social scientists, writers, and political activists on the Left, such as Margaret Mead, Mary Ware Dennett, and Charlotte Perkins Gilman.[18] Women's forums such as Heterodoxy in New York and women's informal clubs, such as the Royal Bengal Bicycle Club, organized by socialist Ann Craton and her friends,[19] kept open the discussion of women's equality, politics, and changing sexual morality. While Left critics ignored women's proletarian and revolutionary novels, the writings of Agnes Smedley, Meridel Le Sueur, and Tillie Lerner (Olsen) found an audience, as they explored the sexual consequences and complications of working-class lives. In more popular arenas, the writings of Ruth McKenney and Elizabeth Hawes gave voice to women's experience and ideas. Within the Communist Party, Grace Hutchins and Mary Inman formulated new arguments on women's double burden that broadened the primarily economic analysis of the Woman Question and the Sex Question. Their work questioned the classic formulations of Left theory and spoke to the effects of ideology, sexuality, and mass culture on women's subordination. What was lost by the 1930s, however, was the means for making sexual politics count in the political agenda of the Left. Within the constraints of the new heterosexual freedom, women were nominally freer to express themselves privately but made little impact on the public stance of Left political parties.[20]

Sexual politics on the Left ran into obstacles when it engaged questions of women's sexual freedom and alternative sexualities. With the exception of such figures as Emma Goldman, few radicals publicly defended homosexuality as sexual choice. Even anarchists thought the subject "most taboo in polite society." Homosexuality invited social ostracism and state repression. As Emma Goldman recalled in *Living My Life* (1931): "Censorship came from some of my own comrades because I was treating such 'unnatural' themes as homosexuality. Anarchism was already enough misunderstood . . . ; it was unadvisable to add to the misconceptions by taking up perverted sex-forms, they argued."[21] The enthusiastic embrace of heterosexual variety and heterosexual liberation among Left theorists did not extend to similar support for either gender equality or lesbian and gay identities. In the end, the Left witnessed and enabled the "Rehabilitation of Monogamy,"[22] as historian Elsa Dixler has argued. The evolution of radical discourse on sexuality throughout the decade revealed an apparent puritanical side of the Left, with its repression, homophobia, and the separation of the "personal" from the "political." Celebrating the renewed cult of masculinity in the depression era, the Left challenged neither its own sexism nor pervasive homophobia. Sexual conservatism colored its public texts and practices, even as the economic crisis wore on. As Stalin reinstituted restrictions on divorce and abortion and re-criminalized homosexuality, many American Communists urged more conservative sexual policies.[23] Shifts in Soviet policy, and the conforming "American" influence of the Popular Front, had an impact on Left views of sexuality. The head of the CP, Earl Browder, staked out his policy in 1937:

> Any manifestation of looseness or penetration into our ranks of bourgeois habits, particularly with respect to personal life, must be rooted out, because it is precisely from such things as this that the enemies recruit in our ranks. It has been an almost invariable result of examination of political degeneration that it almost always is accompanied by personal degeneration. We must begin to examine the private lives of our leading cadres as a necessary and unavoidable part of the guarantee of the political integrity of our Party.[24]

Silence concerning private life more generally prevailed, so that the chasm between personal experience and public discourse, individual behavior and party doctrine, widened over the course of the depression decade. Sexual identities, experiences, and ideas on the Left remained the subject of personal narrative, not political life.

Sexual knowledge, ideas and attitudes about sexuality, on the Left did not simply originate in its reading of political economy. Attitudes also were based on the teachings of families of origin, individual experiences as young adults, discussions in the workplace, and poetry, psychology, and popular culture. Many of the men and women who moved to the Left in the interwar years or who were raised within Left communities were taught about sexuality and biology by their parents or friends. Leftist labor activist Eugene V. Dennett's Irish Catholic immigrant mother explicitly taught him the "unfair burden" of women's double duty, the importance of a women's right to control her body, and the need for safe and legal birth control.[25] Yet, there was an uneven range of knowledge about sex, due to personal reticence, family customs, or shared ignorance. Communist Party organizer Dorothy Healey explained that her own attitudes toward her body and sex evolved out of the explicit and implicit messages of her working-class, Russian-Jewish, socialist mother. Explaining her feelings of shame about her body, Healey stated that they "were something . . . I got from my mother, who very clearly didn't like sex or sexuality. We once had a 'mother-daughter' chat about sex, and the main thing I got from it was a sense of how distasteful she found the whole subject."[26] In contrast Peggy Dennis's working-class, immigrant, Russian-Jewish family appeared to share more positive information and values about sexuality. When she contemplated leaving her husband for Eugene Dennis, she consulted her parents, who offered nonjudgmental guidance.[27]

While it is easy to see family as a source of sexual ideas and values, it is important to acknowledge that many families did not discuss sex with their offspring. John Abt recalled that his father "never did discuss sex" with him, "although once" his father handed John "a magazine article to read—again without discussion—on the dangers of masturbation."[28] Even as married adults, those on the Left frequently turned to each other for help and guidance. Blanche O'Connor wrote her good friend, radical Bets Bickel, to ask about "birth control," the sexual "double standard," and "other questions of interest to women."[29] Dorothy Healey sought out birth control advice from her friend Minnie Carson.[30] Junius Scales recounted that as CP leader in North Carolina, many of comrades "felt close enough to me to discuss their sexual fears, difficulties, and inexperience."[31] Having watched her mother and neighborhood wives have unwanted child after child, radical poet Elsa Gidlow developed a firm belief in women's rights to control their bodies. She sought out birth control information and passed it on to her sisters and their leftist women friends.[32] The shop floor also provided some radicals with an introduction to issues of sexuality. Anarchist Lucy Lang recounted learning "the intimate secrets of life" from her fellow factory girls.[33]

Similarly, leftists recounted getting their ideas and attitudes from popular culture, poetry, and literature. Group Theater cofounder Cheryl Crawford recalled that what she "learned about sex came from a book we found hidden under the dress shirts" of her otherwise "puritanical" father's chiffonier.[34] Communist and Beat poet Harold Norse recalled that he was initiated "into the mysteries" of sexual education by reading aloud, with five other boys, Frank Harris's *My Life and Loves,* which had [very] graphic sexist descriptions of heterosexual intercourse and oral sex. Such literature, combined with his reading of Walt Whitman and Norse's experiences growing up in working-class communities, led him to internalize popular conceptions of masculinity.[35] For radicals, straight and gay, Whitman's affirmation of the "manly love of comrades" and wild sensual avowals opened new horizons of political and sexual identity.[36] As late as the 1930s, the legacy of sexual radicalism, the new sexology, and free love advocacy remained pressing and prescient ideas. They pervaded radical political culture and shaped the way that radicals both arranged and derived meaning from their private lives.[37] Anarchist poet Elsa Gidlow as well as Communist activist and Mattachine Society founder Harry Hay looked to sexologists such as Edward Carpenter for ideas about lesbian and gay identity. For "ideas on the subject of Free Love," radical Floyd Dell "began with Shelley and Plato and Edward Carpenter, not with Greenwich Village." Freud completed Dell's sex education.[38] Popular studies of sex, love and psychology sparked introspection and discussion.[39]

The ascendance of new sexual theory opened up discussion on the Left with the new "scientific" discourse around sexual repression, sexual deviance, and sexual expression. In radical circles as in mass culture, the popularization of Freud led to greater emphasis on sexual intimacy among men and women, focus on sexual intercourse, and marginalization of alternative sexualities. As historian Jeffrey Weeks suggested, this dependence on a "unitary model of sexuality," which was "heterosexual, procreative, and male," constrained sexual choices. The increasing number of "perversions, deviations, paraphilias," which sexologists catalogued and diagnosed, "inevitably marginalized and in the last resort pathologized other sexualities."[40] While Left sexologists expanded the range of sexual identity and practice to include same-sex bonds, few radicals accepted them as legitimate or normal sexual practice.[41]

Whatever their origin, the attitudes of heterosexual leftists towards sex and sexuality varied greatly. Some women on the Left demonstrated Victorian or conservative attitudes.[42] Working-class radical Barbara Nestor joined the Communist Party in the late 1920s. A life-long leftist, she taught her daughters that sexual expression was reserved for marriage and that such expression was distasteful. As her daughter Dorothy Healey later recalled, Nestor stressed that "you don't let a man kiss you unless you were in love with him" and that "no woman could be happy without a man." The end result of this, according to Healey, was "if I kissed a man, I kidded myself into thinking that I loved him, which led to complications."[43] Marrying young and a virgin, Healey evolved her own ideas about sexuality after she joined the Communist Party. Her mother's apparent "prudery" might be attributed to an Orthodox Jewish family of origin and her age, but equally responsible was her experience of the repercussions of heterosexual sexual encounters. Dorothy Healey recalled that her parents' marriage was "tension-ridden" in part because "Mama was constantly getting pregnant." Lacking effective birth control, Barbara bore six children and "performed sixteen abortions on herself."[44] No doubt other leftist women had experiences similar to Nestor and believed that sex was a necessary and unpleasant chore for women.

In contrast, some Left women adopted the attitudes which John D'Emilio and Estelle Freedman defined as the new "sex liberalism." These women, along with their mainstream counterparts, "detached sexual activity from the instrumental goal of procreation, affirmed heterosexual pleasure as a value in itself, defined sexual satisfaction as a critical component of personal happiness . . . , and weakened the connections between sexual expression and marriage."[45] Working-class radical Theodora Gidlow, radical labor activist Thyra Edwards, and Communist Party member Jane Foster exemplified some of the ways leftist women shared in the "sexual liberalism" of the inter-war years. Dora Gidlow, a Canadian-born radical activist, believed heterosexual pleasure was valuable in and of itself and saw sexuality to be a critical component of her development. In a letter to her sister, she explained that engaging in sexual relations was a way of "yielding to the natural need to broaden my life and myself," and gently asked her sister to cease criticizing her: "You deplore my dearth of it [sexual experience] yet object to my acquiring it."[46] Perhaps what differentiated Dora Gidlow from mainstream sex liberals was her independence. "T'will be a long day and night," she wrote, "ere I permit my lovers to . . . vest me with their own creeds."[47] To her, sexual satisfaction was a critical component of a successful marriage, but she idealized neither marriage nor heterosexual relationships.[48]

Brookwood Labor College graduate and radical African American activist Thyra Edwards shared in this modern view of sexuality. She believed that sex was an important part of life and had affairs with fellow activists and casual companions. For her, participation in radical political movements was both political and personal. Her personal correspondence speaks of her political work and of seeking fellow travelers for sex and conversations "naked soul to naked soul."[49] Edwards had both brief and long-term relationships with men, yet also rejected marriage. "I never," she wrote to a friend, "wanted to be married in the routine way most of my friends are."[50]

Other radical women affirmed heterosexual pleasure as a value in itself, defined sexual satisfaction as a critical component of personal happiness, and accepted marriage as a malleable institution. Communist Party activist Jane Foster was an upper-middle-class Northern Californian. Sexually active in high school, she broke up with her "first love and first lover," Lonnie Noble, "because he was morbidly jealous." Radicalized by her exposure to the corrosive racism and sexism in the Dutch East Indies where her husband was a colonial officer, she deserted her husband, returned to San Francisco, and joined the Communist Party.[51] Divorced and living in New York in 1941, she met her future husband George: "If it was not a case of love at first sight, it was certainly sex at first sight." Separated from her husband during the war, she began a sexual relationship with a military lawyer. She explained, "I had no guilt feelings about George because he was on the other side of the world and I was sure that he was not sexually deprived wherever he was."[52] For Foster sex was a critical component of personal happiness and there was no stigma on sex outside of marriage.

Many Radical women did not accept the dictates of mainstream sexual science. According to historian Christina Simmons, that science placed men in control of sex, limited women's rights to withhold intimacy, and "muted female sexuality."[53] Some leftist women, however, did experience the constraints which Simmons described. Communist writer Meridel LeSueur had a twenty-five-year relationship with artist Bob Brown, whom she viewed both as "a weapon of destruction" and as a "weapon of love." Sometimes the cruel and abusive Brown threatened both LeSueur's personal autonomy and her sense of self, diminishing her pride in her writing but at the same time fueling her creativity.[54]

Easier divorce, greater access to birth control, and freer sex expression opened up sexual possibilities for women and, at the same time, brought corresponding pressures to be sexually active and available. Popularized understandings of Freud emphasized heterosexual engagement, bolstered the myth of vaginal orgasm, and characterized alternative sexualities and choices as "repressed" and "deviant." Some radical women were intimidated by accusations of not being "good comrades" if they refused to grant sexual favors. Although initiated into sexual activity by a bisexual woman, Communist activist Vera Buch idealized romantic heterosexual relationships and internalized homophobic attitudes about nonmonogamous same-sex relationships. Heterosexually inexperienced and insecure, Vera Buch allowed Albert Weisbord to control her sexually and emotionally. Having "had little control over" her life, she moved in with him when he proclaimed "I want to live with you on a permanent basis. I believe you have the qualities I want in a partner." To both of them, her consent and "love" were not the issue, his desires were. He played the "dominant role" in their relationship.[55]

Both older and younger generations of radical men were known to have traditional, even conservative, attitudes toward sexuality and its place in their lives. Charles Shipman (known in the CP as "Manuel Gomez") came of age politically during the First World War. He believed that discussions of sexuality and birth control were "out of place" in the revolutionary struggle.[56] When he refused to treat his first wife as an equal or a partner, she left him for another man. During a trip to Russia, Shipman bigamously married his non-Communist eighteen-year-old translator, Natalie. He brought her to the United States where, he recalled, she "adjusted her life to mine as best she could. . . . She went with me to Communist-run picnics, festivities at comrades' homes, and so on, but never to political meetings, public or private."[57]

Some men on the Left saw women, when they saw them at all, as sexual objects rather than as people. Perhaps unintentionally, some Left men emphasized their masculinity and comradeship in retelling stories about regular visits to brothels with other radical men. For these writers, sex with prostitutes was both about receiving sexual gratification and strengthening homosocial community.[58] Tales of sexual exploits with prostitutes and stories of sexual conquest were ways men could impress and compete with other men, and create shared understandings. Recounting having his pocket picked by a prostitute was one man's way of expressing contempt for women as mere receptacles and reemphasizing the war between the sexes. Making radical women the butt of sexual jokes diminished them as human beings and as effective political agents.[59] Hays "Jaze" Jones, an ex-Wobbly and later Communist, tried his hand at writing pornography. Reading his personal correspondence, one gets the impression that while Jones' explicit purpose in writing the pornography was to supply one-handed-reading material, an underlying cause was to bond with his male comrades.[60]

A few radical men kept sex on purely a physical basis, rejecting the emotional intimacy which could accompany sexual relations. The necessity of making or keeping sex "impersonal" was the excuse that Trotskyist Barney Mayes gave for his relationship with his wife, Tess. Although Mayes stated the two had, what was for him, a sexually satisfying relationship, Tess "was essentially a stranger" to him. In his memoir, he wrote that as a young organizer, love "was too strange, individualistic, risky and dangerous." While there was room in his life for using Tess's paycheck and her bed, he could find "no room for" a meaningful relationship. "Sex," he explained, "was as important as food but just as incidental, without any fetishes and undue emphasis. To keep it as impersonal as possible would provide greater compatibility and minimize its interference with one's political activity."[61]

In contrast, some men on the Left explicitly emphasized gender and sexual equality as core values of revolutionary ethics and practice. Middle-class born Jewish-American Communist Hank Rubin, serving as a medic in the International Brigade in Spain, lived up to his belief in gender and sexual equality. Despite "sexual pressures, jumbled hormones, intense curiosity, and desire," he first would not and then could not have sex with prostitutes. He explained that he could not "square" his "professed belief in the equality of women with having sex with a prostitute." For him, prostitution was "a social evil that I didn't want to support."[62] Rubin recalled that in the year and a half he was in the battle zone in Spain, he "was even more worried about dying a virgin than about dying." One evening while on leave from the front, he picked up a prostitute but found himself "embarrassingly impotent." Looking back, he remarked: "I still believe that the shame of paying for something that should result only from shared desire was a central factor in my impotence. The idea of buying what should be given in affection was just as repugnant to me as would have been taking it by force."[63]

Similarly, Filipino-American radical Carlos Bulosan rejected as dishonorable, inhuman, and contrary to radical politics a roommate's sexual conquest of another man's wife. The issue for Bulosan was not the woman's male partner's property rights in her, but her humanity. Bulosan rejected treating either men or women as objects.[64] Obviously, the connection between one's politics and one's sexual attitudes and attitudes about sexual and gender equality varied. Yet a large number of men on the left shared positive views of sex, egalitarian attitudes towards women, and a belief in companionate marriage. IWW member and first-generation Dutch-American Nicolass Steelink's prison correspondence with his wife, Fannia, indicates his love and concern for her, their joint political and business interests, and their egalitarian relationships. Convicted under California's Criminal Syndicalism law in 1920, Nicolass served three and a half years in San Quentin. His correspondence reveals that while he and Fannia did not believe in compulsory monogamy, they were both conscious of gender inequality within sexual relationships and that he distrusted some of his male leftist colleagues because they displayed "woman hate."[65]

Sexual politics among heterosexual leftists was complex. Sex was both enjoyed on the personal level and, at times, used for political purposes. Frequently marriages and sexual unions supported political activity.[66] Both women and men on the Left could and did occasionally use sex in a functional, rather than personal, manner. Re-evaluating her life and sexual relationships from a distance of fifty years, Dorothy Healey revised her initial belief that her sexual behavior in the 1930s was "liberated." After divorcing her first husband, Lou Sherman, Healey "was involved with a number of men."

> My relationships with men were not as uncomplicated as I thought. My "liberation" from conventional standards of female behavior did not consist so much of getting what I wanted in my private life as in not attaching a great deal of importance to what I was missing.[67]

Sex took on a functional form: "I had often slept with men not because I gave a damn about them but because it was the easiest way to establish friendships and because it reassured me of my attractiveness."

For Healey sex could and did become a political tool, rather than a personal choice, spiritual relationship, or act of "love." She recalled:

> There was one guy . . . with whom I lived for about two years. He was a seaman on steam schooners on the west coast. I stayed involved with Dutch for so long . . . because I felt it was my Party duty to do it. We needed to have a seaman stay on the beach. And he was lonely and he was one of our best members and if that's what he wanted, . . . then it was my Party duty to give him what he wanted.[68]

In retrospect, Healey described this as her "'Salvation Army' approach to love and marriage. You're bestowing yourself because that's what somebody else wants and what do you care?"[69] "Party duty," not mutual sexual attraction, motivated Healey's relationship with the sailor, thus sex had become a political labor rather than a personal pleasure. It was not only women who used their sexuality for instrumental purposes. Radical men also used sexuality as a tool for political and professional purposes. Apparently labor reporter and radical Harvey O'Connor sometimes had sex with the women he interviewed. Jessie Lloyd gave Harvey, her brand new lover, the OK to carry on with women "if it would help him in his business."[70]

While sexual relations often began outside the bonds of matrimony, marriage or permanent unions were frequently the result of such relationships. Couples decided whether they would be monogamous or have open relationships. Despite her initial relationship with the strident non-monogamist John Collier, Miriam deFord identified herself as a believer in monogamy, in the idea that there was only one significant life mate for her—Maynard Shipley, for whom she left Collier. Assuring Collier that although she would not sleep with him, she was still his "friend and well-wisher," deFord explained: "Fate made me a monogamist, and you not; you could not be my mate, and I have found him and am supremely happy with him; but you were the first man I ever loved, and you can never be the same to me as a lost acquaintance."[71] She explained in a letter to John, her "love" for him, now platonic, continued: "It is a beautiful feeling, and nothing for later and greater loves to be jealous of."[72] Miriam deFord's monogamy, commitment to maintaining emotional and social bonds with her ex-lover, and condemnation of jealousy were conscious political choices.

While perhaps not all leftists were as conscious in their choices, many shared with deFord a commitment to monogamy within their relationship(s). Communist Party activists LaRue McCormick, Marvel Cooke, and Peggy Dennis appear to have practiced monogamy with their respective partners. While that sexual fidelity may have allowed for occasional brief affairs or "slips," many leftists identified as couples to signify their commitment to their primary partner. Communists Fred and Doris Fine came to terms about their relationship when they were separated for the first time. During his military basic training, Fred had a sexual encounter with a female friend. Fred shamefully apologized for his "indefensible behaviour": "The sensible and mature way to react to the war's impact on one's private life and its attendant problems is surely not to look upon times as these as license for delayed adolescent tomfoolery." Concluding that, "I cant have the marriage and the distortions too," Fred thanked Doris for her "forbearance" and "lack of acrimonious 'spousely' accusations" in their discussions.[73]

For some radicals, a first marriage or partnership laid the groundwork for a second, more successful union. Like many of their generation, they married young and divorced before marrying again later in life. The second marriage or partnership often linked political activism and intellectual comradeship with sexual intimacy. Harvey O'Connor, for instance, married quite young and initially unhappily. Eight years into his marriage, he began an affair with Jessie Lloyd. Harvey and Jessie shared a commitment to labor writing and radical politics as well as a deep physical and emotional attachment. Subsequently Harvey obtained a divorce; and he and Jessie moved in together, creating a partnership which lasted over fifty years. While both Harvey and Jessie professed to having radical ideas about sexuality (Jessie described herself as "a free thinking, polyandrous girl"[74]), in effect, once together, they practiced what amounted to monogamy.

Other leftists did not seek a life partner. Margaret Larkin had a series of relationships, only the first man of which she married. Thyra Edwards had significant relationships as well as casual affairs with a variety of men, but she chose not to marry, as she saw marriage as restricting women's freedom. Some male radicals also rejected marriage. Joe Bianca and Hays Jones were union activists and communists who rejected the institution of marriage, not because it would restrict a woman's freedom, but because it would restrict their own. Wobbly anarchist and actor Ben Legere, who had children outside marriage with anarchist Mathilda Robbins and socialist Barbara Fenigston, had children with another woman, whom he married and subsequently divorced.[75]

Greenwich village radicals such as Floyd Dell, Hutchins Hapgood and Neith Boyce, Jack Reed and Louise Bryant were notorious for both promoting and experimenting in open relationships. The long-term affair between Rose Pesotta and Powers Hapgood was complicated by Hapgood's commitment to his wife, Mary Donovan, and her sexual possessiveness. As Hapgood wrote Pesotta,

> Our relationship deepens and we miss each other. We are growing closer and the more I know you, the more I love you and want to come to you and stay. But I have my children and I can't forget what a comrade Mary has been, participating in labor struggles, sharing jails with me, keeping house, and having a baby on miner's wages. I wish she wasn't so jealous.[76]

Needless to say, Hapgood's open marriage was one where he alone exercised sexual freedom. Such experiences often revealed the pesky contradictions of radical ideals and radical practices. Possessiveness in sexual relationships did not lessen simply because the principals declared the relationship open or refused to subject it to the sanctions of law. Tensions over partners' rights and privileges and the permissible boundaries of sexual love permeated the practice.

Sexual radicals were discomforted by lovers who exercised the same sexual rights. V. F. Calverton, Maynard Shipley, and John Collier all chafed under the knowledge that their primary sexual partner (in each case nonmarital heterosexual unions) found others sexually attractive, personally compatible, and emotionally engaging. As socialist-suffragist Miriam deFord recalled of her lover, "every time a man got interested in me, or I in him, I was 'entirely too fine a person to be having anything to do with that man.' The consequence was that I remained monogamous and he [Collier] not only slept with every woman that I've ever known him to know, but he brought them home. It got rather on my nerves."[77] Nonmonogamy, either formal or informal, practiced through serial monogamy, promiscuity, and extramarital affairs, was one alternative to conventional heterosexual marriage chosen by many in the radical community; homosexuality, a newly visible sexual choice, provided another.

In the radical community of the 1920s through the 1940s, there were a growing number of gays and lesbians active as writers, organizers, and rank-and-file activists. Heterosexual leftists reacted to their presence in a variety of ways. Disapproval of homosexuality was not confined to mainstream culture; homophobia was alive and well in the Left itself. Whether reacting to unwanted sexual advances or to fellow activists' sexual proclivities, leftists could be brutal towards their homosexual colleagues. Mary Heaton Vorse's rejection of Winifred Duncan's sexual advances was harsh and emotionally cruel. Accusing Duncan of being "pathological," Vorse pleaded for her to "stop writing," "stay away," and "cease nagging me and never let me see you or hear from you again."[78] Equally insulted at a sexual overture, writer Adolf Dehn remembered being "startled and disturbed" to realize that *Liberator* editor Claude McKay was "making homosexual" advances. Dehn abruptly cut off all contact with McKay.[79] Katherine Anne Porter, rather than offering support or a friendly ear to her long-time friend and compatriot Josephine Herbst, criticized her for her lesbian relationship with Marion Greenwood. African American journalist and Communist Party member Marvel Cooke explained that while Countee Cullen was a "very sweet person," he did not fit into her radical writing group: "It was rumored that he was homosexual. He just didn't seem to make it, you know, with the virulent crowd that we went with."[80]

Despite knowing gays and lesbians in the Party, some lesbian and gay radicals believed that the CP totally rejected homosexuality and

homosexuals. In 1939 Harold Norse, writing to ex-lover Chester Kall-
man and W. H. Auden, explained his decision to give up the communism
of his college days stating that the Party "doesn't take kindly to writers
and queers anyway. And what if they found out about David and me?
To the salt mines, dear."[81] Los Angeles radical activist Harry Hay
believed that the CP "strictly prohibited homosexuals from joining and
did not acknowledge homosexuality as anything more than the degenerate phase of a decadent system."[82]

Some gay radicals kept their politics separate from their sexual identity, believing in the separation of political and personal, public and private. Composer Aaron Copland, for example, was both a communist
activist and a sexually active gay man who was quiet about his personal life. While Copland lived with his partner, Victor Kraft, and attended
Left social functions with him, Copland did not publicly declare his
homosexuality or see it as a political issue. According to one musicolo-
gist, Copland "was not openly gay," because "he viewed sexuality, along
with family and other personal affairs, as private matters."[83] Ex–IWW
organizer and Heterodoxy member Elizabeth Gurley Flynn's private correspondence simply glossed over her lesbian relationship with Dr. Marie
Equi.[84] Other leftist gay men and lesbians were even more circumspect.
Group Theater director Cheryl Crawford's 1977 autobiography both hid
her lesbianism and downplayed her depression-era political values; poet
Muriel Rukeyser, while openly a communist, kept private who was the
father of her son (conceived outside of marriage) and her bisexuality.[85]

The attitudes and behavior of leftist gays and lesbians varied as much
as those of their heterosexual counterparts. While some lesbians and
gays internalized negative images of their sexuality, others participated
in gay cultural worlds,[86] believed that their homosexuality was normal,
natural and healthy, and acted accordingly. Communist Party member
and composer Marc Blitzstein exemplified gay male leftists who, in historian George Chauncey's terms, rejected "the dominant culture's view
of them as sick, perverted, and immoral."[87] While Blitzstein engaged in
sex exclusively with other men and identified as a homosexual, his sexuality did not interfere in his Cultural Front politics. Perhaps this is
because he chose to marry a woman friend as a "social gesture."[88] Leftist lesbian poet Elsa Gidlow had in common with Blitzstein a full self-
acceptance of her sexuality. Yet whereas Blitzstein married, Gidlow
refrained from such pretense of heterosexuality, believing that "I had a
right to be, to love, according to my nature."[89] Her poetry reflected her
construction of women's same-sex relationships and desires as perfectly
normal and fit for publication in mainstream literary journals.[90]

By all appearances, Anna Rochester and Grace Hutchins approached
their sexuality in the same way that Gidlow did hers. During the First

World War, Hutchins became a Socialist and went to work for the Fellowship of Reconciliation. In 1920 Hutchins and socialist pacifist Anna Rochester became lovers and remained together until Rochester's death in 1966. Both became communists in 1927 and subsequently focused on labor writing and fundraising for Left organizations. As a couple, Rochester and Hutchins formed a loving partnership.[91] They wrote publicly and privately of their love and commitment.[92]

Some gay men in the late 1920s through the early 1940s internalized mainstream American culture's view of them as unhealthy, immoral, and perverted. Evidencing shock at the suicide of gay musician George Edwards, John Collier asked his ex-wife Miriam deFord for the "particulars and details" of Edwards's death. Collier explained:

> I was very fond of Geo Edwards—in spite of our pronounced differences—and respected him for his manly attitude and defense of his unpopular tendencies and principles. I thought that, like Edward Carpenter, he believed in the righteousness of his sexual variations. And I thought that the girl who had been so long in love with him, married him with understanding and acceptance of his congenital ways of sex expression.[93]

Miriam deFord responded that, despite Edwards's defense of his sexual orientation, he allowed himself to be "psycho-analyzed" by what she described as a "totally untrained and incompetent" analyst. He "told George he had cured him of homosexuality and made him normal; on that premise, George married Beth." The marriage was not a success. According to deFord, Edwards realized that the trappings of heterosexuality, including a child, over whom he "was wild," did not make him straight. He returned to seeking sex with men. His wife's response was to demand "slavish adoration," spend money at a "fearfully extravagant" rate, make fun of Edwards's musical pursuits, and grow "sloppy and careless and even dirty, so that George was ashamed to go out with her." The two divorced, and Beth was given custody of their child. Miriam deFord was unclear if Edwards's suicide was brought on by self-loathing after he "gradually . . . began to go back to what he always had been" or by Edwards's despair that "the court allowed him to see his little boy" just once a week.[94] Similarly, poet Harold Norse had problems accepting his own sexuality. Brought out by a bisexual college professor who assured Norse that sex with and love for other men was "natural," not "criminal," sick, or evil, Norse acknowledged he was homosexual but for years believed that somehow he was "abnormal."[95]

The question is whether leftist activists who chose not to come out or to act on their sexual orientation had fully internalized society's view of non-heterosexual activity as depraved. Given conflicting evidence, there is no clear answer. Harry Hay recounted being drawn into the Communist Party through his then lover, gay communist organizer and actor Will Geer. Like Hay, Geer chose to marry in 1938 after having been both a Party activist and actively gay for at least four years. It is unclear if Geer's marriage to Herta Ware signaled an end to his male-to-male sexual activity, or if Geer married because he believed that the Communist Party "strictly prohibited homosexuals from joining."[96] We do know, however, that Geer was somewhat honest with Herta about his sexuality. At Geer's funeral in 1974, perhaps still smarting at having lost Geer to Herta a quarter century before, Harry Hay exclaimed to her, "I had him first." To which she replied, "I had him longest."[97]

Gays and lesbians on the Left, like their heterosexual counterparts, made choices in terms of how they viewed their personal lives, their sexuality, and politics. Alone and celibate in New York in 1920, Elsa Gidlow wrote "As Usual," an ironic poem which emphasized her belief that love was stronger and more important than religious or political ideals. The line, "lovers never think of creeds,"[98] expressed Gidlow's life-long pattern of relationships which crossed class and political boundaries. Her first lover in New York was Muriel Symington, a fellow Canadian immigrant, who was a "British conservative in her feelings and beliefs."[99] Gidlow's second long-term lover, Violet (Tommy) Henry-Anderson was "a loyal daughter of the British Empire" uncomfortable with revolutionary politics. Although Gidlow engaged in the "polemics and politics" of New York's ethnic communities and formed friendships with Indian Nationalists, she explained that "these differences between us did not have any adverse effect on our relationship."[100] Similarly, when their "loyalty to and love of women, influences from our English heritage, mutual devotion to the earth and to gardening" drew Gidlow and Anglo-African Isabel Grenfell Quallo together, Gidlow did not let their racial differences or Isabel's Catholicism keep them separate.[101]

Gidlow's belief that love and relationships should come before politics stood in contrast to Communist Party activist and actor Harry Hay, who would not stay with a lover who did not share his radical idealism. Hay later recalled:

> I was caught up in the Marxist notion that "man makes himself."
> The simple involvements of domesticity, which both Walter and Stanley insisted upon, were simply *not good enough*! On this point, all my lovers and I (except Will Geer and three others I would meet in the future) were at loggerheads.[102]

While Hay searched for a lover and finally settled on a wife who would work by his side in the revolution, other gay and lesbian radicals tried to incorporate their sexuality into their politics in different ways. Marc Blitzstein was consciously aware of the issues involved in sexual politics and the politics of his sexuality. He did not consider his sexual orientation something of which to be ashamed or as contradictory to his revolutionary politics and membership in the CP. While Blitzstein may not have told straight Communist Party men that he was gay, he believed that he should portray all those involved in the revolutionary struggle as "warm" and "healthy about sex"; and he experimented with including gay characters in his work.[103]

As with their heterosexual counterparts, there was considerable complexity in the sexual choices of gay and lesbian leftists. Their practices included celibacy, monogamy, serial monogamy, and nonmonogamy. Weavers singer Lee Hays, according to biographer Doris Willens, chose celibacy.[104] Monogamy or serial monogamy seems to have been the choice of some Left gay couples, including Anna Rochester and Grace Hutchins, their socialist pacifist friends Ruth Erickson and Eleanor Stephenson, and Aaron Copland and Victor Kraft; but monogamy was not the only choice.

Within the nonmonogamous set, there were differences between those who engaged in occasional affairs and those who engaged in promiscuity or, as one historian defined it, "erotic excesses . . . that sometimes had an aspect of desperation more than pleasure."[105] In the first category was Elsa Gidlow who, while primarily serially monogamous, maintained both the theory and practice of open relationships.[106] In contrast to her variations on monogamy, Marc Blitzstein had completely open relationships. He was quite frank about his sexual encounters and his affection for other men. According to Gordon, Blitzstein did not "put any stock in fidelity as an institution"; and most of his friends knew it. He continued to pick up "rough trade" (sailors, soldiers, working-class toughs) and his "habit of going to the Everard Baths." Like many of us, Blitzstein at times had problems separating his intellectual belief in nonmonogamy from jealous reaction when hearing of his lover Bill Hewett's sexual liaisons with other men.[107]

Some gay leftists faced a variety of hazards which set them apart from lesbian and heterosexual activists. Not only did they encounter violence in the form of "queer bashing," but they ran the risk of public humiliation if arrested for soliciting sex, and the additional risk of serious jail time if they were caught or accused of having sex with an underage boy. These were not minor problems; the threats were real. Gay men spoke among themselves of their common fears of picking up the wrong man (or men) in bars or beaches and being assaulted.[108] Poet Harold Norse recalled picking up a "very handsome blond youth" who, it turned out, got his sexual kicks by beating gay men unconscious with brass knuckles.[109] California composer, editor of *New Music,* and radical Paul Cowell served four years in San Quentin when a young man with whom he had been sexually involved turned him in to the police.[110] In the eyes of most radicals, it was one thing to be arrested, convicted, and jailed for union or radical protesting or rent strike activity. But to be arrested in a public bathroom or park for solicitation or to be accused of indecent liberties with a minor could not be construed as in any way furthering the revolution.

Just as politics influenced the sex lives of leftist gays and lesbians, so could their sexuality influence their politics. When in 1939 Harold Norse coined the term "Homintern," he was only playing with language. As Norse explained, he came up with the term as "a takeoff on Comintern (Communist International), it was meant to convey the idea of a global homosexual community," which did not then exist.[111] In 1948 Harry Hay was more serious about creating such an association of gays and linking his communist training and analytic skills with his experience as a gay man. Hay's prospectus for an international gay rights organization, initially called "International Bachelors' Fraternal Order for Peace and Social Dignity," which evolved into the Mattachine Society, was based on the idea that gays were an "oppressed cultural minority" and drew from the "analysis, models, and specific policies that the Party had promulgat[ed]" concerning African-Americans.[112] Not just Harry Hay, but other Mattachine founders and early members had ties to the Left. Chuck Rowland was a World War II veteran who joined the CP while organizing for the American Veterans Committee. He left the party in 1948 for personal rather than political reasons. He was tired of the "total dedication" he believed the party required and "was getting very little sex" and "didn't have a lover." Both he and his then-lover, Bob Hull, a practicing chemist and ex-Communist, joined Hay in organizing Mattachine.[113] Similarly, Jim Kepner recalled that it was his "Marxist background" which led him to believe that gay men, by organizing, could change society's views. He too joined Mattachine.[114] Radical lawyer Pearl Hart transferred her knowledge and experience learned while a lawyer for the Chicago Branch of the American Committee to Protect Foreign-Born to defending the civil rights of lesbians and gays during the 1950s. She wrote "Your Rights If Arrested" for *One* magazine, acted as legal advisor for Mattachine's Chicago Area Council, and organized Mattachine Midwest in the 1960s.[115] Similarly, Elsa Gidlow wrote articles for *The Ladder* and contributed poetry and prose to a variety of early lesbian and feminist journals.[116]

❖ ❖ ❖

This essay illustrates the contradictory and complex character of sexual attitudes, identities, and politics among radicals in the United States between 1919 and 1945. Far from being a single narrative spoken in a singular voice, the sexual history of radicalism was experienced and expressed in diverse ways. The evidence we have presented of tensions between pressures for social conformity and political respectability on the one hand and desires for sexual autonomy and freedom on the other fracture the previously impoverished understanding of the American Left in this crucial period and lay the groundwork for new explorations in Left sexual history. While historians have argued that Left radicals—and communist parties in particular—were sexually repressive, socially conservative, and sexist in their policies toward gender equality and sexual freedom, our research leads us to believe that rhetoric and experience on the Left often stood in opposition to each other. What leftists would privately express or act upon was often not practiced in public nor formulated in policy. This was true both of the Left's implicit tolerance of a range of sexual practices (never consenting to the idea of a single "proletarian revolutionary stance toward sex" and often working with and forming personal bonds among both straight and gay/lesbian radicals) and of the Left's position on the Woman Question. As a matter of practice, the Left may have been more tolerant of gay/lesbian comrades than of public feminists in its ranks. In contrast the depression-era Left embraced masculinist ideas about solidarity and emphasized male bonding.

A second finding emerges from the evidence of Left sexual attitudes and practices. Many post–World War II proponents of women's equality and supporters of sexual emancipation, and especially of gay/lesbian liberation, were schooled in the depression-era Left, despite its reputed sexual conservatism. Learning tools of analysis, political organizing skills, and the language of oppression and liberation, Mattachine Society founders began to formulate ideas about gay liberation. Much feminist theory in the post–World War II era also drew upon the earlier ideas and experiences of the interwar Left.[117] Perhaps most importantly, the political self-respect and cultural self-confidence required of all those who would fight for an alternative sexual future were learned by some on the Left, just as ideas about alternative sexual relationships and identities were fostered in their reading, discussions, and political work.

Throughout American society in the years between World War I and the cold war, men and women experienced new tensions in sexual and gender relations. The cataclysms of war and depression, cultural change in the range of sexual identities and experiences, and emerging political alternatives all helped to transform the sexual order. Those who felt the new pressures most keenly had little knowledge and no experience in how to transform these feelings into political action or even how to name them. The introduction of the new sexology presented some alternatives; so too did ideas and examples drawn from the successful socialist revolution in Russia. More important in developing a sexual politics for the postwar world was the working out in daily practice of sexual relationships and ideas in conjunction with the evolving left politics. In study groups, informal discussions, correspondence and shared reading, both sex radicals and political activists learned tools to analyze and rethink sexual politics and redefine the nature of radical politics. Their "outlaw emotions," to use a phrase from philosopher Alison Jaggar, feelings unsanctioned either by formal left organizations or by the wider society, helped open up the possibilities of both radicalism and sexual politics in the postwar world.

NOTES

1. Thyra Edwards to Etha Bell, 14 April 1934, 1:1, Thyra Edwards Papers, Chicago Historical Society, Chicago. See Rima Schultz, "Thyra J. Edwards," in *Chicago Women, 1770-1990: A Biographical Dictionary,* ed. Adele Hast and Rima Lunin Schultz (Bloomington: Indiana University Press, 2001); Beth Tomkins Bates, "'The Unfinished Task of Emancipation': Protest Politics Come of Age in Chicago, 1925–1943," (Ph.D. diss., Columbia University, 1997), 255–304.

2. Thyra Edwards to Etha Bell, 14 April 1934, 1:1, Edwards Papers.

3. See Mari Jo Buhle, *Women and American Socialism, 1870–1920* (Urbana: University of Illinois Press, 1981); Linda Gordon, *Woman's Body, Woman's Right: A Social History of Birth Control in America* (New York: Grossman Publishers, 1976); Nancy F. Cott, *The Grounding of Modern Feminism* (New Haven: Yale University Press, 1987).

4. This was one of the major complaints of John Darmstadt (pseud. John Collier), "The Sexual Revolution," *Modern Quarterly* 4:2 (1927) reprint (not paginated), Box 2, ff "The Sexual Revolution," Collier Papers, part I, Archive of Labor and Urban Affairs, Wayne State University (hereafter cited as ALUA).

5. See Elsa Jane Dixler, "The Woman Question: Women and the American Communist Party, 1929–1941" (Ph.D. diss., Yale University, 1974), 25–85; Leonard Wilcox, *V. F. Calverton: Radical in the American Grain* (Philadelphia: Temple University Press, 1992), 47–97; Philip Abbott, *Leftward Ho! V. F. Calverton and American Radicalism,* Contributions in Political Science 315 (Westport, CT: Greenwood Press, 1993), esp. 19–56. See also Paula Rabinowitz, *Labor and Desire: Women's Revolutionary Fiction in Depression America,* Gender and American Culture series, (Chapel Hill: University of North Carolina Press, 1992), on treatment of issues of female subjectivity and sexuality as frivolous.

6. Benjamin Vestal Hubbard, *Feminism, Socialism, Suffragism, the Terrible Triplets: Connected by the Same Umbilical Cord, and Fed from the Same Nursing*

Bottle (Chicago: American Publishers, 1915), 83, 8. See also Richard Merrill Whitney, *Reds in America: The Present Status of the Revolutionary Movement in the United States based on documents seized by the authorities in the raid upon the Convention of the Communist Party at Bridgman, Michigan, August 22, 1922, together with descriptions of numerous connections and associations of the Communists among the Radicals, Progressives and Pinks* (1923; reprint, Belmont, MA: Western Islans Pub., 1970; references to reprint edition), 16; Blair Coan, *The Red Web: An Underground Political History of the United States from 1918 to the Present Time showing how Close the Government is to Collapse and told in an Understandable Way* (1925; reprint, Boston: Western Islands Pub., 1969), vii, 104, 180; Samuel Saloman, *The Red War on the Family* (New York, 1922), 32, 65; Elizabeth Dilling, *The Roosevelt Red Record and Its Background,* (Kenilworth, IL: self-published, 1936), 25, 28, 143–44; Elizabeth Dilling, *The Red Network: A Who's Who and Handbook of Radicalism for Patriots* (Kenilworth, IL: self-published, 1934), 27–28, 91–92, 126–27.

7. Saloman, *Red War on the Family,* 25; Whitney, *Reds in America,* 16. See also Coan, *The Red Web,* vii, 104, 180.

8. Saloman, *Red War on the Family,* 67–92; Joseph J. Mereto, *The Red Conspiracy* (New York: Natural History Society, 1920), 163–68. Writer George Seldes traced the original charge that women had been nationalized in the Soviet Union to the London *Times,* according to historian Peter G. Filene, *Americans and the Soviet Experiment, 1917–1933* (Cambridge, MA: Harvard University Press, 1967), 46–47, and n. It appeared in such publications as the *New York Times,* 26 October 1918, 5:5; *Congressional Record,* 65th Congress, 3rd Session, 24 January 1919, 1970–71; and "Nationalization of Women in Russia: New Documentary Evidence," *Current History,* 13 October 1920, 169–71. There were denials as well. See, for example, Jerome Davis, "Nationalization of Women—A Hoax," *New York Times,* 23 February 1919; and "Fair Play for Russia," *The Public* (Chicago), 1 March 1919, both reprinted in Philip S. Foner, ed., *The Bolshevik Revolution, Its Impact on American Radicals, Liberals, and Labor: A Documentary Study* (New York: International Publishers, 1967), 162–65. Filene notes private correspondence on the issue.

9. Whitney, *Reds in America,* 16; Dilling, *Roosevelt Red Record,* 25, 143–44; Saloman, *Red War on the Family.*

10. Dilling, *Red Network,* 221–22; Dilling, *Roosevelt Red Record,* 46–47, 194–201, 221, 249–52, 277–78.

11. V. F. Calverton, *The Bankruptcy of Marriage* (London: John Hamilton, 1931). See also Ben Lindsay and Wainwright Evans, *Companionate Marriage* (New York: Boni and Liveright, 1927). For the historical interpretation, see Christina Clare Simmons, "'Marriage in the Modern Manner': Sexual Radicalism and Reform in America, 1914–1941" (Ph.D. diss., Brown University, 1982); Elaine Tyler May, *Great Expectations: Marriage and Divorce in Post–Victorian America* (Chicago: University of Chicago Press, 1980); John D'Emilio and Estelle B. Freedman, *Intimate Matters: A History of Sexuality in America* (New York: Perennial Library, 1989), 222–300; Carroll Smith-Rosenberg, *Disorderly Conduct: Visions of Gender in Victorian America* (New York: Knopf, 1985), 245–96; George Chauncey, *Gay New York: Gender, Urban Culture, and the Making of the Gay Male World, 1890–1940,* (New York: Basic Books, 1994); Sharon R. Ullman, *Sex Seen: The Emergence of Modern Sexuality in America* (Berkeley: University of California Press, 1997). On sexual frankness, see Ann Douglas, *Terrible Honesty: Mongrel Manhattan in the 1920s* (New York: Farrar, Straus, Giroux, 1995), 30–41.

12. See Dixler, "The Woman Question," 1–29.

13. See, for example, Miriam Allen deFord to Armistead Collier, 18 July 1927, "Have you read Mme Kollontay's [*sic*] *Red Love?*," Box 1, ff "Miriam Allen deFord, Correspondence and Miscellany, 1915–1927," part 1, Collier Papers. Alexandra Kollontai's writings on marriage and divorce are excerpted as an appendix to Saloman, *Red War on the Family*, 166–78, an anticommunist tract, but Kollontai is also discussed approvingly in Calverton, *Bankruptcy of Marriage*, 294–99. See also Louise Bryant, *Mirrors of Moscow* (New York: T. Seltzer, 1923), 111–28; Anna Porter, *A Moscow Diary* (Chicago: C. H. Kerr, 1926); Jessica Smith, *Women in Soviet Russia* (New York: Vangrand, 1928), among others. Ella Winter, *Red Virtue: Human Relationships in the New Russia* (New York: Harcourt, Brace & Co., 1933), captures the changes in the Soviet Union since Stalin's ascent to power. Kollontai's fiction, including *Red Love* (New York, 1927; later published as *The Love of Worker Bees*) and her tracts on *Workers Opposition in Russia* (Chicago: IWW, 1921) and *Communism and the Family* (New York: Western Worker and Toiler, 1920). See also Filene, *Americans and the Soviet Experiment*, esp. 46–47, 141–42, 246–47, on women, the family, free love.

14. Dorothy Ray Healey and Maurice Isserman, *Dorothy Healey Remembers: A Life in the American Communist Party* (New York: Oxford University Press, 1990), 30. Healey may misremember the source of the story. Nadezhda K. Krupskaya, *Memories of Lenin* (New York: International Publishers, 1930), would have been available, but most historical sources credit Clara Zetkin with the tale. See Winter, *Red Virtue*, 115–16; Dixler, "The Woman Question," 14–17, among others. For the original, see Klara Zetkin, *Reminiscences of Lenin* (New York: International Publishers, 1934). On other ideas about sexuality in the USSR, see H. Kent Geiger, *The Family in Soviet Russia* (Cambridge, MA: Harvard University Press, 1968), 61–71.

15. Alexandra Kollontai, "Make Way for Winged Eros: A Letter to Working Youth," in *Selected Writings of Alexandra Kollontai*, trans. with an introduction and commentaries by Alix Holt (Westport, CT: Greenwood Publishers, 1977), 276–92, quote from 285.

16. Darmstadt, "Sexual Revolution."

17. See Wilcox, *V. F. Calverton*, 47–86; Abbott, *Leftward Ho!*, 19–49. Malcolm Cowley's contributions, "Sex Boys in a Balloon," *New Republic* 65 (15 January 1930), and "Oedipus: The Future of Love," *New Republic* 66 (March 1930), demonized Calverton, Dell, and Darmstadt (Collier) as "sex renegades" and their "erotic pantheism" as destructive of revolutionary aims.

18. See Freda Kirchwey, ed., *Our Changing Morality, A Symposium* (New York: Albert and Charles Boni, 1924); V. F. Calverton and Samuel D. Schmalhausen, eds., *Sex in Civilization* (New York: Macaulay Co., 1929); Samuel D. Schmalhausen and V. F. Calverton, eds., *Woman's Coming of Age: A Symposium* (New York: Horace Liveright, 1931).

19. See June Sochen, *The New Woman: Feminism in Greenwich Village, 1910–1920* (New York: Quadrangle, 1972); Judith Schwarz, *The Radical Feminists of Heterodoxy, Greenwich Village, 1912–1940*, rev. ed. (Norwich, CT: New Victoria Pub., 1986); Kate E. Wittenstein, "The Heterodoxy Club and American Feminism, 1912–1930" (Ph.D. diss., Boston University, 1989); Ann Blankenhorn, "Fact-finding," manuscript, 2:2–15, Ann Heber Blankenhorn Papers, ALUA.

20. For a summary of this literature, see Kathleen A. Brown, "The 'Savagely Fathered and Unmothered World' of the Communist Party, U.S.A.: Feminism, Maternalism, and 'Mother Bloor,'" *Feminist Studies* 25:3 (Fall 1999): 537–70. On the writings of LeSueur and Olsen, see Constance Coiner, *Better Red: The Writing and Resistance of Tillie Olsen and Meridel LeSueur* (Urbana: University of Illinois Press,

1995); Rabinowitz, *Labor and Desire*; Michael Denning, *The Cultural Front: The Laboring of American Culture* (New York: Verso, 1997), 136–51; Linn Shapiro, "Red Feminism: American Communism and the Women's Rights Tradition, 1919–1956" (Ph.D. diss, American University, 1996), 155–259.

21. Emma Goldman, "The Unjust Treatment of Homosexuals; 'No daring is required to protest against a great injustice,'" in Jonathan Katz, *Gay American History: Lesbians and Gay Men in the U.S.A., A Documentary* (New York: Thomas Y. Crowell, 1976), 376–77. See also Gert Hekma, Harry Oosterhuis, James Steakley, "Leftist Sexual Politics and Homosexuality," *Journal of Homosexuality* 29:2/3 (1995), special issue, "Gay Men and the Sexual History of the Political Left," 1–40; Hubert Kennedy, "Johann Baptist von Schweitzer: The Queer Marx Loved to Hate," ibid., 69–96.

22. Ella Winter, "No Gold Diggers," *New Masses* 10 (13 February 1934): 27, quoted in Dixler, "Woman Question," 52.

23. The basic argument here is drawn from Dixler, "Woman Question," 1–126, where she traces out the changes in both the Left's ideology and its culture. On homosexuality, see Dixler, 43–48, where she discusses expulsions from the party and the homophobia of the Left. On the masculine "complex" of labor and the Left, see Elizabeth Faue, "The 'Dynamo of Change': Gender and Solidarity in the American Labour Movement of the 1930s," *Gender and History* 1:2 (Summer 1989): 138–58. See Winter, *Red Virtue*, for an American take on the changes in the Soviet Union's gender and family policy under Stalin.

24. Earl Browder, "The People's Front Moves Forward," *Communist* 16 (December 1937): 1101, quoted in Dixler, 40.

25. Eugene V. Dennett, *Agitprop: The Life of An American Working-Class Radical* (Albany: State University of New York Press, 1990), 4.

26. Healey and Isserman, *Dorothy Healey Remembers*, 25.

27. Peggy Dennis, *The Autobiography of an American Communist: A Personal View of a Political Life, 1925–1975* (Berkeley: University of California Press, 1977), 17–18.

28. John J. Abt, with Michael Myerson, *Advocate and Activist: Memoirs of an American Communist Lawyer* (Urbana: University of Illinois Press, 1993), 9.

29. Bets Bickel to Harvey O'Connor, 14 April 1922, 11:60, part 2, Harvey O'Connor Papers, ALUA.

30. Healey and Isserman, *Dorothy Healey Remembers*, 28, 38.

31. Junius Irving Scales and Richard Nickson, *Cause at Heart: A Former Communist Remembers* (Athens: University of Georgia Press, 1987) 176.

32. Elsa Gidlow, *Elsa, I Come with My Songs: The Autobiography of Elsa Gidlow* (San Francisco: Druid Heights Books and Booklegger Press, 1986), 177.

33. Lucy Fox Robins Lang, *Tomorrow is Beautiful* (New York: Macmillan, 1948), 22.

34. Cheryl Crawford, *One Naked Individual: My Fifty Years in the Theatre* (Indianapolis: Bobbs-Merrill Co., 1977), 8, 7, 10, 11.

35. Harold Norse, *Memoirs of a Bastard Angel* (New York: William Morrow and Co., 1989), 40–41, 91.

36. Whitman's homosexuality was certainly acknowledged in sectors beyond Goldman. Dr. W. C. Rivers, *Walt Whitman's Anomaly,* a pamphlet which argued the case, was published in 1913. See Martin Duberman, comp., *About Time: Exploring the Gay Past*, revised and expanded edition, (New York: Meridian Books, 1994), 106–20. On the importance for the gay subculture of Whitman, see Chauncey, *Gay New York*, 104–105, 284–85.

298 ■ Brown and Faue

37. For an overview of the nineteenth-century legacy of sexual radicalism in the United States, see Taylor Stoehr, comp., *Free Love: A Documentary History* (New York: AMS Press, 1979); Hal Sears, *The Sex Radicals: Free Love in Victorian America* (Lawrence: Regents Press of Kansas, 1977); Margaret S. Marsh, *Anarchist Women, 1870–1920* (Philadelphia: Temple University Press, 1981), 65–99; Ellen Carol DuBois and Linda Gordon, "Seeking Ecstasy on the Battlefield: Danger and Pleasure in Nineteenth-Century Feminist Thought," in Carole S. Vance, ed., *Pleasure and Danger: Exploring Female Sexuality* (Boston: Routledge and Kegan Paul, 1984), 31–49. For the European background, see Jonathan Beecher, *Charles Fourier: The Visionary and His World* (Berkeley: University of California Press, 1986); Philip Abbott, "Charles Fourier and the Regime of Love," in his *The Family on Trial: Special Relationships in Modern Political Thought* (University Park: Penn State University Press, 1981), 59–71; Claire G. Moses, "Saint-Simonian Men/Saint-Simonian Women: The Transformation of Feminist Thought in 1830s' France," *Journal of Modern History* 54 (June 1982): 24–67; Barbara Taylor, *Eve and the New Jerusalem: Socialism and Feminism in the Nineteenth Century* (New York: Pantheon, 1983); Saskia Poldervaart, "Theories about Sex and Sexuality in Utopian Socialism," *Journal of Homosexuality* 29:2/3 (1995): 41–67.

38. Floyd Dell to "Dear Darmstadt," 23 March 1927, Box 2: ff "Revolution and Sex, Floyd Dell 1927," part I, Collier Papers; Stuart Timmons, *The Trouble with Harry Hay, Founder of the Modern Gay Movement* (Boston: Alyson Pub., 1990), 27–28; Gidlow, *Elsa*, 72–73; Simmons, "Marriage in the Modern Manner," 58–104; Fishbein, *Rebels in Bohemia*, 74–112. See also Sheila Rowbotham and Jeffrey Weeks, *Socialism and the New Life: The Personal and Sexual Politics of Edward Carpenter and Havelock Ellis* (London: Pluto Press, 1977); Bonnie Haaland, *Emma Goldman: Sexuality and the Impurity of the State* (New York: Black Rose Books, 1993). John Collier laid claim to having read Carpenter at the same time he read Kropotkin. John Darmstadt to Floyd Dell, 16 April 1927, Box 2: ff "Revolution and Sex, Floyd Dell 1927," part I, Collier Papers. Note, however, Ann Blankenhorn wrote that while she "flung" *Love's Coming of Age*, among other books, at her friends to read, she had not read it herself. Ann Blankenhorn, "Chapter 1 Turning to the Left," manuscript autobiography, Box 1, ff 1–21, Ann Blankenhorn Papers.

39. Dorothy (Ray) to Marna Leigh [Phyllis Fenigston], 21 June 1934, Box 27, ff 27:36 Corres; Dorothy (Ray) Healy, 1934, 1966, 1967, part II, Collier papers.

40. Jeffrey Weeks, *Sexuality* (London: Tavistock, 1986), 74–75, quoted in Haaland, *Emma Goldman*, 141.

41. Simmons, "Marriage in the Modern Manner"; Kathy Peiss and Christina Simmons, eds, *Passion and Power: Sexuality in History* (Philadelphia: Temple University Press, 1989), esp. George Chauncey, "From Sexual Inversion to Homosexuality: The Changing Medical Conceptualization of Female 'Deviance,'" 87–117, and Christina Simmons, "Modern Sexuality and the Myth of Victorian Sexual Repression," 157–77; Rowbotham and Weeks, *Socialism and the New Life*; Haaland, *Emma Goldman*; Mari Jo Buhle, *Feminism and its Discontents: A Century of Struggle with Psychoanalysis* (Cambridge, MA: Harvard University Press, 1998), 22–124; Lucy Bland and Laura Doan, eds., *Sexology and Culture: Labelling Bodies and Desires* (Chicago: University of Chicago Press, 1998).

42. Christina Simmons argument that retaining "a Victorian sexual self-definition" was not unusual for women in the 1920s and 1930s fits the experience of these women. D'Emilio and Freedman, *Intimate Matters*, 241; Simmons, "Modern Sexuality and the Myth of Victorian Repression," in *Passion and Power*, 170.

43. Carol Jean Newman interview, quoted in Healey and Isserman, *Healey Remembers*, 38.

44. Ibid., 19. Dorothy's recollected awaking "in the middle of the night once and hearing my mother saying 'No, no, no, not again!'" (20).

45. D'Emilio and Freedman, *Intimate Matters,* 241.

46. Theodora Gidlow to Elsa Gidlow, 17 August 1920, 1: "Gidlow, Theodora . . . (1 of 2)," Gidlow Papers.

47. Theodora Gidlow to Elsa Gidlow, 28 August 1920, 1: "Gidlow, Theodora . . . (1 of 2)," Gidlow Papers.

48. Theodora Gidlow to Elsa Gidlow, May 1922, 1: "Gidlow, Theodora . . . (1 of 2)," Gidlow Papers.

49. Thyra Edwards to Etha Bell, 14 April 1934, 1:1, Edwards Papers.

50. Thyra Edwards to Thelma, 3 November 1939, 1:3, Edwards Papers.

51. Jane Foster, *An Un-American Lady* (London: Sidgwick & Jackson, 1980), 53–54, 68, 74, 81, 82.

52. Ibid., 127, 136, 160.

53. Simmons, "Modern Sexuality," in *Passion and Power,* 169–70.

54. Coiner, *Better Red,* 87–89.

55. Vera Buch Weisbord, *A Radical Life* (Bloomington: Indiana University Press, 1977), 56, 85, 115–16, 120, 136.

56. Charles Shipman, *It Had to Be Revolution: Memoirs of an American Radical,* with a foreword by Harvey Klehr, Studies in Soviet History and Society Series (Ithaca, NY: Cornell University Press., 1993), 19.

57. Ibid., 127, 136, 160.

58. Al Richmond, *Long View from the Left,* 198. See also Herald Ruttenberg, "Monday, April 30, 1934," typewritten notes re 30 April–1 May 1934 Steel Workers Convention, 17:95, part 2, O'Connor Papers; Marjorie Penn Lasky, "'Where I was a Person': The Ladies Auxiliary in the 1934 Minneapolis Truckers' Strike," in *Women, Work and Protest: A Century of U.S. Women's Labor History,* ed. Ruth Milkman (Boston: Routledge and Kegan Paul, 1985), 181–205.

59. See, for instance, "Jaze" Hays Jones to Harvey O'Connor, 26 Sept 1922, 14:48, part 2, O'Connor Papers.

60. "Jaze" Hays Jones to Harvey O'Connor, 24 June 1919, 14: 47, part 2, O'Connor Papers.

61. Barney Mayes, autobiographical manuscript, typewritten (photocopy), untitled, n.d., LARC. Similarly, socialist Marx Lewis and communist Ben Gold had little time for the "collision" of marriage or even affection. See Marx Lewis to Phyllis Fenigston, 23 December 1923, Box 27, ff 27:14, Corres; Marx Lewis, part II, Collier papers; also Phyllis's letter to John Collier on her new lover, Ben Gold: "He said he couldn't give love, and that that was one of the sacrifices he had to make in his life." See Phyllis to "My darling Sweet" (To J.A. in Boston), 11 July 1927, Box 25, ff 25:14, Corres; Phyllis Collier, part II, Collier Papers.

62. Hank Rubin, *Spain's Cause was Mine: A Memoir of an American Medic in the Spanish Civil War,* (Carbondale: Southern Illinois University Press, 1997), 46.

63. Ibid., 134, 135.

64. Carlos Bulosan, *America is in the Heart* (1946; reprint Seattle: University of Washington Press, 1973; reference to reprint ed.), 135–36.

65. Nicolass Steelink to Fannie, 3 June 1920, 1:1, Nicolass Steelink Collection, ALUA. See also Basha de Ward to Harvey O'Connor, 8 December 1932, 9:9, Part 2, O'Connor Papers; and Horace Davis to Harvey O'Connor, 2 July 1952, 13:4, part 2, O'Connor Papers. On companionate marriage see Carroll Binder to Dorothy Walton Binder, 5 October 1923, Binder Papers.

66. Kathleen A. Brown and Elizabeth Faue, "Social Bonds, Sexual Politics, and

Political Community on the U.S. Left, 1920s–1940s," *Left History* 7:1 (Spring 2000): 9–45.

67. Healey and Isserman, *Dorothy Healey Remembers*, 66–67.

68. Ibid., 67.

69. Ibid.

70. Jessie Lloyd to Harvey O'Connor, Tuesday 26 July 1929, 17:3, part 2, O'Connor Papers. Elinor Langer, Josephine Herbst's biographer, provides interesting insight into William Phillips's use the use of sexuality as a political and professional tool. See Langer, *Josephine Herbst*, 198. See Joan Mellen, *Hellman and Hammett: The Legendary Passion of Lillian Hellman and Dashiell Hammett* (New York: Harper Collins, 1996), 40.

71. Miriam deFord to Armistead Collier, 9 May 1921, 25:5, part II, Collier Papers.

72. Miriam deFord to Armistead Collier, 25 September 1922, 25:10, part II, Collier Papers.

73. Fred Fine to Doris Fine, 5 May 1942, 2: "1942 (March–July)," Fred Fine Collection, Chicago Historical Society, Chicago.

74. Jessie Lloyd to Harvey O'Connor, 4 September 1929, 17:1, part 2, O'Connor Papers.

75. On Legere's complex family life and unusual string of sexual unions, see the Collier papers, the Mathilda Robbins papers, and the Ben Legere papers, all in ALUA.

76. Powers Hapgood to Rose Pesotta, 24 February 1937, 10:11, Pesotta Papers, quoted in Elaine Leeder, *The Gentle General: Rose Pesotta, Anarchist and Labor Organizer* (Albany: State University of New York Press, 1993), 133.

77. Miriam Allen deFord, "On the Soapbox," in *From Parlor to Prison: Five American Suffragists Talk about Their Lives,* ed. Sherna Gluck (New York: Vintage, 1976), 159. See Miriam deFord to Phyllis Fenigston, 26 July 1927, Box 27, ff 27:10 Corres; Miriam Allen deFord, part II, Collier Papers.

78. Mary Heaton Vorse to Winifred Duncan, 3 October 1926, box 58: "1926—July–Dec.," Mary Heaton Vorse Papers, ALUA.

79. Adolf Dehn to Wayne Cooper, 14 January, 1964, quoted in Wayne Cooper, *Claude McKay, Rebel Sojourner in the Harlem Renaissance: A Biography,* reprint, (New York, 1990), 150–51.

80. *Interviews with Marvel Cooke, Recorded by Kathleen Currie for The Washington Press Club Foundation as part of its oral history project Women in Journalism* (Washington, D.C.: The Washington Press Club Foundation, 1990), 49–50.

81. "David" is a pseudonym. Norse, *Memoirs of a Bastard Angel*, 77.

82. Timmons, *Trouble with Harry Hay.*

83. Jennifer L. DeLapp, "Copland in the Fifties: Music and Ideology in the McCarthy Era" (Ph.D. diss., University of Michigan, 1997), 76. Or as a biographer of Bernstein put it, Copland "never flaunted his homosexuality in the way certain of his friends did." Humphrey Burton, *Leonard Bernstein* (New York: Anchor Books, Doubleday, 1995), 43.

84. Elizabeth Gurley Flynn to Mary Heaton Vorse, 16 May 1930, box 60: ff "1930, Jan–May," Mary Heaton Vorse Papers, ALUA.

85. Crawford, *One Naked Individual.* On Crawford's lesbian relationship with Dorothy Patton, see Wendy Smith, *Real Life Drama: The Group Theatre and America, 1931–1940* (New York: Alfred A. Knopf, 1990), 47, 172, and 298. See also Jay Plum, "Cheryl Crawford: One Not So Naked Individual," in *Passing Performances: Queer Readings of Leading Players in American Theater History,* ed. Robert A. Schanke and Kim Marra (Ann Arbor: University of Michigan Press, 1997), 239–61.

On Rukeyser, see Jan Heller Levi, ed., *A Muriel Rukeyser Reader*, introduction by Adrienne Rich, xiii, xviii.

86. Chauncey, *Gay New York*; Smith-Rosenberg, *Disorderly Conduct*.

87. Chauncey, *Gay New York*.

88. Ibid., 83.

89. Gidlow, *Elsa*, 166.

90. See for instance Elsa Gidlow, *On a Gray Thread* (Chicago: Will Ranson, 1923).

91. Grace Hutchins to Dearest Mother, 11 July 1927, Box 1: "Letters Sent-Grace Hutchins," Grace Hutchins Papers, Special Collections, Knight Library, University of Oregon, Eugene.

92. Grace Hutchins, "Hutchins, Grace," *The Turtle's Progress,* 1931, Box 1, "Additional Biographical Material," Hutchins Papers. Of their openness about their relationship with heterosexual members of the Left see, for instance, Anna Rochester to Devere Allen, 9 May 1924, Devere Allen Collection, Box C-4, Swarthmore College, Peace Collection, photocopy, Box 1: "Additional Biographical Material," Hutchins Papers; and Grace Hutchens to Harvey O'Connor, 1 August 1928, 14:27, part 2, O'Connor Papers.

93. John Collier to Miriam deFord, 25 September 1925, 25:11, part II, Collier Papers.

94. Miriam deFord to John Collier, 22 December 1925, 25:11, part II, Collier Papers.

95. Ibid., 83.

96. Timmons, *The Trouble with Harry,* 64, 67–69. The only full-length study of Geer is Sally Osborne Norton, "A Historical Study of Actor Will Geer, His Life and Work in the Context of Twentieth-Century American Social, Political, and Theatrical History" (Ph.D. diss., University of Southern California, 1980). Norton fails to take up Geer's sexual orientation.

97. Quoted in Timmons, *The Trouble with Harry,* 289.

98. Elsa Gidlow, "As Usual" (1920), in *Sapphic Songs: Seventeen to Seventy* (Baltimore: Diana Press, 1976), 35.

99. Gidlow, *Elsa*, 145.

100. Ibid., 173–74.

101. Ibid., 326.

102. Emphasis in the original, ibid., 94.

103. Gordon, *Marc the Music*, 198.

104. Doris Willens, *Lonesome Traveler: The Life of Lee Hays* (New York: W. W. Norton, 1988), 78.

105. John Loughery, *The Other Side of Silence: Men's Lives and Gay Identities: A Twentieth-Century History* (New York: Henry Holt and Co., 1998), 53.

106. Elsa Gidlow, "Constancy," in *Sapphic Songs*, 33; Gidlow, *Elsa*, 222, 216.

107. Gordon, *Marc the Music*, 276.

108. See for instance Norse, *Memories of a Bastard Angle*, 90.

109. Ibid., 130. On fears of queer bashing, see ibid., 90.

110. Alan Rich, *American Pioneers: Ives to Cage and Beyond* (London: Phaidon Press Ltd., 1995), 128; Rita Mead, *Henry Cowell's New Music, 1925–1936: The Society, the Music Editions, and the Recordings,* Studies in Musicology, no. 40 (Ann Arbor: UMI Research Press, 1981), 354.

111. Norse, *Memories of a Bastard Angel*, 77.

112. Will Roscoe in Harry Hay, *Radically Gay: Gay Liberation in the Words of Its Founder,* edited by Will Roscoe (Boston: Beacon, 1996), 40. Hay's prospectus for his

proposed organization is reprinted in *Radically Gay,* 63–75; the Mattachine Society's statement of missions and purposes is reprinted in *Radically Gay,* 131–32.

113. Chuck Rowland, oral history, in Eric Marcus, *Making History: The Struggle for Gay and Lesbian Equal Rights, 1945–1990* (New York: HarperCollins, 1992), 27, 32. Similarly, early Mattachine member and *One* editor Martin Block recalled that his family background, a socialist father and an anarchist mother, led him to feel disdain rather than paranoia about FBI surveillance of the movement. Martin Block, oral history, in Marcus, *Making History,* 39.

114. Jim Kepner, oral history in Marcus, *Making History,* 47.

115. Jim Bradford, "Pearl Hart is remembered on the anniversary of her passing," *Chicago Gay Life* 1:20 (19 March 1976); Maria Kuda, "Chicago's Gay and Lesbian History: From Prairie Settlement to World War II," *Outlines* (June 1994); idem, "Pearl Hart, Clinton & the Constitution," *Outlines* (24 February 1999); *Pearl M. Hart, 70th Birthday Celebration, Saturday, April 2, Ballroom, Midland Hotel, Souvenir Journal* (Chicago: Midwest Committee for Protection of Foreign Born, 1960); Del Martin, "New Illinois Penal Code: What does it Mean?" *The Ladder* (March 1962), 1415; "Press Release, Issued by Illinois State Committee, Communist Party," 24 September 1942, in "Pearl Hart" file, Gerber/Hart Library, Chicago. Special thanks to Gerber/Hart archivist Karen C. Sendziak for locating these materials.

116. See "Scrapbook clippings," box 9: "Poetry and Prose of Elsa Gidlow . . . ," Gidlow Papers.

117. On the connection between emerging sex and gender radicalism and the Left, see additionally Daniel Horowitz, *Betty Friedan and the Making of the Feminine Mystique: The American Left, the Cold War, and Modern Feminism* (Amherst: University of Massachusetts Press, 1998); Kathleen A. Weigard, "Vanguards of Women's Liberation: The Old Left and the Continuity of the Women's Movement" (Ph.D. diss., Ohio State University, 1995); and John D'Emilio, "Dreams Deferred: The Birth and Betrayal of America's First Gay Liberation Movement," in *Making Trouble: Essays on Gay History, Politics, and the University* (New York, 1992), 17–56.

12

Consuming the "Orient": Images of Asians in White Women's Beauty Magazines, 1900–1930

Midori Takagi

Within the past twenty years there has been a notable increase in imperial and colonial studies that focus on the nexus of relations between the colonizer and colonized outside of "the imposition of rule by an army."[1] Going beyond the institutional view of imperialism, these studies foreground racial, sexual, and class issues to understand the process of empire building and its impact on the dominant and subordinate societies. Of particular interest to this study are the works that explore the relationship between Western women, race, and colonialism. A few of the many works to have emerged include studies on white women travelers and their observations of colonized countries, British feminism within the context of England's relationship to India, and the impact of imperialism on notions of white motherhood. Historians have made great strides towards understanding the impact of imperialism on British women and, conversely, the women's association with, participation in, and resistance to the Imperial Empire.[2] Research on white middle-class American women's relationship to imperialism, however, is not as extensive. Granted, the United States did not possess as vast an empire as Great Britain, but by 1900 the U.S. exerted enormous influence over dozens of foreign governments and countries including the Philippines, Hawaii, Samoa, and a number of other Pacific Islands. In practice, if not in name, America was an imperial power.

This chapter is part of a broader study of the process through which the United States built and maintained its empire in Asia. But like the newer imperial studies, it seeks to understand the interconnections between gender, race, and colonialism. By foregrounding race and gender, this chapter explores how knowledge about American imperial activities in Asia was produced and disseminated to white middle-class women through advertisements and household tips, and how the image of the colonized "Oriental" became naturalized in American homes.

An analysis of *Ladies Home Journal, Cosmopolitan,* and *Good Housekeeping* between 1900 and 1930 shows that advertisements for home and beauty products featuring the "Orient" and "Orientals"[3] often encouraged white middle-class women to purchase goods as a way to enhance their social standing among their peers; help them establish a social identity apart from their husbands; and uphold American racial, political, economic, and sexual domination of Asians. Ads for soap, for example, encouraged sales based on their products' ability to "civilize" and clean "primitives" in Asia. Advertisers selling "Oriental" furnishings suggested such items would enhance the status of a middle-class family by making the home more exotic. Finally, advertisements for Asianesque perfumes and powders persuaded women to enhance their sexuality as a form of empowerment. While there is no conclusive evidence that white middle-class women absorbed and adopted the values heralded by the advertisements, there is some evidence that advertisers portrayed social values and statements that "carried an ideological bias toward 'system reinforcement.'"[4] In this case the "system" being reinforced was white, middle-to-upper class, male, patriarchal control, and the doctrine of Western progress, modernity, and civilization. But the advertisements did more than simply reflect the "system," they also encouraged white women to use the "Orient" as a way to empower or enhance themselves, to reaffirm the ideological foundations for Western colonization of Asia, which was and is integrally linked to the patriarchal and colonial oppression of American women. Consuming the "Orient," then, made white middle-class women shoppers complicit to, and recipients of, white male imperialism.

By 1900, readers of *Ladies Home Journal, Cosmopolitan,* and *Good Housekeeping* were no doubt familiar with the "Orient." America's presence in Asia dated back to the nineteenth century when the military, missionaries, merchants, commission agents, United States import houses, explorers, and diplomats forced their way into China, Japan, the Philippines, and many of the Pacific islands. In 1844 the U.S. gained access to China and her markets, after American Commissioner Caleb Cushing made veiled threats of war and forced the country to sign the Treaty of Wangxia.[5] Ten years later, the U.S. extracted similar privileges from Japan after sending Commodore Perry and an armed flotilla to sit in Edo bay to "encourage" the Shogunate to open that country's doors to Americans. Using Cushing's methods as a model, Perry successfully opened three ports to U.S. ships and established diplomatic and economic ties to Japan.[6] The United States also played an important role in "opening" Hawaii in 1893 when its military assisted a small group of American-born annexationists to overthrow Queen Lili`uokalani.[7] And in 1898 America took control of the Philippines after Commodore George Dewey surprised and defeated the Spanish squadron in the Manila port during the Spanish-American war.

Asia, as the site of American military exploits, did not, however, make the pages of these women's magazines during the early 1900s. Rather, columnists and advertisers described a Far East practically untouched by the West, but in great need of American modernization, civilization, and technology. Fictional stories spoke of rampant prostitution and infanticide, while advertisements proclaimed "Orientals" lacked proper hygiene and held little value for human life.[8] To combat such primitivism, argued one *Ladies Home Journal* columnist, and to "bring Asia at last into the range and under the influence of modern civilization," required creating a strong American presence in the Far East. And the U.S. in Asia, proclaimed a *Cosmopolitan* writer, would create a "wonderful opportunity for the strenuous individuality of Americans! Thousands of miles of steel rails will be required . . . bridges must be built and irrigation works engineered . . . [as well as] sanitary appliances."[9] At times these pronouncements expressed an altruistic interest in helping Asia, and at other times, they merely provided a justification for colonial capitalism.[10] Regardless of their motivation, the message was clear: the "Orient" was America's "burden."

To underscore this belief, Asians and Asia were consistently portrayed in articles and advertisements as dark, untamed, exotic, and backward. Most commonly "Orientals" were depicted as the opposite of middle-class Anglo-Americans: dark-skinned, child-like, primitive, lacking Christian moral values, cleanliness, domestic hygiene, sexual restraint, and living in remote areas far from "civilized" society. On occasion Asian men were portrayed as menacing and threatening, but in general Asians were depicted as helpless colonial subjects."[11]

Advertisements portrayed Asia's landscape in similar terms: wild and uncultivated. Frequently readers were given a glimpse of a dense jungle, a mountain range, vast untilled fields, or an empty country road. Advertisers provided little explanation about the scenery, thereby adding to a sense of the foreign and unknown. Even illustrations of Asian homes proved disorienting; advertisements generally featured empty tatami-mat rooms without walls, furniture, or fixtures, which left readers without any reference points. Although the technique of showing a room without ceilings or walls was commonly used in advertisements for household products, the fixtures in the rooms (a kitchen sink, a refrigerator, or a bed) immediately alerted readers to the purpose of the rooms and needed little explanation or context. No such information about Asian homes, however, was given.

It made little difference to advertisers that childlike Asians did not exist, or that they did not live in wild jungles or empty rooms because it served an important role in their advertisement campaigns geared towards white middle-class women. In fact, it is the decisive lack of realism in the portrayals of Asians that underscores how the "Oriental" was constructed by advertisers for—to paraphrase James Clifford—the eyes of the privileged.[12]

One of the largest group of advertisers to commodify the "primitive Oriental" as a way to stimulate sales, represented soap manufacturers. Brands such as Ivory Soap, Palmolive, and Jap Rose all invoked the image of the "Orient" or the "Oriental" as part of a sales pitch to gain the attention of women readers. The artwork and information about Asia in each ad served to persuade potential customers of the effectiveness of the products. Yet nowhere in these advertisements did the makers discuss the price of the soap or the potency of the product against competing brands. Instead, by invoking the image of the "primitive," advertisers measured the strengths of their soaps by their ability to "civilize" Asians.

The advertisements for Ivory Soap that featured Asians, for example, often featured their product as an agent of imperial and industrial progress. This could be seen in a 1910 advertisement which portrayed a group of Filipino Igorrotes making the long trek to their remote village from the town of Vigan. According to the text, the purpose of the Igorrotes' two hundred-mile journey was to bring Ivory Soap to their community. The accompanying sketch showed dark-skinned men wearing loincloths, fez-like hats, and nothing else. On their left shoulders they carried crates of Ivory Soap, and in their right hands, they held spears. Clearly it was an arduous journey, for the Igorrotes had to walk barefoot along unpaved roads and over mountain passes while carrying their load. Yet the image, and dialogue written below it, suggested that the trip was well worth it; according to the advertisers, "some people like Ivory Soap so much that they have it brought *nearly half way 'round the globe for them.*"

The image of "Orientals" fetishizing Ivory Soap attempted to lure potential female customers on an emotional level by promising to help supposedly lesser fortunate people. In literal terms, the soap—as a cleansing agent—would wash away the dirt from their bodies, make them healthy, and more aware of their personal hygiene. In metaphoric terms, the soap promised to "convert other cultures to 'civilization'" by changing disorder into order and rationality, and changing "Man the Hunter-gatherer" into "Man the Consumer."[13] American shoppers who purchased Ivory, then, were not merely buying a bar of soap, but a household good invested with great social, political, and cultural power and significance.

In its promise to "civilize the primitives," this Ivory Soap advertisement also reinforced the notion of white western cultural and racial superiority over the "darker" societies by demonstrating what the natives lacked in terms of material goods, standards of living, technology, and even intellectual capability. On a material basis alone, white middle-class women could feel assured of their "elevated" status by the very fact that soap had been a common item in their households for the past century. Furthermore, by 1910 American consumers had the luxury of choosing from a dozen different brands of soap to suit their needs. According to the advertisement it appears the Igorrotes had only just learned of Ivory Soap and only then because the United States had taken possession of the islands a little over ten years before.

The ease with which middle-class women could buy soap also underscored the geographic and technological advantages of American life. "It is not necessary for *you*," the advertisement stated, "to send eleven thousand miles for a cake of Ivory Soap. It is on sale in nearly every one of the three hundred thousand grocery stores in the United States." In contrast to the Igorrotes, white, middle-class women did not live in isolation in the "extremely wild and mountainous country," but in urban areas close to commercial, financial, and cultural centers.[14] Their lives were filled with modern conveniences: mass-produced soap, pre-made clothing, tinned meats, and condensed milk.[15] Furthermore, American women did not have to travel two hundred miles by foot to get to the nearest market, they could drive to the store or have their groceries delivered. Igorrotes, on the other hand, could not ride a bus or even an ox to reach the nearest town.

No doubt geographic location and a lack of transportation technology hampered the Igorrotes' ability to possess soap, but the Ivory Soap advertisement seemed to suggest greater obstacles existed; the Igorrotes lacked the intellectual and moral capacity to make soap and understand the value of it. These attributes were implied by the very image of the barefoot men in loincloths. Since Western culture often interpreted nakedness as a sign of primitivism, the nearly nude Igorrotes signified that they did not or could not grasp concepts and virtues such as shame, modesty, sexual restraint, or self-discipline, and therefore were not prepared for greater technological developments.[16]

Such an implication probably did not surprise many American women readers. The notion that Filipinos and other Asian ethnic groups lacked the intellectual capacity for technological and social development was common during nineteenth and early twentieth centuries. Sir John

Bowring in 1859, for example, described Filipinos as inherently lazy and indolent, and attributed the "backward" conditions in the Philippines to the nature of its people.[17] In 1899 British geographer G. J. Younghusband characterized the new American colony as islands filled with nothing but "large masses of tropical people who are utterly different from the Americans in origin, language, traditions, and habits, with no hope of assimilation."[18] In 1900 Asian "expert" William Elliot Griffis made a similar assessment of Northern Chinese people, calling them "ignorant and poor," and not "given to progress and enlightenment."[19] That same year James D. Phelan, Mayor of San Francisco—as did many nativists, farmers, and labor organizers—proclaimed Chinese and Japanese workers residing in the United States as inferior to whites and called for their removal on the basis that they "are not the stuff of which American citizens can be made."[20]

If there was one marker that explained and rationalized the Igorrotes' "backward" state to white women, it was skin color. For white Americans and Europeans, this was an old and familiar argument that had been used to enslave, subordinate, and disenfranchise nonwhite minorities for centuries. Beginning in the colonial era, many European settlers believed "Red" Indians to be innately savage and that no amount of Christianizing could change them.[21] During slave times, many white Southerners similarly believed Africans' dark skin was proof of the Curse of Ham, which doomed them and their descendants to be the "servant of servants."[22] After the 1850s, biblical justifications were supplemented, if not supplanted, by scientific studies "proving" a connection between race and intelligence.[23] Within this framework, then, the Igorrotes' brown skin became proof of their supposed primitive and debauched state, and reinforced beliefs in a racial hierarchy.[24]

The makers of Ivory Soap, however, were confident that the Igorrotes were not beyond being "saved" (or perhaps conquered). As the advertisement suggests, a cake of "99 44/100 Per Cent Pure" soap could change the course of the Filipinos' future by cleansing and civilizing the natives, taming the landscape, and bringing the people out of cultural and physical isolation.[25] What Ivory Soap offered white middle-class women was a way for them to participate in this campaign to uplift the "Oriental" by appealing to their sense of anxiety and aspiration.[26] The image of "wild" Igorrote men, for example, served to remind white women of the sexual and moral dangers of the untamed "Other" and the need to control them. Purchases of the soap then, became a way for white middle-class women to—metaphorically—help wash out impure thoughts and actions and impose morality and self-restraint on "Orientals."

The campaign to "uplift" Asians also promised women the ability to transcend their roles as housewives. By buying Ivory Soap—the advertisement argued—American women would be maintaining western values of cleanliness, purity, and rational order, as well as spreading "the lesson of imperial progress and capitalist civilization."[27] By invoking the image of the "primitive" male "Oriental," and by not portraying American women washing clothes, the makers of Ivory Soap offered white middle-class women powerful political and cultural roles. Suddenly, they were the bearers of civilized society instead of merely disenfranchised, undervalued, and unpaid domestic workers.

While Ivory Soap makers encouraged sales by portraying "wild" Igorrote men, other products, such as Jap Rose Soap and Quaker Rice Cereal, attracted consumers by invoking the image of an "infantilized Oriental." In each of these other advertisements child-like Asians were shown gleefully consuming American products in playful ways. Jap Rose Soap advertisements, for example, featured young Asian children frolicking among soap bubbles, taking bubble baths and kissing behind a transparent bar of soap, while ads for Quaker Cereal featured mothers and children happily holding bowls of rice cereal.

The image of infants and children smiling and playing was not an uncommon advertising tactic during the early twentieth century. Soap and cereal makers often used these bucolic scenes to link cleanliness and nourishing foods with pleasant family moments. In addition, these images were used to instill a sense of innocence in the products. What could be more "pure" than children playing in a bath or eating breakfast?

The image of Asian children playing offered more than a heightened sense of innocence, however; it also perpetuated the notion that "Orientals" were like children "under control." This was a common technique in advertisements portraying African Americans and Native Americans, scholar Jeffrey Steele notes, "in answer to the more disturbing racial anxieties of the time. . . ."[28] A good example of the infantilizing of Asians could be found in the advertisements for Jap Rose Soap where children were shown amusing themselves playing with American soap bubbles and taking a bath without coercion or supervision. The sense that Asians were like docile children was also referred to in the advertisements for Quaker Cereal. In those ads Asian families were portrayed happily consuming bowls of rice cereal. They were the epitome of "good Orientals" who knew "their place and their proper role—to be unquestioning consumers."[29] There was no look of doubt on their faces as to why they would want or need Quaker Rice Cereal when rice, a staple in the Asian diet, was readily available and considered (by American nutritionists) to be filled with "purity, strength and goodness."[30]

In comparison to the image of the "wild" and "primitive" Igorrote men, the "infantilized Oriental" posed little threat to white middle-class women or to the dominant society. The women and children came across as submissive, vulnerable, and in need of guidance. As a result, the makers of Jap Rose and Quaker Rice did not call upon women consumers to help "tame" Asians, as much as extend a paternalistic—or in this case—maternalistic hand to help nurture "Orientals." So whereas Ivory Soap encouraged white women to become "imperial housewives," Jap Rose and Quaker Rice enlisted American consumers to become "imperial mothers" to protect the "defenseless" Asian families.

While the image of feminized or infantilized Asians continued to be invoked by soap and cereal makers between 1900 and 1930, after 1912 advertisements portraying "Orientals" began to change in tone. The urgent calls to "save" Asians had largely ended; spiritual salvation of the "primitives" was no longer connected to consumerism. In other words, while the earlier ads invited women readers to see Asia as a place where *they could uplift the masses and impose order,* the later ads emphasized what *they could take from Asia to uplift themselves.*

Although it is not clear why advertisements changed in tone, the shift does parallel the increasingly rocky relations between United States and Asia (specifically those with Japan). Japan's defeat of Russia in 1905, and its imperialist activities in Korea (1910) and Manchuria (1911–12), left American and British policymakers extremely uneasy. Japan could be viewed no longer as a "backwards" state, but an ambitious military power that threatened the economic interests of the West in Asia.[31] While this new image of a militaristic Japan did not completely dispel the notion of Asians as "barbarians," it certainly may have dampened American hopes in "rescuing" the Japanese people.

Dampened "rescue" hopes may explain why advertisements in the post–1912 era portrayed the "Orient" and the "Oriental" as objects to be consumed, rather than as consumers. Earlier images of Japanese women holding bowls of Quaker Rice cereal were replaced with pictures of white women surrounded by Asianesque goods.[32] "Oriental" men no longer carried soap back to their villages, but appeared poised and ready to scrub American tabletops and floors. Even Buddha, the Indian religious leader, became an advertising commodity; every jar of Pompeian Day and Night Creams was supposedly "blessed" by the mystic himself.[33]

Asia was now a warehouse of goods to be literally "cut up, salvaged," and disseminated as home furnishings, household goods, and floral scents, that would enhance the lives of white, middle-class women.[34] Fabrics with Japanese designs generally reserved for Japanese kimonos, for example, were now being sold as exotic "curtains, table covers, bedspreads, dress and chiffonier scarfs [sic]."[35] "Quaint Oriental creations" now served as negligee gowns for the spring and summer months.[36] Rare Egyptian beauty secrets and furniture wax from China—once reserved for the privileged—were now accessible to middle-class consumers. There were few "Oriental delicacies" Americans could not purchase for "personal use and presentation purposes."[37] As the makers of Whittall (Oriental) Rugs explained, every home could have "a bit of the Orient. . . ."[38]

In some ways the profusion of "Oriental" home furnishings was a manifestation of increased middle-class concerns with "self-aggrandizement and fulfillment" through interior design.[39] Between 1900 and 1930, middle-class homeowners began acquiring artifacts and decorations that symbolized gentility and reflected, as Anne McClintock explains, "the man's market worth and the wife's exhibition status."[40] Middle-class desires and aspirations have been most evident in the changes made to house floor plans, the rapid popularity of indoor plumbing and electrical lights, and the numerous sales in goods reminiscent of the Spanish and Italian Renaissance periods, European Art Nouveau styles, and of the romanticized "Orient," among other genres.[41]

Marketers of "Oriental" goods, however, promised consumers more than a touch of gentility for their parlours, dining rooms, and bedrooms; they also promised to empower middle-class women by allowing them to express their individuality through choice and selection. The "new" woman could now express her unique qualities by choosing, for example, products scented with "Indian vetivert, ylang-ylang from Manila, and olibanum from the 'Holy Land,'" as opposed to buying plain old soap.[42] According to these advertisements, shopping—the very act of choosing one particular brand over another—was a form of power. Consistently, marketers of "Oriental" goods translated women's power and equality in terms of consumerism. But the makers of these products were not alone. It appears many advertisers made such a claim; as historian Nancy Cott explains, "advertisements worked and reworked the theme that purchasing was an arena for choice and control in which women could exert rationality and express values."[43] A classic example of this would be the Listerine advertisement from the 1930s which suggested that a woman's right to vote was exercised even in the act of choosing a brand of toothpaste.[44]

Also similar to other brands of household and beauty goods, "Oriental" products promised to free women from housework and other time-consuming tasks. Like their less exotic competitors, cleansers supposedly from Asia claimed to ease the drudgery and toil of dusting and mopping. What set Asianesque goods apart from their "American-made" competition, however, was the method of freeing women; these products offered the labor and (what was perceived to be) the essence of the "Orient," as well as the ability to become an "Oriental."

"Oriental" household products such as furniture polish, not only were guaranteed to produce the "hard, dry, brilliant lustre," usually found in wealthy homes, but they also offered the services of an Asian man to do the work.[45] In advertisements for Wizard polish and their competitors "3 in One," it appears a feminized "houseboy" would accompany each purchase. Opening a bottle of the polish, the advertisements proclaimed, is like releasing a genie who will dust your furniture. To underscore this message, every ad featured a Middle-Eastern "genie" rising from the liquid polish with a rag in hand, smiling and happily dusting

The "Oriental houseboy" theme was prominent in advertisements for other products such as Chi-Namel (a play on the words China and enamel) and Jap-A-Lac (a shortened version of Japanese lacquer). According to these advertisements, getting a can of either varnish was like buying a Liliputian-sized Asian who would make your woodwork shine. Every purchase of Chi-Namel was accompanied by an elaborately (and inappropriately) dressed Chinese "elf," while a seemingly submissive young Japanese girl (kneeling with a paintbrush in hand) came with each can of Jap-A-Lac.

Even cooking and baking were no longer chores with purchases of Aladdin Aluminum pots and pans because it was like getting a miniature Chinese cook who stirred and served "flaky pies" and "rich jars of brandied peaches." "Built for a hard life," the tiny, well-dressed Chinese "houseboy" will "serve you faithfully, and "do a season's preserving at one boiling."[46]

The image of an Asian male dusting, cooking, and cleaning linked the supposed liberation of middle-class housewives from the toil of housework and the strict sexual division of labor to the colonization of "Orientals" and their labor. In other words, these advertisements invited white middle-class women to see appropriating Asian labor as the key to their own freedom.

Viewing Asians, particularly Asian men, as "houseboys" was not a stretch of any imagination. Since the late nineteenth century, Asian men (Chinese, Japanese, and Filipino) worked in domestic service. Proportionately the Chinese workforce participated in this industry the most. According to statistics gathered by historians David J. O'Brien and Stephen S. Fugita, 51.2 percent of the Chinese workforce was "engaged in domestic and personal service work" as opposed to only 22.0 percent of the Japanese workforce.[47] It was no coincidence that so many Chinese men worked in domestic service; by the late nineteenth century, Chinese male workers could find few jobs in the fields of mining, manufacturing, agriculture, and railroad building. Hostility and racial violence against Chinese laborers by native white workers caused the former to flee from the rural areas and small towns into larger urban centers. Once lodged in the cities, Chinese laborers found employment only in ethnic enterprises, and in domestic service.[48] It was not uncommon, then, for middle-class households—particularly on the West Coast—to employ an Asian servant.

But "Oriental" household goods offered more than just the labor of Asians, they also promised the essence of the "Orient" as a way for women to escape the trappings and constraints of Victorian culture, to explore their sexual freedom, and become "a different type of woman."[49] Such promises were most notable in the advertisements for oils, perfumes, powders, and creams which proclaimed to have "caught, distilled, and faithfully reproduced" the "Orient."[50] Sen-Yang Powder, Wisteria Blossom perfume, and Florient, Flowers of the Orient scent, for example, all promised to transform the practical and economical middle-class woman into a more sensual and sexual creature who was "deli-cate," "engaging," and "cha-ming" (an "Oriental" play on charming).[51] Fleur D'Orient swore to make women "bewitching."[52] Palmolive Soap even promised to make women as alluring as Queen Cleopatra![53]

While these "Oriental" products simply offered to enhance women's beauty and charm, other products suggested they could enhance their physical sexual desires and desirability. Onyx Hosiery made from "pure Japanese silk" promised to make women's ankles an object of "fascina-tion" for men.[54] One "Oriental" night cream suggested women could have orgasmic-like experiences when using their product by opening their 1930 advertisement with the phrase, "Valerie's breath came in short, excited gasps. . . ."[55]

Increased sexuality could also be gained through the purchase of kimono-style silk wrappers—a very popular item for women in their boudoir. Although images of kimonos and other Asian clothing had occasionally appeared in the magazines prior to the teens, advertise-ments for ready-made kimonos, and articles teaching readers how to sew "Oriental" robes became commonplace. Suddenly robes normally worn by Asian women for special occasions, such as weddings or funerals, and even those worn to clean house, were now appearing in the baths and bedrooms of white American women. These advertisements purposeful-ly framed the kimonos in highly sexualized ways with images of middle-class women powdering their chests and breasts, rubbing lotion on their feet, or helping their husbands into (or out of) their clothes, while the robes slid off their shoulders.

Mattress makers even appropriated the "Orient" to transform the bed-room—a site in the sexual commodification of women—into an "adven-turous" sensual experience. In 1916 the Simmons company added a "suggestion of the Japanese lacquer and decoration" to their new design.[56] Their advertisement featured a large black lacquered bed frame surround-ed by Japanese painted screens. Covering the mattress was a bedspread with a distinctly Asianesque crest in the center. By bringing the "the magic and mystery of the Far East into [the] boudoir," the Simmons Company suggested that sexual relations could be "fun" rather than a "duty."[57]

Framed in this manner, consuming the "Orient" appeared to be a powerful tool that gave white middle-class women a degree of power and authority within the home. Products of the "Orient" gave women an opportunity to explore their sexuality, to view sex for non-procreation purposes, to enhance their (hetero)sexual appeal to men, and to "indulge themselves sensually through the consumption of exquisitely exotic commodities."[58]

Perhaps in minor ways these "Oriental" products did enhance women's power within the home.[59] As the primary purchaser of these commodities[60] (in spite of their dependence on their husbands' or fathers' money), women were able to define an identity "through a style created from those commodities,"[61] which was apart from, and at times in conflict with, their husbands and their authority. With "Oriental" products like the toweling, middle-class women were able enhance the beauty and value of their homes, which may have allowed them to maintain or raise their status within their peer group. Finally, by bringing a Far Eastern allure into the boudoir, white women used "Oriental" products to take the sexual initiative with their husbands or potential mates.

But the consumption of the "Orient" had severe ramifications; through purchases of Far Eastern goods, white women became unwitting "global political actors" in the colonization of Asia and "normalized" or domesticated imperialism of the East.[62] Whether through purchases of Ivory Soap or Jap-A-Lac, American women's interest in helping "our little brown brothers,"[63] or recreating the "Orient" within their homes helped construct an Asia that existed solely for the purposes of being uplifted and appropriated. No thought or care was given to the political, social, and economic desires of the native peoples, or their efforts to resist colonization.

The appropriation and dissemination of "Oriental" goods into the American household also effectively dismissed any of the original significance of the Asian items or their meaning within the Asian cultures. The only importance Japanese toweling or kimonos served, then, was in terms of how these goods promoted middle-class values and enhanced the "liveableness" of their homes.[64]

By suggesting the colonization of Asia as an important key to enhancing the middle-class home, and subsequently, women's power within the home, advertisers encouraged white women to see objectifying and colonizing the "Oriental" as necessary for their own emancipation. This was made most clear in a 1919 Palmolive Soap advertisement, which featured a white woman dressed as (or embodying the) "Oriental," with a dark-skinned man, who was ostensibly a servant. The woman is adorned in (Middle-Eastern) brocades and white silk veils decorated with jewels. She is presented to the reader in a bold sensual manner, with her hands clasped behind her head, and her chest pushed outwards. It is a highly sexualized and boldly defiant stance. To emphasize her "power" as the "Oriental," the advertisement shows the dark-skinned "primitive peasant" kneeling at her feet while offering her a bowl of palm and olive oils.[65]

The woman's position of authority is "justified" in several ways: in terms of body positions, she dominated both the picture and the kneeling male figure; in terms of skin color, her white skin gave her power and control rarely afforded darker-skinned people; and in terms of sexuality, her hypersexualized form made her more alluring and desireable to white men than the feminized Asian male figure. The ad's message clearly equated a white woman's ability to be pampered and to live in luxury with the sexual and racial subordination of Asians, but it also introduced imperialism into the middle-class home as a common occurrence and as a household item, which made middle-class women complicit imperialists. Like the early Ivory advertisements, Palmolive's "Orientalized" white woman served as both symbol and agent of "imperial progress."

Ironically, the supposed empowerment of white women as imperialists served to reinforce the racial and sexual hierarchies that supported white male patriarchal control, which in turn re-inscribed the subordination of women within American society. First, consuming the "Orient" reemphasized constructed gender differences and cultural beliefs that subjugated white women. By negating the notion that women were becoming political equals to men (in terms of suffrage), the Asianesque powders, perfumes, and oils accentuated Victorian ideals of femininity including purity, softness, frailty, and helplessness that mandated patriarchal control and authority. Furthermore, these products emphasized the importance of marriage and a bourgeois social status—social arrangements that have historically oppressed women by placing them under the legal, economic, political, and social control of their husbands. Beauty ads and cosmetic sales, Stuart Ewen explains, simply reminded women that "the imperative of beauty was directly linked to the question of job security—their survival, in fact depended upon their ability to keep a husband. . . ."[66] So while women may have gained a modicum of power within the household by developing personal tastes and making consumer decisions, the purchases of home and beauty goods essentially nullified any emancipatory gains.

While purchases of "non-foreign" (non-"Oriental") beauty and household goods certainly contributed to the sexual oppression of white middle-class women as much as "Oriental" goods, the appropriation of the Far East linked domestic sexual colonization and international racial imperialism in a way non-Asianesque consumerism did not. Consumption of the "Orient," for example, created a space for women in America's imperial activities, and conversely, created a space within the home for the colonization of Asia. The purchase of the Simmons "Japanese" bed, as opposed to a new stove, served as both the metaphor and result of Asian colonization. Metaphorically, the Asianesque bed served as the new site of the "Orient" where western men could legally, physically, economically, and sexually subjugate women (white or Asian), while the placement of Asian goods within the bedroom is a product of American imperialism. As a result, purchases of "Oriental" goods became an important nexus for American consumerism, the cult of domesticity, and the colonization of Asia.

Much more work needs to be done in terms of understanding the gendering of imperial activities in Asia or any other country for that matter. This study demonstrates that far from being isolated from the outer world, national advertising, middle-class women and their consumer habits, and the cult of domesticity served an important function within the American empire. "Orientalizing" one's home or body undeniably held some benefits for middle-class women. Yet it is equally true that consuming the "Orient" re-inscribed and reinforced the subordination and subjugation of white women as well. As a result, the extent of white women's relation to imperialism and the imperialist ideology based on their class and political beliefs, and the range of gains they received from that relationship still need to be explored.

NOTES

1. Sara Mills, "Knowledge, Gender, and Empire," in *Writing Women and Space: Colonial and Post–Colonial Geographies*, ed. Alison Blunt and Gillian Rose (New York: Guilford Press, 1994), 32; Susan Meyer, *Imperialism at Home: Race and Victorian Women's Fiction* (Ithaca, NY: Cornell University Press, 1996).

2. Angela Woollacott, "'All This Is the Empire, I Told Myself': Australian Women's Voyages 'Home' and the Articulation of Colonial Whiteness," *American Historical Review* (October 1997): 1003–29; Cheryl McEwan, "Encounters with West African Women: Textual Representations of Difference by White Women Abroad," in *Writing Women and Space*; Antoinette M. Burton, "The White Woman's Burden: British Feminists and 'The Indian Woman,' 1865–1915," in *Western Women and Imperialism: Complicity and Resistance*, ed., Nupur Chaudhuri and Margaret Strobel (Bloomington: Indiana University Press, 1992); Mona Domosh, "Toward a Feminist Historiography of Geography," *Transactions of the Institute of British Geographers*, n.s., 16 (1991): 95–104; Sara Mills, *Discourses of Difference: An Analysis of Women's Travel Writing and Colonialism* (London: Routledge, 1991); Anna Davin, "Imperialism and Motherhood," *History Workshop Journal* (Spring 1978): 9–65.

3. The creation of the ubiquitous "Oriental" was a Western cultural invention as well. This term blends together all the various ethnic Asian groups thereby making little distinction between and among the different cultures and languages.

4. Roland Marchand, *Advertising the American Dream, Making Way for Modernity, 1920–1940* (Berkeley: University of California Press, 1985), xviii.

5. Tyler Dennett, *Americans in Eastern Asia* (New York: Barnes & Noble, Inc., 1941), 150.

6. Ibid., 268.

7. Robert L. Beisner, *From the Old Diplomacy to the New: 1865–1900* (New York: Crowell, 1975), 104.

8. *Ladies Home Journal,* June 1930.

9. *Ladies Home Journal,* Sept. 1903; *Cosmopolitan,* June 1910.

10. Syed Hussein Alatas, *The Myth of the Lazy Native* (London: F. Cass, 1977), 7.

11. Burton, "The White Woman's Burden," 137.

12. James Clifford, *The Predicament of Culture: Twentieth-Century Ethnography, Literature and Art* (Cambridge, MA: Harvard University Press, 1988), 5.

13. Anne McClintock, *Imperial Leather: Race, Gender and Sexuality in the Colonial Contest* (New York: Routledge, 1995), 223.

14. Ivory Soap, *Ladies Home Journal,* June 1910.

15. T. J. Jackson Lears, "From Salvation to Self-Realization: Advertising and the Therapeutic Roots of the Consumer Culture, 1880–1930," in Richard Wightman Fox and T. J. Jackson Lears, *The Culture of Consumption: Critical Essays in American History, 1880–1980* (New York: Pantheon Books, 1983), 7.

16. This argument was made by American colonists of Native Americans, and of European explorers of Africans. James Axtell, *The European and the Indian* (New York: Oxford University Press,, 1981), 58.

17. Sir John Bowring, *A Visit to the Philippine Islands,* quoted in *Myth of the Lazy Native,* 58–59.

18. G. J. Younghusband, *The Philippines and Round About* (New York: Macmillan, 1899), chap. 13.

19. Ibid., 63.

20. *San Francisco Examiner* May 8, 1900, quoted in Roger Daniels, *Asian America: Chinese and Japanese in the United States since 1850* (Seattle: University of Washington Press, 1988), 112.

21. Axtell, *The European and the American,* 85.

22. Winthrop Jordan, *White over Black: American Attitudes toward the Negro, 1550–1812* (New York: Norton, 1968): 17.

23. Michael L. Blakey, "Scientific Racism and the Biological Concept of Race," *Literature and Psychology* 45½ (1999): 28–43; Dennis Rutledge, "Social Darwinism, Scientific Racism, and the Metaphysics of Race," *Journal of Negro Education* 64:3 (Summer 1995): 243–51.

24. Jordon, *White over Black,* chap. 1; Alatas, *The Myth of the Lazy Native,* chap. 3.

25. *Ladies Home Journal* (June 1910), 2.

26. Lears, *From Salvation to Realization,* 27.

27. McClintock, *Imperial Leather,* 132.

28. Jeffrey Steele, "Reduced to Images: American Indians in Nineteenth-Century Advertising," in *Dressing in Feathers: The Construction of the Indian in American Popular Culture,* ed., S. Elizabeth Bird (Colorado: Westview Press, 1996), 45.

29. Ibid., 56.

30. *Good Housekeeping,* 1910.

31. W. G. Beasley, *Japanese Imperialism, 1894–1945* (London: Oxford Press, 1987), 100–101.

32. A. A. Vantine & Co. Inc., *Good Housekeeping*, vol. 66, 1918.

33. *Ladies Home Journal*, January 1925.

34. Clifford, *The Predicament of Culture*, 12.

35. *Good Housekeeping* 66, 1918.

36. *Good Housekeeping* 64, May 1917.

37. *Good Housekeeping* April 1917.

38. *Good Housekeeping* 63, 1916.

39. Candice M. Volz, "The Modern Look of the Early-Twentieth-Century House: A Mirror of Changing Lifestyles," in *American Home Life, 1880–1930*, ed., Jessica H. Foy and Thomas J. Schlererth (Knoxville: University of Tennessee Press, 1992), 34.

40. McClintock, *Imperial Leather*, 219.

41. Volz, "The Modern Look of the Early-Twentieth-Century House," 44.

42. *Ladies Home Journal*, Feb. 1918.

43. Nancy Cott, "The Modern Woman of the 1920s, American Style," in *A History of Women in the West*, ed., Françoise Thebaud (Cambridge, MA: Harvard University Press, 1994), 89.

44. *American Magazine*, October 1932, in Marchard, *Advertising the American Dream*, 182.

45. Stuart Ewen, *Captains of Consciousness: Advertising and the Social Roots of the Consumer Culture* (New York: Macmillan, 1976), 163.

46. *Good Housekeeping*, April and May 1917.

47. David J. O'Brien and Sephen S. Fugita, *The Japanese American Experience* (Bloomington: Indiana University Press, 1991), 18.

48. Ronald Takaki, *Strangers from A Different Shore* (New York: Penguin, 1989), 239–41.

49. Palmolive Soap, *Ladies Home Journal*, May 1916.

50. *Good Housekeeping*, October 1912.

51. Ibid.; *Ladies Home Journal*, Feb. 1919, April 1919, June 1920, and Dec. 1921.

52. *Ladies Home Journal*, March 1925.

53. *Ladies Home Journal*, May 1916.

54. *Ladies Home Journal*, May 1925.

55. *Ladies Home Journal*, November 1930.

56. *Ladies Home Journal*, April 1916.

57. *Ladies Home Journal*, June 1916; Rayna Rapp and Ellen Ross, "The 1920s Feminism, Consumerism, and the Political Backlash in the United States," in *Women in Culture and Politics: A Century of Change*, ed. Judith Friedlander et. al. (Bloomington: Indiana University Press, 1986), 56.

58. Ibid.

59. There are contesting interpretations of the institutionalization of women's cosmetics and of the beauty culture. Vincent Vinikas, among others, believes that make-up was designed to reduce the superficial similarities between the "New Women" and men. As Vinikas states, "The widespread reintroduction and acceptance of cosmetics in the first decades of the twentieth century was a noticeable revision in the schedule for the depiction of female. This innovation can be interpreted as a ritual of feminization. . . . The use of cosmetics served to modify the recent changes in women's status in America; in applying them, women could both acknowledge recent alterations in gender identity and mute the more threatening ambiguities that

accompanied the emergence of the New Woman." Vincent Vinikas, *Soft Soap Hard Sell: American Hygine in the Age of Advertisements* (Ames: Iowa State University Press, 1992), 57.

60. Studies indicate that women purchased up to 85 percent of the goods sold at retail. Vinikas, *Soft Soap Hard Sell*, 98.

61. Gina Marchetti, *Romance and the "Yellow Peril,"* in *Race, Sex, and Discursive Strategies in Hollywood Fiction* (Berkeley: University of California Press, 1993), 29.

62. Cynthia Enloe, *Bananas, Beaches and Bases: Making Feminist Sense of International Politics* (Berkeley: University of California Press, 1990), xii.

63. General Nelson A. Miles, "Our Little Brown Brothers . . . ," *Cosmopolitan*, October 1912.

64. *Ladies Home Journal*, April 1925.

65. *Ladies Home Journal*, May 1916; April 1919.

66. Ewen, *Captains of Consciousness*, 177–78.

13

Women, Cheesecake, and Borderline Material: Responses to Girlie Pictures in the Mid-Twentieth-Century United States

Joanne Meyerowitz

The proliferation in the mass media of sexual representations of women is, arguably, among the most significant developments in twentieth-century U.S. women's history, the history of sexuality, and the history if popular culture. Stated simply, illustrations and photographs of scantily clad and nude women, once considered disreputable, now grace billboards, calendars, television, movies, and magazines. The exposed female body appears ubiquitously as our primary public symbol of eroticism. Since the protests against *Playboy* magazine in 1969, feminists have repeatedly questioned the meanings of the mass marketing of the female body. In fact, angry debates over mass-produced sexual representations recently split the U.S. women's movement.[1]

Curiously, historians have scarcely addressed this phenomenon. Histories of erotic images generally focus either on illicit pornography or on nudity in the Euro-American fine arts tradition, and histories of censorship tend to dwell on the battles and negotiations between predominantly male moralists and predominantly male modernists and entrepreneurs.[2] In this essay, I shift the focus from pornography and art and battles among men to popular magazines and debates among women. I examine the most widely marketed forms of sexual representation—cheesecake and borderline material—and the vociferous public responses of women.[3] This history demonstrates that commodified sexual representation was a "woman's issue" well before the contemporary feminist movement. As sexual images of women multiplied in the popular culture, women participated actively in constructing arguments to endorse as well as protest them. The open battles between women not only involved moralism, modernism, and mass-marketed culture but also concepts of respectability, female beauty, feminism, racial equality, and maternalism.

This discourse on sexual imagery belongs within a larger context of cultural contests over changing sexual codes. The rise of popular erotic images was one component of a broader transformation toward a modern sexuality that assigned a heightened value to nonprocreative heterosexuality. As sexual mores changed in the late nineteenth and twentieth centuries, sexologists and other experts regulated sexuality by codifying and disseminating new definitions of "normal" and "abnormal" behavior.[4] On a more popular level, the entrepreneurs who mass-produced sexual representations and the consumers who viewed them also constructed and categorized sex. Through the thousands of images they commodified and consumed, they not only defined and redefined what was attractive and arousing; they also distinguished respectable sexual spectacle from the questionable and taboo.

In the early twentieth century, a new language emerged to represent the unstable categories of a new taxonomy of sexual display. The American slang "cheesecake" entered the common parlance around 1915 as a term for publicly acceptable, mass-produced images of seminude women.[5] As "cheesecake" spread through the popular culture, the term "borderline material" came to refer to erotic imagery that stretched the gap between respectable cheesecake and illicit pornography.[6] Cheesecake, borderline material, and pornography did not progressively unveil the reality of sex or of women's bodies; rather, they removed some images of women's bodies from the margins of obscenity to the center of mainstream popular culture. They helped define certain bodily images as clean, healthy, and wholesome, enjoyed by "normal" men and women, and left others as dirty, taboo, and grotesque. The content of cheesecake, borderline material, and pornography changed over time. Not surprisingly, cheesecake pictures in mid-century differed from cheesecake pictures forty years earlier.[7] But into the 1960s the categories themselves provided a widely accepted classificatory schema, a schema at least as important as the oft noted one that distinguishes "art" from "obscenity."[8] The changing content of cheesecake and borderline material, like the changing content of art, marked the shifting and contested boundaries of respectable female sexual display and of normal visual pleasure.[9]

Women joined in this process of classification when they argued for or against the respectability of certain sexual images. Women supporters welcomed a visual rhetoric that they read as a positive post–Victorian rejection of bodily shame and a healthy respect for female beauty. In contrast, women protesters struggled to reassert their diminishing moral authority, to wrest control from the mass market of supply and demand. They publicly denounced the new taxonomy of sexual display which they saw as harmful, especially to women and youth. These contests reveal women not only as objects of sexual representation but also as engaged and embattled participants in the construction of sexual meanings.

Historians of American women, myself included, sometimes portray twentieth-century battles over sexuality as sporadic generational rebellions. In the early twentieth century, for example, the "sexual revolution" often appears as an epochal rift in which middle-class flappers, working-class "charity girls," and feminist "new women" routed older Victorian mores.[10] The battles over cheesecake and borderline material, however, suggest a recurring conflict not resolved as one generation allegedly triumphed over its predecessor. In twentieth-century America, sexuality has repeatedly served as a battlefield for conflicting cultural visions more complicated than generational divides. The disputed meanings of the exposed female body sometimes stood at the center of these fights.

This article begins with a short chronology of the rise of popular sexual representations in the United States and of women's early public responses, both pro and con. It then focuses in depth on mid-twentieth century episodes in which women articulated both their pleasure and their disgust with the commercialized sexual representations found in mass-circulation magazines. In the Post Office hearings on *Esquire* magazine, the battles over "girlie pictures" in *Ebony* and *Negro Digest,* the debates in *Playboy,* and the national campaign against "girlie magazines," women arrayed themselves on opposing sides of an ideological fault line still visible on our current cultural terrain.

A BRIEF HISTORY

Through the first two-thirds of the nineteenth century, popular books, magazines, and newspapers did not include the kinds of bodily images routinely seen in the mass media today. For the nineteenth-century American middle class, public displays of nudity were acceptable under the guise of fine art representation of beauty, but even then, on display in art museums, they sometimes courted censure.[11] Erotic representations of nude and seminude women flourished, though, in the urban underworld of commercialized sex. Saloons decorated with paintings of female nudes, cheap museums with lascivious exhibits, and *tableaux vivants,* or living picture shows with female models decked in tights, arose in neighborhoods where the sex trade throve. Men purchased erotic pictures at steamboat docks and in railway stations, and during the Civil War, soldiers created a mail-order market for pictures of naked women.[12]

After the Civil War, images from the demimonde trickled into the mainstream. As urban commercialized recreation expanded, entrepreneurs promoted sexual entertainments to a wider market. In the late 1860s, the wild success of the musical extravaganza *The Black Crook* and the burlesque troupe Lydia Thompson and Her British Blondes established women's legs as major theatrical attractions and inspired numerous "girlie shows" in the decades that followed. In the same years, sensational scandal sheets, such as the *Police Gazette,* and new magazines, such as *Munsey's,* boosted their circulation with pictures of women in tights, décolleté, and swimwear.[13]

As the commercialization of erotic images proceeded apace, women joined men as voyeuristic observers of the female form, and not just in museums and galleries. Entertainment entrepreneurs worked pointedly to attract "respectable" female customers. Some offered matinee performances and free admission on "ladies' night," and banned drinking, smoking, and soliciting. Advertisers, too, introduced nude and seminude images to sell products marketed specifically to women. From the late nineteenth century on, advertisers in popular magazines, including *Ladies Home Journal,* used idealized, artful images of the female body to promote such products as soap and corsets. By the 1920s, they appealed to women with frankly erotic images. They speculated (correctly, it seems) that sexual representations of women would encourage women to buy the attraction seen in the ads.[14]

By the 1930s, scantily clad women were ubiquitous in the popular culture. Even middle-class family magazines, such as *Life,* regularly featured such photographs, especially of women posing in swimwear.[15] During World War II, Hollywood studios and popular magazines accelerated the distribution when they sent "pin-ups" to soldiers overseas. By the 1940s, the American public generally hailed the "pin-up girls" not as prostitutes but as patriots who boosted the morale of soldiers.[16] The "pin-ups" crossed the boundaries of race and class. By the late 1940s, the *American Federationist,* official organ of the American Federation of Labor, and *Ebony,* a popular African-American magazine, regularly included photos of seminude, white, working-class women and African-American women, respectively.[17]

As some sexual representations entered the popular culture as "cheesecake," entrepreneurs experimented with the more risqué popular forms that came to be known as "borderline material." "Girlie calendars," for example, emerged as a popular commodity during the 1910s, and specialized "girlie magazines," with overtly erotic pictures of nude and seminude women, appeared during World War I and flourished after 1920, during the same years that burlesque evolved into striptease.[18] *Esquire* magazine, first published in 1933, attempted to elevate the netherworld of borderline acceptability to the higher realm of urbane good taste.[19] In the postwar era, *Playboy* followed *Esquire*'s lead with sophisticated articles and ads for middle-class consumer products, but unlike *Esquire, Playboy* included photographs of women's breasts. Its immediate success inspired a rash of imitation, including *Cabaret, Jaguar, Jem, Nugget,* and *U.S. Male. Duke* magazine, another *Playboy* imitator, featured photos of bare-breasted African-American women aimed at African-American men.[20]

With bare breasts available as quasi-legitimate entertainment, pornographers inched toward other taboos. In the 1940s and after, pornographic magazines experimented increasingly with sadism, masochism, fetishism, and lesbianism, and underground stag films more often included scenes of oral and anal sex.[21] As imagery once considered obscene reemerged as "cheesecake" and "borderline material," pornographers searched for different conventions in which to present symbols of illicit sex.

By the mid-twentieth century, then, the female body as sexual symbol permeated American popular culture. As prostitution declined and mass-produced sexual representation increased, the commodification of sexual images seems to have partially supplanted the commodification of sexual acts.[22] In the growing market of sexual spectacle, a new code of mass-produced sexual display provided a rough and shifting classification that ranged from the most acceptable cheesecake to the most taboo pornography.

At virtually every point in this history, protesters challenged the rise of popular sexual representations. After the Civil War, an organized antiobscenity movement, led by Anthony Comstock, captured national attention. In 1873 it triumphed in its efforts for federal antiobscenity legislation. In the years that followed, local "vice societies" worked, with considerable public support, to stem the tide of alleged moral corruption.[23]

From the beginning of this national movement, women's voices joined the rising chorus of outrage. As early as 1869, Olive Logan, a former actress, attacked the new "leg business" of burlesque, or "The Nude Woman Question."[24] By the end of the century, national women's organizations had entered the fray, positioning middle-class women as maternal guardians of the public morals. In 1883, the Woman's Christian Temperance Union (WCTU) took the lead when it created its Department for the Suppression of Impure Literature. By the 1890s, the Department's list of impurities included advertisements that used the female form, "living pictures," "indecent shows and posters," and "photographing of the nude" as well as more highbrow forms of erotica. As part of a national social purity movement, the women wrote legislation, lobbied, collected signatures on petitions, and distributed thousands of pages of anti-vice literature.[25] The women protesters, it seems, believed that public display of the female body "lower[ed] the standard of womanhood, detract[ed] from womanly dignity, and corrupt[ed] the youth of the land."[26]

Through the early twentieth century, middle-class women reformers continued as foot soldiers, patrolling the borders of obscenity. By the 1910s, the General Federation of Women's Clubs (GFWC) had replaced the WCTU as the center of women's organized protest. In the 1910s and 1920s, it condemned, for example, "suggestive stories in magazines," "the vulgar popular song," "obscene literature," and "bathing beauty contests." Its most sustained protests, though, focused on "immoral" popular films and their alleged damage to youth. In 1929, after years of protest against and consultation with Hollywood, the GFWC came to an agreement with the motion picture industry. Prominent middle-class women's organizations, including the GFWC, the Daughters of the American Revolution, and the Business and Professional Women's Clubs, sent women volunteers to preview films and compile lists of recommended movies.[27]

Countering this regulatory movement, a pro-erotica stance emerged more slowly. This position is harder to document than the organized protest; nonetheless, it is clear that by the early twentieth century, as sexual mores changed, increasing numbers of women performed in and attended the new sexual entertainments. Working-class daughters and middle-class flappers wore their enjoyment of sexual entertainment as a badge of their sophistication. Young feminists broke away from the social purity movement, fought for their right to sexual pleasure, and "embraced and romanticized sexual daring."[28] Women observed the new sexual fashions displayed on the stage and screen, and bought the new swimwear and dresses that revealed increasing portions of arm and leg. For these women, perhaps, the thrill of sexual daring derived in part from breaking former taboos. While they asserted their right to participate in the sexual entertainment, they seem to have accepted the already entrenched code of the demimonde in which the female body served as the primary symbol of sexual pleasure.[29]

By the 1920s, a few women began to engage in vocal defense of sexual representations. Most notably, women bohemians protested the suppression of erotic art. Margaret Anderson, publisher of *The Little Review*, captured the tone in 1921 when she and her partner Jane Heap faced obscenity charges for publishing excerpts of James Joyce's *Ulysses*. "[The] judges," Anderson claimed . . . do not know the difference between James Joyce and obscene postal cards. . . . [T]he words 'literature' and 'obscenity' can not be used in conjunction any more than the words 'science' and 'immorality' can." Like Anderson, most pro-erotica intellectuals distinguished obscenity, which they condemned, from art, which they supported.[30] On a more popular level, and without the references to art, this pro-erotica stance appeared by mid-century in women's applause for mass-produced cheesecake and borderline material. "I . . . am a young housewife," one woman wrote, "and I enjoy [*Playboy*] as much as any man! I am sure a lot of other women do too!"[31]

By the mid-twentieth century, Americans lived in what John D'Emilio and Estelle Freedman have labeled a "sexualized society," which valued sexual pleasure as a primary source of personal happiness, for women as well as men.[32] Among the middle class, the social purity movement had declined, and the moralists had lost their biggest battles against modernist art. But the wars over sexuality had hardly ended. From the mid-1930s into the 1960s, massive campaigns against "sexual psychopaths," prostitutes, homosexuals, abortionists, and pornographers pointed to fears of sexuality out of control.[33] Protesters voiced explicit fears that sex in the mass media had undermined moral order, and girlie pictures served as frequent targets of attack. As these mid-century sex wars flared and as girlie pictures multiplied, women entered into heated public debates on the meanings of the exposed female body.

WOMEN READ *ESQUIRE*

In the early 1940s, in the wake of a wave of local protests, Postmaster General Frank C. Walker began to deny discount (second-class) postal rates to dozens of girlie, detective, and adventure magazines. Walker treated these magazines as borderline material: he did not declare them wholly nonmailable, but he did question their contribution to the public good. For the most part, he focused his attack on working-class targets, such as *Sir,* "the poor man's *Esquire.*"[34] Eventually, though, he revoked the second-class mailing privilege of *Esquire* itself. In September 1943, the Post Office claimed that *Esquire* included matters of "obscene, lewd, and lascivious character." It objected especially to the "Varga girls," the popular pin-ups created by illustrator Alberto Vargas.[35]

In October and November 1943, the Post Office Department held hearings to allow *Esquire* to "show cause" as to why the second-class mailing privilege should not be revoked. *Esquire* pulled out all the stops. It published a three-quarter-page advertisement in the *Washington Post,* proclaiming its morale-boosting benefits to U.S. troops overseas. Its lawyers compiled a seventy-one-page "respondent's memorandum" to refute the obscenity charges, and at the hearings prominent witnesses, including H. L. Mencken, testified on the magazine's behalf.[36] When the hearings ended, the Post Office board voted two-to-one in *Esquire*'s favor, but Postmaster General Walker upheld his original decision. The case continued through appeals until it reached the U.S. Supreme Court in 1946 as *Hannegan v. Esquire*. In a unanimous decision, the court proclaimed that the postmaster general could not exercise "a power of censorship abhorrent to our traditions."[37] The decision narrowed the federal power to control the flood of girlie magazines that surged in the 1950s.

In the lengthy Post Office hearings, *Esquire* called in two women witnesses, child welfare activist Edith B. Cook of the Connecticut State Welfare Association, and social worker Rae L. Weissman of the New York City Committee on Mental Hygiene.[38] Cook and Weissman, of course, did not find the magazine indecent. The dour prosecutor for the Post Office felt compelled to state for the record that "questioning a woman" about obscenity caused him "a great deal of embarrassment," but Cook and Weissman approached the mailer without reticence. Cook spelled out a version of history in which pictures of semi-clad women represented a progressive change from a repressive past. "I was brought up in the Victorian method or manner," she stated, "where everything was kept under cover. . . . The young people today . . . are brought up so they knew [sic] most everything. . . . I think it is a good deal better and a purer way to bring them up." In the post–Victorian era, she claimed, "we are a great deal franker and, therefore, sex isn't necessarily impure." She argued that the pictures in question were "very attractive," and not at all immoral, as, she said, "we are used to seeing those things." For Cook, an erotic image was not obscene if it was commonly viewed in public places. She testified that the images in *Esquire* differed little from what one might view in an art gallery, at a beach, or in lingerie advertisements. In sum, Cook saw the pictures in *Esquire* as mild cheesecake which she regarded as a positive and widely accepted feature of modem American life. Testifying as a child welfare expert, she claimed further that *Esquire* would not upset the morals of youth. Both boys and girls, she suggested, admired *Esquire's* pin-ups with no deleterious effect.[39]

Rae Weissman, *Esquire's* second woman witness, sidestepped the issue of sexuality and read the images in *Esquire* as aesthetic symbols. For Weissman, the "Varga girl" represented "the type of physical perfection that . . . few, if any, women are fortunate enough to possess." She found them "pleasing to the eye." Beautiful images, she argued, were preferable to "the ugly and grotesque drawings that some of the artists produce." For Weissman, "grotesque" images might have connoted misogyny, but the voluptuous "Varga girls" served as tributes to female beauty. She went so far as to claim that "most women would derive a deep sense of gratification in the thought that the female form is so beautifully portrayed." Weissman tried to escape the prevalent construction that portrayed the female body not only as art form but also as sex. Under questioning, she denied that normal boys or men would find "the picture of a nude woman" particularly stimulating. Only the abnormal man, with "extreme erotic needs," she said, would "derive unusual or extreme satisfaction from looking at a picture."[40]

Weissman's comments, and Cook's as well, reflect a 1940s variant of the modern woman's unsqueamish approach to the proliferation of erotic imagery: women's bodies were lovely, bodily images were not shameful, and pictures only corrupted the abnormal mind. As to pornography, or "filthy pictures" of the "French post card type," Weissman denied that "the average normal individual would be interested in looking." She thus reinforced the modern sexual code that distinguished healthy cheesecake, attractive to normal men and women, from illicit pornography, appealing only to the abnormal.[41]

On the opposing side, the Post Office called only one woman, feminist Anna Kelton Wiley, a longtime Washington, D.C., activist in the National Woman's Party General Federation of Women's Clubs, and Daughters of the American Revolution.[42] Steadfast in her convictions, Wiley refused to draw the common twentieth-century distinctions between cheesecake, borderline material, and pornography. While she eventually granted that some things are worse than others," she displayed a deep distrust of any sexual imagery. She found *Esquire* "degrading and depressing to women," and she tied her aversion directly to her feminist politics:

> I have spent my life in trying to build up the dignity of women. I have been thirty years in this movement to secure . . . equal rights for men and women . . . and all of this [material from *Esquire*] . . . is contrary to the campaign that we women have . . . sacrificed so much to carry on.

Wiley insisted that images of seminude women debased women because they implied that women "gained their point by chicanery and the lure of sex."[43] For Wiley, sex was not a legitimate public activity. To suggest that women used sex in the public realm detracted from the fight for equal rights because it implied that women advanced themselves differently, and less honorably, than men. Note that Wiley's argument differs from contemporary feminist antipornography positions: she saw the women depicted in *Esquire* as active subjects luring men, not as victims of the voyeuristic male gaze. As she noted more than a year later, she wanted women to depend "more and more on their mental and spiritual capacities and less and less on personal appearance, glamour and charm."[44]

Amidst the wartime celebration of pin-ups, Wiley's disgust with cheesecake seemed old-fashioned, and the lawyer for *Esquire* cast her in the role of the "prudish Victorian matriarch."[45] He presented a picture of a woman in swimwear which Wiley refused to proclaim "decent," and he then revealed that the picture in question was a thirty-year-old photo of swimming champion Annette Kellerman. At that point, Wiley had to grant that the picture was decent. She reiterated her argument. She did not object to bathing suits on the beach or at a pool, but in magazines like *Esquire,* she claimed, they had a different meaning. She responded with the defensiveness of a feminist often ridiculed: "I knew I was going to be trapped . . . and I know I shall be in every column tomorrow. . . . I am trying to be made a prude. I am not a prude."[46] True to her prediction, the *Washington Daily News* mocked her the following day with an article headlined, "The Shapely Annette Shocks, Unshocks a Feminist Leader," and the *Washington Post* labeled her "grim" and lampooned her in a cartoon.[47]

While the women witnesses were not major players in the *Esquire* case, their testimony maps an area of dispute. On one side, Cook and Weissman tried to portray the pictures in *Esquire* as wholesome cheesecake. They described the images as commonly accepted, modern, healthy, and lovely imagery, admired by girls and women as well as by boys and men. They avoided the obvious gender asymmetry that we notice immediately today: that only women were portrayed with their clothes off and that the pictures were created by men for heterosexual male pleasure. Instead, they cleansed the images by associating them with pleasure for all and with the uplifting qualities of health, beauty, and art. On the other side, Wiley attempted to sully *Esquire* by linking it to pornography, low vulgarity, immorality, and prostitution. For Wiley, the rise of modern sexual display was a story of declension, not progress. She saw erotic images of the female body as harmful to all women. In Wiley's vision, a woman's power should emanate from her "mental and spiritual capacities," a form of power she found threatened by the modern emphasis on glamour and allure. But Wiley's version of feminism relied on concepts of sexual purity that reinforced a distinction between good women and bad. In this view, sex was a private act and any woman who made a public display of it was indecent, undignified, and unattractive.

Outside of the hearing rooms, probably few women knew the details of the testimony for and against *Esquire.* Similar issues and similar arguments came up repeatedly though, as other women addressed the explosion of girlie pictures and girlie magazines in the postwar era.

THE RACIAL POLITICS OF CHEESECAKE

The battle over sexual representations erupted again in the mid-1940s when readers of *Ebony* and *Negro Digest* responded to photos of semi-clad African American women. The disputed pictures, as some readers noted, differed little from cheesecake images published in white magazines, such as *Life* and never went beyond the risqué pictures featured in *Esquire*. Nonetheless, from 1945 to 1957, *Ebony* and *Negro Digest* published sixty-seven letters commenting on cheesecake or the controversy surrounding it. The magazines published letters from both women and men (with a few more letters from women), but the letters from men supported cheesecake overwhelmingly (over two to one) while the majority of the letters from women opposed it.[48]

The women who wrote letters to *Ebony* and *Negro Digest* often addressed issues of respectability, beauty, and morality in much the same language that white women did. Black women supporters of cheesecake labeled the pictures "beautiful" and argued that they appeared "in all leading magazines."[49] Women protesters complained that the photos were "offensive and . . . in very bad taste," "disgusting and revolting," and "obscene." "There was no art in these poses—just cheap sensualism," wrote one woman, and the women who posed, wrote another, were "really a disgrace to all women."[50] Mrs. J. M. Washington portrayed sexual representation as a woman's issue:

> I can see no reason whatsoever in picturing a naked body of a woman regardless of her race, creed or color on the cover of a magazine. It shocks me to think of a woman who would permit such a photo to be taken—such little self-pride she must have. It certainly isn't attractive . . . and since most of the supporters of *Ebony* are women, we should have some say about what goes on the cover.

Like white clubwomen, she concluded with a call for "better moral examples to our youth."[51]

But African American women also argued the pros and cons of sexual images within the context of American racism. Since the early years of the slave trade, white men had used racist stereotypes of African "animal" sexuality to justify the sexual exploitation of black women. And some of the most hard-core pornography presented nonwhite women as exotic objects of titillation for white men.[52] From the end of the nineteenth century, middle-class African-American women activists had worked strenuously to counter these racist stereotypes and to publicize a contrasting image of black women as morally pure.[53] At the same time that black women were sexually exploited and sexually stereotyped, though, they were also portrayed as lacking in beauty by the dominant white culture. Through the mid-twentieth century, the cheesecake in Hollywood movies, the most widely circulating magazines, and Miss America contests remained exclusively white. In this context, the debate over cheesecake took on a different political tone, in which supporters wrote of African American women's equality in beauty and opponents wrote to defend African American women's morals.

Support for cheesecake was stated most bluntly by Gladys V. Brown in the March 1947 issue of *Ebony*. "Black women are just as good as other women," she wrote. "Why don't they stop putting women of other races and women that don't look colored inside and outside of the colored magazines?" In this line of argument, the representation of black women's bodies was a sign of racial progress. "I get tired of girlie covers too," wrote another woman, "but you are doing the world in general a great service by making it aware of the beautiful women in our race. . . . It's time our conception of beauty embraced something besides the Nordic type."[54] Several supporters of cheesecake wrote to demand pictures of darker-skinned women, and one woman also addressed the issue of class when she asked for pictures of "a pretty washerwoman," not just professionals.[55] From this point of view, cheesecake did not objectify women for male viewers; it provided democratic social lessons about American racist and classist standards of beauty. One woman berated "the readers who are so ignorant that they can't appreciate the beauty in the cover pages." She applauded *Ebony*'s pictures as a critical social message: "The white man glorifies the pulchritude of his fair sex in his magazines and daily papers. I commend you for taking the lone stand in doing the same for Negro women."[56]

The black women who opposed cheesecake were less likely to view it as democratic lessons in beauty and more likely to see it as damaging symbols of illicit sex. Some called on African Americans to reject the immorality of the white culture. As one woman wrote, "Why copy all the vices of the white man?"[57] For other women, the cheesecake pictures damaged the cause of racial progress by confirming white stereotypes of loose black sexuality. One woman claimed, "the flagrant appeal to the sex-obsessed . . . just help[s] build up the impression many people have of Negroes as morally inferior." This concern with respectability also surfaced in a letter that implicitly distinguished between moral women and the "low type female" who posed for pictures.[58] For the opponents of cheesecake, public sexual display and the "low type female" allegedly depicted were an embarrassment to black womanhood.

By late 1947 reader protest had had an impact. The editors of *Negro Digest* decided to get "a divorce from the 'cheesecake' girls," noting that "efforts to reach out to an audience . . . attracted by . . . sex . . . have frankly not clicked."[59] But in *Ebony* the pictures continued through the 1950s, with some reduction by mid-decade of the most risqué. The unresolved debate demonstrates that the relatively new category of cheesecake remained contested. The defenders of cheesecake saw it as respectable beauty, so respectable, in fact, that the inclusion of African American women counted as racial advancement. In contrast, for the opponents of cheesecake, seminude images reflected negatively on the moral status of African American women and hindered the struggle for racial progress.

SEXUAL FILTH OR SEXUAL FUN

By all accounts, the pictures in *Ebony, Negro Digest,* and even *Esquire* were tepid when compared to the borderline photography in *Playboy*. It is not surprising, then, that the controversy over girlie pictures emerged in force as *Playboy*'s circulation skyrocketed in the 1950s. In the pages of *Playboy* itself, women wrote to praise or condemn the magazine. From its first issue in December 1953 through the end of 1959, *Playboy* published over fifty such commentaries from women; of these letters, around four-fifths lavished praise.[60] The women who supported *Playboy* took an unequivocal stand on their right to read and enjoy a magazine for men, while the women who condemned *Playboy* asserted their authority to denounce girlie magazines, even if women were not the intended audience. On both sides, some of the women wrote with anger: after reading letters from women protesters, a woman supporter proclaimed, "I'm *furious*," and a few months later, a woman who denounced *Playboy* stated, "I'm so mad I could scream."[61]

The few letters from women critics labeled the magazine "filth," "dribble," "a disgrace," and "trash."[62] As in earlier debates, the women critics feared that sexual images undermined the dignity of women. One woman thought the magazine showed "no respect for womanhood," and another accused a woman who posed of embarrassing "all womankind." Respectable women, three stewardesses implied, did not want to see themselves portrayed as a "bunch of sex machines." As one eighteen-year-old wrote from Kansas: "I feel very depressed to think that there are some women who have so little respect for themselves as to pose with their bodies showing. . . . [I]t is lowering the standards of all the nice girls."[63] As in the *Esquire* hearings, these women critics could expect public ridicule: *Playboy*'s editors sometimes appended snide putdowns to the letters, expressing "pity" for one woman's husband, for example, and accusing another woman of "sour grapes."[64] The women who appreciated *Playboy* worked to distance themselves from the women who opposed it. One woman objected to the women critics who attempted to place women "on some sort of pedestal." "I have nothing but pity," she wrote, "for the female who is a lady at all times."[65] These women supporters portrayed themselves as cosmopolitan and distinguished themselves from "the popular notion . . . [of] prim, frustrated, old maids who get shocked and blush at anything 'naughty.'" They claimed to prefer *Playboy* to popular literature aimed at women. *Playboy*, one woman wrote, was "a refreshing change from the whipped-cream pap of the so-called women's magazines."[66]

For some of the women who admired *Playboy*, the pin-ups served as the epitome of female sexual allure. Several such women expressed pride in their own bodies. Some of these women sent in pictures of themselves, and a few asked, as one woman put it, for the "great honor" of serving as "Playmate of the Month."[67] These letter writers identified themselves variously as college students, working women, and wives. In one case, a professional sex worker, Evelyn "Treasure Chest" West of Los Angeles, sent in a picture of herself performing bare chested on a stage; she wrote again a few months later to comment on the many "wonderful letters" she had received from admirers.[68] For these women, the playmates provided the standards to which they compared themselves, usually favorably, and the fantasy to which they aspired.

Other women who appreciated *Playboy* attempted to establish that women enjoyed the "spice of life." These women seemed cognizant of the stigma still attached to openly sexual women, and they marked their letters with forms of identification that underscored their respectability. Various women supporters made references to their religiosity, their husbands, or their children, and one ardent admirer of *Playboy* proclaimed, "I'm an ex-PTA President and a Sunday School teacher."[69] These women, it seems, hoped to establish that commodified sexual pleasure was not for men and prostitutes only. Avowedly heterosexual, they insisted on their right to appreciate a magazine aimed explicitly at men. As one letter writer stated, "I'm strictly a woman, and can prove it, and man, I dig your magazine the most."[70] Only two women requested beefcake photos of men; the other supportive letter writers applauded the magazine just as it was."[71] Although *Playboy* was created by and for heterosexual men, these women adamantly insisted that they too enjoyed it. They rejected a double standard in which men enjoyed sexual titillation while women feigned sexual innocence. They thereby asserted their right to inclusion in what they saw as sexual fun.

The letters to *Playboy* illustrate the depth of the division among women. On one side, women supporters read the magazine as a positive expression of heterosexual pleasure and feminine appeal. Some of these women lambasted the women who opposed *Playboy*. One woman, for example, called a woman protester "a drip" and diagnosed her psychologically as "very unsure of herself." She continued: "These hypocrites who make critics and censors of themselves give me a pain."[72] On the other side, women who protested *Playboy* read the magazine as "irresponsible" smut that raised questions "in terms of morality, purity, and the dignity of woman." These women expressed dismay at the women who posed for pictures. "No," wrote one woman, "I won't even call that type a woman," and she then proceeded to label them "bags."[73] One woman's fun was another woman's filth, one woman's pride in allure was another woman's anger at exposure, and each side disparaged the other.[74]

A NATIONAL CAMPAIGN

The letters to *Playboy* were one small piece of a larger cultural conflict. As *Playboy* and other girlie magazines rose to undisputed success, an avalanche of protest descended. In the 1950s, the booming postwar industry in sexual representations inspired revitalized antiobscenity campaigns in cities and towns across the nation.[75] National antiobscenity efforts received two significant boosts in late 1952. In October, *Reader's Digest,* with a circulation of ten million, published novelist Margaret Culkin Banning's exposé "Filth on the Newsstands." In the past, Banning claimed, girlie magazines had circulated "in barbershops, saloons and Army posts," but now, she protested, they competed "right down at the corner drugstore, with all other forms of reading." Two months after Banning's national exposé, the House of Representatives' newly appointed Select Committee on Current Pornographic Materials held well-publicized hearings. At the hearings, Banning testified that girlie magazines had "no purpose except pictorial prostitution."[76]

As a national movement emerged, the General Federation of Women's Clubs once again came to the fore. The Federation began its postwar protests as part of a national campaign against crime and horror comic books. In the course of investigating newsstands, though, the clubwomen discovered a different genre, "magazines of the 'girlie,' 'male,' 'stag,' and 'confidential' type." In 1955, the federation's monthly magazine announced: "Amid all the hue and cry against crime comics, another empire of prurience is thriving—pornographic magazines." According to an internal report, clubwomen were "encouraged by the effectiveness of the campaign against crime comics" and "aroused and indignant over this newest kind of salacious literature." For the most part, the women did not protest pornography, which was not available on open newsstands. "The great problem existing today," stated one GFWC expose, "is with the borderline material. More specifically, it concerns the flood of so-called girly magazines."[77]

In this campaign, as in earlier ones, a recurring motif was that borderline material corrupted youth. The clubwomen were especially disturbed because children and teenagers had access to such material at newsstands and sometimes received direct solicitations through the mail.

With an emphasis on youth, the GFWC dusted off its longstanding maternalist politics and portrayed borderline as a mother's issue. In an era when few people celebrated the sexuality of children, these women bolstered their role as maternal protectors. One activist described what she saw as the cultural contest:

> In the battle for the minds of our youth, the . . . contestants are the purveyors of harmful literature against the mothers, grandmothers, clubwomen and right thinking women everywhere. The morality of our country can depend upon who is the victor . . . . I'M BET-TING ON THE WOMEN![78]

This maternalist language flourished anew as women constructed the battle against borderline as a battle to save the home. In the anxious climate of the 1950s, the clubwomen addressed fears that the "big business of pornography" had invaded the home and undermined the family.[79] In the GFWC's magazine, Congresswoman Kathryn Granahan wrote: "The American home is the target of the pornographic attack. The American home must also be the center of the counterattack against pornography."[80]

The GFWC called on local women's clubs to form citizens' committees, evaluate magazines, pressure retailers, and lobby for legislation. And so they did. In Coral Gables, clubwomen inaugurated a campaign, and the American Legion Auxiliary "carried the campaign to every community" in Florida.[81] In Cincinnati, representatives from over fifty organizations joined to form the Mothers March Against Obscenity. The women's protest "began in the [local] AFL-CIO League of Women," suggesting that women's outrage against borderline material may well have crossed class lines.[82] In these and numerous other local campaigns, women presented themselves as moral guardians of the young.

But the clubwomen also offered a protofeminist argument. Like other women protesters, they saw girlie magazines as especially harmful to women and girls. The GFWC noted the "enormous circulation [of borderline material] among young women." Young readers asked themselves whether behaving "immorally, immodestly and with no regard for conventions" was "the price of popularity" or "the typical conduct of attractive girls."[83] Mrs. Walter V. Magee, chair of the Community Affairs Division, made the case most strongly:

> It is tragic to think that a sweet young girl is led . . . to believe that the only way in which she may be accepted socially is to display herself, seminude. . . . The pinnacle of achievement is represented . . . as a girl who exposes as much of her body as possible, surrounded by gaping and leering males.

According to Magee, young women had confided to her about the effect of girlie magazines on their husbands. "A young wife and mother," she wrote, "is expected to join the parade of nudity, listen to dirty stories and exploit her person in imitation of [magazine models]." Even worse, preteen girls "worry because they are not curvaceous." In these ways, Magee worried, sexual representations damaged women's sense of themselves and shaped their public and private behaviors.[84]

In their attack on girlie magazines the clubwomen expressed broader postwar fears about mass media and its impact on the moral order.[85] The same fears appeared starkly in a *Ladies Home Journal* forum of 1956, entitled "Do Americans Commercialize Sex?" The participants in the forum, five women and two men, voiced a blasting critique of popular culture. The women, who dominated throughout, not only protested "men's magazines," but also sex in movies, television, advertising, book jackets, jazz records, comic books, and movie magazines. They turned again and again to images of the female body; they protested, for example, "pictures of girls in Bikini bathing suits," "a star in a tight, well-filled flaming-red dress with tons of men following her around," "the Playmate of the month," and "Marilyn Monroe movies." They did not, it seems, want women to depend on physical allure, nor did they want youth to engage in sexual acts. Conflating their concerns with women and youth, they focused on teenage girls who, they repeatedly argued, suffered moral damage from imitating cheesecake pictures.[86] Mrs. Ian D. Marsh of St. Louis went even further and expressed the ultimate fear of moral anarchy: "we can commercialize [sex] and degrade it to the extent that we destroy our own happiness, our marriages, our homes and even our nation."[87]

In their protests against cheesecake and borderline material, clubwomen were not the most powerful combatants; they did not control the magazine industry, the legislatures, the vice societies, or the courts. Nonetheless, individually and in association, they repeatedly asserted their limited cultural authority to challenge the rise of mass-produced female sexual display. And on the local level, the clubwomen and their allies seem to have had some success: they restricted sales on newsstands, promoted harsher antiobscenity legislation, and persuaded police to enforce the laws.[88]

Cheesecake and borderline material arose in the confluence of rising consumerism, burgeoning mass production, and changing sexual mores. They comprised and reinforced a new taxonomy of sexual display that changed the ways that women were seen in public and perhaps also the ways that women saw themselves. And they divided women from one another. In fact, the battles over cheesecake and borderline material hint at a recurring division among American women, an ideological split that did not disappear when the Victorian sexual ethos collapsed. This division cut across racial, generational, and perhaps class lines. Through the mid-twentieth century, some women saw shameless beauty and sexual pleasure in erotic representations of the female body while others saw degradation of women and corruption of youth.

During and after World War II, the division seems to have deepened. The deployment of feminine sex appeal accelerated while the stigma attached to openly sexual women scarcely diminished.[89] In this conflicted climate, women attempted to negotiate older concepts of female morality and newer standards of sexual display. They disagreed on whether cheesecake and borderline material (and the women who posed for pictures) empowered or embarrassed them. On opposing sides, they posited different criteria for what constituted progress and dignity for women, and they held divergent views on the impact of mass-marketed culture.

In recent years, this ideological split has reappeared, in different form, in feminist battles over pornography. As hardcore pornographic films, videos, and magazines have reached a wider national audience, women have entered again into heated debates over the meanings of mass-produced sexual representation. On one side, antipornography feminists protest the subordination of women in pornography constructed by and for men. On the other side, anticensorship feminists defend freedom of speech and insist that sexual images might promise sensual pleasure to women as well as men. These "sex wars" raged in the 1980s and still smolder today. In these ongoing battles, a long-standing ideological rift continues, in new permutations, to haunt the American women's movement.

NOTES

This essay was first presented as a paper at the Organization of American Historians Conference, April 1993. For their advice on earlier versions, I thank Paul Boyer, Anne Boylan, Alice Echols, Estelle Freedman, Christina Simmons, and the students in my graduate colloquium on mass culture. Thanks also to Sarah Heath for research assistance.

1. Dozens of publications generally fall into one of two opposing political camps: "antiporn" feminists demand legislation to combat certain sexual representations, and "anticensorship" feminists object to censorship. For feminist antipornography viewpoints, see, for example, Andrea Dworkin and Catharine A. MacKinnon, *Pornography and Civil Rights: A New Day for Women's Equality* (Minneapolis: Organizing Against Pornography, 1988); Catharine A. MacKinnon, *Feminism Unmodified: Discourses on Life and Law* (Cambridge, MA: Harvard University Press, 1987), part 3; Diana E. H. Russell, ed., *Making Violence Sexy: Feminist Views on Pornography* (New York: Teachers College Press, 1993). For feminist anticensorship

statements, see, for example, Vanda Bursty, ed., *Women against Censorship* (Vancouver: Douglas and McIntyre, 1985); FACT (Feminist Anti-Censorship Task Force) Book Committee, *Caught Looking: Feminism, Pornography and Censorship* (New York: Caught Looking, Inc., 1986); Lynne Segal and Mary McIntosh, eds., *Sex Exposed: Sexuality and the Pornography Debate* (New Brunswick, NJ: Rutgers University Press, 1993); Nadine Strosseir, *Defending Pornography: Free Speech, Sex, and the Fight for Women's Rights* (New York: Scribner, 1994).

2. On the history of pornography, see, for example, H. Montgomery Hyde, *A History of Pornography* (New York: Farrar, Straus, Giroux, 1964); Steven Marcus, *The Other Victorians: A Study of Sexuality and Pornography in Mid-Nineteenth-Century England* (New York: Basic Books, 1974); Al DiLauro and Gerald Rabkin, *Dirty Movies: An Illustrated History of the Stag Film, 1915–1970* (New York: Chelsea House, 1976); Linda Williams, *Hard Core: Power, Pleasure, and the "Frenzy of the Visible"* (Berkeley: University of California Press, 1989), chapters 2 and 3. On nudity in the Euro-American fine arts tradition, see, for example, Kenneth Clark, *The Nude: A Study in Ideal Form* (New York: Pantheon, 1956); John Berger, *Ways of Seeing* (New York: Viking, 1972), chapter 3; Marcia Point, *Naked Authority: The Body in Western Painting, 1830–1908* (Cambridge: Cambridge University Press, 1990); Lynda Near, *The Female Nude* (New York: Routledge, 1990). On censorship battles, see, for example, Robert W. Haney, *Comstockery in America: Patterns of Censorship and Control* (Boston: Beacon Press, 1960); James C. N. Paul and Murray L. Schwartz, *Federal Censorship: Obscenity in the Mail* (New York: Free Press, 1961); Paul S. Boyer, *Purity in Print: The Vice-Society Movement and Book Censorship in America* (New York: Charles Scribner, 1968); Felice Flannery Lewis, *Literature, Obscenity, and Law* (Carbondale: University of Illinois Press., 1976); Walter Kendrick, *The Secret Museum: Pornography in Modern Culture* (New York: Viking, 1987); Edward De Grazia and Roger K. Newman, *Banned Films: Movies, Censors and the First Amendment* (New York: B. B. Bowker, 1982); and the articles in *American Quarterly* (December 1992).

3. Two popular histories of pin-ups address some of the history of cheesecake and borderline material. Especially useful is Mark Gabor, *The Pin-Up: A Modest History* (New York: Universe Books, 1972). See also Ralph Stein, *The Pin-Up: From 1852 to Now* (Chicago: Ridge Press and Playboy Press, 1974).

4. Michel Foucault, *The History of Sexuality, Vol. 1: An Introduction* (New York: Viking, 1978). On the United States in the twentieth century see Christina Simmons, "Modern Sexuality and the Myth of Victorian Repression," in *Passion and Power: Sexuality in History*, ed. Kathy Peiss and Christina Simmons (Philadelphia: Temple University Press, 1989); Estelle B. Freedman, "'Uncontrolled Desires': The Response to the Sexual Psychopath, 1920–1960," *Journal of American History* (June 1987).

5. Gabor, *Pin-Up*, 23. According to Webster's *Third New International Dictionary*, "cheesecake" is "photography or photographs (as in advertisements or publicity) featuring the natural curves of shapely female legs, thighs, or trunk, usually scantily clothed."

6. According to Webster's *Third New International Dictionary*, "borderline" is "not quite meeting or conforming to accepted patterns (as of good taste or morality); esp.: verging on the indecent or obscene."

7. In this essay, I am less concerned with the images themselves than I am with the construction of categories. As Andrew Ross writes: "Cultural power does not inhere in the content of categories of taste. On the contrary, it is exercised through the capacity to draw the line between and around categories of taste; it is the power to define where each relational category begins and ends, and the power to determine

what it contains at any one time." Andrew Ross, *No Respect: Intellectuals and Popular Culture* (New York: Routledge, 1989), 61.

8. On the unstable categories of art and obscenity, see, for example, Abigail Solomon-Godeau, *Photography at the Dock: Essays on Photographic History, Institutions, and Practices* (Minneapolis: University of Minnesota Press, 1991), chap. 10; Carolyn Dean, "Pornography, Literature, and the Redemption of Virility in France, 1880–1930," *Differences* 5, no. 2 (1993): 271–96.

9. The category of cheesecake illustrates the concept of "contained license" that historian Peter Bailey labels "parasexuality," a "safely sensational pattern of stimulation and containment." Peter Bailey, "Parasexuality and Glamour: The Victorian Barmaid as Cultural Prototype," *Gender and History* (Summer 1990): 149, 167.

10. On flappers, see James McGovern, "The American Woman's Pre-World War I Freedom in Manners and Morals," *Journal of American History* (September 1968): 315–33. On working-class "charity girls," see Kathy Peiss, "'Charity Girls' and City Pleasures: Historical Notes on Working-Class Sexuality, 1880–1920," in *Powers of Desire: The Politics of Sexuality*, ed. Ann Snitow et al. (New York: Monthly Review Press, 1983); Joanne Meyerowitz, "Sexual Geography and Gender Economy: The Furnished Room Districts of Chicago, 1890–1930," *Gender and History* (Autumn 1990): 274–96. On feminist "new women," see Ellen Carol DuBois and Linda Gordon, "Seeking Ecstasy on the Battlefield: Danger and Pleasure in Nineteenth-Century Feminist Sexual Thought," in *Pleasure and Danger: Exploring Female Sexuality*, ed. Carole S. Vance (Boston: Routledge and Kegan Paul, 1984); Carroll Smith-Rosenberg, *Disorderly Conduct: Visions of Gender in Victorian America* (New York: Knopf, 1985), 245–96; Leila J. Rupp, "Feminism and the Sexual Revolution in the Early Twentieth Century: The Case of Doris Stevens," *Feminist Studies* (Summer 1989): 289–309.

11. William H. Gerdts, *The Great American Nude: A History in Art* (New York: Praeger, 1974), 46, 78–80, 103; David Pivar, *Purity Crusade: Sexual Morality and Social Control, 1868–1900* (Westport, CT: Greenwood Press, 1973), 237–38. On obscenity before the nineteenth century, see Hyde, *History of Pornography*.

12. Lois W. Banner, *American Beauty* (Chicago: University of Chicago Press, 1983), 111; Robert C. Allen, *Horrible Prettiness: Burlesque and American Culture* (Chapel Hill: University of North Carolina Press, 1991), 73–76, 92–94; Christine Stansell, *City of Women: Sex and Class in New York, 1789–1860* (New York: Knopf, 1986), 174–75; Timothy J. Gilfoyle, *City of Eros: New York City, Prostitution, and the Commercialization of Sex, 1790–1920* (New York: W. W. Norton, 1992), 127–28; John D'Emilio and Estelle B. Freedman, *Intimate Matters: A History of Sexuality in America* (New York: Harper and Row, 1988), 130–32; Hyde, *History of Pornography*, 191.

13. On theater, see Allen, *Horrible Prettiness*; Robert C. Toll, *On With the Show: The First Century of Show Business in America* (New York: Oxford University Press, 1976), 207–31; Banner, *American Beauty*, 115–17, 120–27, 180–87. On magazines, see Frank Luther Mott, *A History of American Magazines*, (Cambridge, MA: Harvard University Press, 1938) 2:325–37, 3:43–44, 4:46–47, 152–53, 608–19, 5:144–53; Gabor, *Pin-Up*, 36, 44, 54–56. On other commodified forms of sexual imagery, such as cigarette cards, stereotypic "picture stories," and mutascope (or flip card) films, see Allen, *Horrible Prettiness*, 260, 266–71. See also Martha Banta, *Imaging American Women: Idea and Ideals in Cultural History* (New York: Columbia University Press, 1987), 180, 205–206, 210. According to Banta, in the late nineteenth century, women (clothed or not) came to represent desire (sexual or not) in both high art and popular culture.

14. On theater, see Lewis A. Erenberg, *Steppin' Out: New York Nightlife and The Transformation of American Culture, 1890–1930* (Chicago: University of Chicago Press, 1981), 67; Kathy Peiss, *Cheap Amusements: Working Women and Leisure in Turn-of-the-Century New York* (Philadelphia: Temple University Press, 1986), 142–45, 148–53. On advertisements, see Mott, *History of American Magazines*, 4:32; Stuart Ewen, *Captains of Consciousness: Advertising and the Social Roots of Consumer Culture* (New York: McGraw Hill, 1976), 178–82.

15. *Life* was first published in November 1936; by the second issue, it included cheesecake photos of women in bathing suits.

16. John Costello, *Virtue under Fire: How World War II Changed Our Social and Sexual Attitudes* (Boston: Little, Brown, 1985), 144–55; Robert B. Westbrook, "'I Want a Girl, Just Like the Girl That Married Harry James': American Women and the Problem of Political Obligation in World War II," *American Quarterly* (December 1990): 587–614. The term "pin-up" was popularized during WWII; see Gabor, *Pin-Up*, 77.

17. The *American Federationist* did not include photographs until the 1940s. The first cheesecake photograph was in the August 1945 issue, p. 26. *Ebony* was first published in 1945; it included cheesecake pictures from the start.

18. Early magazines provoked occasional prosecution under obscenity laws. Gabor, *Pin-Up*, 76; Theodore Peterson, *Magazines in the Twentieth Century* (Urbana: University of Illinois Press, 1956), 338–40.

19. See Gabor, *Pin-Up*, 76–77; Kenon Breazeale, "In Spite of Women: *Esquire* Magazine and the Construction of the Male Consumer," *Signs* (autumn 1994): 1–22.

20. Barbara Ehrenreich, *The Hearts of Men: American Dreams and the Flight from Commitment* (Garden City, NY: Anchor Press, 1983), 42–51; John Brady, "Nude Journalism," *Journal of Popular Culture* (Summer 1975): 151/53–161/63, esp. 158/60; *Newsweek*, November 7, 1955, 68, 71. On imitators, see *Time*, September 24, 1956, 71; Gabor, *Pin-Up*, 78, 109. For gay men, the beefcake in physique magazines, such as *Vim* and *Physique Pictorial*, provided analogous visual stimulation (without full frontal nudity); see *One: The Homosexual Viewpoint* (December 1957): 21.

21. Peterson, *Magazines in the Twentieth Century*, 338–40; Di Lauro and Rabkin, *Dirty Movies*, 98, 100.

22. On the decline of prostitution, see Gilfoyle, *City of Eros*, 306–15.

23. For a good general history, see Boyer, *Purity in Print*, 24.

24. Olive Logan, *Apropos of Women and Theatres* (New York: Carlety, 1869), 152–53. See also Allen, *Horrible Prettiness*, 122–27. Women's rights activists often opposed public displays of nudity, but by the 1880s they were condemning Comstock for his overly zealous prosecutions of reformers. For feminist attacks on Comstock, see Lucinda Chandler, "Un-American Institutions," *Woman's Tribune*, January 14, 1888; *Woman's Journal*, May 2, 1891, 138.

25. At the urging of the WCTU, the new National Congress of Mothers also protested degrading "pictures and displays," and the Women's Board of Home Missions and the Women's Sabbath Alliance gave their "hearty endorsement" to the WCTU's efforts. "Promotion of Purity in Literature and Art," in Minutes of WCTU National Convention, 1896, 354–58; "Promotion of Purity in Literature and Art," in Minutes of WCTU National Convention, 1897, 442–50, at Frances E. Willard Memorial Library, Evanston, Ill. (also available on microfilm in the "Temperance and Prohibition" collection produced by the Ohio Historical Society). On the WCTU's activism in this area, see also Alison M. Parker, "'The Desecration of the Woman's Form': The Woman's Christian Temperance Union and Pro-Censorship Activism"

(paper presented at the Organization of American Historians Conference, Anaheim, Calif., 1993); Pivar, *Purity Crusade,* 182–84, 235–38.

26. This statement was made in 1899 by the Illinois Federation of Women's Clubs; quoted in Mott, *History of American Magazines,* 4:32. See also Elizabeth Blackwell, "The Moral Education of the Young in Relation to Sex," in *The Sexuality Debates,* ed. Sheila Jeffreys (New York: Routledge, 1987), 388.

27. 1914, Resolution 4; 1920, Resolution 36; 1924, Resolution 27; 1925, Resolution 12 in Resolutions Notebook, GFWC Archives, Washington, D.C. On the GFWC battle against obscene magazines in the 1920s, see also Nellie B. Miller, "Fighting Filth on Main Sheet," *The Independent* 115 (October 10, 1925), 411–12, 428. For the GFWC's early condemnation of films, see 1916, Resolution 3; 1918, Resolution 36; 1922, Resolution 18 in Resolutions Notebook, GFWC Archives, Washington, D.C. For summaries of GFWC activities concerning the regulation of films in the 1920s, see *General Federation News* (December 1923), 3; *General Federation News* (January–February 1925), 21; *General Federation News* (December 1925), 11; *General Federation News* (January–February 1926), 11. The women's preview committees, in Hollywood and New York City, continued their work at least through the 1950s. See Mrs. P. E. Willis, "Nothing But the Best," *General Federation Clubwoman* (May 1949), 13; Raymond Moley, *The Hays Office* (Indianapolis, 1945), 143–45; Garth Jowett, *Film: The Democratic Art* (Boston: Little, Brown, 1976), 178–80.

28. DuBois and Gordon, "Seeking Ecstasy on the Battlefield," 41. On women and the new eroticism, see also McGovern, "The American Woman's Pre-World War I Freedom in Manners and Morals"; Elizabeth Ewen, "City Lights: Immigrant Women and the Rise of the Movies," *Signs* (Spring 1980), supplement, S45–S65; Peiss, *Cheap Amusements,* 45–76; Erenberg, *Steppin' Out,* 60–87; Meyerowitz, "Sexual Geography and Gender Economy"; Nancy F. Cott, *The Grounding of Modern Feminism* (New Haven, CT: Yale University Press, 1987), 41–49.

29. In the early twentieth century, at least one woman noted the contradiction in heterosexual women attending performances created for heterosexual male pleasure. She requested more men on stage, or "equality of opportunity for emotional satisfaction." Mary Vida Clarke, "Sauce for the Gander and Sawdust for the Goose," *The Dial* (December 14, 1918), 542, 543. By the 1920s, there were at least some popular beefcake images of men, such as movie star Rudolph Valentino, directed at heterosexual women, but beefcake was never as widespread nor as contested as cheesecake. On Valentino, see Gaylyn Studlar, "Discourses of Gender and Ethnicity: The Construction and De(con)struction of Rudolph Valentino as Other," *Film Criticism* (winter 1989): 18–35; Miriam Hansen, *Babel and Babylon: Spectatorship in American Silent Film* (Cambridge: Cambridge University Press, 1991), part 3.

30. See Margaret Anderson, "'Ulysses' in Court," *The Little Review* (January–March 1921): 22. On pro-erotica intellectuals, see Boyer, *Purity in Print*; Joan Hoff, "Why Is There No History of Pornography?" in *For Adult Users Only: The Dilemma of Violent Pornography,* ed. Susan Gubar and Joan Hoff (Bloomington: Indiana University Press, 1989), 20–23, 27–28.

31. Letter from Alice Soriano, *Playboy* (September 1954): 4.

32. D'Emilio and Freedman, *Intimate Matters,* 326–43.

33. Freedman, "'Uncontrolled Desires'"; Allan M. Brandt, *No Magic Bullet: A Social History of Venereal Disease in the United States Since 1880* (New York: Oxford University Press, 1985); John D'Emilio, *Sexual Politics, Sexual Communities: The Making of a Homosexual Minority in the United States, 1940–1970* (Chicago: University of Chicago Press, 1983); Rickie Solinger, "Extreme Danger: Women

Abortionists and Their Clients before *Roe v. Wade*," in *Not June Cleaver: Women and Gender in Postwar America, 1945–1960,* ed. Joanne Meyerowitz (Philadelphia: Temple University Press, 1994); D'Emilio and Freedman, *Intimate Matters,* 280–84.

34. On local protest, see Courtney Riley Cooper, "This Trash Must Go!" *Forum* (February 1940): 61–64. On Walker's campaign, see Press Releases, Information Service, Post Office Department, 1942 and 1943, in bound volumes, Post Office Department Library. Post Office Building, L'Enfant Plaza, Washington, D.C.; Post Office Department, Annual Report of the Postmaster General for the Fiscal Year Ending June 30, 1942 (Washington, D.C.: Government Printing Office, 1942), 11–13; *PM* (July 16, 1943): 5.

35. District Court of the United States for the District of Columbia, *Esquire v. Frank C. Walker, Postmaster General, Transcript of Proceedings Before Post Office Department,* Civil No. 22722, National Archives, Post Office Department Records, Record Group 28, 46:2, 1, 14.

36. *Washington Post,* October 5, 1943; Cravath, de Gersdorff, Swaine and Wood, "Respondent's Memorandum for Use of Board at Hearing," National Archives, Post Office Department Records, Record Group 28, 46:1. For press reports on the hearings, see National Archives, Post Office Department Records, Record Group 28, 46:3.

37. "Press Release on Postmaster General Frank C. Walker's Decision to Revoke Second-Class Mailing Privileges," December 31, 1943, National Archives, Post Office Department Records, Record Group 28,46:1; *New York Times,* February 5, 1946; *Hannegan v. Esquire, Inc.,* 327 U.S. 151.

38. *Esquire* also solicited depositions from prominent academics Mary Ellen Chase and Marjorie Hope Nicholson. The depositions stated that college-age women would not suffer moral damage from reading *Esquire.*

39. *Esquire v. Frank C. Walker,* 957, 960–61, 964, 965.

40. *Esquire v. Frank C. Walker,* 991, 997, 999.

41. *Esquire v. Frank C. Walker,* 999.

42. Wiley was also active in the Housekeepers' Alliance, Woman's Civic Club, Washington Institute of Mental Hygiene, and Twentieth-Century Club. While Cook and Weissman held expert status in the fields of child welfare and mental hygiene, Wiley placed herself squarely in the female voluntarist camp.

43. *Esquire v. Frank C. Walker,* 1689, 1686, 1688–89.

44. Quoted in Leila J. Rupp and Verta Taylor, *Survival in the Doldrums: The American Women's Rights Movement, 1945 to the 1960s* (Columbus, OH: The Ohio State University Press, 1990), 64.

45. On the "prudish Victorian matriarch" stereotype, see Simmons, "Modern Sexuality."

46. *Esquire v. Frank C. Walker,* 1691–92.

47. *Washington Daily News,* November 6, 1943 (available in National Archives, Post Office Department Records, Record Group 28, 46:3); *Washington Post,* November 6, 1943.

48. These numbers, of course, do not necessarily reflect differences between women and men. The magazines may well have published letters selectively, and the apparent gender differences may reflect the magazines' choices about which letters to include. Both *Ebony* and *Negro Digest* were published by John H. Johnson Publications.

49. Letters from Mrs. Eva Young Brown, *Ebony* (August 1947): 7; Mrs. Julia Robinson, *Ebony* (January 1946): 51.

50. Letters from Mary Barrara, *Ebony* (May 1947): 3; Daphne A. Grigsby,

Ebony (August 1947): 4; Harriet E. Dayson, *Ebony* (May 1949): 8; Mrs. T. E. Clark, *Ebony* (August 1947): 4; Mrs. Loretta Powell, *Ebony* (December 1954): 10.

51. Letter from Mrs. J. M. Washington, *Ebony* (August 1950): 6–7.

52. Deborah Gray White, *Ar'n't I a Woman: Female Slaves in the Plantation South* (New York: W. W. Norton, 1985), 29–46; D'Emilio and Freedman, *Intimate Matters,* 132.

53. Paula Giddings, *When and Where I Enter: The Impact of Black Women on Race and Sex in America* (Toronto: Bantam Books, 1984), 85–89; Hazel V. Carby, "It Jus Be's Dat Way Sometime: The Sexual Politics of Women's Blues," *Radical America* (June/July 1986): 12; Darlene Clark Hine, "Rape and the Inner Lives of Black Women in the Middle West: Preliminary Thoughts on the Culture of Dissemblance," *Signs* (summer 1989): 912–20; Hazel Carby, "Policing the Black Woman's Body in an Urban Context," *Critical Inquiry* (Summer 1992): 738–55.

54. Letters from Gladys V. Brown, *Ebony* (March 1947): 6; Esther P. Oliver, *Negro Digest* (April 1948): 98.

55. Letter from Miss L. C. Henry, *Ebony* (February 1947): 50; for other letters supporting dark-skinned women, see letters from Mrs. Cleoria H. DeLaine and Helen Brown, *Ebony* (August 1947): 4. For responses to these women, see letters from Mrs. Marcella Hunt, *Ebony* (April 1947): 3; and Bernice Miller, *Ebony* (January 1951): 7.

56. Letter from Helen L. Beaumont, *Ebony* (March 1948): 9.

57. Letter from Daphne A. Grigsby, *Ebony* (August 1947): 4; see also letter from Muriel Donnelly, *Ebony* (December 1945): 51.

58. Letters from Lillian Dowdell, *Ebony* (August 1947): 6; Dorothy Giles, *Ebony* (September 1947): 5.

59. Editorial, *Negro Digest* (November 1947): 8.

60. I am counting only those letters that made general commentaries on the magazine, its pin-ups, or its appeal to women. I do not include the numerous letters from women that praised or condemned specific articles.

61. Letters from Layde Pettio, *Playboy* (August 1956): 4; "A Virgin," *Playboy* (November 1956): 7.

62. Letters from "An Executive Secretary," *Playboy* (December 1954): 3; Mrs. L. D. Frateschi, *Playboy* (February 1955): 3; Mrs. N. A. Quasebarth, *Playboy* (April 1955): 3; Mrs. C. W. Potter, *Playboy* (May 1956): 6.

63. Letters from Mrs. Ruby Carpenter, *Playboy* (May 1956): 6; Eleanor Heimbeckner, *Playboy* (September 1957): 5; Dorothy Chapman, Khaki Ross, and Shirley Hoffecker, *Playboy* (October 1957): 4; Debra A. Martin, *Playboy* (October 1955): 4.

64. Letters from Mrs. N. A. Quasebarth; Mrs. A. B. Mayfield, *Playboy* (September 1959): 16.

65. Letter from Layde Pettio.

66. Letter from Betty Gay Swan, *Playboy* (December 1954): 3; Anne E. LeCroy, *Playboy* (June 1957): 7. See also letter from Billie O'Doherty, *Playboy* (November 1956): 7.

67. Letter from Susan Counter, *Playboy* (September 1956): 8.

68. Letters from Evelyn "Treasure Chest" West, *Playboy* (April 1954): 3; and (July 1954): 3.

69. Letters from Mrs. Ray Hitch, *Playboy* (February 1955): 4; Mrs. Katherine E. Williamson, *Playboy* (May 1956): 6.

70. Letter from Joni Laiole, *Playboy* (October 1955): 4. For a lesbian's appreciation of girlie magazines in the 1950s, see Elizabeth Lapovsky Kennedy and Madeline D. Davis, *Boots of Leather, Slippers of Gold: The History of a Lesbian Community* (New York: Routledge, 1993), 215.

71. For letters requesting beefcake, see letters from Carol B. Montgomery *Playboy* (November 1956): 7; "Name withheld on request," (March 1959): 5.

72. Letter from Mrs. Ray Hitch.

73. Letters from Mrs. Eva Printz, *Playboy* (May 1956): 6; Debra A. Martin.

74. The oppositional letters in *Playboy* do not necessarily indicate a neat dichotomy of opposing views among women in general. Many women (most of whom did not write letters to girlie magazines) no doubt stood somewhere in the middle, attempting to steer a middle course between the negative referents of prudish "drips" and whorish "bags" presented in the letters to *Playboy.*

75. See J. Edgar Hoover, "The 'Big Business' of Pornography," *General Federation Clubwoman* (October 1959), 16–17, 23–24; Haney, *Comstockery in America,* 98.

76. Margaret Culkin Banning, "Filth on the Newsstands," *Reader's Digest* (October 1952): 115–19. On the House Committee, also known as the Gatbings Commmittee, see *Publisher's Weekly,* May 17, 1952, 2007–2008; December 13, 1952, 2318–21; December 27, 1952, 2436–37; January 10, 1953, 125–27. For Banning quote, see *New York Times,* December 4, 1952, 26.

77. Mrs. Walter V. Magee, "Crime Comics," *General Federation Clubwoman* (September 1956): 10; "Morals at Stake on Your Newsstand," *General Federation Clubwoman* (October 1955): 8; "Objectionable Publications: The Problem," 1, typewritten report in Program Records, 1956–58, Youth Division, General Federation of Women's Clubs Archives, Washington, D.C.; "The 'Big Business' of Pornography," *General Federation Clubwoman* (May/June 1960): 50. On the national comic book campaign, see James Gilbert, *A Cycle of Outrage: America's Reaction to the Juvenile Delinquent in the 1950's* (New York: Oxford University Press, 1986).

78. Magee, "Crime Comics," 10.

79. In 1959 and 1960, the *General Federation Clubwoman* ran a series of articles entitled "The Big Business of Pornography."

80. Kathryn Granahan, "The Big Business of Pornography," On maternalist politics in the early twentieth century, see Seth Koven and Sonya Michel, "Maternalist Politics and the Origins of the Welfare States in France, Germany, Great Britain, and the United States, 1880–1920," *American Historical Review* (October 1990): 1076–1108.

81. O. K. Armstrong, "How Coral Gables Cleaned Up Its Newsstands," *Parents' Magazine* (December 1957): 76, 78; Mrs. Walter V. Magee, "A Year of Achievement," *General Federation Clubwoman* (March 1958): 22.

82. *Cincinnati Enquirer,* November 4, 1958, A7; see also *Cincinnati Post,* February 25, 1958, 1; *Cincinnati Post and Times-Star,* August 6, 1958, 60. For brief reports of other local actions, see "Let's Abolish Pornography," *General Federation Clubwoman* (March 1960), 16–17.

83. Mrs. Arthur Crom, "The 'Big Business' of Pornography—A Moral Threat To Our Youth," *General Federation Clubwoman* (September 1959): 30.

84. Mrs. Walter V. Magee, "Our Scandalous Newstands," *General Federation Clubwomen* (September 1959): 30.

85. On these fears in the postwar era, see Gilbert, *Cycle of Outrage,* 77–126, 143–77.

86. For earlier concerns about the impact of images on young women, see Lea Jacobs, *The Wages of Sin: Censorship and the Fallen Woman Film, 1928–1942* (Madison: University of Wisconsin Press, 1991), 3–5.

87. "Do Americans Commercialize Sex?" *Ladies' Home Journal* (October 1956): 68, 69, 198–204.

88. On women as instigators of local antiobscenity movements, see also Alfred C. Kinsey et al., *Sexual Behavior in the Human Female* (Philadelphia: W. B. Saunders, 1953), 663. For reports of successful local actions, see Magee, "A Year of Achievement"; "Let's Abolish Pornography."

89. Marilyn E. Hegarty, "'Patriots, Prostitutes, Patriotutes': The Mobilization and Control of American Women's Sexuality during World War II" (Ph.D. diss., Ohio State University, 1998).

NOTES ON CONTRIBUTORS

Ruth M. Alexander is professor of history and department chair at Colorado State College. She is the author of *The 'Girl Problem': Female Sexual Delinquency in New York, 1900–1930* and coeditor of *Major Problems in American Women's History.*

Norma Basch is professor of history at Rutgers University, Newark. She is the author of *Framing American Divorce: From the Revolutionary Generation to the Victorians.*

Kathleen A. Brown is associate professor of history at St. Edwards University in Austin, Texas.

George Chauncey is professor of history at the University of Chicago. He is the author of *Gay New York: Gender, Urban Culture and the Making of the Gay Male World, 1890–1940* and coeditor of *Hidden From History: Reclaiming the Gay and Lesbian Past.*

Lucie Cheng is professor of sociology at the University of California, Los Angeles. She is the co-editor of *Labor Immigration under Capitalism: Asian workers in the United States before World War II.*

Cornelia Hughes Dayton is associate professor of history at the University of Connecticut at Storrs. She is the author of *Women before the Bar: Gender, Law, and Society in Connecticut, 1639–1789.*

Lisa Duggan is an associate professor of history at New York University. She is the author of *Sapphic Slashers: Sex, Violence and American Modernity* and coeditor of *Our Monica, Ourselves: The Clinton*

Affair and the Public Interest and *Sex Wars: Sexual Dissent and Political Culture.*

Elizabeth Faue is professor of history at Wayne State University. She is the author of *Community of Suffering and Struggle: Women, Men, and the Labor Movement in Minneapolis, 1915–1945* and *Writing the Wrongs: Eva Valesh and the Rise of Labor Journalism.*

Ramón A. Gutiérrez is professor and chair of ethnic studies at the University of California, San Diego. He is the author of *When Jesus Came the Corn Mothers Went Away: Power and Sexuality in New Mexico, 1500–1846.*

Martha Hodes is associate professor of history at New York University. She is the author of *White Women, Black Men: Illicit Sex in the Nineteenth-Century South* and editor of *Sex, Love, Race: Crossing Boundaries in North American History.*

Kathleen Kennedy is associate professor of history at Western Washington University. She is the author of *Disloyal Mothers and Scurrilous Citizens: Gender and Subversion during World War I* and editor, with Frances Early, of *Athena's Daughters: Television's New Warrior Women.*

Joanne Meyerowitz is professor of history at the University of Indiana and editor of the *Journal of American History.* She is the author of *Women Adrift: Independent Wage Earners in Chicago, 1880–1930* and the editor of *Not June Cleaver: Women and Gender in Postwar America, 1945–1960.*

Peggy Pascoe is Beekman Associate Professor of History at the University of Oregon. She is the author of *Relations of Rescue: The Search For Female Moral Authority in the American West, 1874–1939.*

Jacqueline Peterson is professor of history at Washington State University. She is the coeditor of *New Peoples: Being and Becoming Metis in North America.*

Midori Takagi is associate professor at Fairhaven College of Western Washington University. She is the author of *Rearing Wolves to Our Own Destruction: Slavery in Richmond, Virginia, 1782–1865.*

Sharon Ullman is associate professor of history at Bryn Mawr College. She is the author of *Sex Seen: The Emergence of Modern Sexuality in America.*

INDEX

97–98, 104–108; and self-control,
92–93; and sexual imagery,
334–37
Mothers March against Obscenity,
335
Munsey's, 323
murder: and adultery, 95; and lesbianism, 167–73
My Life and Loves, 279
Myrdal, Gunnar, 235, 236–37

Narpa, Francisco, 11–12
Nation, The, 276
National Association for the
Advancement of Colored People
(NAACP), 238
Navajo Indians, 6
Navy, the United States: and female
impersonators, 190–91; homosex-
uality in, 188–95, 198; investiga-
tion of homosexuality by, 187–88,
199–201; and men's first experi-
ences with homosexuality, 193–94;
recognizing homosexuals in,
191–92; and "trade" men,
196–98; use of decoys by, 187–88,
198–201, 203–4, 205, 208–9
Nedersen, Susanna, 263
Negro Digest, 322, 330–32
Nestor, Barbara, 280
New Masses, The, 276
New Mexico, 5–9, 20–22
New Music, 292
Newport, R. I., 188–91, 207–8
Newport Ministerial Union, 187, 201,
203
Newport Recruit, 190
New York, N.Y., 189, 205, 256
New York State Reformatory for
Women, 250–51
New York Sun, 178
New York World, 168
Nightingale, Abigail, 55–56, 60, 66
Noble, Lonnie, 281
Norse, Harold, 279, 288, 289, 292
Nugget, 324

O'Brien, David J., 312
O'Connor, Blanche, 279
O'Connor, Harvey, 285, 286
Ojibwa Indians, 30
O'Meara, Walter, 29
One, 292

Ortega, Geronimo, 17–18
Oshahgushkodanaqua (Ojibwa
woman), 35–36
Ottawa Indians, 30
Overton, John, 100
Oxford English Dictionary, The, 54

Painter, Nell, 48
Palmolive soap, 306, 313, 314, 315
Parsons, Louisa, 253–54
Parton, James, 83
Pascoe, Peggy, 162
Pattee, Samuel L., 223–24
peasants: and arranged marriages, 13;
and honor, 9–11
Peiss, Kathy, 252
Perez, Andrea, 233–35
Perrot, Nicolas, 33
Perry, William, 304
Pesotta, Rose, 286
Peterson, Jacqueline, 3, 29
Phelan, James D., 308
Philippines, the, 305, 306–8
Phillip II, King, 8
Phillips, Addie, 176
physical appearance and race, 30,
236–37, 308
Pitt-Rivers, Julian, 9
Playboy, 320, 322, 324, 332–34
poetry and songs: romance in, 17–20;
on sexuality, 279, 290
Polentz, Sophie, 255, 260–61, 265,
266
Police Gazette, 323
politics. *See also* radicalism: and
advertising, 311; and Christianity,
86–87; during the Civil War,
115–17, 223; and marriage,
47–48, 83–86; and the media, 85,
87–95; nineteenth-century,
83–108, 116–18; and privacy,
89–92, 288; and public response
to scandals, 83–84, 86; and race,
116–18, 123–25, 240–41; and
republicanism, 90–91; and sexuality, 87–108, 116–18, 123–25,
273–78, 282–83, 284–85, 292–94;
and state attempts to regulate sexuality, 161–62; and women,
106–108
Pomfret, Conn., 50–53, 57–62
Poovey, Mary, 94
Popular Front, 278

Stalin, Joseph, 277–78
State Laws Limiting Marriage Selection Examined in the Light of Eugenics, 230
Stearnes, George, 118
Steele, Jeffrey, 309
Steelink, Nicolass, 284
Stephenson, Eleanor, 291
Sterling, Ilene, 263
Strang, Jesse, 95
Symington, Muriel, 290

Thomas, Clarence, 240
Thompson, Lydia, 323
Traynor, Roger, 234–35
Truth's Advocate and Monthly Anti-Jackson Expositor, 87

U. S. Male, 324
Ulysses, 325
Unitarianism, 87
University of California, Berkeley, 235

Vanity Fair, 175
Van Kirk, Sylvia, 29
Vargas, Alberto, 326–28
venereal diseases, 146, 255–56
View of General Jackson's Domestic Relations, 87–88
Vorse, Mary Heaton, 287

Waldstein, Ella, 250–51, 255, 259, 264
Walker, Frank C., 326–27
Ward, Freda, 168
Ware, Herta, 290
Washington, Mrs. J. M., 330
Washington Daily News, 329
Washington Post, 326, 329
Wayward Minor Act, 256–57
Weekly Marylander, 92, 97
Weeks, Jeffrey, 280
Weisbord, Albert, 282
Weissman, Rae L., 327–28
Well of Loneliness, The, 182, 183
Weltfish, Gene, 227
West, Evelyn, 333
Western House of Refuge for Women, 252
Whipple, Elsie, 95
Whitman, Walt, 279
Wicks, H. M., 276
Wiley, Anna Kelton, 328–29

Wilkins, Nanette, 264
Willens, Doris, 291
Williams, Ebenezer, 65, 67–68
Williams, Emma, 176–77
Wilson, Woodrow, 188
Woman's Christian Temperance Union (WCTU), 324
women. *See also* imagery, sexual; lesbianism: abuse of, 254, 255, 263; accusing men of rape, 122–23; advertising directed at, 304–16; and the antiobscenity movement, 324–25, 328–29, 331, 332–37; and arranged marriages, 11–13; and birth control, 120, 274, 278, 279, 280; Chinese prostitute, 134–53; and colonialism, 303, 314–16; committed to reformatories, 251–67; and cross-dressing, 170–75, 173–75, 181–82; and death after abortions, 50–51, 55–57; as domestics, 263, 264–65; dominating men, 119–22; early-twentieth-century, 251–67; expected behavior for, 31–33, 64–65, 87, 93–94, 106–108, 121–22, 165–66 256–57, 261–64; fur traders, 29; and gender identity, 167–72, 181–83; and ideals of beauty, 38–39, 327–28, 330–32; imported for prostitution, 132–35; as indentured servants, 136–37, 141–42; influential in marriage, 28–29; and interracial relationships, 115–25, 254–55; kidnapped, 136, 145, 150; and menstruation, 32, 34, 35; Metis, 28–40; middle-class, 47, 304–16, 324–25; and murder, 95; nontraditional, 33–34, 121–22, 165–66, 258, 266–67; and politics, 106–108, 277; portrayed in advertising, 314–15; pregnant out of wedlock, 58–59, 120–21, 146–48, 254, 258, 264; prophesy by, 33, 34–36; and prostitution, 131–53, 255, 266; and puberty, 33, 34; punishment of, 52, 251–52, 259–60; and radicalism, 276–77, 279; running away from home, 265–66; as semiskilled laborers, 144; and sexual double standards, 50–53, 64–65, 72, 118, 254, 278, 333; sold into prostitution, 133;